ESSAYS IN IRISH LABOUR HISTORY

Elizabeth and John W. Boyle in 1963, with their daughter Elizabeth (courtesy of Liz Curtis)

ESSAYS IN IRISH LABOUR HISTORY

A Festschrift for
Elizabeth and John W. Boyle

EDITORS
FRANCIS DEVINE, FINTAN LANE
AND NIAMH PUIRSÉIL

In association with the Irish Labour History Society

IRISH ACADEMIC PRESS
DUBLIN • PORTLAND, OR

First published in 2008 by Irish Academic Press

44 Northumberland Road,
Ballsbridge,
Dublin 4, Ireland

920 NE 58th Avenue, Suite 300
Portland, Oregon,
97213-3786

www.iap.ie

This edition copyright © 2008 Irish Academic Press
Chapters © individual authors

British Library Cataloguing in Publication Data
An entry can be found on request

ISBN 978 0 7165 2825 8(cloth)
ISBN 978 0 7165 2826 5(paper)

Library of Congress Cataloging-in-Publication Data
An entry can be found on request

All rights reserved. Without limiting the rights under copyright reserved alone, no part of this publication may be reproduced, stored in or introduced into a retrieval system, or transmitted, in any form or by any means (electronic, mechanical, photocopying, recording or otherwise) without the prior written permission of both the copyright owner and the above publisher of this book.

Printed by Biddles Ltd, King's Lynn, Norfolk

Contents

Notes on the Contributors	vii
Preface	ix

1. A Gentle Flowering: Elizabeth and John W. Boyle, Historians and Labour Activists
   Francis Devine — 1

2. Envisaging Labour History: Some Reflections on Irish Historiography and the Working Class
   Fintan Lane — 9

3. Popular Protest and a 'Moral Economy' in Provincial Ireland in the Early Nineteenth Century
   John Cunningham — 26

4. 'Remembering who we are': Identity and Class in Protestant Dublin and Belfast, 1868–1905
   Martin Maguire — 49

5. Sheep in Wolves' Clothing: Labour and Politics in Belfast, 1881–1914
   Emmet O'Connor — 65

6. The Dublin Building Trades Lockout of 1896
   Charles Callan — 83

7. Outwork, Truck and the Lady Inspector: Lucy Deane in Londonderry and Donegal, 1897
   Kevin J. James — 103

8. Striking for the Right to be Late at Work: Workers' Resistance to Employers' Time Discipline in Lurgan Power Loom Factories, 1899–1914
   Mats Greiff — 118

9. The Belfast Shipyards and the Industrial Working Class
   John Lynch — 135

10. The IRA and Trade Unionism, 1922–72
   Brian Hanley   157

11. Catholic Stakhanovites? Religion and the Irish Labour Party, 1922–73
   Niamh Puirséil   178

12. Writers of the Left: Politics and Culture in Ireland during the 1930s
   Paul O'Brien   200

13. Money Matters in the Lives of Working Women in Ireland in the 1940s and 1950s
   Elizabeth Kiely and Máire Leane   219

14. The Decline of the Collaborators: the Ulster Unionist Labour Association and Post-war Unionist Politics
   Henry Patterson   238

Index   257

Notes on the Contributors

Charles Callan is a former long-time secretary of the Irish Labour History Society (ILHS) and the author of several articles on the history of the painting and decorating trades.

John Cunningham is a lecturer in history at the National University of Ireland, Galway. His publications include *Labour in the West of Ireland: Working Life and Struggle, 1890–1914* (Belfast: 1995) and *'A Town Tormented by the Sea': Galway, 1790–1914* (Dublin: 2005).

Francis Devine works as a tutor in SIPTU College and is a former president of the ILHS and a former editor of *Saothar*, the journal of Irish labour history. His publications include *Acting for the Actors: Dermot Doolan and the Organisation of Irish Actors and Performing Artists, 1947–1985* (Dublin: 1997), *Understanding Social Justice: Paddy Cardiff and the Discipline of Trade Unionism* (Dublin: 2002), *An Eccentric Chemistry: Michael Moynihan and Labour in Kerry, 1917–2001* (Dublin: 2004) and, with Norman Croke, *James Connolly Labour College, 1919–1921* (Dublin: 2007).

Mats Greiff lectures in history at the University of Malmö in Sweden. He has written several articles on Irish labour history.

Brian Hanley lectures in history at the National University of Ireland, Maynooth. His previous publications include *The IRA, 1926–1936* (Dublin: 2002).

Kevin J. James lectures in history at the University of Guelph in Canada. His publications include *Handloom Weavers in Ulster's Linen Industry, 1815–1914* (Dublin: 2007).

Elizabeth Kiely lectures in the Department of Applied Social Studies at University College, Cork.

Fintan Lane is a former editor of *Saothar*, the journal of Irish labour history. His publications include *The Origins of Modern Irish Socialism,*

1881–1896 (Cork: 1997), *In Search of Thomas Sheahan: Radical Politics in Cork, 1824–1836* (Dublin: 2001), *Long Bullets: A History of Road Bowling in Ireland* (Cork: 2005) and, as co-editor, *Politics and the Irish Working Class, 1830–1945* (Basingstoke: 2005) and *Politics, Society and the Middle Class in Modern Ireland* (Basingstoke: 2008).

Máire Leane lectures in the Department of Applied Social Studies at University College, Cork.

John Lynch lectures in history at Queen's University, Belfast. His previous publications include *A Tale of Three Cities: Comparative Studies in Working-Class Life* (Basingstoke: 1998) and *An Unlikely Success Story: the Belfast Shipbuilding Industry, 1880–1935* (Belfast: 2001).

Martin Maguire lectures at the Dundalk Institute of Technology. His publications include articles on the Dublin Protestant working class and *Servants to the Public: A History of the Local Government and Public Services Union, 1901–1990* (Dublin: 1998).

Paul O'Brien writes on the relationship between literature, history and politics. His publications include *Shelley and Revolutionary Ireland* (London: 2002).

Emmet O'Connor lectures in history at the University of Ulster. He is a former editor of *Saothar* and his publications include *Syndicalism in Ireland, 1917–1923* (Cork: 1988), *A Labour History of Waterford* (Waterford: 1989), *A Labour History of Ireland, 1824–1960* (Dublin: 1992), *James Larkin* (Cork: 2002) and *Reds and the Green: Ireland, Russia and the Communist Internationals, 1919–43* (Dublin: 2004).

Henry Patterson lectures in history at the University of Ulster. His publications include *Class Conflict and Sectarianism: the Protestant Working Class and the Belfast Labour Movement, 1868–1920* (Belfast: 1980), *The Politics of Illusion: A Political History of the IRA* (London: 1997) and *Ireland since 1939: the Persistence of Conflict* (London: 2006).

Niamh Puirséil is currently joint-editor of *Saothar*, the journal of Irish labour history, and lectures in history at University College, Dublin. Her publications include *The Irish Labour Party, 1922–1973* (Dublin: 2007).

Preface

The Irish Labour History Society (ILHS) was established in 1973 with a constitutional obligation to 'promote the knowledge of Irish labour history and of Irish people abroad and labour history in general; the appreciation of the importance of labour history in the educational curriculum; and the preservation of the records and reminiscences, oral and written, relating to the current and past experiences of the working class and its organizations.' The society has diligently attempted to fulfil these obligations, despite the handicaps of a chronic lack of resources, financial and human, and an essential reliance on voluntary commitment from its committee, members and supporters.

At a recent ILHS Publications Committee meeting, Charles Callan recalled the early difficulties the society endured in its effort to maintain the publication of our journal, *Saothar*. At a committee meeting in 1980, the late Paddy Bergin, having just seen the proofs of *Saothar*, vol. 6, going to press, remarked: 'All the same, if we manage to publish up to *Saothar* 10, the society will have achieved something.' Twenty-seven years on, thirty-one volumes of *Saothar* have been published, a comprehensive Index to *Saothair* 1–24,[1] twelve issues of the *Studies in Labour History* series,[2] and, through the mechanism of the Irish Manuscripts Commission, Sarah Ward-Perkins' invaluable *Select Guide to Trade Union Records in Dublin*.[3] In addition, there have been annual conferences, scores of lectures, exhibitions and events, and, not least, the permanent premises in Beggar's Bush, housing the ILHS Archives, a 10,000-volume library, and much ephemera.[4] The hugely valuable archive of primary trade union and labour movement documents and individual papers would, in most cases, undoubtedly have been lost were it not for the ILHS and its work, all, it must be remembered, achieved by essentially voluntary efforts. While ILHS policy is subject to change over time, a detailed statement of the society's intentions and a listing of material held both featured in a special labour history issue of *Irish Archives* in 2003.[5] In addition, of course, annual updates on activities and holdings in the ILHS Archives are provided in *Saothar*.

It must be observed that the indispensable financial and material support of the trade unions – given without qualification or condition – has underpinned all of our efforts and provided the ILHS with a strong base within the Irish labour movement, in contrast to its marginal and largely ignored position with Irish academic history circles. The society would, as always, of course, welcome a stronger involvement and contribution from academic historians. Indeed, the society would appreciate any interest from new members, researchers or those simply interested in labour history who have discovered us through this publication. We can be contacted at our offices at the ILHS Museum & Archives, Beggar's Bush, Haddington Road, Dublin 4 or through our website – http://www.ilhsonline.org

Any success is due in large measure to the massive contribution made by our members and committees over the past thirty-five years, a commitment embodied in John W. and Elizabeth Boyle, who never allowed distance to diminish their interest or to prevent attendance at a number of AGMs. The society is thus pleased to produce this collection of essays to honour their memory. The Boyles were active and enthusiastic members of the ILHS from its formation in 1973. As historians and activists, they embodied that unique blend of scholarship and organization that has distinguished our society from many of its international, sister societies. Both received obituaries in *Saothar*, and their lives are dealt with fully in the opening essay of this book.[6]

After Elizabeth Boyle's death in November 1995, John made a bequest to the ILHS in her memory. After John's own death in 1998, it seemed appropriate that the bequest then be used in both their names. John, whose magnum opus, *The Irish Labor Movement in the Nineteenth Century* (1988), was the pinnacle of his work, wrote some pioneering material in Irish labour history. Son of a bottler in Guinness, he never abandoned his working-class roots through a long academic career that took him from Trinity College, Dublin, where he was an exceptional student, to teaching at the Royal Belfast Academical Institute, then to Queen's University, Belfast, and, finally, to the University of Guelph, Ontario, in Canada. Elizabeth Morwood returned to Belfast from India after her mother's death and married John in 1942.

The Boyles were active in the Northern Ireland Labour Party (NILP), John serving on the executive and Elizabeth as head of the NILP Women's Council. Frustration at the lack of progress within the party on the civil rights campaign led to their resignation. These 'wrong politics' led to John being labelled as 'an anti-union, Fenian Protestant' and this limited his career prospects, ultimately determining him to emigrate to

Preface

Canada in 1972, initially as Associate Professor of History at Mount Allison University, New Brunswick. As with so many Irish who felt themselves' forced to go', it was a wrench, but they quickly adapted and both became active in the New Democratic Party (NDP). John wrote extensively on aspects of Canadian social and labour history in the nineteenth century, particularly the contribution made by Irish immigrants. His command of French provided an entrée to the two strands of Canadian society and a rich understanding of the complexities of their new society. Elizabeth maintained a broad involvement in human rights, civil liberties, the women's movement and Third World support organizations.

Despite living 3,000 miles away, the Boyles maintained strong connections with Ireland. Acknowledging their support for the ILHS and John's long service on the *Saothar* Editorial Advisory Board, at the ILHS AGM in 1990 they were presented with a hand-crafted copper plaque by Inchicore Works coppersmith Dermot Barrett, displaying the foundation emblem of the Irish Trades Union Congress and inscribed: 'To John and Elizabeth Boyle for their contribution to the making and recording of Irish labour history'. This Festschrift further recognizes that contribution with a unique collection of essays in Irish labour history. The editors, Francis Devine, Fintan Lane and Niamh Puirséil, are to be congratulated for persuading such an eclectic and distinguished body of contributors to submit material; the willingness they found was a further mark of the respect in which the Boyles are held.

Before concluding, on behalf of the ILHS Committee, I wish to formally record our thanks to the Boyles for their initial bequest and to their daughter, Liz Curtis, for her patience, support and interest in the project, not least with the provision of illustrative material. The ILHS is grateful to Irish Academic Press for their management of the publication and professionalism at all stages of the promotion and production of the book. Many served on the ILHS Committee as this project was discussed and planned, but mention must be made of our late president, Hugh Geraghty, who so tragically died in 2006 and of former president Jack McGinley, who was involved in the early stages of the project. Finally, we acknowledge the Boyles for their academic contributions and for their financial and intellectual commitment to the task of rescuing Irish labour history.

Brendan Byrne
President
Irish Labour History Society
December 2007

NOTES

1. Francis Devine, *An Index to* Saothar, *Journal of the Irish Labour History Society and other ILHS Publications, 1973–2000* (Dublin: ILHS, 2000).
2. Anthony Coughlan, *C. Desmond Greaves, 1913–1988: An Obituary Essay* (1990, reprinted 1991); Manus O'Riordan, *The Voice of a Thinking, Intelligent Movement: James Larkin Junior and the Ideological Modernisation of Irish Trade Unionism* (1995, reprinted in updated edition in 2001); Francis Devine, *Acting for the Actors: Dermot Doolan and the Organisation of Irish Actors and Performing Artists, 1947–1985* (1997); Bill McCamley, *The Third James: James Fearon, 1874–1924: an Unsung Hero of Our Struggle* (2000); Anton McCabe, *'Stormy Petrel of the Transport Workers': Peadar O'Donnell, Trade Unionist, 1917–1920* and Francis Devine, *Navigating a Lone Channel: Stephen McGonagle, Trade Unionism and Labour Politics in Derry* (2000); Helga Woggon, *Silent Radical – Winifred Carney, 1887–1943: a Reconstruction of her Biography* (2000); Helga Woggon, *Ellen Grimley (Nellie Gordon) – Reminiscences of her Work with James Connolly in Belfast* (2000); Francis Devine, *Understanding Social Justice: Paddy Cardiff and the Discipline of Trade Unionism* (2002); Joseph Deasy, *Fiery Cross: the Story of Jim Larkin* (2004); Francis Devine, *An Eccentric Chemistry: Michael Moynihan and Labour in Kerry, 1917–2001* (2004); Francis Devine and Manus O'Riordan, *James Connolly, Liberty Hall and the 1916 Rising* (2007); and Norman Croke and Francis Devine. *'More Permanent than Bronze: More Enduring than Stone: the James Connolly Labour College, 1919–1921, and Workers' Educational Institute, 1925–1927* (2007). Copies of all of these pamphlets are available directly from the ILHS.
3. Sarah Ward-Perkins, *Select Guide to Trade Union Records in Dublin* (Dublin: 1996).
4. See 'Irish Labour History Society Archives & Museum', *Saothar*, vol. 15 (1990), pp. 97–100, for details and images of the opening of the Labour History museum and archive in the former Beggar's Bush barracks.
5. Francis Devine, 'The Irish Labour History Society and archives', 'An index to sources for labour historians in *Saothar* – a working journal, an update', *Irish Archives*, vol. 9, n.s. (Winter 2003–4), pp. 5–10, 79–82.
6. Francis Devine, 'Elizabeth Boyle', *Saothar*, vol. 21 (1996), pp. 11–12, and 'J.W. Boyle', *Saothar*, vol. 24 (1999), pp. 7–10.

A Gentle Flowering: Elizabeth and John W. Boyle, Historians and Labour Activists

FRANCIS DEVINE

John William Boyle and his wife Elizabeth were two of the Irish Labour History Society's (ILHS) most consistent, staunchest and generous supporters. This long-awaited volume of essays is testimony to that support, as it is part-funded by a bequest made to the ILHS by John after Elizabeth's death in 1995. After John's death in 1998, such was their natural indivisibility that it seemed appropriate to utilize the bequest in both their memories.

JOHN W. BOYLE – LABOUR HISTORIAN

J.W. Boyle was born in Dublin on 4 October 1914, the son of a bottler in Guinness's brewery.[1] A bright child, young John's educational opportunities were severely limited by this background, but such denials firmly implanted in him the socialist beliefs to which he was to remain ever true. Eventually, a scholarship gained him access in 1933 to Trinity College, Dublin. Even with the scholarship, Boyle never forgot the support of his two sisters, their actions sensitizing him to the sacrifices common to all women of his generation and class and infusing his politics with a feminist perspective. He graduated with a first class honours degree in Modern Languages and Economic and Political Science in 1937. He was awarded a gold medal and graduate research prize in recognition of his outstanding scholarship. He went on to complete both an MA in Old French and an MLitt in Anglo-Norman Poetry in 1939, before commencing a lengthy tenure as a senior assistant in the Department of English and History at the Royal Belfast Academical

Institute ('Inst'). From 1946 until 1955, he tutored on a part-time basis in the Department of Extra-Mural Studies, Queen's University, Belfast, and, in 1965 became a special lecturer, part-time, in the Department of Economic and Social History. Extra-mural work was particularly gratifying to Boyle, as he met worker-students who, like himself in the 1930s, were struggling to access third-level education, realize their potential and simply enjoy the thrill of learning and self-exploration that he so valued. He was awarded his doctorate by Trinity in 1961 for a study of the labour movement from 1800 to 1907, the thesis later being the foundation of his *magnum opus*, *The Irish Labor Movement in the Nineteenth Century* (1988).[2]

Emmet O'Connor, in a historiographical review of Irish labour history, referred to Boyle's treatment of nineteenth-century labour as 'a magisterial opus of the old school, sternly fixed on labour organization'.[3] There are still only a handful of general works on Irish labour history, and Boyle's is the most comprehensive treatment of the neglected nineteenth century.[4] John Foster described Boyle's work as 'path-breaking' and remarked that its 'most significant contribution' was to provide the 'basis for a comprehensive understanding' of how Irish labour developed in the 'absence of an industrial proletariat'.[5] Boyle's approach has been criticized as anglo-centric and, initially perhaps, Irish labour historians did attempt to find evidence of an essentially English construct of labour's development within Ireland.[6] However, Boyle's work took Scotland rather than England as a comparator in attempting to explain matters. He held to a particularly Connollyite model, seeing national self-determination as the 'first task' before the construct of national trade union and political organization could move to the greater tasks. Foster recognized that Boyle did 'not adopt an easy academic separation of nationality and class', that he understood the 'importance of the material base for class formation' and that 'to this extent imperialism, whether formal or informal, inflicts a continuing loss'. Rather than being over-critical of Boyle's work as 'old-fashioned', Foster instead thought it a 'matter of congratulation that a lifetime's work should be drawn together in a volume, which in its perceptions, balance and realism takes these issues back into the heart of labour history'.[7] They still do, and Boyle was to acknowledge, at least in correspondence and conference contributions, that trade unionism's own 'imperialism', the absorption of Irish craft trade unionism by British-based, essentially English, amalgamated unions awaited the liberating forces of the rise of the unskilled, Larkin and the Irish Transport and General Workers' Union, Connolly and the demand for national self-determination, that were to be beyond his eighteenth- and nineteenth-century foci. As with Connolly, Boyle refused to separate the cause of Ireland from the cause of labour, and his conception of labour and labour movement was inclusive of radical republicanism.

Boyle's scholarship covered a broad spectrum and is partially indicated by the select bibliography that follows. His knowledge of the Belfast labour movement in the late nineteenth and early twentieth centuries was substantial – one wonders if he actually knew the members of Belfast Trades Council of 1890–1914 personally. He had a finely honed ability to discern and analyze the tensions of craft and unskilled, and the sectarianism that divided Ireland's then most advanced and deeply organized working class. His life experience equipped him with a capacity to understand the pressures on the various factions as they evolved and impacted upon and collided with each other. Naturally, he applied similar tools to his analysis of contemporary events in Ireland. Both Boyles deplored sectarian division, condemned all forms of destructive violence and sought continuously to stress the commonality in the pursuit of unity – a unity that they undoubtedly thought would bring peace and fresh, more progressive perceptions of identity and mutual respect. They took encouragement from the emerging achievements of the peace process in Northern Ireland.

ELIZABETH MORWOOD BOYLE

It was in Belfast that John met and married Elizabeth Morwood, who should never be remembered simply as John W. Boyle's wife.[8] Such would be to offend her memory and to seriously misunderstand the integral and interdependent nature of their creative and supportive relationship. Elizabeth and John were clearly friends and lovers, comrades and soul mates, and it was a joy to be in their company. Elizabeth Morwood was born on 24 January 1908 during a smallpox epidemic in India, where her father, James, a County Derry man, served as a doctor in the Indian Medical Service. Her mother, Mary Bell, an American from New Orleans and California, had met James romantically on a Red Sea passage as they first steamed eastwards from Europe. Elizabeth's childhood memories of the poverty in the subcontinent bred an enduring interest in and concern for Third World development, aid and debt relief. James performed many successful cataract operations under trying and primitive conditions, and it was hugely ironic that, having returned to Belfast, he should lose his own sight during a poorly conducted cataract operation. Elizabeth, consequently, always supported Operation Eyesight, taking great, private pleasure from the letters of thanks she received from families in many countries, whose relatives had received restored vision.

Elizabeth Boyle was an intrepid campaigner and supporter of progressive causes. Among the organizations in which she involved herself were Oxford Canada Share Plan, which bought milling machines for women in developing countries; Help the Aged; Match International Centre, a support agency for international women's rights; American Civil Liberties, Southern California; Foster Parents Plan of Canada – she had adopted an Indian child and assisted its parents support their child until her death; Inter Pares; and Casa Alianza. Behind all this was an informed concern born of avid reading, intellectual and political curiosity, but, above all else, a fundamental human interest.

Elizabeth's political formation began in the 1930s when she supported the Spanish Republic against Franco and, at one stage, was among protesters baton-charged by mounted police in London. She persuaded her father to put up refugee Basque children. Her identification with political prisoners saw her organize for Amnesty International in Canada, founding branches in Sackville and Guelph, and remaining a lifetime activist. Politically, she would say, she was 'always left'. At Girton College, Cambridge, she was a member of the Labour Club. Later she was active in the Independent Labour Party and, when back in Belfast, the Northern Ireland Labour Party (NILP). In Canada, along with John, she was an enthusiastic member of the New Democratic Party (NDP), readjusting her political sights to the *realpolitik* of North America. She was an undemonstrative stalwart, an addresser of envelopes, a knocker on doors, a telephone caller and writer of appeals, a largely unseen but essential part of any political team.

After graduation, Elizabeth Morwood assisted in a women's hostel and taught in the Sadler's Wells (now Royal) Ballet School. She wrote *The Irish Flowerers* (1971), still the standard work on the subject, outlining the history of lace-making and embroidery and the women who supplemented their small-farmer husbands' income.[9] The book sold out and is much sought after today on internet book sites. After marriage to John, Elizabeth pursued a supportive role that he saw as marking her out as the 'most unselfish person I ever knew'. However, he did not take any part of her for granted and, like her lace-making, theirs was a gentle flowering that bloomed from first spring till winter frosts. After her death, he was distraught and his sense of loss was incalculable.

THE BOYLES IN CANADA

The Boyles, John and Elizabeth, were indivisible and, for anyone meeting them, they became 'John and Elizabeth' or 'Elizabeth and John'. Theirs was truly a partnership, both bringing what the other lacked, each drawing strength and security from the other.

Belfast, however, did not provide a satisfactory living. In 1966, John became an associate professor in the Department of History, Mount Allison University, New Brunswick, Canada, and in 1972 he was appointed to the post of professor of history at the University of Guelph, Ontario, a position he held until retirement in 1984. This emigration, about which both expressed some regrets, was, they felt, a consequence of the limited opportunities in Irish academia and the common disapproval of those 'holding the wrong politics'. In Queen's, John's involvement in the NILP saw various applications for promotion rejected and his being labelled an 'anti-Union, Fenian Protestant'.[10] Prospects were further diminished by police searches of the Boyles' home and threats to their personal security. John had been elected to the NILP executive and Elizabeth was head of the NILP Women's Council. In the end, frustration at the lack of progress within the NILP on the developing issue of civil rights led to the Boyles' resignation.

In Canada – initially a very alien environment – the Boyles were made welcome. John adapted quickly and was soon writing of Canadian social and labour history in the nineteenth century, particularly immigrant Irish involvement. Both John and Elizabeth became NDP activists, commenting on the 'missionary' nature of socialist agitation in their newly adopted homeland. The uphill struggle of socialist evangelizing in Ireland no doubt stood them in very good stead! They engaged in many other progressive causes and activities.

Colleagues of J.W. Boyle remembered him for his 'dedication', 'integrity' and 'wholeness of character'. His strength, they felt, was to show others that 'life is seamless, and that our own individual and collective thoughts and actions can improve those things that unite us as human beings.'[11] John always pursued that unity. He was an unassuming man and, for all his academic qualifications, achievements and titles, when asked by comrades or colleagues to sign nomination papers that required both signature and occupation, he wrote simply, 'John Boyle, teacher'.[12] Teaching was his true vocation, and many have reason to be very grateful that he chose to give them time to learn and develop in his presence.

Despite their years in Canada, John and Elizabeth Boyle remained very European. Their essential Irishness – like that of their beloved

United men – was similarly flavoured with continental considerations and concerns. Linguistic abilities gave them easy access to European culture and thought, and frequent trips – they were avid and enthusiastic travellers – provided opportunities for research and the exchange of ideas. John's francophile inclination allowed for a diverse and yet balanced insight into and understanding of Canadian society that would distinguish him from many monoglot, anglo-centric immigrants. The Boyles respected all cultures, and their concerns for Inuit and other native Canadians occasionally brought disagreements with colleagues.

THE BOYLES AND THE IRISH LABOUR HISTORY SOCIETY

The Boyles were ardent supporters of the ILHS. John wrote copious, informative letters to society activists and was a supportive member of the *Saothar* Editorial Advisory Board from its inception in 1979. He addressed various ILHS conferences, the last in 1994 at the event that marked the centenary of the Irish Trade Union Congress/Congress of Irish Unions/Irish Congress of Trade Unions. On that occasion, he made little of his eighty years and was seldom to be seen without a circle of enthusiastic students, seeking his opinion and advice or asking questions merely to savour the erudition of the reply. There was agreement that his presence had, yet again, graced the event. To record the society's respect, the ILHS made a presentation to the Boyles at its annual general meeting in 1990. It was a plaque crafted by the late Dermot 'Derry' Barrett, a Cork-born coppersmith from Inchicore Works, which depicted the original emblem of the Irish Trade Union Congress and carried the apt inscription, 'To John and Elizabeth Boyle for their contribution to the making and recording of Irish labour history'. It cannot be forgotten that the Boyles were labour activists as well as historians.

Elizabeth Boyle died on 16 November 1995, leaving John bereft. His letters after her death were poignant, his broken heart and sense of loss massively apparent. His bequest, in Elizabeth's name, to the ILHS followed. I am sure they discussed the matter, so typical was it of their lifetime of support for various progressive causes. John himself passed away three years later on 16 November 1998. It seems absolutely appropriate that the bequest should now be used in both their memories.

The Boyles are missed by family, friends, comrades and colleagues, and the warmth of the tributes paid bore testimony to this. On a personal note, I miss his correspondence. Even though it was very uneven, John persisted in writing letters that were always a true pleasure, literary in style (and often in content too), personal and involving, informative and challenging – a rare treat. 'Our man in Canada' and his neat, tiny hand-writing are gone, as are his quiet consideration, droll humour and occasional, easy-paced mischievousness. Conversation was better than a letter, packed with references and quotations, laden with examples of corporate or individual behaviour and provocative questions.

The ILHS hopes that, with this volume, the Boyles' daughter, Elizabeth, and her family will appreciate how much we valued their parents and grandparents. Irish labour history felt it had seen the passing of a pioneering figure, that the uncertain seas of research had been denied a guiding light. Most of all, there is still simply a sense that we all lost two gentle friends and comrades who enriched so many lives.

SELECT BIBLIOGRAPHY OF THE WRITINGS OF JOHN W. BOYLE

'Segregation in Northern Ireland', *Irish Times*, 11–12 July 1956.

'Industrial conditions in the twentieth century', in T.W. Moody and J.C. Beckett (eds), *Ulster Since 1800: A Social Survey* (London: 1957).

'In search of Yeats', *Threshold*, 1, 1 (1957) [translation and annotation of an article by André Rouyer (T.N.P.) on a French production of three Yeats plays].

'Citizen Tone', *Threshold*, 1, 4 (1957).

'The Rural Labourer', *Threshold*, 3, 1 (Spring, 1959) [broadcast as a Thomas Davis lecture on Radio Éireann].

'The resurrection of Griffith', *Threshold*, 3, 4 (1959).

'The Rise of the Irish Labour Movement, 1880–1907', unpublished PhD thesis, Trinity College, Dublin (1961).

'The Belfast Protestant Association and the Independent Orange Order, 1901–1910', *Irish Historical Studies*, vol. xiii no. 50 (1962–3).

'Le dévelopement du movement ouvrier Irelandais de 1880 á 1907', *Le Mouvement Social*, no. 52 (Juillet–Septembre, 1965).

(As editor) *Leaders And Workers* (Cork & Dublin: 1965; reprinted Cork: 1978).

'The sum of things' in ibid., pp. 1–10.

'William Walker' in ibid., pp. 57–66.

'Irish labor and the Rising', *Éire-Ireland*, 2, 2 (Fall, 1967).

'Belfast and the origins of Northern Ireland', in J.C. Beckett and R.E. Glasscock (eds), *Belfast: Origins and Growth of an Industrial City* (London: 1967).

'Connolly, the Citizen Army and the Rising', in Kevin B. Nowlan (ed.),

The Making of 1916: Studies in the History of the Rising (Dublin: 1969).

'Irish Protestant nationalism in the nineteenth century', *Dalhousie Review*, 49, 4 (Winter, 1969–70).

'A Fenian Protestant in Canada: Robert Lindsay Crawford, 1910–1922', *Canadian Historical Review*, 52, 2 (June 1971).

'Ireland and the First International', *Journal of British Studies*, 11, 2 (May 1972).

'The Irish TUC', *Bulletin of the Society for the Study of Labour History*, 41 (Autumn 1980) [review essay].

'The scholar's pleasant life: the history of Irish education', *History of Education Quarterly*, 11, 2 (Summer, 1981) [review essay].

'A marginal figure: the Irish rural labourer', in Samuel Clark and James S. Donnelly (eds), *Irish Peasants: Violence and Political Unrest, 1780–1914* (Dublin: 1983).

The Irish Labor Movement in the Nineteenth Century (Washington, DC: 1988).

'Workers in union: a coming of age', *Saothar*, vol. 14 (1989) [review essay].

'A Biography of my Wife, Elizabeth Boyle, née Marwood, 1908–1995' (Guelph: 1998) [unpublished memoir circulated to family and friends].

NOTES

1. See Francis Devine, 'J.W. Boyle', *Saothar*, vol. 24 (1999), pp. 7–10.
2. See John Foster, 'Completing the first task: Irish labour in the nineteenth century', *Saothar*, vol. 15 (1990), pp. 65–9, for a review of this work.
3. Emmet O'Connor, 'Labour history in other lands: Ireland', *Labour/Le Travail*, no. 50 (Fall, 2002), pp. 243–8; available at www.historycooperative.org/journals/llt/50/0-connor.html.
4. See Jessie Dunsmore Clarkson, *Labour and Nationalism in Ireland* (New York: 1925); Charles McCarthy, *Trade Unions In Ireland, 1894-1960*, (Dublin: 1977); Arthur Mitchell, *Labour in Irish Politics, 1890-1930*, (Dublin: 1974); and Emmet O'Connor, *A Labour History of Ireland 1824-1960*, (Dublin: 1992).
5. Foster, 'Completing the first task', p. 65.
6. See Francis Devine and Emmet O'Connor, 'Marxism, modernisation and memory', *Saothar*, vol. 15 (1990), pp. 2–4.
7. Foster, 'Completing the first task', p. 69.
8. See Francis Devine, 'Elizabeth Boyle', *Saothar*, vol. 21 (1996), pp. 11–12.
9. *The Irish Flowerers*, (Belfast: 1971); she had previously published 'Irish embroidery and lacemaking, 1600–1800', *Ulster Folk Life*, no. 12 (1966), pp. 52–65.
10. Stuart Dixon, 'John Boyle: a celebration', read at the funeral of J.W. Boyle.
11. Terry Crowley, 'John Boyle, 1914–1998', read at the funeral of J.W. Boyle.
12. Ruth Kaufmann, 'Tribute to a teacher', *TAB – The Action Bulletin of Guelph-Wellington New Democratic Party* (January 1999).

Envisaging Labour History: Some Reflections on Irish Historiography and the Working Class

FINTAN LANE

The history of the Irish working class, like many facets of Irish social history, remains under-researched and an explosion of interest within academia seems unlikely in the short term. Indeed, a recently published 340-page guide to new research on nineteenth-century Ireland covered 'labour history' as a specific sub-discipline in one paragraph (within a chapter on 'political history').[1]

In some circles, a myth has arisen that Irish history-writing, as a scholarly pursuit, scarcely existed before the 'scientific' historiographic shift initiated in the 1930s by the British-trained academics Robert Dudley Edwards and Theodore William Moody. It would be a mistake to underestimate the influence of Edwards, Moody and the group of professional historians who contributed to *Irish Historical Studies* (founded in 1938), but it would be wrong equally to ignore the progenitors of a discipline that has been practised in Ireland, with varying degrees of competence and integrity, for hundreds of years. This essay intends to track, in broad terms, the treatment of workers and the working class by Irish historians since the late nineteenth century; it will also explore possible explanations for the weakness of 'labour history' as a sub-discipline and will assess the current state of research and writing on the Irish working class.

LABOUR AND EARLY IRISH HISTORIOGRAPHY

A professorship of oratory and history was established in Trinity College, Dublin, as early as 1724, but it was not until the late nineteenth century that the subject came into its own within Irish academia.[2] Indeed, even at that stage, most history-writing was conducted by non-academic middle-class men and women, who generally had implicit or explicit nationalist and unionist agendas; the professionalization of history as an academic discipline was at a nascent stage and the small university sector was much less important as a locus of historiography than it increasingly became as the twentieth century unfolded. It is clear that the tiny number of university-educated historians had much less effect on popular consciousness than those who operated outside the academy and its cultural *milieu*.

Academic history-writing was shaped in the late nineteenth and very early twentieth century by university-educated – and predominantly male – scholars, whose focus was fixed firmly on political history and whose work acted to legitimate the state. For eminent academic historians, such as W.E.H. Lecky (1838–1903), who were alert to political developments in Britain and on the continent, the labour movement and socialist ideas were less something to be studied than a malignant spectre haunting Ireland; indeed, Lecky's profound hostility to contemporary socialist and democratic doctrines impacted on his historical writings, impelling him towards a more robust defence of the status quo and, in the Irish context, of political unionism.[3] He believed that the Land League and Irish agrarianism of the late nineteenth century were motivated by socialistic ideas, and this informed his rejection of home rule and of Gladstonian compromise. Right-wing intellectuals, such as Lecky, were startled by the growth of oppositional working-class movements but never studied them in depth as historical subjects. In so far as any scholarly Irish 'labour history' was written in the late nineteenth century, it was produced by economic statisticians such as the English academic Arthur Lyon Bowley (1869–1957), whose long-run survey of wages in Ireland, while imperfect, is still of interest to social historians.[4]

In general, the Irish university *milieu* and broader middle-class intelligentsia displayed little positive interest in the 'socialist revival' of the 1880s and 1890s, and consequently there were no leftist historians equivalent to those – such as the Fabians Beatrice and Sidney Webb – who pioneered labour history in England.[5] The 'new ideas' in the salons of Dublin and Cork were those of cultural nationalism rather than socialism. There were, nonetheless, flickers of curiosity: Charles Hubert Oldham and T.W. Rolleston, who founded the *Dublin University Review* in 1885, showed some interest in the Socialist League, a British organization with a Dublin branch, and Oldham, on the advice of Michael Davitt, even took out a subscription to the group's monthly newspaper, *The Commonweal*.[6] W.B. Yeats evinced a similar interest in the Socialist League, as did the minor Cork poet Stephen Foreman.[7] The fact that

William Morris, the celebrated poet, novelist and artist, was a leader of the group was almost certainly behind this fleeting flirtation with socialism by members of Ireland's literati. Indeed, Morris was invited to speak at a gathering of the Contemporary Club in Dublin in April 1886.[8] Ultimately, however, Irish middle-class intellectuals remained aloof from the socialist and labour movements.

Outside of academia, those researching and writing history were often committed nationalists or unionists, who, consciously or unconsciously, sought to naturalize contentious interpretations of Ireland's colonial experience. A great deal of non-academic Irish historiography was written purposely with an eye on the present and as part of a wider exercise in nation-building. Historians such as A.M. Sullivan, Thomas Dunbar Ingram and Margaret Cusack were politically committed and wrote partisan studies to buttress the claims of competing bourgeois ideologies; the history of Irish urban and rural workers never registered as a serious concern. Of course, this lack of attention to the working class was not a peculiarly Irish problem, but it was exacerbated by the complete absence of a left-wing intelligentsia in late nineteenth-century Ireland. In 1869, the prominent German socialist Friedrich Engels, who visited Ireland on several occasions, began writing what was designed to be a voluminous history of the island; this could have been a fascinating study, as he proposed to bring it up to his own day, but, unfortunately, he abandoned the project in early 1870. The surviving preparatory notes, however, indicate that he intended to pay little attention to the working class and it was planned primarily as an anti-imperialist polemic.[9] In many ways, Engels' historical concerns differed little from contemporary Irish historians in that his research centred on resistance to British rule and its implications; he was intrigued by Ireland largely because of its impact on Britain and its empire, and not because of any interest in internal social change and class formation. Importantly, Ireland, as a predominantly agricultural country, did not possess the large-scale industrial working class that Engels saw as crucial for socialist revolution.

In fact, the class structure of nineteenth-century Ireland was quite different from that of, say, Britain or Germany, where 'labour history' emerged in the slipstream of strong labour and socialist movements that were rooted organically in substantial urban working classes. In the second half of the nineteenth century, outside of the north-east, the majority of Irish waged workers were engaged in agricultural work, were poorly organized and rarely members of trade unions or political labour associations.[10] As John W. Boyle remarked in 1983, these men and women – composing a rural proletariat – were the 'marginal figures' of

Irish society, ignored by political elites and historians alike.[11] This strong dominance of agriculture was not always the case; indeed, early industrialization in parts of the island during the late eighteenth and early nineteenth centuries meant that in 1821, roughly two-fifths of workers were 'chiefly employed in trades, manufactures, or handicraft' rather than in agricultural work.[12] However, this proportion decreased, as deindustrialization severely undermined some manufacturing sectors – particularly textiles outside of Ulster – and other manufacturing areas failed to develop. The years before the Great Famine saw a *relative* decline in Irish industry and, with the exception of north-east Ulster (which enjoyed strong growth in industrial output), the decades after the famine were marked by industrial stagnation.[13] Linked to this was the relatively slow pace of urbanization, which meant that, as late as 1911, just over one third of Irish people – middle class and working class – lived in towns with a population of 2,000 or more. Leinster, including Dublin, not surprisingly, had a higher rate of urbanization, but, even there, less than 48 per cent of people lived in an urban context, though this was a significant increase on the 22.43 per cent recorded in 1841. Table 1 accentuates the provincial disparities and clearly indicates that urban workers were very much a minority segment of the national population.[14]

TABLE 1:
POPULATION OF IRISH TOWNS OF 2,000 OR MORE INHABITANTS, AS A PERCENTAGE OF TOTAL POPULATION, 1841–1911

Year	Leinster	Munster	Ulster	Connaught	Ireland
1841	22.43	16.15	9.46	5.65	13.89
1871	36.00	21.88	19.29	7.16	22.20
1891	40.07	22.44	27.62	7.31	26.44
1911	47.25	25.58	38.38	8.13	33.50

Source: Census of Ireland, 1841–1911.

In such circumstances, the industrial power of the urban trade unions was curtailed, though this did not stop the spread of unionization in the late nineteenth and early twentieth centuries. Indeed, with the emergence of 'new unions' in Dublin and elsewhere in the early 1890s, unskilled workers were brought into the trade union movement, in which they had been scarcely represented previously. Nonetheless, with a weak urban working class and a large but unorganized rural working class, Ireland in the nineteenth century did not produce a strong *political* labour movement from which a stratum of labour or socialist intellectuals might emerge. Consequently, leftist class politics did not constitute a major discourse within the public sphere; subversive politics – the bedrock of any significant counter-public sphere and the driving force behind what Antonio Gramsci termed 'counter-hegemony' – were associated with politico-cultural nationalism, which had limited social ambitions.

CONNOLLY AND IRISH LABOUR HISTORY

The first significant Irish labour historian was a product of the small but enthusiastic socialist movement in Britain. In fact, James Connolly (1868–1916), the son of poor Irish emigrants to Scotland, was the mirror-opposite in many ways of the academics then engaged in professionalizing the writing of history, though he bore some resemblance to the more numerous non-academic nationalist and unionist historians in that he viewed the past as a political weapon. In terms of social background, he came from the lower echelons of the urban working class and his was not a story of rags to riches; he lived in precarious socio-economic circumstances for much of his life: the 1901 census, for example, shows him, his wife and six children living in one room in a tenement house at 54 Pimlico in Dublin.[15] Connolly was a former soldier, an autodidact, an unskilled labourer turned printer turned full-time political activist and, later, trade union organizer, and his work on labour history was intimately entwined with his commitment to socialism. His early researching and writing was conducted in snatched moments between providing for his family and political organizing.

From his arrival in Ireland in 1896, as an organizer for the Dublin Socialist Society, Connolly's interest in history was motivated by his desire to link the labour movement to the struggle for national independence. Indeed, by 1897, in his pamphlet *Erin's Hope: The End and the Means*, he was arguing that a type of Celtic communism, based on the 'clan' system, had existed prior to the intervention of British imperialism, sustaining itself as late as the seventeenth century, and providing a model for a future socialist society on the island; in essence, his argument was that socialism was 'natural' to Ireland, while feudalism and capitalism were foreign imports, a neat reversal of the dominant anti-socialist view, which associated socialist ideas with cranks, faddists and foreign-born agitators. However, Connolly's tendentious description of pre-colonial Irish society has received little support from scholars of the period, though Peter Berresford Ellis, an ardent Connollyite, made a sustained effort to buttress Connolly's argument in his polemical and impressionistic *A History of the Irish Working Class* (1972). Ellis begins his book with the assertion that '[t]he clash between the Celtic communistic social system and the crushing slavery of the Anglo-Norman feudal system marked the beginning of the struggle of the Irish working classes', an ahistorical judgement to be sure, but one that stands as evidence of Connolly's continuing influence on some non-academic history-writing.[16]

Connolly's *Labour in Irish History* (1910), published by Maunsel and Co. in Dublin, constitutes a seminal text in Irish historiography; it was the first book to focus on the history of the Irish working class. He adverted to this singularity at the outset of his first chapter:

> It is in itself a significant commentary upon the subordinate place allotted to labour in Irish politics that a writer should think it necessary to explain his purpose before setting out to detail for the benefit of his readers the position of the Irish workers in the past, and the lessons to be derived from a study of that position in guiding the movement of the working class today. Were history what it ought to be, an accurate literary reflex of the times with which it professes to deal, the pages of history would be almost entirely engrossed with a recital of the wrongs and struggles of the labouring people, constituting, as they have ever done, the vast mass of mankind. But history, in general, treats the working class as the manipulator of politics treats the working man – that is to say with contempt when he remains passive, and with derision, hatred and misrepresentation whenever he dares evince a desire to throw off the yoke of political or social servitude. Ireland is no exception to the rule. Irish history has ever been written by the master class – in the interests of the master class.[17]

As a Marxist, Connolly argued for a class analysis of Irish history; his central thesis in the book was that the 'Irish question is a social question', requiring the 'people' – a somewhat ambiguous entity that emphatically did not include the capitalists and middle class – to struggle against the 'invaders' for 'mastery of the means of life, the sources of production'.[18] 'Paradoxical as it may seem,' he had declared in 1900, 'I am a patriot because I am a socialist, and a socialist because I understand the true meaning of the word patriotism.'[19] *Labour in Irish History* is class politics swaddled in language instantly recognizable by Irish nationalists.

Aindrias Ó Cathasaigh, in a recent article, has tracked the development of the book from articles published by Connolly in socialist newspapers, as far back as 1898, and it is clear that, in political terms, it is of a piece with his early efforts to blend the national and labour agitations.[20] In fact, by 1910, he was consciously projecting his history-writing as part of the contemporaneous Gaelic revival:

[W]e believe that this book, attempting to depict the attitude of the dispossessed masses of the Irish people in the great crisis of modern Irish history, may justly be looked upon as part of the literature of the Gaelic revival. As the Gaelic language, scorned by the possessing classes, sought and found its last fortress in the hearts and homes of the 'lower orders', to reissue from thence in our own time to what the writer believes to be a greater and more enduring place in civilisation than of old, so in the words of Thomas Francis Meagher, the same 'wretched cabins have been the holy shrines in which the traditions and the hopes of Ireland have been treasured and transmitted.'

The apostate patriotism of the Irish capitalist class, arising as it does upon the rupture with the Gaelic tradition, will, of course, reject this conception, and saturated with foreignism themselves, they will continue to hurl the epithet of 'foreign ideas' against the militant Irish democracy.[21]

The outcome was a book that is less a history of the Irish working class than an outline analysis of the place of working people in the struggle against British rule; it is radical 'people's history', focusing on the lower classes but scarcely touching on the organized labour movement or on the non-political aspects of working people's lives. In its approach, it fits within an established nationalist paradigm, diverging significantly from the 'story of Ireland' only in the chapters on William Thompson and the Ralahine co-operative. Paradoxically, it is both a critique of Irish nationalism and an affirmation of its historical concerns.

POST-CONNOLLY LABOUR HISTORY

The execution of Connolly for his role in the 1916 rising meant that, despite his radical leftist politics, he acquired, in death, a political influence far more extensive than he had in life. Inevitably, this led to a scramble for ideological ownership of his 'legacy' and vigorous disagreements regarding the content of his politics, often centring on just how 'nationalist' he really was, if at all.[22]

Coincidentally, Connolly's new status as a national martyr occurred shortly before a wave of labour militancy and massive trade union expansion, linked to the political economy of the First World War and its aftermath.[23] In addition, a new socialist organization was formed in 1917 – the Socialist Party of Ireland (SPI) – that, as Emmet O'Connor has remarked, became 'the best connected, best resourced Marxist party in Irish history ... [and] it operated during a very propitious period'.[24] Importantly, this 'propitious period' for radical left activism was not unique to Ireland, and across Europe there was working-class unrest and exponential growth for revolutionary socialist organizations; the Russian revolution of 1917 stands out but, as Geoff Eley has highlighted, mass actions by elements of the European working class were occurring before the Bolsheviks seized power, with the German, Italian and Austrian movements 'setting their own pace'.[25] Germany teetered on the edge of social revolution, while, closer to home, Britain saw significant labour unrest. Ireland, consumed as it was by its own nationalist revolution, did not experience a dramatic swing to the left, but the political climate did change and, until the beginning of the 1920s, socialist ideas were less coldly received. The SPI never became a mass organization; nonetheless, its membership size, in the low hundreds, and connections to the trade union movement represented a substantial advance on previous socialist groups on the island. Moreover, for a brief few years, otherwise moderate trade unionists were happy to associate themselves – in word if not in deed – with the Bolshevik revolutionaries. Likewise, workplace occupations carried out at the time significantly labelled themselves 'soviets', and red flags appeared prominently at workers' demonstrations.[26]

This heightened activism naturally led to increased intellectual interest in the labour movement and, consequently, in its history. In late 1919, the SPI was instrumental in establishing a 'James Connolly Labour College' in Dublin, which offered courses on labour history; one of the lecturers was SPI activist Malcolm MacColl, a Scottish Christian socialist, who went under the name 'Joseph M. MacDonnell' while living in Ireland.[27] In 1921, MacDonnell published a pamphlet titled *The Story of Irish Labour*, which was almost certainly based on his notes from the James Connolly Labour College lectures; the pamphlet was republished by the Cork Workers' Club in 1974. The college, based in the same building as the SPI office at 42 North Great George's Street, survived until 1921, though it virtually ceased operating after November 1920 following raids by British paramilitary forces – the Auxiliaries – during which substantial damage was done and the library and other material confiscated.[28]

A significant biography of Connolly himself was inevitable and it duly appeared in 1924, from the pen of Desmond Ryan, who had participated in the 1916 rising as an aide to Patrick Pearse.[29] More important, however, was the publication in 1919 of a study by Ryan's journalist father and erstwhile SPI member, William Patrick Ryan, titled *The Irish Labour Movement from the Twenties to our own Day*, which – part history, part current affairs – was a considerable improvement on Connolly's *Labour in Irish*

History. W.P. Ryan, an advocate of the Gaelic revival with socialist convictions, followed Connolly in omitting an academic apparatus (references and bibliography), but, on the final page of his book, he does broadly identify his 'authorities and sources', which ranged impressively from parliamentary and trade union papers to personal interviews and pamphlets, newspapers and other material held by the National Library.[30] A more significant difference between Ryan's book and Connolly's is the attention paid to labour conflict and, specifically, to the emergence and trajectory of trade unionism in Ireland; it contains much information on workers' struggles through the nineteenth century. However, it is also distinctly teleological in approach, declaring bluntly that the labour movement had 'reached its first decisive manifestations with [Jim] Larkin, Connolly and their comrades'.[31] This is clearly the judgement of a zealous admirer of Connolly and Larkin rather than that of an even-handed historian. The book also should be seen as a product of the cultural nationalist movement of the time, with Ryan at pains to portray Connolly and the militant labour movement as authentic promoters of a Gaelic nation: Larkin was 'quick to see the importance of the Gaelic idea', while Connolly 'stood for Gaelicism ... and for industrial unionism'.[32]

Despite significant weaknesses in Connolly's *Labour in Irish History* and Ryan's *The Irish Labour Movement*, these two books revealed a hidden history that academic historians continued to ignore. In fact, it was 1925 before a scholarly tome was produced on Irish working-class history – and this was written by an American academic. Moreover, unlike the Connolly and Ryan books, which reached a popular market, Jessie Dunsmore Clarkson's *Labour and Nationalism in Ireland* (1925), published by Columbia University, had a short print run and was almost impossible to obtain in Ireland. Clarkson's detailed study is more reflective and less politically didactic than its predecessors, not simply because of his scholarly discipline, but because it was written after the conclusion of the Irish revolution and the labour ferment of 1917–23. Clarkson, for example, was downbeat about the prospects for Irish organized labour and suggested that, in its now weakened state, its primary objective should be to consolidate, educate and rebuild thoughtfully.[33] In general, and unsurprisingly, he was less prescriptive than Connolly and Ryan.

The Clarkson book was a false dawn; it was very poorly circulated and did not encourage further scholarly studies. Instead, labour history for the next few decades was transmitted intermittently via political pamphlets of the 'Connolly school' (including re-publications of Connolly's own work) and by individuals, such as Thomas A. Jackson, who were connected to the British communist movement. Unfortunately,

Jackson's most notable work, *Ireland Her Own* (1946), was a vulgar Marxist–Leninist appraisal of Irish nationalism and not a study of the Irish working class; Connolly is mentioned only to be squeezed into a Leninist box, with Jackson declaring that Connolly's supposed position on the 'complementary' nature of socialism and nationalism in an oppressed country was 'finally vindicated by the teaching of Lenin and Stalin'.[34] Despite such crude appropriation, Jackson's book sold well on the Irish left for many years because of its robust anti-imperialist politics. A better and more sophisticated book, in a similar vein, was the Austrian Marxist Erich Strauss' *Irish Nationalism and British Democracy* (1951).

Between the 1920s and 1960s, the historiography of the Irish working class scarcely developed, with reprints of *Labour in Irish History* and journalistic articles in left-wing and labour newspapers and magazines providing most readers with their information on the topic. There were a few useful publications, such as R.M. Fox's various popular studies and the trade unionist John Swift's substantial *History of the Dublin Bakers and Others* (1948), but, in general, it was as if time stood still.[35] In the 1960s, there was slight progress with the publication of well-researched and important biographies of Connolly (by the English orthodox communist activist C.D. Greaves) and of Larkin (by the US historian Emmet Larkin).[36] These two books, though strictly focused on individual leaders, marked a turn towards more seriously researched Irish labour history, which gathered pace in the 1970s. However, the Greaves and Larkin studies did not rupture a virtual consensus among Irish-based academic historians that workers as historical actors received walk-on parts in mainstream historiography primarily through references to the 1913 lockout and Connolly's involvement in the 1916 rising.

LABOUR HISTORIOGRAPHY SINCE THE 1970s

The 1970s saw major developments in the field of Irish labour history. A sketchy, and sometimes inaccurate, but useful non-academic survey of Irish trade unionism, drawing partly on published and unpublished scholarly work, was made available by Anvil Books at the beginning of the decade, reaching a large general readership; this was Andrew Boyd's *The Rise of the Irish Trade Unions, 1729–1970* (1972), which continued to sell well for many years afterwards. In terms of scholarly research, there was substantial progress, with the formation in 1973, by an amalgam of academics and labour activists, of the Irish Labour History Society (ILHS) and the publication of two 'institutional' surveys: Arthur Mitchell's *Labour in Irish Politics, 1890–1930* (1974) and Charles McCarthy's *Trade*

Unions in Ireland, 1894–1960 (1977). Mitchell was an academic from the United States, who has continued to publish on aspects of Irish history; McCarthy was a lecturer in industrial relations in Trinity College, Dublin, and, hence, his was the first book-length study of labour history by an Irish-based academic. Interestingly, McCarthy was not the product of a university history department – prior to joining the staff in TCD, he had been a full-time trade union official.[37]

Alongside these landmark books, the 1970s saw a substantial increase in scholarly articles and local studies on working-class history, with the launch in 1975 of *Saothar*, the annual journal of the ILHS, providing a forum for new work.[38] Without *Saothar*, it is likely that a great deal of research by non-academics, university-based scholars and postgraduate students would have gone unpublished; *Irish Historical Studies*, the leading history journal on the island, has published, in eighty years of existence, no more than a handful of papers on working-class history and, for most of that time, its focus was determinedly on political history, narrowly understood. Although, the ILHS has gone through short periods of vibrancy and longer periods of stasis over the past thirty-five years, its mere existence, as a stable point of contact, and the annual appearance of *Saothar* have remained essential in sustaining and promoting an interest in labour history; it has created a niche public sphere within which practitioners can find encouragement, even if much of the interaction is through reading and contributing to the journal rather than engaging directly with the society. On some levels, the ILHS has failed to develop, thus limiting its intervention. It is associated, understandably in some respects, with the formal labour movement and, consequently, *Saothar* is wrongly seen by many, and treated by some, almost as a 'house journal', whose role is to pay pious homage to the working-class past, with an especial loyalty to the trade union movement.[39] This approach, of course, leads to the production of hagiographies and sanitized histories rather than the critical engagement that should be central to all history writing.

The 'cultural turn' and the postmodernist wave that affected labour history elsewhere in the 1970s and 1980s had almost no impact on the ILHS and was scarcely visible in *Saothar*; in some ways, this was no bad thing, but, less positively, the dulled to non-existent effect resulted not from a thoughtful rejection, but from a negative lack of curiosity, which extended to theoretical discourses in general, except those that dealt with the problematic of Northern Ireland. In this, the labour history community was no different to the denizens of Irish university history departments, who were similarly minded. One important development that failed to enthuse the Irish labour and social history professions was the emergence in Germany, and elsewhere, of *Alltagsgeschichte* (the 'history of everyday life'), which critiqued traditional historiographic methodologies, attempted to learn from related fields – sociology and anthropology, in particular – and led to the production of some fascinating micro-histories of working-class life. Though, arguably, there is a danger that some such studies implicitly diminish the importance of macro-histories and the role of politics, and hence, at a stretch, constitute a kind of postmodernist infection, there is no doubt that *Alltagsgeschichte* is an enriching innovation.[40]

The determined emphasis on 'traditional' empirical history-writing is entirely understandable from one perspective: Irish labour historians have had a lot of catching up to do. Since the 1980s, a growing number of institutional histories have appeared of individual trade unions, and much work has been completed on prominent figures, particular moments (such as the 1913 lockout) and on radical political movements (such as those motivated by socialism and left-republicanism).[41] Nonetheless, the factual gaps in our knowledge are being filled very slowly. For example, a detailed survey of the working class in nineteenth-century Ireland remains to be written, though a useful beginning was made by John W. Boyle's *The Irish Labor Movement in the Nineteenth Century* (1988); Boyle's book, although a splendid piece of research, concentrates on organized labour and, for the most part, on the large urban centres of Dublin and Belfast. The first-ever collection of scholarly essays on the history of the Irish working class, *Politics and the Irish Working Class, 1830–1945* (edited by Lane and Ó Drisceoil), appeared as late as 2005, while, even more remarkably, the first thorough history of the Irish Labour Party (written by Niamh Puirséil) did not come out until 2007.[42] James Connolly's biography and political legacy (or legacies), on the other hand, have been the subject of innumerable studies; like rabbits, more than a few researchers in labour history remain trapped in his headlights.

Despite the leisurely rate of production, the past two decades have seen a gradual accumulation of scholarly works on the history of the Irish working class. Particularly from the 1990s, the scope of labour history research has broadened, with the appearance of comparative studies, such as John Lynch's *A Tale of Three Cities: Comparative Studies in Working-Class Life* (1998); investigations of the impact of legislation, such as Desmond Greer's and James W. Nicolson's *The Factory Acts in Ireland, 1802–1914* (2003); and long-run local and regional studies of particular sections of the working class, such as Maura Cronin's *Country, Class or Craft? The Politicisation of the Skilled Artisan in Nineteenth-Century Cork*

(1994) and Kevin James's *Handloom Weavers in Ulster's Linen Industry, 1815–1914* (2007). A little-noticed but very useful book that is worth reading in conjunction with James's study is Jane Gray's *Spinning the Threads of Uneven Development: Gender and Industrialisation in Ireland during the Long Eighteenth Century* (2005).[43] Far too little has been written on gender and, more specifically, on working-class women and the role of women within the labour force, and the appearance of *Women and Paid Work in Ireland, 1500–1930* (2000), edited by Bernadette Whelan, indicated some critical areas that await further research.[44] Anthropology has also made a contribution to working-class historiography, with the publication of Marilyn Silverman's mistitled *An Irish Working Class: Explorations in Political Economy and Hegemony, 1800–1950* (2001), a study of working people in Thomastown, County Kilkenny. Indeed, a number of local studies have appeared, though regional studies, such as John Cunningham's *Labour in the West of Ireland: Working Life and Struggle, 1890–1914* (1995), are less common; arguably, Ulster has been better served than most regions.[45]

Perhaps the most important book to be published was Emmet O'Connor's *A Labour History of Ireland, 1824–1960* (1992), which provided a badly needed overview that should have facilitated the emergence of courses on labour history within Irish academia. However, despite the availability of this textbook, university history departments continued to largely overlook the history of the working class and, even now, specific courses are a rarity; the number of university-based historians who have 'labour history' as their primary specialism is still very low. Indeed, it would be interesting to see a sociological background study done on those who do write labour history from within Irish academia, as one suspects that most derive their motivation and interest from elsewhere: for example, how many are engaged, or once were, with labour or leftist politics? How many are the sons or daughters of trade union or leftist activists? How many come from working-class communities with strong associational traditions? It would be absurdly reductionist to expect that a neat correlation will always be found – it will not – but, with so little working-class history taught in Irish universities, it is likely that the passion of the few often has its *fons et origo* elsewhere: labour history, manifestly, has come from below.

CONCLUDING THOUGHTS

Mainstream Irish historiography, as is clear from the literature survey mentioned at the outset of this chapter, has yet to fully integrate the research and information made available by labour historians over the past few decades. Likewise, university history departments have failed, thus far, to recognize the area as crucial; the experience of working people should be a fundamental element in any attempt to holistically apprehend the Irish past. This failure is linked to a wider avoidance of class as an explanatory factor among Irish public intellectuals and, in particular, within the elite political culture, where bourgeois nationalists historically have privileged ethnic identity and nation, with class wishfully dismissed as irrelevant in the Irish context. Fianna Fáil – the populist 'party of government' in the Republic of Ireland – has been especially anxious to maintain its cross-class constituency by undermining explicit class politics; Todd Andrews, a founding member of Fianna Fáil, summed up this mentality in the following terms:

> I believed … that we had in Ireland a classless society except for the remnants of Anglo-Irish gentry, and their imitators. After the Treaty, many of those left: those who remained, with notable exceptions, accepted the state but rejected the nation. The Free State regime warmly adopted this alien element, gave them seats in the Senate and proceeded to re-build a native ascendancy around them. The election of a Fianna Fáil government in 1932 put a stop to t is process. This restoration of the classless society is one of its rarely recognized contributions to the national well-being. What class consciousness exists in Irish society is merely tuppence halfpenny looking down on tuppence.[46]

In a similar vein, Charles Haughey, then leader of Fianna Fáil, with classic anti-intellectual reasoning, asserted in 1987 that socialism is 'an alien gospel of class warfare, envy and strife, is also inherently unIrish and therefore unworthy of a serious place in the language of Irish political debate.'[47] Bertie Ahern took a different tack in 2004 when he moved to strip the issue of class politics of all meaning by, rather implausibly, declaring himself a 'socialist'.[48] The nervous approach to class in Irish political culture has been reflected in academia.

In addition, misconceptions still exist with regard to the contours of labour history, which is defined narrowly by some as primarily the study of organized labour, with a special focus on industrial relations and political history. This is a hopelessly inadequate vision for labour history, which needs to embrace the entire history of the working class, from politics to leisure, from workplace behaviour to family relations, from socio-economic conditions to socio-cultural values. Indeed, a strong argument could be made for dispensing altogether with the term 'labour history', which seems to exclude rather than include, and referring instead to the 'history of the working class' or 'working-class history'. In 2003, on the inside cover of *Saothar*, we defined it thus:

> By the 'history of the working class', we mean waged and unwaged workers, their lives, work, economic conditions, social and cultural relationships, leaders, organisations, movements, values and ideas. Studies of anti-labour movements, such as strike-breaking organisations or anti-socialist groups, are also of relevance. We are particularly interested in studies that focus on the 'everyday life' of workers and their families.

Moreover, the study of the history of the working class cannot be conducted as if this class floated in a vacuum; classes do not exist alone, they change and shift as part of a relationship with other social classes and in the context of the prevailing mode of production. Consequently, while research on the working class is essential, the ultimate object of 'labour history' must be to assist in the construction of holistic general histories that appreciate the centrality of class in our past and present.

NOTES

1. Gearóid Ó Tuathaigh, 'Political history', in Laurence M. Geary and Margaret Kelleher (eds), *Nineteenth-Century Ireland: A Guide to Recent Research* (Dublin: 2005), pp. 21–2. However, a chapter on women's history by Maria Luddy, the inclusion of which reflects the vitality of that area, does contain a useful overview of research on waged women workers; see M. Luddy, 'Women's history', pp. 48–51.
2. R.B. McDowell and D.A. Webb, *Trinity College, Dublin, 1592–1952: An Academic History* (Dublin: 2004), pp. 44–5.
3. Donal McCartney, *W.E.H. Lecky: Historian and Politician, 1838–1903* (Dublin: 1994), p. 101.
4. Bowley was one of the intellectual founders of the London School of Economics, where he taught from 1895 to 1936. A liberal, he was sympathetic to Fabian socialism as a young man and did significant research on the economic condition of nineteenth-century workers in Britain and Ireland. On Ireland, see A.L. Bowley, 'The statistics of wages in the United Kingdom during the last hundred years, Part III, Agricultural wages continued: Ireland', *Journal of the Royal Statistical Society*, vol. LXII (June 1899) and 'The statistics of wages in the United Kingdom during the last hundred years, Part IV, Agricultural wages concluded: earnings and general averages', *Journal of the Royal Statistical Society*, vol. LXII (September 1899).
5. Sidney and Beatrice Webb published their seminal *The History of Trade Unionism* in 1894. The Webbs, whose specialism (like Bowley's) was economics and not history, were founders in 1895 of the London School of Economics. Sidney was later an MP for the British Labour Party.
6. C.H. Oldham to Manager, *The Commonweal*, 30 August 1885, Socialist League Papers, International Institute of Social History, Amsterdam.
7. Fintan Lane, *The Origins of Modern Irish Socialism, 1881–1896* (Cork: 1997), pp. 132–3, 160.
8. Ibid., pp. 128–31; Fintan Lane, 'William Morris and Irish politics', *History Ireland*, 8, 1 (Spring 2000), pp. 22–5. In England, the Irish *émigré* George Bernard Shaw also began his long association with the political left at this time; he was connected with Fabianism but had some interaction with Morris's Socialist League.
9. See the material published in *Ireland and the Irish Question: A Collection of Writings by Karl Marx and Frederick Engels* (New York: 1972), pp. 171–269.
10. On the nineteenth-century rural working class, see John W. Boyle, 'A marginal figure: the Irish

rural labourer', in Samuel Clark and James S. Donnelly (eds), *Irish Peasants: Violence and Political Unrest, 1780–1914* (Dublin: 1983), pp. 311–38; and Fintan Lane, 'Rural labourers, social change and politics in late nineteenth-century Ireland', in Fintan Lane and Donal Ó Drisceoil (eds), *Politics and the Irish Working Class, 1830–1945* (Basingstoke: 2005), pp. 113–39.
11. Boyle, 'A marginal figure', p. 311.
12. Cormac Ó Gráda, *Ireland: A New Economic History, 1780–1939* (Oxford: 1994), p. 273.
13. For an interesting discussion of these issues, see Ó Gráda, *Ireland*, pp. 273–348. On north-east Ulster, which experienced industrial growth rather than relative decline, see Philip Ollerenshaw, 'Industry, 1820–1914', and Henry Patterson, 'Industrial labour and the labour movement, 1820–1914', in Liam Kennedy and Philip Ollerenshaw (eds), *An Economic History of Ulster, 1820–1939* (Manchester: 1985).
14. Preceding figures and following table are drawn from data in A.J. Fitzpatrick and W.E. Vaughan (eds), *Irish Historical Statistics: Population, 1821–1971* (Dublin: 1978), p. 27.
15. Fintan Lane, 'James Connolly's 1901 census return', *Saothar*, vol. 25 (2000), pp. 103–6. The most detailed biography of Connolly is Donal Nevin's *James Connolly: 'A Full Life'* (Dublin: 2005).
16. Peter Berresford Ellis, *A History of the Irish Working Class* (London: 1985 edn), p. 11. Ellis also remarked, in the preface to the 1972 edition, that his book aimed to trace 'the struggle of the Irish working classes from their original communistic society, through the various stages of their struggle for national and social emancipation' (ibid., p. 8).
17. James Connolly, *Labour in Irish History* (Dublin: 1910), pp. 1–2.
18. Ibid., p. 214.
19. Quoted in W.K. Anderson, *James Connolly and the Irish Left* (Dublin: 1994), p. 41.
20. Aindrias Ó Cathasaigh, 'James Connolly and the writing of *Labour in Irish History* (1910)', *Saothar*, vol. 27 (2002), pp. 103–8.
21. Connolly, *Labour in Irish History*, pp. xi–xii.
22. See Helga Woggon, 'Interpreting James Connolly, 1916–23', in Lane and Ó Drisceoil, *Politics and the Irish Working Class*, pp. 172–86.
23. On the context of this upsurge in labour activity, see Emmet O'Connor, *A Labour History of Ireland, 1824–1960* (Dublin: 1992), pp. 94–116.
24. Emmet O'Connor, 'True Bolsheviks? The rise and fall of the Socialist Party of Ireland, 1917–21', in D. George Boyce and Alan O'Day (eds), *Ireland in Transition, 1867–1921* (London: 2004), p. 211.
25. Geoff Eley, *Forging Democracy: The History of the Left in Europe, 1850–2000* (New York: 2002), p. 138.
26. On labour radicalism during this period, see Emmet O'Connor, *Syndicalism in Ireland, 1917–1923* (Cork: 1988); D.R. O'Connor Lysaght, 'The Munster soviet creameries', *Irish History Workshop*, vol. 1 (1981), pp. 36–49; Liam Cahill, *Forgotten Revolution: Limerick Soviet, 1919* (Dublin: 1990); Conor Kostick, *Revolution in Ireland: Popular Militancy, 1917 to 1923* (London: 1996); and Conor Kostick, 'Labour militancy during the Irish War of Independence', in Lane and Ó Drisceoil, *Politics and the Irish Working Class*, pp. 187–206. Kostick arguably overstates the revolutionary potential of the labour unrest; many general studies, on the other hand, overlook or underestimate the real and potential impact of the labour movement between 1917 and 1923.
27. On MacDonnell and the James Connolly Labour College, see Norman Croke and Francis Devine, *James Connolly Labour College, 1919–1921* (Dublin: 2007). Also, on workers' education in Ireland, see Andrew Boyd, *Fermenting Elements: the Labour Colleges in Ireland, 1924–1964* (Belfast: 1999).
28. O'Connor, 'True Bolsheviks?', pp. 220–1.
29. Desmond Ryan, *James Connolly: His Life, Work and Writings* (Dublin: 1924).
30. W.P. Ryan, *The Irish Labour Movement from the Twenties to our own Day* (Dublin: 1919), p. 266.
31. Ibid., p. 10.
32. Ibid., p. 10.
33. J. Dunsmore Clarkson, *Labour and Nationalism in Ireland* (New York: 1925), pp. 477–8.
34. T.A. Jackson, *Ireland Her Own* (London: 1946), p. 356. Leninists, particularly of the orthodox communist strain, have always been anxious to associate Connolly with their political tradition. However, while clearly a Marxist, Connolly's leanings were towards syndicalism and there is no evidence that he was sympathetic to the theories of Vladimir Lenin and his then relatively obscure Bolshevik party. Nonetheless, the Leninists were quick to claim him as one of their own with, for example, the communist T.J. O'Flaherty, brother of the writer Liam O'Flaherty, insisting in 1926 that Connolly was 'a true Leninist before that word was coined into the English language', while agreeing with G. Schüller of the Communist International, who claimed that Connolly 'understood ... and put into practice the basic theories of Leninism'. See G. Schüller,

James Connolly and Irish Freedom (Cork: 1986; originally pub. Chicago: 1926), pp. 3, 5. C. Desmond Greaves in his 1961 biography of Connolly carried on this tradition of Leninist appropriation, regardless of the evidence to the contrary.
35. Richard Michael Fox, an English socialist married to Irish writer Patricia Lynch, wrote a number of journalistic volumes on the Irish left: the most interesting are *The History of the Irish Citizen Army* (Dublin: 1943), *James Connolly: the Forerunner* (Tralee: 1946), *Jim Larkin: the rise of the Underman* (London: 1957) and *Louie Bennett: Her Life and Times* (Dublin: 1958).
36. C. Desmond Greaves, *The Life and Times of James Connolly* (London: 1961) and Emmet Larkin, *James Larkin, 1876–1947: Irish Labour Leader* (London: 1965).
37. He had previously published a detailed study of contemporary Irish industrial relations, which is now an important source for labour historians of that period: Charles McCarthy, *The Decade of Upheaval: Irish Trade Unions in the Nineteen Sixties* (Dublin: 1973).
38. For work published in *Saothar*, between 1975 and 1999, see Francis Devine (ed.), *An Index to Saothar, Journal of the Irish Labour History Society, and other ILHS Publications, 1973–2000* (Dublin: 2000).
39. This tendency is exemplified, perhaps, by the 'Studies in Irish Labour History' pamphlet series produced by the ILHS, mostly in conjunction with SIPTU, Ireland's largest trade union.
40. On *Alltagsgeschichte*, see Alf Lüdtke (ed.), *The History of Everyday Life: Reconstructing Historical Experiences and Ways of Life* (Princeton, N.J: 1995). On related developments in the United States, see James B. Gardner and George Rollie Adams (eds), *Ordinary People and Everyday Life: Perspectives on the New Social History* (Nashville, TN: 1983).
41. Many histories of individual trade unions have now been published, most of which resulted from 'official' commissions by the unions themselves; examples include C. Desmond Greaves, *The Irish Transport and General Workers' Union: The Formative Years, 1909–1923* (Dublin: 1982); Sean Redmond, *The Irish Municipal Employees Trade Union, 1883–1983* (Dublin: 1983); Garry Sweeney, *In Public Service: A History of the Public Service Executive Union, 1890–1990* (Dublin: 1990); Martin Maguire, *Servants to the Public: A History of the Local Government and Public Services Union, 1901–1990* (Dublin: 1998); John Logan (ed.), *Teachers' Union: The TUI and its Forerunners, 1899–1994* (Dublin: 1999); and Marie Coleman, *IFUT: A History* (Dublin: 2000). In addition, see Seamus Cody, John O'Dowd and Peter Rigney, *The Parliament of Labour: 100 Years of the Dublin Council of Trade Unions* (Dublin: 1986) and Donal Nevin (ed.), *Trade Union Century* (Cork: 1994).
42. Niamh Puirséil, *The Irish Labour Party, 1922–73* (Dublin: 2007).
43. Also see Jane Gray, 'Gender and uneven working-class formation in the Irish linen industry', in Laura L. Frader and Sonya O. Rose (eds), *Gender and Class in Modern Europe* (Ithaca: 1996), pp. 37–56; and W.H. Crawford, *The Impact of the Domestic Linen Industry in Ulster* (Belfast: 2005).
44. For some examples of recent research on women and the working class, see Mary Jones, *These Obstreperous Lassies: A History of the Irish Women Workers' Union* (Dublin: 1988); Theresa Moriarty, *Work in Progress: Episodes from the History of Irish Women's Trade Unionism* (Dublin: 1995); Mary E. Daly, *Women and Work in Ireland* (Dundalk: 1997); Mary Cullen and Maria Luddy (eds), *Female Activists: Irish Women and Change, 1900–1960* (Dublin: 2001); Rosemary Cullen Owens, *Louie Bennett* (Cork: 2001); 'The economy from 1850' and 'The labour movement in Ireland, 1800–2000', in Angela Bourke et al (eds), *The Field Day Anthology of Irish Writing, Volume V, Irish Women's Writing and Traditions* (Cork: 2002), pp. 530–66; Rosemary Cullen Owens, *A Social History of Women in Ireland, 1870–1970* (Dublin: 2005); and Maria Luddy, 'Working women, trade unionism and politics in Ireland, 1830–1945', in Lane and Ó Drisceoil, *Politics and the Irish Working Class*, pp. 44–61.
45. Studies on Ulster workers, however, tend to focus on the industrial area in and around Belfast; see, for example, Henry Patterson, *Class Conflict and Sectarianism: the Protestant Working Class and the Belfast Labour Movement, 1868–1920* (Belfast: 1980); Graham Walker, *The Politics of Frustration: Harry Midgley and the Failure of Labour in Northern Ireland* (Manchester: 1985); John Gray, *City in Revolt: James Larkin and the Belfast Dock Strike of 1907* (Belfast: 1985); Austen Morgan, *Labour and Partition: the Belfast Working Class, 1905–23* (London: 1991); Terence Bowman, *People's Champion: The Life of Alexander Bowman* (Belfast: 1997); and Catherine Hirst, 'Politics, sectarianism and the working class in nineteenth-century Belfast', in Lane and Ó Drisceoil, *Politics and the Irish Working Class*, pp. 62–86.
46. C.S. Andrews, *Man of No Property* (Cork, 1982), pp. 256–7.
47. Quoted in Diarmaid Ferriter, *The Transformation of Ireland, 1900–2000* (London, 2004), p. 697.
48. *Irish Times*, 13 November 2004.

3

Popular Protest and a 'Moral Economy' in Provincial Ireland in the Early Nineteenth Century

JOHN CUNNINGHAM

The editor of the *Londonderry Journal* took the opportunity provided by the 1811–12 subsistence crisis to offer a lesson in political economy. Quoting approvingly from Adam Smith, he urged that a bad situation not be made worse by inappropriate intervention. While it was regrettable, he wrote, that 'the poorer classes impute their distresses to the corn merchant and the farmer, and cast such a degree of odium upon them that the one is induced to re-sell his grain in the port where he had purchased it, and the other to hoard it up',[1] their reaction was understandable. But it was not only poor people who had the capacity to adversely affect circumstances at such times:

> Even the wealthy and better informed part of the community join in the cry, and excite rather then discourage the clamours of the populace, and sometimes countenance tumultuous risings of the people, which generally terminate in the destruction of ... the very article of which they stand so much in need.[2]

No rising was anticipated in Derry, where 'civilization and respect for the laws are to be found in greater perfection than any other part of the world', but caution was necessary nonetheless, given what had happened in the city as recently as 1808, when:

> the Corporation and a Society of the most respectable inhabitants of the city, all influenced by the most pure and laudable motives, purchased a quantity of oatmeal for the purpose of retailing it to

James Connolly and Irish Freedom (Cork: 1986; originally pub. Chicago: 1926), pp. 3, 5. C. Desmond Greaves in his 1961 biography of Connolly carried on this tradition of Leninist appropriation, regardless of the evidence to the contrary.
35. Richard Michael Fox, an English socialist married to Irish writer Patricia Lynch, wrote a number of journalistic volumes on the Irish left: the most interesting are *The History of the Irish Citizen Army* (Dublin: 1943), *James Connolly: the Forerunner* (Tralee: 1946), *Jim Larkin: the rise of the Underman* (London: 1957) and *Louie Bennett: Her Life and Times* (Dublin: 1958).
36. C. Desmond Greaves, *The Life and Times of James Connolly* (London: 1961) and Emmet Larkin, *James Larkin, 1876–1947: Irish Labour Leader* (London: 1965).
37. He had previously published a detailed study of contemporary Irish industrial relations, which is now an important source for labour historians of that period: Charles McCarthy, *The Decade of Upheaval: Irish Trade Unions in the Nineteen Sixties* (Dublin: 1973).
38. For work published in *Saothar*, between 1975 and 1999, see Francis Devine (ed.), *An Index to Saothar, Journal of the Irish Labour History Society, and other ILHS Publications, 1973–2000* (Dublin: 2000).
39. This tendency is exemplified, perhaps, by the 'Studies in Irish Labour History' pamphlet series produced by the ILHS, mostly in conjunction with SIPTU, Ireland's largest trade union.
40. On *Alltagsgeschichte*, see Alf Lüdtke (ed.), *The History of Everyday Life: Reconstructing Historical Experiences and Ways of Life* (Princeton, N.J: 1995). On related developments in the United States, see James B. Gardner and George Rollie Adams (eds), *Ordinary People and Everyday Life: Perspectives on the New Social History* (Nashville, TN: 1983).
41. Many histories of individual trade unions have now been published, most of which resulted from 'official' commissions by the unions themselves; examples include C. Desmond Greaves, *The Irish Transport and General Workers' Union: The Formative Years, 1909–1923* (Dublin: 1982); Sean Redmond, *The Irish Municipal Employees Trade Union, 1883–1983* (Dublin: 1983); Garry Sweeney, *In Public Service: A History of the Public Service Executive Union, 1890–1990* (Dublin: 1990); Martin Maguire, *Servants to the Public: A History of the Local Government and Public Services Union, 1901–1990* (Dublin: 1998); John Logan (ed.), *Teachers' Union: The TUI and its Forerunners, 1899–1994* (Dublin: 1999); and Marie Coleman, *IFUT: A History* (Dublin: 2000). In addition, see Seamus Cody, John O'Dowd and Peter Rigney, *The Parliament of Labour: 100 Years of the Dublin Council of Trade Unions* (Dublin: 1986) and Donal Nevin (ed.), *Trade Union Century* (Cork: 1994).
42. Niamh Puirséil, *The Irish Labour Party, 1922–73* (Dublin: 2007).
43. Also see Jane Gray, 'Gender and uneven working-class formation in the Irish linen industry', in Laura L. Frader and Sonya O. Rose (eds), *Gender and Class in Modern Europe* (Ithaca: 1996), pp. 37–56; and W.H. Crawford, *The Impact of the Domestic Linen Industry in Ulster* (Belfast: 2005).
44. For some examples of recent research on women and the working class, see Mary Jones, *These Obstreperous Lassies: A History of the Irish Women Workers' Union* (Dublin: 1988); Theresa Moriarty, *Work in Progress: Episodes from the History of Irish Women's Trade Unionism* (Dublin: 1995); Mary E. Daly, *Women and Work in Ireland* (Dundalk: 1997); Mary Cullen and Maria Luddy (eds), *Female Activists: Irish Women and Change, 1900–1960* (Dublin: 2001); Rosemary Cullen Owens, *Louie Bennett* (Cork: 2001); 'The economy from 1850' and 'The labour movement in Ireland, 1800–2000', in Angela Bourke et al (eds), *The Field Day Anthology of Irish Writing, Volume V, Irish Women's Writing and Traditions* (Cork: 2002), pp. 530–66; Rosemary Cullen Owens, *A Social History of Women in Ireland, 1870–1970* (Dublin: 2005); and Maria Luddy, 'Working women, trade unionism and politics in Ireland, 1830–1945', in Lane and Ó Drisceoil, *Politics and the Irish Working Class*, pp. 44–61.
45. Studies on Ulster workers, however, tend to focus on the industrial area in and around Belfast; see, for example, Henry Patterson, *Class Conflict and Sectarianism: the Protestant Working Class and the Belfast Labour Movement, 1868–1920* (Belfast: 1980); Graham Walker, *The Politics of Frustration: Harry Midgley and the Failure of Labour in Northern Ireland* (Manchester: 1985); John Gray, *City in Revolt: James Larkin and the Belfast Dock Strike of 1907* (Belfast: 1985); Austen Morgan, *Labour and Partition: the Belfast Working Class, 1905–23* (London: 1991); Terence Bowman, *People's Champion: The Life of Alexander Bowman* (Belfast: 1997); and Catherine Hirst, 'Politics, sectarianism and the working class in nineteenth-century Belfast', in Lane and Ó Drisceoil, *Politics and the Irish Working Class*, pp. 62–86.
46. C.S. Andrews, *Man of No Property* (Cork, 1982), pp. 256–7.
47. Quoted in Diarmaid Ferriter, *The Transformation of Ireland, 1900–2000* (London, 2004), p. 697.
48. *Irish Times*, 13 November 2004.

3

Popular Protest and a 'Moral Economy' in Provincial Ireland in the Early Nineteenth Century

JOHN CUNNINGHAM

The editor of the *Londonderry Journal* took the opportunity provided by the 1811–12 subsistence crisis to offer a lesson in political economy. Quoting approvingly from Adam Smith, he urged that a bad situation not be made worse by inappropriate intervention. While it was regrettable, he wrote, that 'the poorer classes impute their distresses to the corn merchant and the farmer, and cast such a degree of odium upon them that the one is induced to re-sell his grain in the port where he had purchased it, and the other to hoard it up',[1] their reaction was understandable. But it was not only poor people who had the capacity to adversely affect circumstances at such times:

> Even the wealthy and better informed part of the community join in the cry, and excite rather then discourage the clamours of the populace, and sometimes countenance tumultuous risings of the people, which generally terminate in the destruction of ... the very article of which they stand so much in need.[2]

No rising was anticipated in Derry, where 'civilization and respect for the laws are to be found in greater perfection than any other part of the world', but caution was necessary nonetheless, given what had happened in the city as recently as 1808, when:

> the Corporation and a Society of the most respectable inhabitants of the city, all influenced by the most pure and laudable motives, purchased a quantity of oatmeal for the purpose of retailing it to

the poor at reduced prices ... For a time, their efforts had the desired effect; but mark the end. Considerable supplies originally destined for this port were ordered to others ... and while Belfast market, which had been allowed to take its natural course, declined considerably after benefiting by the supplies intended for us, the price of ours advanced.[3]

In 1808, the *Journal* had approved of mayoral intervention, and if the editorial line had changed in the meantime, it was not a singular shift, for there was much debate in early nineteenth-century Ireland – just as there was in England and elsewhere – about the proper response to popular distress.[4]

Whether the *Londonderry Journal* editor's knowledge of the predilections of the poor during hard times was acquired from the pages of Adam Smith or from his own experience of Irish crowds is a question that must be asked. E.P. Thompson, whose seminal 1971 article, 'The moral economy of the English crowd in the eighteenth century', triggered immense interest in food disturbances and in market culture generally, concluded that the 'classical' food riot was not a significant feature of the Irish scene, but later modified his position somewhat. On the basis, mainly, of a description in John Wesley's journal of the behaviour of an anti-export 'mob' at Jamestown County Sligo, Thompson posited that the '"classical" food riot was certainly known to the eighteenth-century Irish', but, guided by the absence of the phenomenon from Irish historiography, accepted that there must have been a 'weakening of the tradition as the century wore on'.[5] Recent writers on the subject, otherwise unsympathetic to Thompson's arguments, have accepted this view.[6] However, there is evidence pointing to a vibrant 'moral economy' with regard to the marketing of food into the early nineteenth century, and in research on the town of Galway considerable evidence was found of its durability up until the famine, and even of a residual presence afterwards.[7] Incidental evidence indicating that Galway was not exceptional provided the impetus to establish the extent of provincial urban Ireland's moral economy in the early nineteenth century. But in order to determine whether a 'moral economy' was a significant factor in Irish social relations of the early nineteenth century, we must first summarize Thompson's thesis.

The historic importance of ensuring that urban populations were cheaply fed was reflected in regulatory mechanisms of the mercantilist era – in laws against monopolistic food-marketing practices, such as forestalling, regrating and engrossing; in the appointment of market juries by local authorities so as to protect consumers from exploitation by dealers; in proscriptions on distilling and on food exports from districts affected by scarcity. Such mechanisms came to be regarded as an administrative and ethical imperative by urban elites, and as vital shields against hunger by urban crowds, with the result that a type of social contract came into being. The mobilizations usually referred to as 'food riots' were the crowd's way of drawing attention to breaches of this social contract. That they were rarely as disorderly as implied by the term was indicated by the practice of *taxation populaire* – the seizure of over-priced produce, its sale at a 'fair price' by the crowd, and the payment of the reduced amount to the owner.

Such demonstrations occurred in towns, or at least places where there were markets, and mainly at times of general scarcity, when shortages gave opportunities to speculators, and when soaring prices gave market customers reasons to believe that they were being defrauded. As the *Londonderry Journal* suggested, food disturbances were often treated indulgently by the authorities, being differentiated from sometimes similar activity on the part of agrarian secret societies, which, it has been shown, had their own version of a moral economy.[8] While the focus of this article is on urban Ireland, reference will be made to a number of rural mobilizations whose clear purpose was to reduce food prices. Regulatory crowds, generally, were composed of the working poor, and they considered themselves to be acting righteously in drawing to attention market abuses. Indeed, for most working-class people of the pre-industrial and early industrial eras, the marketplace was a more fruitful arena for economic bargaining than the workplace.

In labelling the social relationship described as the 'moral economy', Thompson was deliberately drawing a contrast with the 'political economy' of the theorists of contemporaneous capitalism, who abhorred all interference in markets, whether by assertive crowds or meddlesome market jurors. (Thompson did acknowledge that the term 'moral economy' was used in a similar sense as early as 1837 by Chartist leader, Bronterre O'Brien (1805–64), who, incidentally, may have witnessed the food disturbances of 1817 in his native Granard.)

For the political economists, a high price for a scarce commodity was an effective rationing mechanism, compelling the improvident poor to be sensibly thrifty, and the increasing influence of their ideology was shown in the repeal of the parliamentary legislation prohibiting forestalling, and in increasing disregard for by-law injunctions. As time went on, popular demonstrations did not win redress as easily as heretofore, because local elites were tending to renounce the social contract (and were facilitated in suppressing 'disorder' by improved transport and by a more interventionist state). It was a slow process, however, and vestiges of the moral economy survived for two generations after the publication of *Wealth of Nations*.

Changes in the economic context had their own effects. The provincial grain trade received a stimulus from the bounties paid by the Irish parliament in the late eighteenth century, encouraging dealers to supply the almost insatiable Dublin market, while the extension of the canal network opened up trade with the interior.[9] In this context, and one of growing demand for food from Britain, fresh grounds for concern about the local food supply presented themselves during the half century before the Famine. Such concern resulted in protests of 1800–1, 1808, 1812, 1817 and, the evidence seems to indicate, on several occasions during the 1820s, 1830s and early 1840s. These protests were sufficiently widespread as to justify a revision of the judgement of the editors of the volume *Crowds in Ireland*, when they state that 'scarcity crowds appear to have been far fewer prior to the Famine than they had been in the eighteenth century.'[10]

THE EIGHTEENTH CENTURY BACKGROUND

Several writers have described popular interventions in the urban marketplace during periods of distress in the middle part of the eighteenth century. In his treatment of responses to distress in 1728–9, James Kelly referred to the ban on food exports by the Irish Privy Council, a measure which did not prevent disorder, because it did not prevent food being moved within Ireland. In the south, where the harvest had been ample, prices were nonetheless high because of demand from Ulster, where it had not. Imposing *taxation populaire*, and preventing grain ships from sailing from the port, the Cork crowd brought about a considerable reduction in local prices (albeit at the cost of at least six lives), sparking off 'province-wide food riots'.[11] David Dickson catalogued anti-export demonstrations during the terrible Famine of 1740–1 in Dublin, Dungarvan, Carrick-on-Suir, Youghal, Cork, Kinsale, Galway, Sligo, Belfast, and Drogheda. In Drogheda, a 'crowd' seized a vessel laden with oatmeal and destined for Scotland in April 1740, removing her sails and rudder, and surrendering control only when the urban authorities undertook to prohibit all food exports. Not all such 'negotiations' in 1740, however, had a congenial outcome.[12] Eoin Magennis's research on the crisis of 1756–7 uncovered anti-export mobilizations in Waterford, Wexford, Cork, Galway and Drogheda, and riotous attacks on grainstores and/or suspected forestallers in Belfast, Dundalk, Dublin, and Wexford. He cited a report from Waterford of April 1757, when a 'mob' seized a large quantity of oatmeal and 'retailed it out' in the market. Though it was not explicitly spelled out, the fact that the contraband was taken to the public market indicates that this was an example of *taxation populaire*, rather than of simple appropriation. And although the comfortable classes disapproved strongly of 'direct action' by the people, both charitable and public bodies throughout the island intervened in the food market in 1756–7, with a view to relieving distress and maintaining public order. Evidently guided by a Mark Harrison, a detractor of E.P. Thompson's, Magennis was hesitant regarding whether the evidence he offered proved 'the existence of an Irish "moral economy"' in the eighteenth century,[13] but, if taken in conjunction with the work of the other writers mentioned, it seems to point strongly in that direction, bearing in mind Thompson's own declaration of purpose:

> ... to reconstruct a paternalistic model of food marketing, with protective institutional expression and with emergency routines in times of dearth ... and to show how, in times of high prices and of hardship, the crowd might enforce, with a robust direct action, protective control and the regulation of prices, *sometimes* [author's emphasis] claiming a legitimacy derived from the paternalist model.[14]

Emmet O'Connor referred to anti-export mobilizations in Waterford in 1732 and 1744, and research is likely to provide examples from later in the eighteenth century, especially since anti-export disturbances were among the phenomena which were specifically provided for in the 1772 legislation which is regarded as 'effectively Ireland's first Riot Act'.[15]

Roger Wells, an authority on English markets, has researched the Irish subsistence crisis of 1799–1801, one complicated by prevailing political circumstances. It was an episode, he argued, that 'revealed various confrontations between moral and market economies'. There was an administration committed to the free movement of provisions, but constrained by the need to persuade 'public opinion' regarding political union; there were military commanders, clergymen and editors throughout the country who believed that forestallers and regraters bore responsibility for the famine prices in their own neighbourhoods; there were agrarian militants and urban crowds which took steps to prevent provisions leaving their communities and to set their price. Having offered ample evidence of the existence of moral-economic behaviour, and informed by detailed knowledge of contemporaneous occurrences in England, Wells argues that the weight of evidence indicates that there were 'classical' food riots involving *taxation populaire* in several Irish towns during 1799–1801. The want of conclusive proof, he maintained, was due to scantiness of surviving sources by comparison with England.[16]

THE CRISIS OF 1808

A severe frost and heavy snowfall throughout the island in late October/early November 1807 destroyed a large proportion of the potatoes remaining in the ground – the part of the crop retained by the rural poor for their subsistence.[17] The resulting shortfall led to high prices for staples in spring, and consequent alarm, expressed at meetings of 'the inhabitants' of Lurgan, Strabane, and Derry. In Lurgan, monthly subscriptions were sought for a fund to subsidize bread prices for the 'labouring classes', so as to bring 'provisions more within the reach of their means, without relaxing their endeavours to help themselves'. The 'working classes', according to the *Freeman's Journal*, 'are much more to be sympathized with than the importunate beggars, who, by artifice of one kind or another, extort more by begging than can be made by modest industry'. For the *Londonderry Journal*, the 'liberality', which it said was 'manifested in various parts of the country', was 'honourable to the national character'.[18]

From Dublin came reports of forestalling, alongside indications of exceptional interest in the regulation of food and fuel markets on the part of the mayor and other officials. Reminding newly-appointed market jurors of the 'necessity of paying attention to their duty', the recorder of Dublin 'recommended them rather to take those persons by surprise when they went to search for unwholesome food or light bread, than to make a parade, which gave the alarm, and afforded time to the fraudulent dealer to evade justice'.[19]

In Belfast, in early May, a crowd threatened to take violent action to force down provisions prices. Soldiers were deployed, and a magistrate, assisted by several 'respectable gentlemen', persuaded the people to disperse – presumably, undertakings were given that distress would be alleviated.[20] In Bagenalstown, County Carlow, the 'extravagant' price of potatoes sparked a riot, of which no details were found, and in the barony of St Molins, in the same county, a threatening notice was brought to the attention of Brigade Major Hoare:

> This is timely notice and fair warning to all those people who has potatoes or meal for sale or can spare them. By any means to give

them to every person that goes to ask them. Otherwise they will be punished alive, then burned, and destroyed positively. They may believe it. Philip Kavanagh of Drana, Patt and Charles Kavanagh of Ballycronogan, and the Foleys and Thomas Doyle of said town ... Paddy Pine of Ballybegstafford, he ought to take warning be his neighbour Commins, that poor nager that was overjoyed at the distress of the poor and even mocked at beggars in place of giving them alms – he has prayers enough, but no charity.[21]

Andrew Commins, the resident of Ballybegstafford who is referred to in the notice, was an elderly man whose house had been burned in the night. The claim he subsequently lodged with the Grand Jury included the sum of £31.10.0 for thirty-five barrels of potatoes.[22]

In Kilrush, County Clare, nightly meetings were held in early June 'for the avowed purpose of keeping down the price of potatoes', and price-setting notices were posted at Catholic churches.[23] Regarding similar activity in the barony of Kenry, County Limerick, Bolton Waller noted that it was 'considered by some as meritorious', even by 'well-intentioned men ... satisfied that anything short of subversion of His Majesty's government should occupy the minds of the populace'. Such people, he went on, 'forget that mobs don't stop in Ireland – they've interfered here about land and the quantities of labour'. But it was not just 'the populace' that was intervening in the market thereabouts, for the military captain at Askeaton seized potatoes and 'commanded that money paid by soldiers' wives for potatoes over his regulations should be returned to them'.[24]

Possibly the most serious of the 1808 disturbances occurred in Galway town on 21 April, when 'the populace rose' to prevent the departure of the *Anne* with seventy tons of oatmeal for Derry. The vessel's sails were confiscated by the crowd in the presence of the mayor, complained the exporter's agent, and neither he nor the military commander took any steps to recover them.[25]

THE CROWD IN 1812

Unrest in response to high food prices in 1812 caused considerable concern in elite circles, not least because it coincided with Luddist machine breaking across the channel. If the anxieties of the people were not assuaged, warned Dublin's *Evening Herald*, there would be outbreaks 'similar in violence to those which swept the manufacturing districts of England'.[26] Before this warning of mid-March, there had already been mobilizations to prevent the movement of food, and there would be dozens of others throughout Ireland between then and high summer. In order to address the widespread nature of the mobilization and to convey something of elite attitudes to both shortages and unrest, it will be convenient to group developments under geographical headings, as follows: (i) inland waterways; (ii) County Cork; and (iii) seaports.

(i) *Inland waterways*: By mid-March, Dublin's food supply was threatened by attacks on traffic along the main line and branches of the Grand Canal, which had linked Dublin with Shannon Harbour since 1804 (and places closer with the capital before that). Writing from Sallins on 12 March, and referring to 'outrages' in Edenderry and Philipstown, Richard Griffith (1784–1878) – then young geologist, later eminent surveyor – predicted 'much more serious disorders', explaining: 'The canal has been attacked ... because it furnishes great facility to the transportation of potatoes to the capital, and, I think, introduced a considerable speculation in these necessary articles in its neighbourhood.'[27] On the following day, a merchant wrote to Dublin Castle, describing disorder in his general vicinity: the canal had been drained by miscreants outside Tullamore, and 'the mob' was on the loose in Kildare town. From Rathangan came reports that a boat had been stopped, and its cargo placed 'under the Mobb', which had divided it for safe-keeping between a number of houses.[28] At Carlow quay, on the Barrow line of the canal, a notice threatened that any boat bringing meal or potatoes to Dublin would be sunk, and boatmen observed the interdiction.[29]

Elsewhere in the region, magistrates were reluctant to intervene against hungry crowds, and even an investigating committee of directors of the canal company did not contradict the popular analysis of the cause of scarcity:

> Your committee feel that no actual want of provisions in the country has been the real cause of those acts of violence – that an artificial want appeared in some of the towns on your line owing to the speculation of individuals who purchased potatoes and oatmeal for the advanced market of Dublin together with the improper conduct on the sale of provisions by forestallers in those towns.[30]

On Monday, 27 April the people of Carrick-on-Suir assembled in response to the ringing of the town's bells in order to reduce food prices. The first targets were several corn stores, which had their roofs removed and their various grains mixed together (so as to hinder their sale at market). For want of an 'active magistrate' – according to one local notable – the crowd was able to commit 'considerable mischief', but eventually magistrate Harry Briscoe read the Riot Act and directed the army to intervene. The crowd dispersed, but the confiscated meal was not recovered. Rather, it was deposited in stores belonging to a Mr Murray, pending its sale 'at a moderate price to be fixed by themselves'. Next, according to a news-paper report, horses and cars were requisitioned and the people proceeded to rural areas, from whence they procured quantities of potatoes 'by violence', and obliged some farmers to swear that they would send their potatoes to the market, and sell them at 5d per stone (a price that was about 50 per cent above normal, but a price-fixing crowd in nearby Waterford, it will be seen, considered 10d to be reasonable in the circumstances of 1812). Negotiations ensued between representatives of the crowd and Briscoe, the outcome of which was an undertaking to send fifty barrels of potatoes to the market to be sold for 5d a stone. The town was quiet on the following days, but the governing element remained apprehensive, and magistrates in the county sought advice from the chief secretary's office regarding the appropriateness of employing the Riot Act in response to likely future outbreaks.[31]

(ii) *Cork*: At the *Mercantile Chronicle*, editor Eneas McDonnell was reluctant to add to public alarm by discussing in his paper the possibility of a subsistence crisis, but he was persuaded that the dissemination of accurate information would tend to allay fears, so he conducted an investigation into the county's food supply. McDonnell (1783–1858) – whose family was involved in the grain trade at Westport and who himself would later gain prominence in Catholic politics – accepted that the *bona fides* of people like his brother might be suspect, so he circulated a questionnaire throughout Cork's seventeen baronies among the Catholic clergy – men who had 'daily intercourse with their parishioners', and a 'well-known regard for ... the poor in general'.[32]

The responses to the questionnaire – a selection of which were published – indicated that scarcity was acute in some places, and not in others. McDonnell clearly had less faith in the capacity of the market to distribute the necessities of life than had his contemporary at the *Londonderry Journal*:

> If the present supply of provisions in this county be suffered to remain therein, and to be used exclusively for the food of man, it will be found sufficient ... provided attention be devoted to the proper distribution thereof – namely, by causing those baronies which it appears can spare potatoes ... to forward them in fair proportions to the few districts where apprehensions are justifiably entertained, and also by inducing the holders of potatoes to forward their stock.[33]

The 'overholding system' was not pervasive, he continued diplomatically, but he urged 'the gentlemen of the county ... by a discreet exertion of influence such as their own sense may direct, [to] endeavour to persuade the holders of potatoes to be satisfied with reasonable profits'.³⁴ Dublin Castle's informants in the county provided evidence of the operation of an 'overholding system', and of efforts to conquer it: from Kilworth came reports of farmers being sworn not to take their potatoes to market by 'night-time visitors' – presumably other farmers with an interest in the price of potatoes; from Midleton, by contrast, came accounts of 'nightly assemblies of some hundreds ... styling themselves Caravats with a pretence of reducing the price of potatoes'.³⁵

Food continued to leave the county, prompting a hungry throng from the town of Skibbereen to tramp three miles along the River Ilen in the direction of Baltimore on the night of 22–23 April, to capture a sloop loaded with potatoes for Dublin, and to unload it onto small boats, before depositing the cargo in the town's market house, from where it was still being sold at a reduced rate more than a week later. Bernard Marmion, owner of the potatoes, had persuaded magistrates to accompany him to the scene, but he found them to be ineffective. For their parts, the magistrates insisted they had done all they could: risking their lives in 'an old crazy leaky boat', promising to secure lenient treatment for all involved if the potatoes were surrendered, and undertaking to call a public meeting to organize relief measures. Further steps were precluded, according to magistrate Timothy O'Driscoll, because the crowd included armed yeomanry, and there would have been 'great bloodshed' if he had called out the military.³⁶ The apparent involvement of members of the West Carbery infantry raised eyebrows further afield, but Colonel Aurish, in Bandon, assured his superiors that there was no particular cause for concern:

> It is almost impossible for any mob to assemble without having some yeomanry of the party, as they constitute so large a portion of the inhabitants of the western part of the county. If any excuse may be made for such impropriety of conduct, it may be placed under the head of dire necessity, for certainly they were in a state of starvation ...³⁷

(iii) *The seaports*: Between March and July 1812, anti-export crowds are recorded as having assembled in Galway, Waterford, Drogheda and Belfast. The Galway events of late March have been adequately detailed elsewhere, and will not be considered here.³⁸

In mid-April, with potatoes retailing at 18d a stone, the poor of Waterford were in despair. On learning that two sloops bringing potatoes from Clonakilty to Dublin were sheltering in Passage East, large numbers of people made their way there, and forced the captains to take their vessels to the city quays, where they were greeted by a triumphant crowd. A magistrate intervened, offering the captains a premium of twenty-five guineas to 'quietly' bring the potatoes to market. The captains consented.[39] Further subsidies were offered by the corporation and a committee of merchants, enabling potatoes to be sold at 10d a stone, 'by permission', according to a sardonic observer, 'of the sovereyn people'.[40]

On the morning of Monday, 4 May 1812, 3,000 people marched to Drogheda's quay, where the *Stag* was loading oatmeal and wheat for Whitehaven in Cumbria. From the vessel, the cargo was taken to the marketplace, the intention being that it be 'retailed to the poor at the market price', whereupon the crowd returned to unload the Liverpool-bound *Duke of Richmond*. On this second occasion, the crowd was interrupted by soldiers. Next, the stores of those 'men who had purchased for the purpose of retailing at a high price to the poor' were targeted, though the premises of 'the known and respectable merchants' were left alone. By early evening, 'great quantities' of meal and potatoes were in the possession of a magistrate in the marketplace – entrusted to his care by the multitude. Word reached the marketplace that the *Duke of Richmond* was hoisting sail, whereupon the crowd rushed to the shore. Local officials remained apprehensive, and sought clarification regarding whether the ban on exports of provisions applied to cargoes destined for other parts of the United Kingdom.[41]

Through the month of June, the *Belfast Newsletter* reassured its readers that the threatened subsistence crisis was over. Potato prices were falling daily, it reported early in the month, and the shilling loaf at the public bakery had been increased in weight by a quarter pound. On the 23rd, amidst other editorial hyperbole, it 'rejoiced' at having seen 'fine new potatoes' in the market, and 'congratulate[d] the public' on a further fall in the price of oatmeal. By 10 July, however, the paper was scolding 'the giddy and thoughtless multitude' for recent disturbances in Antrim town and in Belfast, reminding them of the 'most benevolent exertions of the rich' and arguing that 'if farmers and others find that their meal is to be taken from them by violence when they bring it to market, they will bring no more of it'.[42] A Belfast crowd, estimated at 5,000, had assembled at dusk on 9 July, and remained through the night, seizing meal from cars leaving the town and taking possession of a vessel at the quay. Following the reading of the Riot Act, order was restored by the Dumfrieshire regiment – though without firing on the crowd –

and cavalry reinforcements arrived to prevent further outbreaks. On 11 July, the seized vessel was allowed to leave the port with its cargo, and two 'ringleaders' were lying in Carrickfergus gaol. Thomas Drinkwater, a drummer with the merchants' infantry corps, was one of them.[43]

There are grounds for suspecting that there were food disturbances of 1812 that left no mark on the historical record. If Eneas MacDonnell is a guide, there were newspapermen who exercised self-censorship lest a report of a disturbance lead to imitation; if there were those who, out of local pride or embarrassment, played down the depredations of their 'own' crowd, it is likely that there were others who neglected to inform outside authority about them; if, as Bolton Waller believed, there were well-to-do people who considered price-fixing to be 'meritorious', they would hardly have registered complaints about it. But, despite the gapped character of the evidence, the events of 1812 are indicative of a widespread moral economic tradition: firstly, popular mobilizations occurred in all four provinces; secondly, there was variety in the objectives of crowds – most of them came together to prevent exports, but there was price-fixing also, and some anti-forestalling measures. This suggests a developed tradition (something explicitly mentioned only in relation to Galway[44]), as does the response of the authorities, which was so mild in instances as to be almost complicit in the efforts at regulation.

In 1813, food supplies were at more normal levels, but there were attempts to prevent the removal of food from a number of communities, nevertheless; in January, at Mullingar on the Royal Canal, anonymous letters were received by boatmen, warning them against bringing potatoes to Dublin; on the Grand Canal, in July, there were 'various depredations' to prevent the sending of provisions to Dublin. Further north, in Bangor, County Down, in late March, anti-export rioters targeted cars bringing potatoes towards the port, an episode in which members of Bangor's yeomanry were implicated. Soldiers had to be brought from Belfast because neighbouring yeomanry corps ignored orders to intervene. Later, when 'ringleader' Robert Sutherland of the Bangor Militia was arrested, his comrades attempted to rescue him.[45]

SOCIAL TURMOIL IN 1817

The subsistence crisis of 1817 was caused by a poor harvest resulting from exceptionally low temperatures in the western hemisphere during 1816 – conditions attributable to the global dispersal of volcanic dust following a cataclysmic eruption in April 1815 in the Indonesian archipelago. With circumstances aggravated by high unemployment due to economic disruption in the wake of the Napoleonic wars, 1817 saw unrest throughout Europe. For the Irish poor, the year ushered in a period of particular difficulty, possibly the worst during the century between the great famines of the 1740s and the 1840s.[46]

'So early as January', according to the *Dublin Evening Post*, there were 'meetings held in several of the country parts of Ireland to provide for the distresses of the poor'.[47] At one such meeting, in Drogheda on 15 January, it was agreed that the relief committee should follow Derry precedent, and accept loans as well as donations from the town's 'inhabitants' (the term referred to people of means, distinguishing them from the 'populace'). At the same meeting, the mayor announced that £50 remained unspent from the fund established for the same purpose in 1812.[48]

If there were meetings of 'inhabitants' in January, discontent was already manifesting itself in actions of the 'populace' in various places, and they would continue into the summer. The events will be examined in three phases, (i) January; (ii) February and March; and (iii) late May and June.

(i) *January*: The Drogheda meeting referred to above may have been prompted by an 'inclination' on the part of the resident 'manufacturing classes ... to parade the streets with emblems of distress'.[49] More seriously, there had been an attack 'by a numerous and tumultuous mob' on a convoy of cars carrying grain, just outside the nearby village of Wilkinstown. The owner, one Charlton, was a magistrate and was consequently empowered to order his escort from the 45th regiment to shoot into the crowd, with the result that a man was killed.[50] Almost 200 miles away, meanwhile, a meeting of several thousand of Cork's journeymen tradesmen demanded intervention to alleviate hunger.[51] In Galway on 9 January, and in Tuam two days later, there were further disturbances. The Galway events were described in a letter from interested merchants to William Gregory, Galway landlord and under secretary at Dublin Castle:

> A considerable mob paraded the town on Thursday last and broke the windows of Mr Moore's house, a respectable merchant who was shipping oatmeal contrary to their wish. They also broke his carts and threw his weights and scales into the river. They broke the windows of the principal flour mill and those of the stores of Mr Burke ... We trust that His Excellency will be pleased to give such directions to the magistrates of Galway as shall in future insure protection to the exportation of grain ...[52]

These 'shameful proceedings' according to the *Belfast Newsletter*, were deserving of 'the most serious reprehension', especially given the intended destination of the affected cargo: 'Would the mob of Galway allow the people of Derry to famish rather than permit a shipload of meal to be carried to them? Let them reverse the case, and say how they would feel.'[53]

Stung by adverse comment, Galway's mayor protested. There was no 'riotous insubordination', he insisted, merely a 'solitary and exaggerated instance ... from an insulated quarter of our suburbs'. He had been criticized by merchants, but such difficulty as had arisen was caused by the weakness of these same individuals who had submitted to an insignificant 'mob'. The mayor's defence may have been disingenuous, but it does assist in the identification of the leadership of Galway's crowd. The 'suburb' he referred to can only be the Claddagh, home to an Irish-speaking fishing community that was prominent in other social protest of the period, and this conjecture is supported by the inclusion of a call to 'assist the fishermen' in a threatening notice of early March 1817, when there was a further anti-export mobilization, and indeed by references in accounts of other assemblies in support of a 'moral economy' in pre-Famine Galway.[54] (Eiríksson described an attack on the village of New Quay in the Burren by Claddagh fishermen, in more than thirty boats, with the objective of forcing merchants and farmers there to supply the Galway markets rather than markets to the south.[55])

In the southern part of County Donegal, unrest also broke out during January, and continued into February. On the market-house in Donegal, a notice threatened Alexander Davis that if he did not 'fetch potatoes to this town, he will be levelled',[56] and from the parishes of Inver and Killaghtee, in the barony of Banagh – 'far removed from a magistrate, not one being resident' – came reports of 'nightly meetings', from whence people went forth to the houses of those believed to have grain or potatoes, and forced them to give undertakings to sell at the next market, at the 'fair price' set at the meetings.[57] Between Castlefin and Claudy in Tyrone, self-styled 'levellers' were also abroad. But the 'evil', according to a complainant, was 'not confined to the midnight, as in the full of day, they assemble in number, armed with pikes, guns, swords, &c, under the pretence of seizing illicit grain likely to be used for the purpose of distillation'. There was activity also in nearby Stranorlar, on the part of bands of 'Still-hunters', hundreds strong, 'who dignify themselves with the name of police'.[58] For anti-distillation crowds of 1817, their 'legitimizing notion' derived from proclamations against distilling that had been enforced during previous subsistence crises, but not on this occasion.[59]

(ii) *February and March*: During February, relief efforts continued: in

Ennis, a committee appealed for support for the 'labouring poor and of the respectable tradesmen'; in Waterford, the relief committee provided fuel and straw for bedding and established a soup kitchen capable of dispensing 8,000 quarts of soup daily.[60]

Disturbances also continued. In Newry, a crowd which assembled in response to the sound of a horn on the mornings of 12 and 13 February targeted premises and vessels implicated in the export of potatoes to England, but its efforts to fix the price of potatoes at the market were thwarted by magistrates.[61] From the midlands, it was reported that 'the poor class of persons' had mobilized in Granard and in adjacent market towns to prevent the removal of potatoes 'to distant counties'.[62] Of developments in Athlone, the following description from a merchant's letter of 25 February appeared in the press:

> Dear Joe: Town in a sad way since yesterday morning – a mob of several hundred paraded the whole town and broke open all the stores that had either potatoes or meal stored in them; ours was the last that was broken open and they carried away a parcel of both meal and potatoes and commenced selling them in the market place ... By the advice of Lord Castlemaine and several others I have agreed to sell out the potatoes to the poor people at 4d per stone, there will be some loss on them, but I see no alternative. The worst is that the boat still cannot be loaded as the mob say they still will not let her take anything away, and even if she got safe away out of the canal here, the people along the Shannon are determined not to let a boat pass with provisions on board ... I feel it is probable I will have to sell out the meal here. I am shouted at and mobbed in all directions as I go along the street. I have just heard they have done in like manner in Moate.[63]

On the same morning, at Ballina, several hundred people went to see Colonel King, military commander, bringing with them carts of seized meal, and advising him 'in the most violent and outrageous manner' that they would not allow provisions to leave Mayo. His efforts at remonstration having failed, King called out the North Mayo Militia and the 68th regiment, and conflict ensued at Ardnaree bridge, where a greatly expanded crowd was obstructing carts bringing food to Sligo port. On being showered with stones, the soldiers fired over the people's heads, which only 'made them worse', wrote the colonel, justifying his order to 'level lower'. Two were killed, but for King, it was 'gratifying to know that one of them was a distinguished leader'. After the confrontation at the bridge, the premises of those involved in the meal trade were broken open.[64] Some days later, a deputation of Ballina tradesmen petitioned the colonel, while at the market the poor prevented the sale of potatoes to anyone not resident in the town or vicinity.[65] With regard to Mayo generally – having taken the above events into account – Desmond McCabe argued that 'no exact counterpart to the English food riot can be made out'.[66] One might argue otherwise.

That the authorities in Waterford remained pro-active is indicated by a report of early March that the mayor had sent a representative to check weights in the grocers' shops. Some were found to be greatly 'under standard'. For the *Waterford Chronicle*, this was useful as a 'serious warning' to those engaged in such sharp practice, and, even more importantly, 'the poor will also learn from it that their interests are carefully attended by those whose duty is to protect them from imposition'.[67](The remark was later echoed by the *Kilkenny Moderator*: 'Acts [of charity] must convince the lower orders that their distresses are not unheeded by those of their fellow citizens to whom providence has been more liberal.'[68])

From Armagh, 'considerable speculation' was reported in early March, with merchants buying up oats in the expectation that prices would rise further. This was serving to 'exasperate' the poorer people and they had responded by administering 'unlawful oaths', something which did not greatly worry Dublin Castle's local informant, because 'these depredations have chiefly in view deterring farmers and other from asking higher prices for provisions than [the crowd] choose to fix, and also [the farmers] frequenting markets out of their own immediate neighbourhoods'.[69]

Attacks on the canal network became widespread during March. At Thomastown Harbour on the Royal Canal, and at several other points near Mullingar, excited crowds assembled, boatmen were assaulted and quantities of food were carried off.[70] On the Grand Canal, between Philipstown (Dangan) and Edenderry, 'the mob' interrupted the provisions trade for a period of two weeks by cutting the canal bank. In the vicinity of Rathangan, several attacks occurred, involving hundreds of people, in the course of which a man called Golden was killed by soldiers. The disposition of the crowd was described by one witness:

> The people who attend on these occasions are unawed, not at all disguised, nor do they think themselves guilty of any crime – they really go about the business deliberately as if they were exercising their domestic industry ... There does not appear to be the least inclination to riot, or to exercise any wanton acts of cruelty.[71]

Responding to demands from merchants, the lord lieutenant ordered that military parties be posted short distances apart along the entire length of the Grand Canal.[72]

After mass in Tralee on Sunday, 2 March, arrangements were made to prevent the removal of oats from the area, and on the following morning, 600 tradesmen 'mustered in a body' and marched to the nearby port of Blennerville. The authorities did not intervene, but a Mr Day, having seen damage inflicted 'on the rigging of a fine English brig' and wishing to prevent 'further mischief', promised that loaded grain would be taken ashore and 'ground into meal for the poor', an undertaking he justified on the basis that it saved several vessels from being 'knocked to pieces'.[73]

(iii) *Late May and June*: There was a hiatus in the unrest during the month of April and the early weeks of May, which may be attributed to extensive charitable and regulatory interventions, to weariness among those who had been involved in protests, and perhaps to apprehension following the killing of protestors at Wilkinstown, Ballina, and Rathangan. There was no slackening in the relief efforts, however, with considerable public collections being reported from Limerick and Cork, preparations being made to import potatoes from England, and a £150,000 loan being voted by parliament for the relief of Irish distress. This last allocation was disparaged as utterly inadequate, since it represented only 10 per cent of the total amount voted for the United Kingdom at a time when Ireland's population was about 30 per cent of the whole and its distress more acute.[74]

Throughout June 1817, 'markets continue[d] to rise and disturbances to extend', in the words of London's *Times*. So extensive, indeed, did unrest become that the regional press became less reticent about reporting it. In describing the turn of events, the *Londonderry Journal* noted that 'riots of a similar nature' had occurred in various parts of France, and commented on 'tumultuous risings' in England.[75]

Of the June disturbances, several were in places where there had been conflict in the January–March period. There was another 'rising' against exporters in Drogheda and a third mobilization in the town of Galway which, in the event, was on a smaller scale than 'the contemplated rising of the mob' that the authorities had been preparing for. In the vicinity of Galway, there were protests in Gort and Loughrea – the last dispersed only when soldiers fired on the crowd.[76] From Granard and Armagh, from the midland waterways, and from towns throughout the South, further anti-export and anti-overholding interventions were reported.[77] There were ongoing efforts to prevent food leaving County Meath for Dublin, prompting some 'gentlemen and farmers' to establish a vigilante force. In a number of centres, where municipal and charitable intervention had kept a lid on things until mid- to late May, the frustrations of the people could no longer be contained.

One such place was the city of Kilkenny, where, through the columns of the *Kilkenny Moderator*, a self-styled 'friend' advised the poor of the city in early June that they should be patient, congratulated them on having been 'very temperate', and promising that their social superiors would continue to look out for them. However, the patience of Kilkenny's poor had limits, and on Friday, 6 June, serious unrest began. The initial flashpoint was the closure of a subsidized potato store when it was overwhelmed by customers. Soon afterwards, a consignment of oatmeal was seized and divided among the multitude. Disturbances continued through the weekend: on Saturday, there were efforts to prevent supplies from leaving the town, but these were thwarted by the mayor, who read the Riot Act and called out the military. Subsequently, there was a raid on a grainstore owned by a Mr Bradly – evidently one of those held responsible for the plight of the people, for forty barrels of his oats were thrown into the Nore.[78] (Such wilful destruction of food was derided by commentators, but it was a widespread phenomenon, intended by the perpetrators to be seen as the exemplary punishment of a malefactor by disinterested enforcers of justice.)

Order was restored by Monday, and maintained, for a period, by the 16th regiment, which was despatched to the city (replacing the 94th, which had been removed to Kildare in response to earlier disturbances).[79] Meanwhile, part of the working class distanced itself from what occurred – conceivably on the suggestion of one or more 'friends' – and the following appeared as an advertisement in the *Moderator*, with solecisms retained so as to establish authenticity:

> We, the trade & labouring classes of Kilkenny do hereby return our sincere and most grateful thanks to the Earl of Desart and all the other gentlemen of this city & county who has so bountifully and timely contributed to reskue us from the most frightful death of famine, which would be the fate of us and our distressed familys had it not for their great humanity, an we heer by express our abhorance of the disorderly conduct exercised by some refractory & foolish people in stopping the free intercourse of provisions ... and we also sincerely promise that we will in futur use our utmost Indeavours to prevent and put a stop to any tumult or such procedure as should give pain or alarm to our great Delivourers. Sind on behalf of all this 11th day of June 1817.[80]

Between the composition of the message and its publication on 19 June, however, there were further outbreaks.[81] But not everyone was overly concerned. Reporting on events in Kilkenny –and similar ones in Waterford – John Beevor, yeomanry brigade major, wrote that things were 'politically quiet', despite 'symptoms of momentary disturbances ... fortunately of a short duration and unattended by any aggravating circumstances' which had been kept in check by 'the exertions of the civil power and the large subscriptions of the wealthy inhabitants'.[82]

The disturbances in the south-west, which have been described elsewhere, began in mid-May with attacks on stores in Ennis, spreading to Clarecastle, Bunratty and Newmarket-on-Fergus. The outbreak has been labelled 'primitive' by one authority, and indeed our sources focus on the plundering of stores – where there was grain intended for the port of Limerick, via the river Fergus – but it is possible that the sources do not tell the full story. Certainly, later disturbances in County Clare drew on a repertoire of protest which was consistent with a developed moral economy.[83] In early June, unrest spread to Limerick to the disappointment of that city's *Evening Post*: 'Our caution and advice have been disregarded,' lamented the editor, 'and the people, instead of waiting upon the magistrates ... have on the contrary hastily and illegally acted for themselves, breaking stores and plundering the property of others during past two days.'[84]

Matters proceeded, along the Clare pattern, with stores being broken open, and rioters 'filling their bags, sheets and aprons with oats'. Oatmeal belonging to the Poor Fund Society was taken, and boats containing grain for transport by canal to Dublin were raided. Magistrates and garrison were unable to intervene to any great effect initially, due to the 'rapid movement of the mob', but ultimately fifty rioters were arrested and a man named Walsh was injured by soldiers' gunfire. More tragically, a young boy 'was literally ground' by mill machinery. To bring an end to the disturbances, the authorities found it necessary to impose martial law measures, including a curfew and the closure of public houses.[85]

Proceedings in Cork were rather different to those in Limerick. Having removed a portion of a ship's cargo, and lodged it in the marketplace, the crowd secured the permission of the owners to land the remainder. In the presence of the mayor, the high constable and others, another half dozen vessels were similarly treated over two days, and scores of corn dealers and merchants had their supplies also taken to the marketplace, where they were sold at a reduced price. All of this, according to a *Cork Reporter* journalist who was present, was accomplished without any violence.[86]

CONCLUSION

The concept of 'moral economy' has been employed to describe a diversity of social phenomena since the 1970s, but it has been applied here in a way that is consistent with the original sense. And, given that even Thompson himself had doubts about the applicability of his hypothesis to Irish circumstance, it has been necessary to provide thick description of the widespread unrest of 1812 and 1817. The evidence offered points strongly to an Irish moral economy surrounding the marketing of food in which crowds in all regions of the island drew on the full repertoire of protest strategies as summarized in one authoritative work on the English moral economy: 'price fixing in the marketplace; the compulsion of farmers to bring food to the marketplace; the stoppage of foodstuffs in transit; and the seizure and/or destruction of foodstuffs.'[87] True, most of the conflicts discussed saw the 'populace' pitted against merchants attempting to remove food from distressed communities at times of extreme scarcity, and there is an absence of descriptions of 'ordinary' conflict between their customers and forestalling or regrating market stallholders, but that does not prove that such did not occur in Ireland, merely that it was infrequently reported during the period under review. Indeed, references to four such episodes in Galway were discovered for the period 1829 to 1842, and it is likely that close studies of the local press in other places for the few decades before the famine – when coverage of local affairs was expanding greatly – will yield many others.[88]

In the difficult years of 1812 and 1817, the impression is that the protesting crowds had considerable success. In some cases, the owners of meal and potatoes were compelled to sell at prices that were considered 'fair', and in others, food intended for export was retained for local consumption. And almost invariably, unrest led to ameliorative initiatives by the charitable. Of course, there were interventions by market jurors and relief committees in places where there was no obvious unrest, but the disposition of the crowd – or its behaviour during previous shortages – was not irrelevant in these instances either. The fear of disorder was a powerful incentive to philanthropy, but it was not the only factor influencing elite reactions to unrest, for it is evident, both from the behaviour of some officials and from the tenor of their reports, that there was considerable sympathy for the plight of the poor, and even some lingering acceptance of the necessity for interference in the 'free intercourse of provisions'. As two medical men, commenting on events throughout Ireland during 1817, put it: 'the wants of the majority of such rioters were real, and their conduct resulted from motives of self preservation.'[89]

NOTES

1. *Londonderry Journal*, 28 April 1812.
2. Ibid.
3. Ibid.
4. Ibid., 31 February 1808.
5. Thompson's article, published in *Past and Present*, vol. 50 (1971), appeared in his *Customs in Common*, (Harmondsworth: 1991), pp. 185–258, alongside 'The moral economy reviewed', pp. 259–351.
6. 'Introduction', in Peter Jupp and Eoin Magennis (eds), *Crowds in Ireland, c.1720–1920* (Basingstoke: 2000), pp. 26, 28.
7. John Cunningham, '*A Town Tormented by the Sea*': *Galway, 1790–1914* (Dublin: 2004), pp. 86–101, 126–35, 141, 197.
8. Michael R. Beames, *Peasants and Power: the Whiteboy Movements and their Control in Pre-Famine Ireland* (Brighton: 1983), pp. 89–101; James S. Donnelly, 'The social composition of agrarian rebellions in early nineteenth-century Ireland: the case of the Carders and Caravats, 1813–16', in P.J. Corish (ed.), *Radicals, Rebels and Establishments* (Belfast: 1985), pp. 151–69; P.E.W. Roberts, 'Caravats and Shanavests: whiteboyism and faction fighting in East Munster, 1802–11', in Samuel Clark and James S. Donnelly (eds), *Irish Peasants: Violence and Political Unrest, 1780–1914* (Dublin: 1983), pp. 64–101; Andrés Eiríksson, 'Crime and popular protest in County Clare, 1815–52', unpublished Ph.D. thesis, TCD 1991, passim; D. McCabe, 'Law, conflict and social order: County Mayo, 1820–1845', unpublished Ph.D. thesis, UCD 1991, pp. 190–213.
9. L.M. Cullen, 'Eighteenth-century flour milling in Ireland', *Irish Economic and Social History*, vol. iv (1977), pp. 5–25; Roger Wells, 'The Irish Famine of 1799–1801: market culture, moral economies and social protest', in Andrew Charlesworth and Adrian Randall (eds), *Markets, Market Culture and Popular Protest in Eighteenth-Century Britain and Ireland* (Liverpool: 1996), pp. 163–7.
10. Jupp and Magennis, 'Introduction', p. 28.
11. James Kelly, 'Harvests and hardship: famine and scarcity in Ireland in the late 1720s', *Studia Hibernica*, vol. 26 (1991–2), pp. 84–9.
12. David Dickson, *Arctic Ireland* (Belfast: 1997), pp. 26–9, 34, 55.
13. Eoin Magennis, 'In search of the "moral economy": food scarcity in 1756–57 and the crowd', in Jupp and Magennis, *Crowds in Ireland*, pp. 199–206.
14. Thompson, *Customs in Common*, pp. 260–1.
15. Emmet O'Connor, *A Labour History of Waterford* (Waterford: 1989), p. 8; Neal Garnham, 'Riot Acts, popular protest, and Protestant mentalities in eighteenth-century Ireland', *The Historical Journal*, 49, 2 (June 2006), p. 415.
16. Wells, 'The Irish Famine of 1790–1801', pp.163–93, and his *Wretched Faces: Famine in Wartime England, 1793–1801* (Gloucester: 1989), passim.
17. *The Census of Ireland for the year 1851, Part v, Tables of Death*, vol.1, H.C. 1856, xxix, pp. 168–9.
18. *Londonderry Journal*, 12 April, 18, 31 May 1808; *Freeman's Journal*, 18 May 1808.
19. *Freeman's Journal*, 12 March, 28 April 1808.
20. *Cork Mercantile Chronicle*, 11 May 1808.
21. National Archives, State of the Country Papers, 1409/10.
22. Ibid.
23. Ibid., 1188/1-2, 1207/5–7.
24. Ibid., 1188/30.
25. Ibid., 1192/1; *Freeman's Journal*, 27 April 1808.
26. Quoted in *Ramsey's Waterford Chronicle*, 17 March 1812.
27. State of the Country Papers, 1409/43.
28. Ibid., 1409/27.
29. Ibid., 1409/7.
30. Ruth Delaney, *The Grand Canal of Ireland* (Dublin: 1995 edn), p.78. The conclusions of the committee were echoed in a report from the military commander in Listowel, County Kerry. Reflecting on the extravagant cost of provisioning his force, he stated his belief that 'speculation is the cause of the poorly supplied markets'. (State of the Country Papers, 1404/20).
31. *Waterford Chronicle*, quoted in *Leinster Journal*, 29 April 1812; State of the Country papers, 1406/16–17; P.C. Power, *Carrick-on-Suir: Town and District, 1800–2000* (Carrick-on-Suir: 2003), p. 23

32. *Cork Mercantile Chronicle*, 13 April 1812. With regard to the arrival of relief supplies and the departure of cargoes of grain during the subsistence crisis of 1822 in Mayo, Eneas McDonnell's brother Matthias explained: 'In truth, the vessels had met each other going out and coming in. A man may have engaged his vessels for two months before and he must go on with his business, no matter what the consequences may be' (cited by McCabe, 'County Mayo, 1820–1845', p. 190).
33. Ibid.
34. Ibid.
35. State of the Country Papers, 1404/1–10.
36. State of the Country Papers, 1404/11–24.
37. Ibid.
38. Cunningham, *Galway*, p. 86.
39. *Leinster Journal*, 15 April 1812.
40. Ibid., 18 April (quoting from *Waterford Mirror*).
41. State of the Country Papers, 1409/49.
42. *Leinster Journal*, 10 June 1812; *Belfast Newsletter*, 23 June, 10 July 1812.
43. State of the Country Papers, 1403/2.
44. Cunningham, *Galway*, p.86.
45. State of the Country Papers, 1535/20, 1536/9, 1537/55.
46. John Dexter Post, *The Last Great Subsistence Crisis in the Western World* (Baltimore: 1977); Cormac Ó Gráda, *Éire roimh an nGorta: An Saol Eacnamaíoch* (Dublin: 1985), p.13; F. Barker and J. Cheyne, *An Account of the Rise, Progress, and Decline of the Fever lately Epidemical in Ireland* (Dublin: 1821), 2 vols, passim; T. O'Neill, 'Poverty in Ireland, 1815–45', *Folk-life*, vol. 11 (1973), pp. 22–33; David Dickson, 'The gap in famines: a useful myth?', in M.E. Crawford (ed.), *Famine: the Irish Experience, 900–1900: Subsistence Crises and Famines in Ireland* (Edinburgh: 1989), pp. 96–111.
47. Cited in *Census of Ireland, 1851, Part v, Tables of Deaths*, vol.1, 1856 xxix, p. 178.
48. *Belfast Newsletter*, 17 January 1817. In Ennis, the discovery that a sum remained from a fund of 1801 prompted the following resolution: 'That in the event hereafter, of any part of this Fund remaining, after supplying the wants of the poor, it be given in charge to the Committee, to vest same in government debentures, so as to accumulate, with a view to applying it to a similar purpose for which this present meeting is convened, and that on any future occasions of general distress arising, a respectable meeting of the inhabitants of Ennis do have it in their power to dispose of same' (*Ennis Chronicle*, 12 February 1817).
49. *Ennis Chronicle*, 18 January 1817.
50. State of the Country Papers, 1829/33–35.
51. *Londonderry Journal*, 14 January 1817.
52. State of the Country Papers, 1833/2.
53. *Belfast Newsletter*, 17 January 1817.
54. Cunningham, *Galway*, pp. 86–98.
55. Eiríksson, 'County Clare', p. 71.
56. *The Times*, 23 January 1817.
57. State of the Country Papers, 1832/4 (1817).
58. Ibid., 1832/17–18.
59. A proclamation of 1817 issued by the lord lieutenant was of an advisory character: 'Whereas from the present very high prices of oatmeal and potatoes which constitute the chief food of the lower orders of the people of the United Kingdom ... it is expedient that those articles of food should be as far as possible reserved for the lower orders of the people. Now we ... do earnestly exhort and recommend all masters of families who are not in the lower classes of life, not to suffer any potatoes whatsoever to be consumed in their respective families. And we do also, in like manner, exhort and charge all persons who keep horses, especially horses for pleasure, to diminish as much as possible the consumption of oats in their subsistence' (*The Times*, 17 June 1817).
60. *Ennis Chronicle*, 5, 12 February 1817; *Kilkenny Moderator*, 10 February 1817.
61. *Kilkenny Moderator*, 20 February 1817.
62. State of the Country Papers, 1838/17. A reference elsewhere to 'Northern men' (State of the Country Papers, 1824/20) indicates which 'distant counties' were meant.
63. *Cork Mercantile Chronicle*, 3 March 1817.
64. State of the Country Papers, 1833/18.
65. *Kilkenny Moderator*, 6 March 1817. A similar disposition was reported from the barony of Clanmaurice, County Kerry, where those who were not ordinarily resident were enjoined to

leave, so as to save scarce provisions (State of the Country Papers, 1838/23).
66. McCabe, 'County Mayo, 1820–1845', pp. 193, 199.
67. *Kilkenny Moderator*, 15 March 1817 (quoting from *Waterford Chronicle*, 8 March 1817).
68. Cited by Marilyn Silverman, *An Irish Working Class: Explorations in Political Economy and Hegemony, 1800–1950* (Toronto: 2001), p. 19.
69. State of the Country Papers, 1838/22
70. *Kilkenny Moderator*, 6, 11 March 1817.
71. *Cork Mercantile Chronicle*, 14 March 1817.
72. *Kilkenny Moderator*, 11 March 1817.
73. *Limerick Evening Post*, 6 March 1817.
74. Ibid., 17 April, 5 May 1817; State of the Country Papers, 1838/36.
75. *The Times*, 7 June 1817; *Londonderry Journal*, 17, 24 June 1817.
76. State of the Country Papers, 1838/51; Cunningham, *Galway*, p. 95.
77. State of the Country Papers, 1824/7, 26, 40, 1838/19; *Limerick Evening Post*, 12 June 1817; *Kilkenny Moderator*, 19 June 1817.
78. *Kilkenny Moderator*, 7, 10 June 1817.
79. Ibid., 11 March, 12 June 1817.
80. Ibid., 19 June 1817.
81. State of the Country Papers, 1824/6.
82. Ibid., 1838/49.
83. Eiríksson, 'Co. Clare', pp. 61–4, 194–206; J. Power, *A History of Clarecastle and its Environs* (Ennis: 2004), pp. 414–18, and *An Ennis Miscellany* (Ennis: 1990), pp. 95–116.
84. *Limerick Evening Post*, 9 June 1817.
85. Ibid., 9, 12 June 1817.
86. *Kilkenny Moderator*, 12 June 1817; *Londonderry Journal*, 17 June 1817.
87. Andrew Charlesworth and Adrian Randall, 'The moral economy: riots, markets and social conflict', in Andrew Charlesworth and Adrian Randall (eds), *Moral Economy and Popular Protest: Crowds, Conflict and Authority* (Houndmills: 2000), p. 3.
88. Cunningham, *Galway*, pp. 89–90, 95–6. See, for example, 'Galway starvation riots', http://vas-sun.vassar.edu/~sttaylor/FAMINE/ILN/Galway/GalwayRiot.html (accessed 12 December 2006). For an Irish moral economy, post-1817, see the following: Eiríksson, 'County Clare', and his 'Food supply and food riots', in Cormac Ó Gráda (ed.), *Famine 150: Commemorative Lecture Series* (Dublin: 1997), pp. 67–94: W. Fraher, 'The Dungarvan disturbances of 1846 and sequels', in Donald Brady and Des Cowman (eds), *The Famine in Waterford, 1845–50* (Dublin: 1995), pp. 137–52; David Lee, 'The food riots of 1830 and 1840', in Debbie Jacobs and David Lee (eds), *Made in Limerick: History of Industries, Trade and Commerce*, vol.1 (Limerick: 2003), pp. 55–65; T. Donovan, 'Bread or blood', *The Old Limerick Journal*, no. 32 (1995), pp. 64–7.
89. Barker and Cheyne, vol. 1, pp. 40–1.

4

'Remembering Who We Are': Identity and Class in Protestant Dublin and Belfast, 1868–1905

MARTIN MAGUIRE

In his 1962 article on independent orangeism, John W. Boyle initiated a debate on the relationship between religion, class and politics in Protestant Edwardian Belfast.[1] This topic was elaborated further by Boyle in his monograph on the Irish labour movement.[2] In Edwardian Belfast religion was the central element in the political, social and cultural life of all classes. Boyle's article showed that amongst the Protestant working class of Belfast, within an identity that was overwhelmingly sectarian in its expression, class could and did assert itself. The struggle between a Conservative middle class establishment and working-class independent orangeism was interpreted as a struggle over who should wield power in the wider society of Protestant Edwardian Belfast; the working class or the commercial bourgeoisie. As a result of this debate Protestant working-class loyalism is no longer interpreted simply as a counter to nationalism. It is recognized as a distinctive Belfast working class political culture, shaped more by negotiation within Protestantism than by confrontation with the Catholic working class. This article reviews the impact of that seminal article and then goes on to offer a comparative examination of Belfast and Dublin Protestant working class culture and politics.

PROTESTANT WORKING-CLASS CONSCIOUSNESS

The first upsurge of Protestant working class mobilization in Belfast was the formation of the Orange and Protestant Working Men's

Association (OPWA) in 1868. This association, composed exclusively of Protestant artisans, was formed to support the maverick orangeman William Johnston. Johnston had led an orange parade in defiance of the Party Processions Act and had roundly attacked the establishment in the Grand Orange Lodge and the Conservative party for their cowardly acquiescence in the suppression of orange parading. For his role in organizing a parade from Newtownards to Bangor in July 1867 (attended by 40,000), Johnston was sentenced to one month in prison, thus securing his status as a champion of the orange democracy. Supported by the OPWA, Johnston took a Belfast seat from the established Conservative candidate in the general election of 1868. Standing in opposition to what he portrayed as the Conservatives' abandonment of orange and Protestant principles and the betrayal of the Protestant rank and file, Johnston put himself forward as the champion of the working class Protestant values that had been espoused by the original founders of the Orange Order. For Boyle, the election of Johnston marks the emergence in Belfast of an independent working-class Protestant tradition.[3] However, class-consciousness, rooted in working-class opposition to the dominance of capital, was limited by sectarianism to support for dissident conservatism. Johnston, a barrister and landlord, ultimately proved to be more loyal to his own class than to the class that ensured his election.

A class-conscious Protestantism continued to be preached by Arthur Trew, the founder of the Belfast Protestant Association (BPA). Trew was an open-air preacher of intense evangelical, anti-Catholic sermons. In 1901 he was jailed for an attack on a Catholic procession in Belfast city. Thomas Sloan, a shipyard worker, took his place. Sloan's particular target was the 'sham Protestants' in the orange and Conservative establishment. In Sloan's view, the working class was the only class that maintained Protestant principles. At the 12 July meetings of 1902, he publicly heckled Edward Saunderson MP, the Belfast grand master and leader of the Irish Unionists at Westminster.

William Johnston, who had long been reabsorbed into the ranks of Conservatism, died in the same year and the BPA were determined to run a Protestant working-class candidate for the vacant seat. Assisted by Richard Braithwaite, secretary to the BPA and a well-known sectarian preacher, Sloan won the South Belfast seat against the official Unionist-Conservative candidate by a majority of eight hundred votes. During his election campaign Sloan attracted the support of Alex Boyd, trade union activist in the Municipal Employees Association, member of the Belfast Trades Council and regarded as a militant on behalf of the working class. Boyd was later a supporter of Larkin in the 1907 strike in Belfast.

To Boyd, Sloan was the more attractive candidate despite his sectarianism, because he was working class with a good record on labour issues. After taking the South Belfast seat, Sloan went on in 1903 to found the Independent Orange Order (IOO) as a breakaway from the Orange Order. The first imperial grand master of the IOO was Robert Lindsay Crawford, a Dublin journalist prominent in evangelical Protestant agitation against High Church practices in the rituals of the Church of Ireland. Crawford drafted the Magheramorne Manifesto, adopted by the IOO in July 1905. The manifesto, addressed to 'all Irishmen whose country stands first in their affections', called for the secularization of Irish education and the end to Irish Unionist subservience to the English Conservative government's Irish policy.[4] It was interpreted by Boyle as evidence for a movement of the Protestant working class toward a non-sectarian nationalism. Boyle then went on to interpret the IOO as the battleground for the future of Belfast working-class Protestantism in a struggle between the forces of a radical Protestant democracy, represented by Robert Lindsay Crawford, and reactionary sectarianism, represented by the Belfast Protestant Association.[5] For Boyle, the demise of Crawford and the marginalization of the IOO in Ulster unionism was the regrettable result of the defeat of a 'liberal, non-sectarian, strongly democratic nationalism' represented by the Magheramorne Manifesto.[6]

Boyle assumed that the cultural and ideological conflict represented by independent orangeism had to be an expression of more fundamental economic conflict. Hence he focused on the implications for the Belfast labour and trade union movement of independent orangeism. In his analysis class-consciousness in the working-class was necessarily opposed to sectarianism, and the rise of the former must signal the decline of the latter. The real struggle was that between capital and labour and the false struggle was between Catholic and Protestant workers. As the struggle between capital and labour intensified it ought to tend toward working-class unity. Boyle interpreted the influence on the working class membership of the IOO of Lindsay Crawford and the Magheramorne Manifesto as such a progression.

Boyle's conclusions on the radicalism of the Ulster Protestant working class have been subject to considerable revision, most especially by Henry Patterson in an article written some twenty years later. Patterson maintained that the Magheramorne Manifesto was in fact the expression of a particular working-class form of sectarianism and that its seeming radicalism was essentially rhetorical, demanding as it did that the Catholic masses jettison their existing cultural traditions.[7] More recently, the IOO and the Magheramorne manifesto have been interpreted as an attempt to move toward a secularist opposition to clerical power, Catholic and Protestant, by the 'two great democracies' of the working class.[8] For the purposes of this article, significance is attached to the fact that the conflict between the working-class and middle-class Protestantism was originally cultural; the refusal of the establishment to endorse working-class parading in defiance of the Party Processions Act. This suggests that the cultural symbols and rhetoric expressing working-class Protestant views of community, that were an embarrassment to the middle class, are to be taken seriously.

HISTORY, MEMORY AND 'BEING PROTESTANT'

In the study of the culture of commemoration in Ireland, the injunction to 'remember' is more usually associated with the Irish nationalist and republican tradition.[9] However, much of the nationalist cult was an appropriation of the far older culture of commemoration of Irish Protestantism. In fact, Irish Catholic and Protestant traditions borrow cultural forms of expression from each other all the time. Growing from diverse confessional and ethnic rootstocks of English, Scottish and continental backgrounds, Irish Protestantism developed a rich culture of historical remembering and commemoration to express its own unique identity.[10] Irish Protestantism developed as an exceptionally introspective culture, and 'remembering who we are' became of central importance to an Irish Protestant understanding of itself as a community and its place in Ireland. Also, where membership of the established Anglican church was required for full access to the patronage and power of the state and therefore excluded the substantial numbers of Presbyterian and other dissenting Protestants, 'remembering who we are' created as well as maintained solidarity.

History was used to mobilize and endorse an Irish Protestant identity. Historical remembering meant participating in rituals of commemoration that had a two-fold emphasis. Firstly, it constructed a providential narrative of Protestant Irish history, emphasizing Catholic treachery repeatedly checked by divine intervention and thereby justifying the ascendancy of Protestantism. Although Protestant Ireland had been victorious, remembering meant reflecting on how different it might have been were it not for God's favour. Secondly, it displayed an extravagant loyalty to the Protestant monarchy. Transcending denominational differences, a list of commemoration days was strung along a calendar of dates, about twenty in all in the year, including not only the anniversaries of the

1641 rebellion and the victories of the Williamite wars that established Protestant ascendancy in Ireland, but also the Hanoverian succession to the throne that secured a Protestant monarchy in Britain and Ireland.[11] The rituals of commemoration sustained the bonds of the Protestant community as well as setting its boundaries, both metaphorically and physically. That the rituals of commemoration featured marching and parading as well as church services also served to militarize the imagining of the Irish Protestant community. The establishment of the Orange Order in 1795 merely formalized what was already a deeply imbedded tradition of militant orangeism within Irish Protestantism.

Under the influence of Peelite conservatism and evangelical preaching, Irish Protestantism was reshaped during the nineteenth century as Irish conservatism. Irish conservatism had a difficult relationship with the older orange tradition. Whilst historical remembering and commemoration emphasized Protestant solidarity, that solidarity was now strained by the intrusion of class differences. The dominance of free market principles and competition with Catholics led to increasingly complex class structures and the growth of inequality and poverty within Protestant Ireland. The differentiation between Catholic and Protestant was eclipsed by class differences within Protestantism. The reality of 'well-off' Catholics and poor Protestants led to a new understanding of the meaning of 'being Protestant'. Increasingly in Protestant Ireland, 'remembering who we are' referred not to historical commemoration but to modes of behaviour and an embourgeoisement of the meaning of being Protestant. That meant acculturating working-class Protestants to the values and practices of respectable society. The assertion of Protestantism as social elitism compensated for the fact of being a minority and the reality of a decline in political power. On the other hand, the assertion of social superiority demanded that the culture of lower-class Protestants and their exuberant sectarianism should be suppressed. Rituals of remembering and commemoration declined in importance as Irish Protestant political identity developed a singular focus on the Act of Union, and its ethnic identity focused on a severely evangelical form of Protestantism.[12] The rituals of commemoration, sustained by the orange and loyal institutions, narrowed to those sites and dates associated with the Williamite victories, most importantly the Battle of the Boyne and the Siege of Derry. The order came under suspicion and was suppressed by Peelite and Melbourne administrations. However, this movement from sectarianism toward respectability was not without resistance. Despite suppression, orangeism survived as a working-class Protestant tradition, surfacing in occasional sectarian confrontations such as Dolly's

Brae in 1849 and Johnston's defiant parade from Newtownards to Bangor in 1867. Within that popular tradition orangeism and Protestantism were one, and faithfulness to the 'glorious and immortal memory' was the measure of Protestant integrity. Evangelicalism within the working class legitimized sectarianism and an aggressive rejection of Catholic claims to inclusion.

The most salient difference in the relationship between religion and class in Protestant Dublin and Belfast was the pattern of segregation. Unlike Belfast, Dublin did not have recognizably Catholic or Protestant areas. A comparison of the Catholic and Protestant residents in each of Dublin city's twenty wards shows quite a high degree of similarity in the distribution of the two population groups.[13] What Dublin did have, however, were recognizably middle-class areas in the suburbs and working-class areas in the inner city. One of the effects of nineteenth-century urban expansion was to segregate physically the different social classes, leading to the emergence of social, not sectarian, segregation patterns. The flight of the middle class to the suburbs was a flight from the working class. In contrast to Belfast, the differences in the dispersal of the city of Dublin's Catholic and Protestant populations were the result of socio-economic rather than sectarian forces. Between the census of 1871, the first to record religion and occupation, and that of 1911 the Protestant male workforce of Dublin, estimated at approximately 10,000 with about the same number of lower middle class of clerks and shopkeepers, was shown to be indeed in slow decline.[14] In contrast the middle-class suburban parishes show a remarkable stability in their populations into the middle of the twentieth century.[15]

The areas of work and charity created the greatest opportunities for contact between middle- and working-class Protestants, but these contacts served to emphasize class differences rather than foster cross-class Protestant solidarity. Many of the charities that intervened in the Protestant working-class communities were formed in the later nineteenth century and were denominationally exclusive; a response to the fear that poverty made the supposedly irreligious working class vulnerable to proselytism. One of the oldest of the charitable organizations linking the middle and working class was the Association for the Relief of Distressed Protestants (ARDP). It was established in 1836 to 'afford relief to necessitous members of any Protestant denomination who shall not reside as a member of a family with a person not a Protestant'.[16] These interventionist charitable organizations were the main source of contact between middle- and working-class Protestants in mid-nineteenth-century Dublin, but the relationship was unequal and paternalistic. As charitable enterprises became the only contact with the working class, 'giving' became deformed into a weapon for social control and was used to impose middle-class patterns of behaviour and discipline on the working class. The ability to choose those worthy of assistance, and to exclude the unworthy, was itself a display of social power and an exercise in status which affirmed rather than transcended class differences.[17]

SECTARIAN SOLIDARITY AND CLASS INTERESTS

Despite the numerical and economic dominance of Belfast, Dublin continued to see itself as the organizational and cultural centre of Protestant Ireland.[18] However, while the political identity of the Protestant middle class was based on unionism, historically it has been the urban working class that has been the voice of militant and uncompromising Protestantism. The increasing emphasis on a political identity of unionism and a retreat from the politics of sectarianism is signalled by the decline in Dublin orangeism and the culture of sectarian parading. In 1887, there were claimed to be four thousand orangemen organized in ten lodges in Dublin. The annual returns for the Dublin lodges show that by the Edwardian era orangeism was inert; the same affiliation fee was being paid, the same officers listed, year after year. The cause of this decline was the retreat of middle-class Protestants from association with plebeian orangeism.[19]

The Protestant working class expected that sectarian solidarity would transcend class interests and, most practically, guarantee Protestant employment. In the early nineteenth century the Protestant working class of Dublin, organized in the Dublin Protestant Operative Association (DPOA), was confidently assertive of its identity both as a class and as the champion of sectarian evangelical Protestantism. Led by the militantly evangelical Reverend Tresham Dames Gregg, the DPOA laid the blame for the economic depression of the late 1830s and early 1840s at the door of the passing of Catholic emancipation and the abandonment of Protestant principles in the government of Ireland.[20] The depression in trade was especially marked in the textile industries of Dublin, traditionally associated with Protestant artisans. Gregg's uncompromising 'No-Popery' convictions allied with an intense providentialism and Biblical literalism interpreted economic distress as divine punishment for the advance of Catholicism in the social and political life of Dublin. Catholic emancipation and municipal reform had severed the link between the state and the established Church. Divine retribution must inevitably follow. In his apocalyptic anti-Catholic preaching, he had the enthusiastic support of the Dublin Protestant working class, who remained loyal to him through the 1840s and 1850s, despite the censure of the Church of Ireland authorities.[21]

The enfranchisement of the working class created the opportunity for a re-assertion of Protestant working-class independence. The City and County of Dublin Conservative WorkingMens' Club (CWC) was formed in 1883 at a time when a working-class identity was being upheld in political life.[22] The CWC was expected to enlist 'Protestant working men of conservative and constitutional opinion' in the work of mobilizing the Protestant working-class vote in the cause of conservatism. The club was an initiative of the 'Howth set', a middle-class coterie of unionist intellectuals grouped around Randolph Churchill. Churchill was, at the time, considered a champion of the Tory working man. The CWC appealed to the working-class sense of solidarity and cohesion. The Protestant working class believed that sectarian solidarity should transcend particular class interests and political loyalty would guarantee Protestant employment. This was the basis of the CWC, formed to mobilize the newly enfranchised Protestant working class in support of Conservative candidates.[23]

The founders of the CWC intended that its main function would be to assist in the time-consuming work of maintaining the voter register. With the extension of the franchise to the working class it was recognized that close attention to the voter register to include supporters and exclude opponents would be vital to electoral success. Protestant working-class residents of those neighbourhoods would provide detailed intelligence on the movement of lodgers into and out of the neighbourhoods, and their politics. However, in contrast to the hopes of their middle-class sponsors, time and again the club's working-class membership showed that it preferred the excitement of street mobilization and riot to the tedium of electoral canvassing. The club claimed to be the inheritor of the DPOA tradition.[24] In 1886 members of the management committee ended up in court on charges of riotous assembly and discharging of firearms after a confrontation with a nationalist mob ended with volleys of gunfire being fired at the mob from within the club premises.[25] Though the club did have as its object the 'provision of rational recreation' for the Protestant working class, for the membership leisure meant beer and billiards. In contrast to the emphasis on conservatism and class that was implied in its title, the CWC membership saw itself primarily in terms of religion rather than class, identifying with a wider Protestant community. The club refused membership to Catholics (even if Conservative) and remained suspicious of any contact with Catholic workingmen's clubs.

At the core of its sense of the political community to which it belonged was not conservatism nor class but a militant and uncompromising assertion of Protestantism, especially an evangelical and Low-Church Protestantism. Hence, members willingly turned from heckling nationalists in the elections to barracking 'ritualists' in the High-Church parishes.[26]

RESISTING HOME RULE

In the aftermath of the 1886 home rule crisis and in the first stages of the plan of campaign, the CWC attempted to seize the leadership of Protestant Ireland in united resistance to Catholic agrarian agitation. A meeting of the club resolved that:

> As a meeting of loyal Irishmen we feel reluctantly compelled to declare that the time has now come when to further avoid the struggle forced upon us by the enemies of law and order would be to brand ourselves as moral and political poltroons. We hereby solemnly pledge ourselves that in the bitter crisis into which our country is now cruelly plunged by relentless agitation our warmest sympathy and support shall be constantly tendered to the gallant men who uphold the law and to the executive which administers it. Resolved that in order to give that sympathy and support organised expression throughout the country this meeting hereby authorises the political committee of the Conservative Workingmen's Club to confer with the members of other loyal bodies in Dublin with a view to issuing an address to our countrymen relative to the painful crisis and promoting such further unity of action amongst all loyal bodies in Ireland (without abandonment of their present titles, status or policy) as shall from day to day and week to week best express the feelings and wishes of the loyal and really industrious classes in Ireland; in protesting against lawlessness and in gaining and retaining the sympathy of the British people.[27]

The call to action led to the formation of the Union and Industries Defence Federation, to be led by the Protestant working-class loyalists of Dublin. The analysis offered by the CWC suggested that as the prosperity of the working class depended on the consumption of the upper classes, and as their security depended on the union, the defence of the political and social status quo was essential to survival and future prosperity. The federation failed, not due to the 'want of social status to which loyalists are so accustomed to look for in everything', as was suggested by a disgruntled member, but due to the flawed analysis of the situation. The federation echoes the traditional response of the Protestant working class to political crisis, which was a call to mass militancy rather than to electoral campaigning. However, it was the Orange Order that led in that form of militancy. The frank sectarianism of the CWC and its proposed federation was an embarrassment to the Dublin Conservative establishment's attempt to present the union as a non-sectarian issue. The landlords were quite sanguine about the intention of the Conservative government on Irish land policy. Especially, however, the proposed federation revealed the gulf between the situation of the Dublin Protestant working class dependent, as skilled artisans, on the wealthy gentry and the situation of the Belfast industrial proletariat. Beyond the circle of its proposers in the CWC, the Union and Industries Defence Federation offered nothing to other Protestants, least of all the working class of Belfast.[28]

The first decade of the 1900s, the period central to Boyle's interpretation of Belfast's Protestant working-class politics, saw an opportunity for the reassertion of militantly Protestant working-class activism in Dublin politics in opposition to middle-class conservatism. The first episode in which militantly Protestant opinion asserted itself in Dublin was the 1900 election in South Dublin, when Horace Plunkett was driven from his parliamentary majority by a split vote created by a rival Unionist candidate, Elrington Ball.[29] Plunkett's commitment to the union could never be doubted and he was considered a supporter of Dublin industries. What earned Plunkett such enmity was the lack of sympathy (that he never bothered to hide) for his Protestant loyalist constituents. Plunkett had been targeted at the Dublin 12 July demonstration of the Dublin orange lodges as a supporter of a government that was betraying the Protestant principles that underlay the Act of Union. The demonstration passed a resolution pledging 'by every means in our power only to support parliamentary candidates who will place Protestantism before party'.[30] The Dublin lodges of the Orange Order circulated a questionnaire to parliamentary candidates that underlined Protestantism as the central issue in Dublin popular unionism. This was a tactic later used by the BPA in Belfast in 1905.[31] The questionnaire asked the candidates to support legislation to suppress ritualism in the Church of England and to promise, if elected, to vote against any proposal to establish or endow a Roman Catholic university for Ireland. The authors and organizers of the questionnaire were Robert Linsday Crawford and Richard Braithwaite.[32] The CWC supported Elrington Ball, though the management committee stifled debate. As Jackson in his history of the 1900 election observes, the confrontation between Plunkett and Ball was the confrontation between an urbane unionism (that had an appeal to the Catholic middle class) and tribal toryism (that appealed especially to the Protestant working class), in which the latter won.[33] The belief that the Conservative government had effaced Protestantism from its policies in Ireland was seemingly confirmed to the members of the CWC by two developments in 1901: the attempt to modify the Accession Declaration and the harassment of Dr Long, a lay preacher in Limerick.

With the death of Queen Victoria in 1901 came the necessity of enacting a coronation, an event that had last occurred in 1837. The coronation ceremony involved the sovereign taking an oath and declaration which, in parts, referred to Catholic belief and practices as superstitious and idolatrous and bound the sovereign to maintain the Protestant reformed religion as established by law.[34] A commission of the House of Lords was established to rephrase the oath, expunging the offensive references to Catholicism without diminishing the security offered to Protestants. The CWC protested against any attempt to dilute the Protestant foundation of the crown and called on the loyalists of the United Kingdom and all Unionist MPs to reject any attempt to tamper with the declaration.[35] The attempt to change the oath was abandoned and it survived undiluted until, at the insistence of George V, it was modified for his accession in 1910.

Street preaching was a venerable tradition in evangelical Irish Protestantism, an activity which caused controversy and often some embarrassment to respectable Protestants. One of the most enduring of these preachers was Dr R.H. Long of Limerick. A son of Dr John Long, archdeacon of Cashel, he was a lay preacher with the Irish Church Mission at the dispensary run by the mission in Limerick, where medicines were accompanied by Bible readings and preaching. The Limerick Redemptorist, Fr Tierney, led a picket on the dispensary from 1898. By 1901 the Dr Long case had become a *cause célèbre* after the Limerick district court appeared to endorse boycotting of Dr Long and dismissed charges of assault on him. The Dublin Orange Order lodges and the CWC vented their fury on the entire unionist establishment; Lord Chief Justice O'Brien who attacked the Irish Church Mission, Edward Carson for not bringing up the issue in the House of Commons, Wyndham for his remark that Dr Long's insistence on proselytizing was regrettable and the entire administration for abandoning the Protestants of Ireland.[36]

The suspicion that the Conservative government was intent on eroding the status of Protestantism extended to Irish unionists collaborating with a tainted administration. These suspicions led to a revolt within

Belfast loyalism, in which the IOO was a catalyst, which led to a realignment of classes within the Ulster Unionist Council. In Dublin, the revolt of 1900 had not merely purged Plunkett, it had effectively annihilated southern representative unionism altogether. Within the Protestant working class of Dublin, it was assumed that a Conservative government ought to have as its first principle a Protestant state and a Protestant throne. The union was simply the constitutional support for that principle. Hostile to unionist politicians that did nothing to actively promote Protestantism, the view was taken by these militantly Protestant activists that losing seats was a small price to pay for asserting fundamental truths and scattering compromisers. Having purged the parliamentary representation of Dublin of 'sham Protestants', the attack shifted to municipal politics.

The Local Government (Ireland) Act 1898 had instituted a new structure of popularly elected local councils voted yearly on a broad franchise. For Dublin loyalists, these elections provided another forum in which principled men could expose 'sham Protestants'. Unlike the *Irish Times*, which treated the municipal elections as pitifully parochial, Lindsay Crawford saw them as a crucial arena of contention with a 'species of Protestant ambitious of public honours and prepared to sacrifice every principle dear to Protestantism if by this means he can win the good will of his opponents and thereby climb to power'.[37] Through 1903 and 1904, as the IOO was emerging as a significant political force in Belfast, a group centred around Lindsay Crawford was active in Dublin municipal ward politics. Belfast and Dublin's Protestant working class were united in a shared commitment to the centrality of Protestantism, not the union, to identity.

The first target of Lindsay Crawford was William West, the official Unionist candidate for the south city ward elections in January 1903. Crawford, along with leading Dublin orangemen, supported the candidacy of Frank Donaldson, the secretary of the Dublin Grand Lodge. Crawford and Donaldson were determined to oust the established figures in the Unionist Registration Association on Dawson Street and prevent, as they saw it, the eclipse of Irish Protestantism. As the struggle against the establishment was taken to other wards, it led to pitched battles between the rival supporters and, not surprisingly, the loss of seats. In 1904, following a vacancy in the St Stephen's Green parliamentary division, Lindsay Crawford persuaded Michael J.F. McCarthy to seek the Unionist nomination. McCarthy was popular amongst Protestants for his books on Catholic Ireland; *Five Years in Ireland* (1901) and *Priests and People in Ireland* (1902). In these books McCarthy analyzed Ireland's economic backwardness as being due to the dominance of Catholic priests and the culture of Catholicism, especially in education. Patterson credits McCarthy with being a powerful influence on Lindsay Crawford.[38] McCarthy had one issue only to put before the electorate; 'whether Ireland was to be a priest-ridden land hastening to senility and decay with no prospect of regeneration'.[39] In his campaign for the nomination, he had not only the backing of Lindsay Crawford but also that of the leading Ulster unionists and orangemen, including Edward Saunderson. A faction within the CWC also supported him, though not all. He was eventually forced to withdraw from the contest. It was soon after that Lindsay Crawford moved north to take up his role as grand master of the IOO.

The redirection of energies into the localities, which in Ulster led to the formation of the UUC, led to the emergence of a vigorous local unionism that was unashamedly parochial and populist. But, whereas in Belfast the IOO was able to ensure that working-class Protestants were of consequence, in Dublin middle-class Protestants eclipsed the working class. The revolt in the local government constituencies was contained by the creation of a Unionist Municipal Reform Party. The objective of the Reform Party was to gain for the Protestant middle class the leadership of local government by articulating an unswervingly local programme of value for money in administration. As such, it had considerable success in the suburban townships, but it had little to offer the Protestant working class.[40]

CONCLUSION

For the Protestant working class, Protestantism was a total worldview, which explains the paradox by which the working class was often lax in its religious observance but fiercely loyal to a Protestant identity. The Protestant working class of Belfast and Dublin always interpreted class issues in sectarian terms. For the Protestant working class, sectarianism was an empowering ideology and culture, not the result of bourgeois manipulation, and one expressive of a strong class-consciousness. In contrast to its own loyalty to Protestantism, the bourgeois unionist establishment was seen as vacillating and compromising and too loyal to the Conservative party. This contestation for power within Irish unionism led to the establishment, in 1905, of the Ulster Unionist Council. The Ulster unionist movement was compelled to come to terms with Protestant working-class loyalists who proved adept at pressure-group politics. The political culture of Ulster unionism responded to working-class aspirations and endorsed its sectarian cultural expression in a relationship between the Protestant middle and working class that was much more than crude manipulation of the simple-minded. The result was the invented tradition of 'Ulster' unionism that validated sectarianism and united the Protestant working class and middle class within political and cultural values of sectarian solidarity. The culture of orangeism was used to construct and negotiate that identity. Since Boyle's 1962 article, a sophisticated historical analysis of the dynamics of class relationship within the politics and culture of Ulster unionism has been developed. In fact any historical analysis of Ulster unionism today assumes that class tensions within Protestantism are more important to understanding and analysis than opposition to nationalism.[41]

It is assumed that Belfast Protestant working-class loyalism was an expression of localism, a uniquely Ulster reaction to uniquely Ulster concerns. Peter Gibbon has argued that the specific character of Ulster unionism was the result of the uneven development of Irish capitalism; industrial, advanced Protestant Ulster developed unionism while Catholic agrarian, under-developed southern Ireland developed nationalism.[42] This argument has led in turn to the development by the British and Irish Communist Organisation of the 'two-nations' thesis of an Irish Catholic and a British Protestant nationality in Ireland.[43] In fact, it seems that class conflict occurs in Ulster whilst a feudal conflict against clericalism is what occurs in the rest of Ireland. Whilst there is a wealth of analysis of class and Protestantism in Ulster, the Irish Protestant experience beyond Ulster has not been subject to class analysis to the same extent. Analysis of southern Protestantism has usually been focused on quantifying and describing the experience of decline.

Discussion on class and Protestantism in southern Ireland has been traditionally dominated by a focus on the landowning gentry class, a class whose lives were devoted to hunting, shooting, gambling and adultery. This imagining has shaped much of the historiography of southern Protestantism, giving it a melancholic plot structure shaped by a consciousness of crisis and decline, as the recent history by R.B. McDowell is titled, and a drift into extinction. The figures that did most to shape this degenerative history of southern Protestantism are the writers Elizabeth Bowen and William Butler Yeats. Bowen, in her grand tragedies, narrated the decline of the 'big house', which become a metaphor for the decline of Protestant Ireland. William Butler Yeats famously described southern Irish Protestants as 'no petty people' and one of the ancient stocks of Europe. But, as Louis MacNiece pointed out, most of the 'big houses', apart from 'an obsolete bravado, an insidious bonhomie and a way with horses', had no culture worth speaking of.[44]

Crisis and decline, a drift toward extinction, is, interestingly, an historiographical emplotment that Irish Protestantism shares with the Irish language, and just like the Irish language, this decline is greatly exaggerated. Despite the iconic status of the 'big house', Irish Protestantism was in fact mainly an urbanized culture of the working and middle classes. These were the plain Protestants with no pretensions to ancient stock or breeding. In contrast to the melancholic vapourings at the loss of country houses, with their leaking internal gutters and dry rot, the memoirs of these middle-class and working-class Protestants show energy, dynamism and confidence. Moreover, in contrast to Ulster Protestants, the memoirs of these plain Dublin Protestants show an acute consciousness of social class, more acute in fact than a consciousness of sectarian difference.[45] This is because the middle class has shaped the culture of Protestantism outside of Ulster in the twentieth century. 'Remembering who we are' has become a reminder of Protestant respectability and not a call for Protestant solidarity.

NOTES

1. John W. Boyle, 'The Belfast Protestant Association and the Independent Orange Order, 1901–10', *Irish Historical Studies*, xiii, 50 (September 1962), pp. 117–52.
2. John W. Boyle, *The Irish Labor Movement in the Nineteenth Century* (Washington: 1988).
3. Ibid., pp. 72–4.
4. An edited text is available in Arthur Mitchell and Padraig Ó Snodaigh (eds), *Irish Political Documents, 1869–1916* (Dublin: 1989), pp. 118–20.
5. Boyle, 'The Belfast Protestant Association and the Independent Orange Order'.
6. Boyle, *The Irish Labor Movement*, p. 295.
7. Henry Patterson, 'Independent Orangeism and class conflict in Edwardian Belfast', *Proceedings of the Royal Irish Academy*, vol. 80, section C, no.4 (1980); *Class Conflict and Sectarianism: the Protestant Working Class and the Belfast Labour Movement, 1868–1920* (Belfast: 1980).
8. Peter Murray, 'Radical way forward or sectarian cul-de-sac? Lindsay Crawford and Independent Orangeism reassessed', *Saothar*, vol. 27 (2002), pp. 31–42; Peter Murray, 'Lindsay Crawford's "Impossible Demand"? The southern Irish dimension of the Independent Orange Order project', NIRSA working paper, (February 2002) available on www.may.ie/nirsa; Siobhan Jones, 'The *Irish Protestant* under the editorship of Lindsay Crawford, 1901–6', *Saothar*, vol. 30 (2005), pp. 85–94. For the term 'two great democracies', see the correspondence preserved in National Library of Ireland (NLI), Ms.11,415, 'Letters and papers of Robert Lindsay Crawford.
9. For example, see Laurence M. Geary (ed.), *Rebellion and Remembrance in Modern Ireland* (Dublin: 2001); Ian McBride (ed.), *History and Memory in Modern Ireland* (Cambridge: 2001); Lawrence McBride (ed.), *Images, Icons and the Irish Nationalist Imagination* (Dublin: 1999); Anne Dolan, *Commemorating the Irish Civil War: History and Memory, 1923–2000* (Cambridge: 2003).
10. For the development of the Irish Protestant commemorative tradition, see, Jacqueline R. Hill, 'National festivals, the state and "Protestant ascendancy" in Ireland, 1790–1829', *Irish Historical Studies*, vol. xxiv (1984), pp. 30–51; T.C. Barnard, 'Crisis of identity among Irish Protestants, 1660–85', *Past and Present*, vol. 127 (1990), pp. 39–83; T.C Barnard, 'The uses of 23 October 1641 and Irish Protestant celebrations' *English Historical Review*, vol. 106 (1991), pp. 889–920; James Kelly, '"The Glorious and Immortal Memory": commemoration and Protestant identity in Ireland, 1660–1800', *Proceedings of the Royal Irish Academy*, vol. 94, section C, pp. 25–52 (1994).
11. Kelly, 'Commemoration and Protestant identity', pp. 42–3.
12. Alvin Jackson, *Ireland, 1798–1998* (Oxford: 1999), pp. 58–68, 215–44.
13. Martin Maguire, 'A socio-economic analysis of the Dublin Protestant working-class. *Irish Economic and Social History*, vol. 20 (1993), pp. 35–61, Table 2.

14. Ibid., Table 1.
15. Ibid., p. 52.
16. Representative Church Body (RCB), Dublin, Library ms. 485, 'Association for the Relief of Distressed Protestants (ARDP), 1836–1977, articles of association'; G.D. Williams, *Dublin Charities* (Dublin: 1902); Kenneth Milne, *Protestant Aid: A History of the Association for the Relief of Distressed Protestants* (Dublin: 1989).
17. Martin Maguire, 'The Church of Ireland and the problem of the Protestant working class of Dublin, 1870s–1930s', in Alan Ford, James McGuire and Ken Milne (eds), *As By Law Established: the Church of Ireland since the Reformation* (Dublin: 1995) pp. 195–203.
18. Jackson, *Ireland, 1798–1998*, p. 231.
19. NLI, ir363g17, Orange Lodge of Ireland, general half-yearly meetings, 1901–1911.
20. J.R. Hill, 'The Protestant response to Repeal: the case of the Dublin working class', in F.S.L. Lyons and R.A.J. Hawkins (eds), *Ireland Under the Union: Varieties of Tension* (Oxford: 1980), pp. 35–68; J.R. Hill, 'Artisans, sectarianism and politics in Dublin, 1829–48', *Saothar*, vol. 7 (1981), pp. 12–27.
21. John Crawford, '"An overriding providence": the life and ministry of Tresham Dames Gregg (1800–81)', in T.G. Barnard and W.G. Neely (eds), *The Clergy of the Church of Ireland, 1000–2000* (Dublin: 2005), pp. 157–68.
22. RCB Library, ms. 486, Records of the City and County of Dublin Conservative Working Men's Club 1883–1987, annual report 1883.
23. On the history of the Conservative Workingmen's Club, see Martin Maguire, 'The organisation and activism of Dublin's Protestant working class, 1883–1935', *Irish Historical Studies*, xxiv, 113 (May 1994), pp. 65–87.
24. Martin Maguire, 'The Dublin Protestant Working Class, 1870–1932: Economy, Society, Politics', unpublished MA thesis, University College Dublin, 1990, p. 67.
25. Ibid., pp. 117–21.
26. John Crawford, *St Catherine's Parish, Dublin, 1840–1900: Portrait of a Church of Ireland Community* (Dublin: 1996), pp. 49–50.
27. Maguire, 'Dublin Protestant Working Class, 1870–1932', pp. 123–5.
28. Ibid., p. 130.
29. Alvin Jackson, 'The failure of unionism in Dublin, 1900', *Irish Historical Studies*, xxvi, 104 (November 1989) pp. 377–95.
30. *Irish Times*, 13 July 1900.
31. Boyle, *Irish Labor Movement*, pp. 354–5.
32. R. Lindsay Crawford and Richard Braithwaite, *Orangeism: Its History and Progress – A Plea for First Principles* (Dublin: 1904).
33. Jackson, 'The failure of unionism in Dublin', p. 95.
34. Rev. H. Fishe, *The Crusade against the Coronation Oath and Protestant Declaration* (Dublin: 1901).
35. RCB library, ms.486, CWC political committee minutes, 9 July 1901.
36. Maguire, 'Dublin Protestant Working Class, 1870–1932', pp. 150–1.
37. *Irish Protestant*, August 1901.
38. Patterson, 'Independent Orangeism and class conflict'.
39. *Dublin Daily Express*, 2 March 1904.
40. Maguire, 'Dublin Protestant Working Class, 1870–1932', pp. 159–172.
41. Alvin Jackson, 'Irish unionism', in D. George Boyce and Alan O'Day (eds), *The Making of Modern Irish History: Revisionism and the Revisionist Controversy* (Dublin: 1996), pp. 120–40.
42. Peter Gibbon, *The Origins of Ulster Unionism* (Manchester: 1975), p. 12.
43. Jackson, 'Irish unionism', pp. 132–3.
44. Louis MacNiece, 'The poetry of W.B. Yeats', p. 97, quoted in Declan Kiberd, *Inventing Ireland: the Literature of the Modern Nation* (London: 1995), p. 449.
45. Robin Tobin, '"Tracing again the tiny snail track": southern Protestant memoir since 1950'. *Yearbook of English Studies* (January, 2005).

5

Sheep in Wolves' Clothing: Labour and Politics in Belfast, 1881–1914

EMMET O'CONNOR

On 7 January 1910, the *Northern Whig* reported Colonel R.H. Wallace, grand master of Belfast orangemen, attacking the Labour election campaign in North Belfast in vintage style:

> Any candidate who opposes the properly selected Unionist candidate and calls himself a Unionist acts the part that Lundy took at the Siege of Derry and every man who votes for such a person votes for Home Rule ... They are wolves in sheep's clothing who seek to hand the keys of our fortress over to our enemies.

The Labour candidate, Robert Gageby, might well have pleaded that he was a sheep in wolves' clothing. A moderate and a justice of the peace, who had formerly been commended to the municipal electors of the Shankill ward by the *Belfast News-Letter*, he closed his campaign with the boast that the Conservatives had not proven that he was 'against the Union or that he was a Socialist'.[1] Originally a Liberal, Gageby was a Labourite only because the Liberals did not represent his Unionism, and the Conservatives did not represent his trade unionism.[2] But in standing for the British Labour Party, he inevitably took on the livery of a party which was largely in favour of home rule. Here, in a nutshell, was Belfast Labour's dilemma.

The reactionary character of Unionism has been affirmed in a variety of studies on labour, including some quite hostile to nationalism.[3] A more vexed question is whether Unionist workers were inherently reactionary, or driven into reaction by an insensitive, uncomprehending Labour movement. The historiography of contemporary Belfast Labour politics has been transformed since 1980, when Patterson's penetrating *Class Conflict and Sectarianism* rejected the view of working-class Unionism as the product of bourgeois manipulation, and made a compelling case for the material basis and relative autonomy of working-class Unionism. Yet, if we accept Patterson's conclusion that 'no form of class politics could have been developed which would have threatened the integration of the Protestant bloc, [and] which did not come to terms with Protestant working-class resistance to nationalist demands',[4] does it follow that a form of class politics was possible which approved of 'resistance to nationalist demands'? If so, why did Belfast Labour take a path which led it into conflict with Unionism?

Most historians who have addressed this question directly in the period under review argue that Labour was led astray by nationalism, echoing Patterson's contention that Ulster might have developed a history of 'political class conflict' had it not been for 'the tendency of many socialists to link socialism to an independent and unitary thirty-two county state'.[5] Particular criticism is made of James Connolly's uncompromising advocacy of socialist republicanism in Belfast between 1911 and 1914. Patterson attaches great weight to Connolly's 'inadequate analysis' of Unionism. Collins blames Connolly for crippling Belfast trades council in 1912. Morgan portrays Belfast socialists as victims of 'nationalist myopia' as much as of 'Unionist violence'. Black contends that northern Labour alienated itself from the bulk of workers by identifying with nationalism in 1912 and after.[6]

This essay argues that there is little evidence for these interpretations. It was an abiding concern of Belfast Labour to accommodate pro-Union elements and avoid association with 'nationalist demands'. Nationalists qua nationalists were not influential within the city's Labour circles, and Connolly's views are something of a red herring, however offensive revisionists might find them. Given the structural basis of local trade unionism and the prevailing anglo-centrism, British Labour was much more significant and much more problematic because of its attitude to the Irish question. The essential difficulty of Belfast Labour lay not with nationalism, or the nationalist/unionist divide. It lay, as Gageby's campaign illustrates, with the tension between Labourism and Unionist insistence on sectarian solidarity.

THE STRUCTURAL BASIS OF LABOUR

As the nineteenth century progressed, Belfast changed from a town of some 20,000 people into a major centre of manufacture with (in 1911) almost 387,000 souls. In the process, its fortunes diverged markedly from 'the south and west' – as the southern provinces were called – where manufacture and population suffered steady decline. While both Belfast and Dublin enjoyed a sizable trade in food, drink and tobacco, Belfast nearly monopolized other sectors of manufacture in Ireland. In 1907, the Belfast region accounted for £19.1 million of Ireland's £20.9 million worth of manufactured exports, excluding food and drink. This performance was based mainly on a high degree of specialization within the British economy, especially in textiles and clothing and engineering and shipbuilding, so that Belfast's industrial links were primarily with Britain rather than the south. For its part, the south mirrored these relations, being tied to Britain rather than the north. Detachment from the south was reinforced by pockets of related manufacture throughout east and mid Ulster, which enhanced the north's sense of difference.[7]

In Labour, as in capital, Belfast gravitated towards Britain. The process was incremental, beginning in engineering in 1820, extending to the building and repair trades in the late nineteenth century, and becoming general after 1914. By 1920, of some 100,000 trade unionists in what became Northern Ireland, about 80 per cent belonged to British, 15 per cent to local, and 5 per cent to Dublin-based unions, proportions that would remain fairly stable throughout the century.[8] The political consequences of anglicization deserve further study. Up to 1914, one can detect a bi-polarity in trade unionism between textiles – the biggest employment sector – and the metal trades – the biggest sector of union membership. Textile unions were local, small, weak, and supportive of the trades council and, to a lesser extent, the Irish Trades Union Congress (ITUC). Unions in the metal trades were British-based, well organized, and under-represented in the council and Congress. The variance can be explained by differences in bargaining power, or by the sectionalism for which the metal trades unions were infamous, but it is likely that the strength of orangeism in shipbuilding and engineering discouraged association with the council and, more especially, with Congress.[9] Police estimated in 1912 that of nearly 20,000 shipyard workers, 6,000 were active in Unionist clubs and orange lodges in their workplaces. Shipyardmen were prominent in sectarian disturbances in 1857, 1864, and 1901; in the workplace expulsions of 1886, 1893, 1912, and 1920; and in leading worker protests against home rule in 1886 and 1914, against the anti-conscription campaign in 1918, and against Labour's election campaign in 1921.[10]

Where British unions established an early and complete dominance was in hegemonizing labour thinking. 'Trade unionism is largely a thing of English growth and development introduced into this country,' said the president of the ITUC in 1908.[11] It was not important that the president was John Murphy, a Belfast printer and lieutenant of William Walker: almost any of his audience would have said the same. The secular model and British orientation of trade unionism was not seriously challenged by either confessional or Dublin-based unions. The Catholic minority in Belfast made little impression on the pattern of labour organization, though sectarianism affected its character. Catholics accounted for 8 per cent of the population in 1784, and 43 per cent in 1848. Their proportion then fell to 24 per cent by 1911. While the decline can be explained by boundary extensions – the Catholic community grew in numbers – there is some evidence that from the 1860s, when Belfast's accelerated growth was powered by iron shipbuilding, Catholics found it increasingly difficult to enter the skilled labour market.[12] The marginality of Catholics in skilled occupations meant that they were marginal too in trade unionism.

Neither was Belfast much troubled by political resistance to British trade unionism. The creation of the ITUC in 1894, with an all-Ireland remit, implicitly rejected the British Trades Union Congress (BTUC) as an effective lobby for Irish workers, but it did not alter the prevailing tendency to follow British thinking on organization and politics. By 1900, some 75 per cent of Ireland's trade unionists belonged to British unions and, north and south, they saw themselves as a region of the British labour movement.[13] An Irish labour movement hardly existed before the foundation of the Irish Transport and General Workers' Union (ITGWU) in 1909. Yet, even when Irish unions enjoyed a resurgence, after 1917, their impact on Belfast was slight, despite the major growth of trade unionism in Ulster during the war years and the brief economic boom that followed.[14] Clearly, the ITUC's backing for nationalism from 1918 did not in itself win support in Ulster for Dublin-based unions. Nationalism – as distinct from the national question – created very few problems within trade unionism in Ulster. That the basis for a pro-Union labour movement was so strongly grounded in the economy, union organization, and mentalities, makes it all the more curious that Labour and Unionism did not reach an accommodation.

LOCAL LABOURISM

Founded in 1881, the United Trades Council of Belfast would provide the agency of local Labour politics up to 1918. During the 1880s, membership did not exceed 5,000, and the council was composed largely of local craft unions in textiles and clothing, construction, and diverse other trades.[15]

While the council became more broadly based in the 1890s, it never enjoyed the committed backing of the metal trades. In 1899, out of fifty-seven affiliates and a membership of 19,000, twenty-five were local, with a membership of 8,000, and of these nine linen unions accounted for 5,000 members.[16]

Political issues were commonly accepted as a legitimate concern of trades councils, and the contradiction that would bedevil Belfast in this respect preceded the first home rule crisis. Most delegates were Conservatives, the Liberals being seen as appeasers of Irish nationalists. Moreover, in so far as working-class representation in politics had been raised in Belfast, it had been promoted by radical orangemen, who acted occasionally as a ginger group within Toryism. An early example was the formation of the Belfast Protestant Working Men's Association in 1868 at a rally in solidarity with 'the indomitable' William Johnston of Ballykilbeg, a landlord and senior orangeman imprisoned for defying the Party Processions Act. Standing for the association in the next Westminster elections, Johnston won a smashing victory over the Conservatives. But while he appealed to workers newly enfranchised in 1867, he stood primarily as a militant opponent of the Party Processions Act – under which orange parades had been banned – and subsequently mended his fences with the Conservatives and the Grand Orange Lodge. As would be seen later in the case of Tom Sloan, working-class Protestants 'could compete with Conservative candidates [only] if they outbid them on commitment to Protestantism'.[17]

Neither radical orangeism nor ties with the Conservatives offered avenues of advance acceptable to Belfast trades council: both ran counter to the values of British Labourism, which itself could be described at this time as social Liberalism. The Liberals were regarded as the party of labour, most British trade unionists were Liberal-Labourites, or Lib-Labs, and Belfast trades council's usual contact at Westminster was the BTUC leader and Lib-Lab MP, Henry Broadhurst.[18] To preclude contention, discussion of 'politics' – by which was meant party politics – was forbidden at council meetings. When its Liberal secretary, Alexander Bowman, contested North Belfast in the general election of 1885, he stood on a Labour ticket, to avoid embarrassing the council. And though nominated by its president, he was not endorsed by the council.[19] An obvious lesson of Bowman's choice of platform was that the only political options open to trade unionists in Belfast were Conservatism or Labourism, but a forgotten lesson was that local considerations had to come before British affiliations.

William Gladstone's conversion to home rule shocked Belfast Liberals, and presented the trades council with its first major controversy. To refute Gladstone's claim that only the upper classes of Ireland opposed home rule, local Liberals despatched a group of trade unionists to Westminster to lobby MPs 'supposed to be identified with the interests of the artisans and working classes'. While the trades council dissociated itself from the deputation, a letter from Bowman to Broadhurst expressing his personal support for home rule was too much for council delegates. The ensuing furore compelled Bowman to resign as secretary. The council confirmed its detachment from Liberal Labourism in declining to affiliate to the BTUC's Labour Electoral Committee in 1887, and hazarding no more than a tentative connection with the successor Labour Electoral Association.[20] The defeat of Liberal-Labourism had not been difficult. The Liberals had little working-class support in Belfast.[21] Independent Labourism would pose a more relentless challenge to Unionists.

The 1890s saw Belfast trades council realize a measure of stability and progress. Influenced by new unionism – the upsurge of militant general unionism that swept across the United Kingdom between 1889 and 1891 – the council made its first effort to transcend sectarianism during a lock-out of linen-lappers in 1892. Twelve thousand workers marched in solidarity, led by bands from both communities, and with union officials sporting orange and green rosettes. Long before Connolly's arrival in Belfast, sectarian differences were being denounced as a bosses' device to divide and conquer, even by Murray Davis, a Conservative on the trades council:

> Too long they had allowed themselves to be led by men who, instead of educating and improving the working class, had endeavoured to separate them and to keep them at each other's throats. But the working men were being educated: day after day they were learning the lesson that it did not matter whether their colours were black, orange, or green, they could still come together to promote their interests.[22]

One year later, Samuel Monro, president of the trades council, would recall the demonstration with pride and tell the BTUC that trade unionism might be the 'ism':

> ... whose mission it shall be to free our unhappy land from the terrible incubus of religious bigotry and political intolerance, which have been the means of separating into hostile camps those who should be brethren.[23]

Jim Larkin would say much the same in 1907.[24] It was generic stuff.

There were some genuine grounds for optimism. Unlike 1886, the shipyard unions called mass meetings to condemn the expulsions that accompanied the second home rule crisis, albeit at the prompting of employers, and the trades council survived the crisis unscathed, apart from what would be remembered for the 'green sash' incident.[25] The semi-mythical incident occurred when Belfast hosted the 1893 BTUC, and the trades council marked the close of Congress with a rally on Saturday 9 September. The House of Lords had rejected the home rule bill the previous day, and the British speakers were advised to be discreet. Before ascending the platform, a bemused Will Thorne, leader of the National Union of Gasworkers and General Labourers, was persuaded to remove a sash in his union's colours of red, white, and green. The stewards had pleaded that 'there's too much green in it'.[26] As feared, the meeting was broken up by loyalist heckling about British Labour's attitude to home rule. It is instructive that Belfast folklore would recall the trouble as erupting spontaneously at the sight of Thorne on the platform in a green sash. In what might serve as a parable for how historians have misread the past, the folk memory substituted local animosities for the key antagonism between Unionism and British Labour, and turned the story into, for nationalists, a joke about loyalist paranoia, and, for loyalists, a joke about English naivety.[27] It was British Labour too that forced Belfast trades council into an exclusively Irish congressional context at this time. The council had hoped to associate with both the BTUC and ITUC until the former, to clip the socialist presence, debarred trades council delegates from 1895.[28]

An extension of the municipal franchise in 1897 encouraged Belfast trades council to contest elections, primarily to advance its grievances about the maladministration of the city, particularly its public health problems.[29] Six members were returned to the sixty-strong Belfast Corporation, 'all of them', noted the *News-Letter* with satisfaction, 'on a platform which has more to do with the interests of trade unionism than with the interest of any political party', and all subvented by the trades council to discourage corruption and keep them 'non-party'.[30] 'The labour party, as they are sometimes called ... comported themselves with credit to themselves and benefit to the artisans of the community,' according to the stridently Conservative *Belfast Evening Telegraph* in 1899.[31] Socialists on the trades council took a more jaundiced view of their councillors' cosy relationship with the 'deadhead' Unionist city fathers. The election in 1899 of Murphy as president, and Walker as assistant secretary, heralded a new era of British Labourite ascendancy.

BRITISH LABOURISM

In 1903 Belfast trades council agreed to form a branch of the Labour Representation Committee (LRC). Founded in London in 1900, the LRC would be known as the Labour party from 1906. By 1905, the officers of the Belfast LRC and the trades council were interchangeable.[32] Walker was the key man. Since the zenith of new unionism, socialists had been struggling to establish a presence in Belfast in the face of violent loyalist opposition. A branch of the British Independent Labour Party (ILP) – forerunner of, and then a left faction within, the Labour party – had been launched in the city in 1892. Dressed in the bohemian style beloved of fin de siècle socialists, Walker showed courage as well as style evangelizing for the ILP on the Custom House steps, Belfast's speaker's corner. 'His speech was his fortune', in an age when the gift was prized. It was a measure of Walker's renown that, on his election to Belfast Corporation in 1904, Kilkenny trades council immediately offered him the presidency of that year's ITUC, waiving the traditional privilege of the hosts to have a local man in the chair.[33] By now the Belfast ILPers had faded away, and Walker, having cut his hair and swapped his floppy tie for a trademark high white collar, was happier with the more moderate LRC.

The initiative came at a uniquely opportune conjuncture of local and national factors. The politicization of British unions was accelerated by the law lords' restriction of trade union rights in the *Quinn v. Leathem* case, in which Belfast was closely involved, and the Taff Vale judgment. The trades council had seen its municipal representation fall to three in 1902, and it was anxious to recover its losses while reducing the financial burden involved. Dissident orangeism was enjoying a revival. Tom Sloan, a semi-skilled shipyard worker, had captured South Belfast from the Unionists in 1902 to become the city's first working-class MP. In 1903, he launched the Independent Orange Order, which was founded to combat Tory appeasement of nationalists and 'Romanization' in the Anglican Church, but evolved into a vaguely liberal vehicle of working-class resentment of the 'fur coat brigade'. That same year, Alex Boyd, a prominent Independent Orangeman, organizer of the Belfast Municipal Employees' Association, and a future vice-president of Belfast LRC, won a municipal by-election.[34] It would be embarrassing if the trades council could not be more critical of the 'deadheads' than orangemen. *British* Labourism, or 'Walkerism' as it has come to be called in the Belfast context, was intended to solve that problem, enabling Labourites to be both anti-Unionist and pro-Union.

It was a doomed policy: more a stratagem than a strategy. It is true that the home rule issue was in abeyance, was not a matter of principle for the British LRC, and Labour was not as identified with Irish nationalism as the Liberals. But the Conservatives would not be in government forever. Another home rule crisis was inevitable, and most LRC leaders were in favour of devolution, seeing it as a straightforward matter of democracy.[35] Belfast trades council's backing for the LRC was a watershed, and created a hostage to fortune. In liquidating local Labourism, Walker set the trades council on a collision course with the national question.

The revisionist portrayal of Walker as an 'orthodox British socialist', advancing standard socialist arguments against nationalism, and flawed only in sharing the British tendency to underestimate the power of ethnicity, defies credibility.[36] Walker's position on home rule provoked widespread protest within the LRC in Britain.[37] Walker may have wanted to be a typical Labourite, but he believed that a political career in Belfast required compromise with Unionist prejudices. His infamous endorsement of a Belfast Protestant Association questionnaire in the North Belfast by-election of 1905 was not an aberration. The Belfast LRC consistently advertised its Protestant orientation, and the *Belfast Labour Chronicle*, published jointly by the trades council and the LRC from 1904 to 1906, echoed orange stereotypes in its repeated assertions that home rule would mean 'Rome rule' and economic ruin. In practice, Walker showed that a secular British Labourism could not be replicated successfully in Ireland. His near victories in North Belfast in 1905 and 1906 need to be kept in perspective. While the Conservatives bankrolled a major electoral campaign, they had a poor candidate in Sir Daniel Dixon, and Labour gleefully rattled the skeletons in his closet. Labour was fighting its best constituency, with its best man, at the best possible time. Walker had the backing of Boyd, whose Independent Orangemen disrupted Dixon's meetings. And the general election in 1906 saw a big swing against the Tories.[38]

Nor, for once, can London be faulted for indifference. From the inception of the Belfast LRC, leading British luminaries visited Belfast in support. Party secretary Ramsay MacDonald, MP, was Walker's agent in 1905, and Arthur Henderson, MP, one of his principal speakers. It was a mixed blessing, as the Conservatives swooped on the home rule proclivities of British Labour. When another by-election followed in North Belfast in 1907, only pressure from London persuaded Walker to run again. Now describing himself as 'The people's candidate', he refused agents and literature from London for their unfamiliarity with the 'peculiarities' of Belfast, and made no mention of the Labour party in his campaign.[39] After a third defeat, Walker abandoned hope of a seat in Belfast, and concentrated on developing his prospects in Britain.

Lionized for his polemic with Connolly in 1911, Walker has been 'ideologized', and Walkerism glorified as a 'socialist Unionist' antidote to Connollyism. The parallels are not exact. Walker did not try to blend socialism and Unionism as Connolly tried to fuse socialism and republicanism. He turned instead to British Labourism for a theoretical argument against Irish nationalism. It was thin camouflage for squaring Labour with a pro-Union position, and most of his colleagues saw it simply as that: as the best tactic against the Unionists. Thomas Johnston, a founder of the Belfast Socialist Society, conveyed their pragmatism to MacDonald in 1905: '[we] won't interfere in the Home Rule question until we are compelled – and then the majority of our members would favour that policy I think.'[40] Walker was exceptional too in his sensitivity about nationalism, and often found himself in a minority because he was so stiff-necked. One example was the toast at the ITUC banquet in 1904, when he and Murphy kept their seats as other Ulster delegates, 'thinking no evil', rose to drink to 'Ireland a nation'.[41] *Honi soit qui mal y pense?* The Unionists were not impressed. They opposed Gageby in 1910, as trenchantly as they had challenged Walker, and he was defeated by a substantial margin.

IRISH LABOURISM?

As revisionists would have it, Connolly pushed the Belfast ILP – revitalized in 1907 in the wake of the big dock strike – and the trades council into supporting home rule. The ILP was divided and the council found itself damned in the Unionist press as 'a Home Rule clique' and ceased to be representative of the mass of Protestant workers.[42] In reality, the ILP gave no more than partial and brief support to Connolly, while the trades council remained marginally pro-Union, avoided a stand on home rule, never voted on partition, and tried repeatedly not to offend Unionist opinion. But troublesome questions could not be disposed of as easily as in 1886 and 1893. What made them so viscous was not Connolly, but the way in which they affected the British Labour Party and the ITUC. The former welcomed the home rule bill at Westminster. The latter narrowly approved Walker's policy of backing the British Labour Party for the last time in 1911. In 1912, the expectation of an Irish parliament swung Congress behind an Irish Labour party.

When Connolly settled in Belfast in 1911, no Labour councillors remained on the corporation.⁴³ At Easter 1912, four of the city's five ILP branches agreed to join with the Socialist Party of Ireland in a new all-Ireland venture, the Independent Labour Party (of Ireland) (ILP(I)). It was undoubtedly an achievement on Connolly's part, even if North Belfast, formerly Walker's own and by far the largest branch, stayed away. However, given his consistent lack of success in building all his Irish parties – the Irish Socialist Republican Party, the Socialist Party of Ireland, and the ILP(I) – it is probable that other factors weighed more heavily with the ILP: the apparent inevitability of home rule, British Labour policy on Ireland, and apprehension about the exclusion of Ulster. Connolly's fear that partition would lead to a 'carnival of reaction' was exceptional only in its eloquence. That same reaction would soon cause the ILPers to resile. By 1913, they had abandoned the ILP(I), and, according to Nevin: 'It had virtually no influence [in Belfast], least of all in the labour-trade union movement.'⁴⁴

More dubious again was Connolly's impact on the trades council. Even before the home rule crisis, unions were drifting away from the council, possibly alienated by the growth of syndicalism, or the emergence of alternative industrial relations procedures. The number of affiliates fell from sixty-three in 1907 to forty in 1911. It would fall to thirty-two in 1913.⁴⁵ It was unfortunate timing that the council produced, in D.R. Campbell and Tom Johnson, two leaders of national calibre in a period when prudence demanded a retreat into apolitical localism. Campbell served on the ITUC executive, from 1909 to 1918, was ITUC president in 1911, and treasurer from 1912 to 1918. In 1920 he declined an offer to become secretary of the Irish Labour party, not wishing to leave Belfast, and the job went to Johnson, a member of the ITUC executive in 1913–14, and a determinant of Congress policy from 1916.⁴⁶ Neither were Connollyites in the sense of being socialist republicans. Both had been Walkerites, and, like Walker in 1903, wanted to be part of the wider labour movement.

Despite the traditional inclination of the trades council to support colleagues of prominence, there were just two instances when Campbell carried the council against conservative opposition. The first of these was in November 1911, when Walker challenged his nomination as a delegate to the British Labour Party's annual conference on the ground he had favoured an Irish Labour party at the 1911 ITUC. Campbell had not spoken in the debate, but had encouraged the prospect in his presidential address.⁴⁷ He secured a nomination by defeating George Greig, a strong critic of Irish Labourism, by twenty-two to eighteen votes.⁴⁸ We can only speculate on how many voted for Campbell because he was outgoing president of Congress. Campbell's second, and final, victory came on 21 September 1912, when, by eleven to nine votes, the trades council endorsed a circular from the ITUC calling for 'independent representation of labour upon all public boards'.[49] Undoubtedly, Unionists saw the proposal as backing for an Irish Labour party, and, by extension, home rule, but it was not the end of the story. In March 1913, the council resolved not to send delegates to the forthcoming ITUC 'on the grounds that the political resolution, passed at last year's congress [at Clonmel], was not acceptable to members of that Council and was impracticable'. The 'Clonmel decision', it was felt, had led to a decline in attendance at council meetings.[50] When, in February 1914, Campbell proposed participation in an all-Ireland conference on labour representation, the council agreed to a local conference only, which itself was cancelled when the Electrical Trades' Union threatened to disaffiliate.[51]

No sooner had Belfast trades council opted for self-exclusion from Irish Labour than it was faced with the prospect of Ulster's exclusion from the home rule bill. Characteristically, it avoided the issue until April 1914, when it received an ITUC invitation to a national protest meeting in Dublin. Johnson and Connolly urged support. Murphy, the council's Walkerite secretary, thought exclusion would leave 'the workers in North East Ulster ... more than ever in the grip of the sweating employer', but advised caution. The council then voted fourteen to three to refer the matter to the executive, which resolved that 'in the present state of divided public opinion, no meeting should be held'.[52] The council meanwhile re-affiliated to the ITUC, and at the annual congress in June, Connolly's resolution condemning partition was passed by eighty-four votes to two, with eight delegates unrecorded: seventeen delegates from Belfast, three from the rest of Ulster and four from Britain attended the congress. The debate reflected the common opinion – so often attributed to Connolly alone – that partition would weaken Labour or was a device to that end. Campbell's remark that 'Belfast trades council [had] never voted on Home Rule' (true), 'but had emphatically protested against partition' (untrue) had a rhetorical validity in contrasting divided opinions on the former with near unanimity on the latter. Of three other Belfast speakers on the motion, one affirmed his indifference to home rule and vehement hostility to exclusion, one expressed his abhorrence of both measures, and Frank Hall, Typographical Association, who must have cast one of the two votes against, said that 'he was not in favour of exclusion from the point of view of the interest of the Irish worker ... but he could not support the resolution, because of the men who sent him there'.[53]

Of course Belfast Labour was not the same as Belfast labour. It never had been, the more so in relation to the ITUC. Belfast residents accounted for 22 per cent of delegates to the annual congresses between 1894 and 1914, well below the representation the city might have claimed. These delegates were drawn from forty-five unions, of which just eight had a presence at more than half of the annual congresses. Belfast's involvement with the ITUC strengthened steadily up to 1910, as the city sent more delegates from more unions and won more representation on the parliamentary committee: it then weakened only marginally up to 1913, a reflection of the way loyalties were polarizing around Labourism and Unionism. The fact remains that Belfast delegates at the 1914 congress were from thirteen unions with a small membership in the city.[54] Campbell and Johnson stood at the apex of a triple distortion. The council was over-representative of textile and craft societies outside the metal trades; that bias was further distilled in affiliations to the ITUC; and human nature dictated that those who engaged with Congress were more likely to share its values. Was there an alternative to alienating the majority? Why did Belfast trades council not defend partition as the democratic choice of Ulster? As we have seen, Labourism was one half of the answer; labour Unionism was the other half.

LABOUR UNIONISM

The labour question had been a flickering theme in Unionism since 1886, when Belfast's anti-Gladstonian Liberals sent Westminster an embassy of trade unionists. 'Labour Unionists' came into common currency during the third home rule crisis to describe Unionist clubs that were predominantly working class. For the Ulster Unionist Council, 'labour Unionism' was of use primarily in the propaganda war in Britain, to counter Liberal or nationalist arguments that Unionism was a movement of landlords and businessmen, and strengthen Tory demands for a general election. Unionist politicians ignored official Labour, and had repeatedly spurned overtures from the ITUC. Contacts with Belfast trades council withered with the emergence of the LRC.[55] No less than 102 delegations of British working men visited Ireland in 1914 on 'Home Rule study tours'. As these tended to come from Conservative Associations, more dedicated efforts were made to reach trade unionists. On 7 April, the Unionist press carried an appeal to British colleagues, signed 'On behalf of the overwhelming body of trade unionists in Ulster' by twenty men, members mainly of unions in the shipyards.[56] In May, 'a body of Belfast working men' was included in a Unionist team despatched to canvass in the North East Derbyshire by-election.[57]

Sectarian solidarity was too valuable politically to permit a similar charm offensive in Ireland. Irish Protestants outside the moral community of loyalism were traitors, and weeding them out of employment was 'a matter of long-standing discussion in Orange and Unionist circles'.[58] In July 1912, some 3,000 workers were expelled from the shipyards and engineering plants; in retaliation, it was claimed, for an assault by Hibernians on a Presbyterian Sunday school outing in Castledawson. Unlike previous expulsions, radicals of all religions were targetted, and about 600 expelled men were Protestants, victimized for being Labourites, Liberals, or Independent Orangemen. Campbell helped to organize an expelled workers' committee, which raised relief funds and lobbied the authorities to protect those willing to go back to work.[59] The ITUC's parliamentary committee made similar representations to John Redmond and the British Labour party.[60] But Campbell could not persuade Belfast trades council to associate itself with the expellees. Instead it suggested that he act discretely. Though Unionist leaders had condemned the violence, the council declined to mention the disturbances in its annual report for 1912, deciding that any reference would stir up controversy. The timidity was all the more remarkable as the council had scant influence in the employments directly affected, where the most powerful labour body was the Federation of Engineering and Shipbuilding Trades. Only when Harland & Wolff threatened to close the yard did the federation's district committee repudiate the 'lawlessness' and 'terrorism', and its affiliates promise to curb the hot-heads. While normality returned in August, few of the expellees got their jobs back.

What would be hailed in retrospect as the symbolic birth of Labour Unionism took place at a 'monster demonstration' in the Ulster Hall on 29 April 1914, convened by Thompson Donald and William Grant, both former officers of Shipwrights' Association, and Joseph Cunningham, sometime secretary of the Belfast district council of the Amalgamated Society of Engineers.[61] There were predictable sideswipes at Redmond, the Liberals, and Catholic clerics, but the focal point of criticism was Labour. Interestingly, the speakers ignored the ITUC, saving their scorn for Belfast trades council, and MacDonald and his MPs, growing fat on £400 a year. MacDonald's parliamentary philippic on the 'Curragh mutiny', and his appeal to the government – 'pass Home Rule as quickly as possible and take the consequences' – had been reported prominently in Belfast.[62] Of the 'various members' of the British Labour party invited to attend, only one had bothered to send an acknowledgement. Cunningham moved the resolution:

> That this meeting desires in the strongest possible manner to protest against the attitude of the British Labour Party and members of parliament in supporting the Home Rule Bill [and repudiates] the pretensions of the Belfast Trades Council to represent the trade unionists of Belfast ... we call upon our fellow trade unionists to refrain from giving to this so-called council and the Labour party any moral or financial support whatsoever.

Other motions affirmed the destructive effect of home rule on the prosperity of Belfast, and called on the BTUC to receive a loyalist delegation. There was an unmistakeable tone of incredulity in the speeches that British Labour men would submit the industrious folk of Ulster to the thriftless, disaffected, priest-ridden south. British workers would have been equally bemused by the sectarianism which peppered the rhetoric. 'They did not pretend to speak for the Roman Catholic trades unionists,' said John Keown, Plasterers' Society, who concluded that home rule 'represented the advance of Roman Catholicism, and would not benefit the country in any way (Cheers)'.[63]

In contrast with its supine stand on the expulsions, Belfast trades council responded stoutly, as all shades of opinion on the council closed ranks against Labour Unionism. Anticipating the language of the Northern Ireland Labour Party, Murphy wrote to the press, pointing out that the council had never taken a stand on home rule or exclusion as 'we never regarded the matter essentially as a labour problem'.[64] On the council itself he declared that the Ulster Hall meeting 'was representative of Unionism but not of trades unionism'.[65] In this respect at least, he was substantially correct. Though Labour Unionism acquired a formal footing in 1918 with the launch of the Ulster Unionist Labour Association and the Ulster Workers' Trade Union, neither won the confidence of the Protestant working class, which, on matters of wages and conditions, showed an overwhelming preference for existing unions.[66]

CONCLUSION

On 4 May 1914, Sir Edward Carson conveyed to Grant his gratitude for the Ulster Hall rally. 'I find it difficult,' he added, 'to offer any explanation as to why your fellow trade unionists in Great Britain have paid so little attention to your resolve not to allow your position to be degraded by placing you under a Parliament in Dublin.'⁶⁷ If Carson was baffled, it said more about him than those he wished to censure. British Labour could hardly champion democracy and oppose home rule. And, in Labour eyes, the case against partition was even stronger than that for home rule, all arguments for exclusion being outweighed by the tactics through which the Unionists eventually triumphed: sectarian solidarity and an alliance with the Conservatives. This same thinking, not nationalism or Connolly, guided Belfast Labour. Labour Unionism, with its seething resentment of official Labour and forthright Toryism, was not an option.

By the time of the third home rule crisis, Belfast Labour faced the choice of following its counterparts in Dublin and London or withdrawing into apolitical localism. It had tried the latter initially, and pointedly so after the first home rule crisis. It was ironic that Walker should have flushed it out of what was probably the one way of escaping the constitutional question. However, for Walker, British Labourism was a means not merely of reconciling Labour and the Union, but of modernizing local trade unionism. What kind of Labour movement would Belfast have if it cut itself off from the wider world? The question was raised again by the prospect of an Irish Labour party during the third home rule crisis. The trades council dithered and sought to take a nuanced stand. Formally, it took no position at all on home rule or exclusion, though it was evident that a narrow majority of delegates opposed the former and almost all opposed the latter. The subtleties were lost on Unionists, for whom it was enough that most Belfast Labourites were Protestants outside the fold.

NOTES

1. Austen Morgan, *Labour and Partition: the Belfast Working Class, 1905–23* (London: 1991), pp. 85–6.
2. To distinguish them from trade unionists, the usual convention is adopted here of referring to supporters of the Union with Britain with a capital 'U', whether members of the Unionist Party or not. Similarly, to distinguish them from the mass of labour, activists in trade unions, trades councils, or Labour political groups are referred to as 'Labour' or 'Labourites'.
3. For a succinct review of the Socialist debate on the Northern Ireland question see Terry Cradden, *Trade Unionism, Socialism, and Partition: The Labour Movement in Northern Ireland, 1939-1953* (Belfast: 1993), pp. 1–22.
4. Henry Patterson, *Class Conflict and Sectarianism: the Protestant Working Class and the Belfast Labour Movement, 1868–1920* (Belfast: 1980), p. 148.
5. Henry Patterson, 'Industrial labour and the labour movement, 1820–1914', in Liam Kennedy and Philip Ollerenshaw (eds), *An Economic History of Ulster, 1820–1939* (Manchester: 1985), p. 180.
6. Patterson, *Class Conflict and Sectarianism*, p. 144; Peter Gerard Collins, 'Belfast trades council, 1881-1921' (D.Phil, University of Ulster, 1988); Morgan, *Labour and Partition*; Boyd Black, 'Reasessing Irish industrial relations and labour history: the north-east of Ireland up to 1921', *Historical Studies in Industrial Relations*, 14 (Autumn, 2002), pp. 45–97.

7. See L.A. Clarkson, 'Population change and urbanisation, 1821–1911', in Liam Kennedy and Philip Ollerenshaw (eds), *An Economic History of Ulster, 1820–1939* (Manchester: 1985), pp. 137–54; Michael Farrell, *Northern Ireland: The Orange State* (London: 1976), p.18; L.M. Cullen, *An Economic History of Ireland Since 1660* (London: 1987), pp. 16–62.
8. Black, 'Reassessing Irish industrial relations and labour history', pp. 77–8, 92.
9. Patterson, *Class Conflict and Sectarianism*, pp. 23–9.
10. Patterson, *Class Conflict and Sectarianism*, pp. 88–9; Ronnie Munck, 'The formation of the working class in Belfast, 1788–1881, *Saothar*, vol. 11 (1986), p. 84; Patterson, 'Industrial labour and the labour movement, 1820–1914', p. 178.
11. University of Ulster, Magee College (UUMC), *Report of the Fifteenth Irish Trades Union Congress, 1908*, p. 27.
12. Black, 'Reassessing Irish industrial relations and labour history', pp. 52–61.
13. John W. Boyle, *The Irish Labor Movement in the Nineteenth Century* (Washington, DC: 1988), pp. 125–6.
14. Emmet O'Connor, *Syndicalism in Ireland, 1917–23* (Cork: 1988), pp. 173–7.
15. Collins, 'Belfast trades council', pp. 10–16.
16. J. Dunsmore Clarkson, *Labour and Nationalism in Ireland* (New York: 1978 edn), p. 348.
17. Catherine Hirst, 'Politics, sectarianism, and the working class in nineteenth-century Belfast', in Fintan Lane and Donal Ó Drisceoil (eds), *Politics and the Irish Working Class, 1830–1945* (London: 2005), p. 77; see also Patterson, *Class Conflict and Sectarianism*, pp. 1–18.
18. Collins, 'Belfast trades council', pp. 27, 42.
19. Terence Bowman, *People's Champion: The Life of Alexander Bowman, Pioneer of Labour Politics in Ireland* (Belfast: 1997), p. 38.
20. Collins, 'Belfast trades council', p. 42; Boyle, *The Irish Labor Movement in the Nineteenth Century*, p. 157.
21. Patterson, *Class Conflict and Sectarianism*, p. 15.
22. Quoted in ibid., p. 15.
23. *Belfast News-Letter*, 6 September 1893.
24. Patterson, *Class Conflict and Sectarianism*, p. 71.
25. *Belfast News-Letter*, 28–9 April 1893.
26. Will Thorne, *My Life's Battles* (London: 1927), pp. 158–9. See also the *Belfast News-Letter*, 11 September 1893, and Bob Purdie, 'Riotous customs: the breaking up of Socialist meetings in Belfast, 1893–1896', *Saothar*, vol. 20 (1995) pp. 32–40.
27. For a loyalist version of events see Emmet O'Connor and Trevor Parkhill (eds), *Loyalism and Labour in Belfast: The Autobiography of Robert McElborough, 1884–1945* (Cork: 2002), pp. 9, 36, 42.
28. Emmet O'Connor, *A Labour History of Ireland, 1824–1960* (Dublin: 1992), pp. 58–9.
29. Patterson, *Class Conflict and Sectarianism*, p. 40.
30. Boyle, *The Irish Labor Movement in the Nineteenth Century*, p. 168.
31. Bowman, *People's Champion*, pp. 128, 136.
32. Collins, 'Belfast trades council', p. 121.
33. Henry Patterson, 'William Walker, labour, sectarianism and the Union, 1894–1912', in Lane and Ó Drisceoil, *Politics and the Irish Working Class*, pp. 154–9; Fintan Lane, *The Origins of Modern Irish Socialism, 1881–1896* (Cork: 1997), pp. 192–6; Bob Purdie, 'An Ulster Labourist in Liberal Scotland: William Walker and the Leith Burghs election of 1910', in Ian S. Wood (ed.), *Scotland and Ulster* (Edinburgh: 1994), p. 122; Boyle, *The Irish Labor Movement in the Nineteenth Century*, pp. 280, 282–3.
34. John W. Boyle, 'The Belfast Protestant Association and the Independent Orange Order', *Irish Historical Studies*, vol. xiii (1962), pp. 117–52; Henry Patterson, 'Independent Orangeism and class conflict in Edwardian Belfast', *Proceedings of the Royal Irish Academy*, 80, section C, 1 (1980), pp. 1–27; *Belfast Labour Chronicle*, no. 50, November 1904.
35. Geoffrey Bell, *Troublesome Business: The Labour Party and the Irish Question* (London: 1982), pp. 1–15.
36. See Purdie, 'An Ulster Labourist in Liberal Scotland', p. 133; Stephen Howe, *Ireland and Empire: Colonial Legacies in Irish History and Culture* (Oxford: 2002), pp. 187–8.
37. Bell, *Troublesome Business*, pp. 17–19.
38. On Walker's elections, see Patterson, 'William Walker, labour, sectarianism and the Union, 1894–1912', pp. 161-5; Collins, 'Belfast trades council', pp. 127–31.
39. John Gray, *City in Revolt: James Larkin and the Belfast Dock Strike of 1907* (Belfast: 1985), p. 39; J.W. Boyle, 'William Walker', in J.W. Boyle (ed.), *Leaders and Workers* (Cork: 1966), pp. 62–3.

40. Thomas Johnston to J. Ramsay MacDonald, October 1905, quoted in Patterson, *Class Conflict and Sectarianism*, p. 75.
41. *Belfast Labour Chronicle*, 12 September 1905. For other examples, see UUMC, *Report of the Sixth Irish Trades Union Congress*, 1899, pp. 42–3; Collins, 'Belfast trades council', p. 91; Public Record Office of Northern Ireland (PRONI), Belfast & District Trades Union Council, minutes, 18 November 1911, MIC/193/5.
42. Morgan, *Labour and Partition*, pp. 145–78; Collins, 'Belfast trades council', pp. 183–218; Patterson, *Class Conflict and Sectarianism*, pp. 80–1; Black, 'Reassessing Irish industrial relations and labour history', p. 80.
43. Morgan, *Labour and Partition*, pp. 68–9.
44. Donal Nevin, *James Connolly: 'A Full Life'* (Dublin: 2005), p.429.
45. PRONI, Belfast & District Trades Union Council, balance sheets, 1899–1928, D/1050/6/F1.
46. Donal Nevin (ed.), *Trade Union Century* (Dublin: 1994), pp. 437–45; Collins, 'Belfast trades council', pp. 316–17.
47. UUMC, *Report of the Eighteenth Irish Trades Union Congress, 1911*, p. 13.
48. PRONI, Belfast & District Trades' Union Council, minutes, 18 November 1911, MIC/193/5.
49. Patterson, *Class Conflict and Sectarianism*, p. 81.
50. Collins, 'Belfast trades council', p. 191.
51. Morgan, *Labour and Partition*, p. 164.
52. PRONI, Belfast & District Trades Union Council, minutes, 2 April 1914, MIC/193/5; Collins, 'Belfast trades council', p.194.
53. UUMC, *Report of the Twenty-First Irish Trades Union Congress, 1914*, pp. 70–3, 108–10.
54. Based on UUMC, ITUC annual reports, 1894–1921.
55. UUMC, *Report of the Ninth Irish Trades Union Congress, 1902*, pp. 24–5; *Report of the Tenth Irish Trades Union Congress, 1903*, p. 31; *Report of the Eighteenth Irish Trades Union Congress, 1911*, p. 18; Boyle, *The Irish Labor Movement in the Nineteenth Century*, pp. 3, 12–14.
56. *Belfast News-Letter*, 7 April 1914.
57. Morgan, *Labour and Partition*, p. 216.
58. Gray, *City in Revolt*, p. 238.
59. Morgan, *Labour and Partition*, pp. 127–39 provides the most detailed account of the expulsions.
60. UUMC, *Report of the Twentieth Irish Trades Union Congress, 1913*, pp. 11, 13.
61. For a biographical note see Bob Purdie, 'Trade and Ulster Unionist: Senator Joseph Cunningham'.
62. *Northern Whig*, 26 March 1914.
63. *Belfast News-Letter, Northern Whig*, 30 April 1914.
64. *Belfast News-Letter*, 5 May 1914.
65. *Belfast News-Letter*, 8 May 1914.
66. O'Connor, *Syndicalism in Ireland*, pp. 178–9.
67. *Belfast News-Letter*, 7 May 1914.

6

The Dublin Building Trades Lockout of 1896

CHARLES CALLAN

INTRODUCTION

The most significant Dublin dispute before the great lockout of 1913 was in the building trades in 1896. Although evidence is insufficient to form a complete account, what is known is worth consideration and record.[1] The lockout lasted 18 weeks from 1 May to 28 August 1896, involving 4,500 workers and the loss of 114,000 working days.[2] Probably up to 30,000 people, including dependents, were directly affected. It was a trial of strength, a quest for dominance by the employers. They attempted to cast future industrial relations in a style that suited employer interests. In effect, the employers adopted trade union methods. At the outset of the lockout, one newspaper noted that 'the labour war in Dublin began this morning'.[3]

'New unionism' had a brief flowering in Dublin from 1889 to about 1893. The existing local and 'amalgamated' unions were concentrated in particular trades. Most were exclusive, had high membership contributions and a range of benefits. 'New unionism' aimed to organize general workers, with low contributions and few benefits, other than dispute pay. The 'old unions' tended to be conciliatory and avoid confrontation. The methods of the 'new unionism' were mass organization, militancy and sympathetic action, if necessary.

The period saw a rise in union membership and in the number of strikes in Dublin. Thousands joined the 'new unions' and some immediate gains were made. By the mid 1890s, most of the 'new unions' had, however, contracted or disappeared. The main Dublin union to survive was the United Builders Labourers of Ireland. Founded in 1889, it had 2,000 members and won an extra 1d. per hour for bricklayers' labourers. By the early 1890s, its membership was down to 1,000. Besides the 'new unionism', the years 1886–94 saw the establishment of the Dublin Trades Council and Labour League (DTCLL) in 1886, the short-lived Irish Trades and Labour Federation in 1889, the first May Day demonstration in 1890 and the creation of the Irish Trade Union Congress in 1894. Employers' organizations also emerged at that time. In 1889, there were strikes involving carpenters and joiners and bricklayers and, in the same year, the Master Builders' Association (MBA) was formed.

On Friday, 1 May 1896, a breakdown in discussions between the MBA and the Amalgamated Society of Carpenters and Joiners (ASCJ) was reported.[4] The union had been demanding an extra 2s. per week. The breakdown precipitated what was probably the first industry-wide dispute in Ireland and affected all Dublin building unions to a greater or lesser extent. The core issues affecting all the trades were essentially the same, although MBA demands impacted in different ways on each trade. Notably, the unions involved did not co-ordinate their response nor did they engage in picketing, other than for one day. While the lockout affected all trades from 1 May, some settled terms before the end of August – the carpenters and joiners on 1 August, brick and stone layers on 21 August, and plasterers, stonecutters and slaters on 28 August. The building labourers, the largest group, suffered the greatest loss. They were involved from the beginning, had no resources and gained nothing in the end.

Working and living conditions were primitive even by the standards of the time. Unemployment and uncertainty was a feature of life. The building trades were particularly prone to seasonal factors. The months from September to March, with short daylight hours and bad weather, were lean times for many. Besides the lack of daylight, the materials used did not lend themselves to use in poor weather conditions. Winter conditions were exacerbated by it being the most expensive time, when clothing, heat and light were required and provisions were at their most expensive. About one in eight of Dublin's 'industrial' workers were in the building trades. In total the trades – carpenters, bricklayers, masons, slaters, plasterers, plumbers, painters, glaziers and others – numbered 6,619 in 1891, rising to 7,484 in 1901. Labourers numbered 13,223 in 1891, rising to 14,728 over the same decade.[5] Most of those involved in the 1896 dispute were skilled workers. Although their lives were blighted by intermittent, seasonal unemployment, they were much better off than unskilled workers. Over a year a building tradesman, even if unemployed for half the time, had an income similar to what general workers were paid for a whole year.

The MBA was aggressive from its inception and was among the first organizations to introduce and practice sympathetic industrial action. In 1892, the DTCLL gave evidence to the Royal Commission on Labour of attempted 'black listing' by one building firm:

> Leinster Building Works, Grand Canal Street, Dublin
>
> Dear Sir,
>
> We presume you are aware that our carpenters are at present on strike since Monday 22 Inst (June 1891). We take the liberty of giving you a list of their names on other side, and ask your assistance in this matter by not employing any man whose name appears on list.
>
> Signed,

The circular listing '40–50 men' was not reproduced in the report.

By the 1890s, Dublin's building workers had a long tradition of union organization. Unions fell into two types. The local unions operated in specific trades, with memberships counted in hundreds, and were confined to the city and district. Most major Irish towns had local unions. Unlike in Britain, no attempt appears to have been made to federate or co-operate.[7] From the 1860s, some British 'amalgamated' unions had branches in Dublin's building trades; most of these branches had existed as local unions. In some trades, the position was weakened by the existence of more than one union. In some instances where local unions did not become amalgamated branches, the amalgamated unions established rival organizations. The aims of local and amalgamated unions were essentially the same: protecting wages and conditions, controlling who worked in the trade, combating the abuses of boy labour, providing friendly society benefits, and, when the opportunity arose, to gain increased wages and reduced working hours.

Amalgamated unions, usually with large memberships and impressive assets, appeared invulnerable. They held an attraction for Irish workers as amalgamated union membership guaranteed access, and the transfer of credits and benefits, to other branches in Ireland or Britain if a member migrated. However, amalgamated unions were bureaucratic, zealous in protecting resources and the union as an institution. They rarely initiated campaigns for improvements and the well being of the union was rarely jeopardized by local disputes, no matter how important the issues were to the members. They tended to seek compromise and the settlement of conflicts, even when such disadvantaged local membership. Local independent unions, in Ireland and Britain, were more inclined to militancy, especially in defence of existing conditions. They were more likely to be prepared to risk everything in fighting for their members.

HOURS, WAGES AND LEGAL STATUS

Neither the DTCLL[8] nor the ITUC[9], then, regarded themselves as having a role or co-ordinating function in industrial disputes. When Charles O'Reilly and John Simmons, DCTLL president and secretary, presented evidence before the Royal Commission on Labour in 1892 they claimed the DTCLL had seventy affiliates with 7,000 skilled and 4,000 unskilled workers.[10] On the matters of hours and wages, they stated that carpenters' hours had 'recently' been reduced to fifty-four following a four-week strike but 'in general' were fifty-four per week in 'summer'. In the bricklaying and painting trades the hours were fifty-seven. Weekly wages 'in general' were said to have been 33s. and in the building trades they claimed that '25s. or 26s. would be nearer the mark'. If such was the case, they were undoubtedly a yearly average, for they also claimed that building workers received up to 38s. per week in 'summer'. They stated that 'unskilled labour' was paid 15s. per week.

Two building employers gave evidence to the Royal Commission that confirmed the DTCLL figures. Samuel H. Bolton reported that rates averaged 7½d. to 8d. 'for skilled labour [and] varies in different

TABLE 1:
DUBLIN BUILDING TRADE WAGES AND WORKING HOURS, 1892

Occupations	Former Hours	Summer Hours	SummerWages	Average Wages
General (all)	-	57	34-35s	33s
Building trades (all)	-	54	38s	25s-26s
Carpenters	61¾	54	38s	25s-26s
Plasterers	61¾	54	38s	25s-26s
Bricklayers	-	57	38s	25s-26s
Painters	-	57	38s	25s-26s
Unskilled	-	-	-	15s.

Source: *Royal Commission on Labour*, vol. 30, pp. 49–51, 390.

trades' for a fifty-four-hour week. Such would have meant wages of from 33s.9d. to 36s. per week. They paid 'about 1d. or 2d. per hour extra' for overtime, and double pay for night and Sunday work. They paid by the hour, with little piece or sub-contracted work.[11] The firm T. & G. Martin stated 'machine hands' (woodcutting machinists) and carpenters were paid from 24 to 36s., cabinetmakers up to 50s., unskilled workers 16 to 20s. and French polishers (probably women) 9s. per week.[12] Weekly hours were fifty-four with no extra overtime rate. They also claimed they provided clothing and had a sick pay provision.

While unions had some legal status by the late nineteenth century, most of their activities remained illegal. No framework existed for the processing or settlement of industrial disputes and from the 1860s unions were demanding conciliation facilities. Following the Royal Commission on Labour report, the Conciliation (Industrial Disputes) Act, 1896 was enacted, providing for conciliation and, if necessary, arbitration.[13] The Board of Trade (BOT) could establish boards representing both sides of an industry under a BOT-appointed chairman. Where agreement could not be reached, the BOT could appoint an arbitrator. Other developments in the 1890s included the adoption by parliament of the 'Fair Wages Clause' of 1891, whereby those engaged on publicly funded works were obliged to observe locally established terms and conditions, the unsuccessful Employer's Liability Bill, 1893 and the pending Workmen's Compensation Act, 1897.[14] These developments may have accounted for the outbreak of employer organization in the 1890s as much as the emergence of the new unionism.

The 1890s also saw the inauguration of Dublin's electricity supply and electric tramway system. Both had implications for working hours and conditions. In many circumstances, working hours in winter were no longer dictated by daylight. Those on shorted 'winter' hours were paid less, as they were paid by the hour. That the availability of artificial light immediately became an industrial relations issue is demonstrated by a strike of twenty-five stonecutters in Rathmines in late 1895. The employer, John Good, the MBA secretary, refused to provide light. The new tramways had implications for the 'boundary' and 'travelling time' allowances. The 'boundary rules' and 'travelling time' were key elements in working agreements. The 'boundaries' for most trades were the Grand and Royal Canals and the Phoenix Park gate. Further boundaries, up to seven miles beyond, were specified with differing payments applying. On work beyond the seven miles boundary, 'country money' rules applied. While the trams reduced 'travelling time', the allowances remained the same.

THE LOCKOUT BEGINS

The craft unions restricted work in their trade to their members, but the MBA approach, though similar, was more subtle. Craft union policies centred on the inclusion of members and the exclusion of others, entry to the trade through apprenticeship, hours, rates and other issues defined in 'working rules'. The MBA employers pursued the same objectives for their own purposes and tried to use the craft unions against their competitors. Such was demonstrated by their attempt to induce unions to charge higher rates to non-MBA firms. There was then a general mutuality of interest between the craft workers and the employers. It was accepted that what was good for employers was good for workers too. Craft union ideology was summed up by the mottos inscribed on many of their banners which, with variations, proclaimed they existed for 'Defence – Not Defiance'. The perceived mutuality of interest was illustrated by the fact that individual employers supported some labour movement initiatives, including the establishment of the DTCLL and ITUC. In 1891, Alderman Meade, MBA president, was one of the guarantors for the DTCLL Trades' Hall in Capel Street.[15]

On Thursday, 30 April 1896, the main building unions held meetings to consider their position. There was no central or co-ordinating committee at any time during the dispute and, other than on one day, no picketing took place. The day after the lockout began, the May Day demonstration was held in the Phoenix Park on Sunday, 2 May. None of the speeches or resolutions reported referred to the lockout. As the main objective of the May Day demonstrations was an eight-hour day for all workers, it was odd that a major dispute concerning working hours was not mentioned. Some building unions were notable by their absence. Those present in large numbers were: Carpenters and Joiners (1,250) with the Phibsborough Brass Band; Stonecutters (400) with both the Glencullen Stonecutters Band and St Patrick's Brass Band; Amalgamated House Painters (130) with the Dublin (Barrack Street) Band; and the United Labourers with their own brass band. The Slaters' and Plasterers' unions sent delegates. Part of the main resolution passed concerned working hours and stated that:

This mass meeting of Dublin workingmen again declares that the reduction of hours of labour is the most important and urgent reform needed in the interests of the general population, and expresses itself in favour of working hours being internationally reduced to the limit of eight per day ...

It went on to condemn the working hours of 'female shop assistants as grossly excessive and discreditable to our common humanity'. However, many building unions opposed reductions in working hours if it meant a loss of earnings.

The issues in dispute differed from trade to trade; some were union and some employer demands. The main issues were working hours in summer and winter, hourly rates for both periods, hourly rates charged by the unions to non-MBA employers, working with members of other unions, the provision of electric light, productivity and sub-contracting. At the start of the lockout, the MBA was a small but powerful organization representing twenty employers. By the end of the dispute, it had forty members. There were eighty-four building contractors listed in the Dublin directory in 1896. Building employers fell into several categories: building contractors, builders merchants, trade contractors (plumbers, painters) and those employing men on building and maintenance work (local authorities, breweries, bakeries).

The original MBA members were all major employers. In 1892, Samuel H. Bolton of Rathmines employed 250–300 men, about twenty apprentices and 300–400 'unskilled workers', while T. & G. Martin employed 272 craftsmen and general workers, forty apprentices and ten women.[16] They were two of the bigger firms, but there were others of similar size. Although there were far more employers outside the MBA when the lockout commenced, the MBA firms were undoubtedly the main employers. Most employers outside the MBA accepted the union's demands, if only on an interim basis. The MBA operated from John Good's SG Brunswick Street office and held their meetings at the Grosvenor Hotel on Westland Row. Good[17] played a leading role in Dublin lockouts and strikes between 1895 and 1931. Alderman Michael Meade, MBA president, was a major employer and owned (albeit good quality) tenements, also operated from South Great Brunswick Street.

Some MBA members, including George Crampton, James Donovan and W & J Roberts, did not lock out their workers. Major employers of painters and other trades, including Thomas Dockrell, Brooks Thomas, J.F. Keatinge and H. Sibthorpe, disassociated themselves from the lockout.[18] All the latter were members of the Dublin Guild of Master Painters (DGMP). They informed the public through the press that their rates

TABLE 2:
RATES & HOURS IN SOME NON-MBA FIRMS

Trades	Weekly Wage	Weekly Hours	Hourly Rate
Carpenters Joiners	36s.	54	8d.
Plasterers	36s.	54	8d.
Slaters	36s.	54	8d.
Bricklayers	38s.3d.	54	8½d.
Scaffolders	21s.	54	-
Labourers	20s.	54	-

Source: *Freeman's Journal*, May, 1896.

already complied with union demands. Eighteen other building firms agreed to union claims, as did D'Arcy's brewery and Kennedy's bakery. Many other employers publicly added their names to this list. A morale boost for the unions happened a week into the lockout when, on 7 May, the City Council recommended meeting the union claims for its building trade employees on an interim basis.

The most numerous trades involved were the carpenters, the ASCJ, with 1,400 members. They met on 30 April at the Mechanics Institute, Lower Abbey Street (although they had their own hall in Gloucester Street) and heard reports from their chairman, Edward O'Neill, and secretary, Joseph Clarke. The meeting lasted from 7.30 p.m. to 1.15 a.m. All but one of the employer's proposals were accepted by the ASCJ. They accepted a compromise hourly rate of 8d. (reducing their claim by ½d. whilst the employers increased their offer by ¼d.) for a fifty-four-hour, six-day week for the thirty-nine 'summer' weeks. They ASCJ did not accept the proposal for a forty-five-hour week during the thirteen 'winter' weeks, mid December to mid March. They had sought a reduction of hours from fifty-seven hours to fifty-four and an increased rate from 8d. to 8½d.[19] Such would have meant a weekly increase of 3d. They also denounced Tim Harrington MP for a speech made at a North Dublin Poor Law Guardians meeting opposing the union's claims and suggesting the demands had their origin outside Ireland.[20] It was claimed that Harrington was a supporter of the 'Free Labour Association', a British body that provided 'scabs' to employers during disputes.[21]

GENERAL LOCKOUT

The ASCJ were prepared to compromise, 'not as a matter of justice, but to avoid a dispute or unpleasantness and to save the public inconvenience and the citizens' loss'. However, the effect of the employer's proposal would have reduced carpenters wages from 34s. to 29s. per week during the 'winter' months. A meeting between the ASCJ and MBA on 2 May brought no resolution. The same day, although backdated, the following notice was posted at workplaces:

> On and after tomorrow the 1st prox, all men employed by this firm to resume work at 6.30 in the morning until 5.30 in the evening, all to be paid at 1.45 p.m. on Friday, 30th April, 1896.[22]

The unions regarded this as a general lockout. The employers gave no notice, although existing agreements required three months' notice of change on either side. All but one of the unions claimed they had given three months' notice of their desire for changes. On 3 May, 1,000 carpenters were immediately affected. The ASCJ boasted of having over £100,000 invested and 54,000 members in 704 branches 'all over the world'.[23] Their weekly dispute pay was to be 15s. or 16s., and, it was intimated, it would be increased if the dispute lasted. Their claim that there was demand for skilled men at 10d. per hour in Belfast, Glasgow and Manchester must have been upset by the impact of the London building trades' dispute in mid May, involving 50,000 workers.[24]

The Ancient Guild of Incorporated Brick and Stone Layers' Trade Union (AGIBSL) had 820 members and met the same evening at their hall on Cuffe Street to hear reports from their secretary, Michael Ennis. Their members had been paid off and had removed their tools from the jobs. They were outraged by the employers' breach of faith regarding notice, as they had observed the agreement. They refused to meet the employers and when they wrote stating they would accept a fifty-four-hour week at 8½d. per hour, they received no reply from the MBA. Their existing conditions were a fifty-seven and a half-hour week at 8d. per hour. They were prepared to accept a fifty-four-hour week if the other trades agreed, as they 'would not obstruct an all around agreement'. In 1885, they had secured an extra ½d. per hour, which brought their rate to 8d. and weekly pay from 35s.7½d. to the current 38s. The proposed 'winter' hours would reduce their weekly income to 36s. The MBA demands on the bricklayers included other issues. They wanted four apprentices per firm, for 'as things stood' apprentices were 'only enrolled through the society'. They wanted AGIBSL members to work with those in other bricklayers' unions. The union insisted that 'men from other districts' take out local membership, as was common practice in most trades. The MBA demanded a standard work rate of eighty-five bricks per hour. The union countered that such was impossible due to the different classes and type of work. The MBA also demanded that the union charge an extra ½d. per hour to non-MBA employers. The union objected to this 'as tending to put down private enterprise'. They also rejected a proposal that members be allowed to sub-contract work to other members.[25] By 5 May, in addition to 200 bricklayers who had already gone to Britain, a further thirty had left 'on last night's boat'. The migrants were reportedly being paid 10d. and 10½d. an hour 'cross channel'.[26]

Plasterers, probably the Regular Stucco Plasterers,[27] met at the Trades' Hall, Capel Street, and heard reports from their president and secretary, Harry Murtagh and James O'Neill. Although the Operative Plasterers were active in Ireland in the 1890s, it is unclear if it had members in Dublin.[28] Their position was similar to that of the bricklayers. They too had left work that evening with their gear, and their decision was 'instantaneous'. They had given notice on 5 January, applicable from 1 May, claiming an increase of 1s. to bring weekly pay from 35s. to 36s. They claimed that over the past year they had been paid from 38s. to 40s. per week. What they were offered, 7¾d per hour for the hours proposed, would have given them 34s.10½d. in 'summer' and 29s.4d. in 'winter'. The employers insisted that working hours were determined 'by the light available'. The MBA proposals were rejected 'in toto'. About 100 plasterers were affected and a weekly levy of 6s. was applied to those still working. The levy would have allowed 12s. weekly strike pay, although it may have been augmented from existing funds. By 5 May, seventy-six of their 356 members were locked out.

There were two slaters' unions in Dublin in the 1890s: the Regular Operative Slaters' Society and the National Operative Slaters and Tilers. The executive of 'The Operative Slaters' Society'[29] met at 37 Wellington Quay. Bernard Sheppard and William Haskins, president and secretary, reported there was no change in the employer's attitude. As they had not given the three months' notice required, they decided to go along with what was agreed across the trades, with one proviso: they insisted on being paid by the day and not by the hour. Eighteen of their 130 members worked in MBA firms.[30] A weekly 4s. levy applied to working members to support those locked out. By the end of the first week thirty members were locked out. The levy would have produced £20 weekly, whereas strike pay at 15s. for thirty members would have cost £22.10s. The involvement of the Operative Stonecutters of Ireland[31] was not reported until 12 May. At an executive meeting held at 37 Wellington Quay their secretary, Christopher Clancy, reported that fifty of their 250 members were locked out. Forty had 'gone away', leaving ten to be supported by the union. The United Operative Plumbers' Association (of Great Britain & Ireland) did not regard themselves as being involved as they 'received no circular'. However, as two members were already locked out, they expected to be affected if the dispute lasted.

On 30 April over 1,000 members of the United Builders' Labourers of Ireland (UBLI)[32] attended a meeting at the Labourers' Hall, 57 Francis Street. Their general secretary, Daniel Farrell, reported, and after a 'warm' discussion the MBA proposals were rejected. They had claimed 5d. for 'hod men' and 4½d. for all others, with hours reduced from fifty-seven to fifty-four, which would have meant 22s.6d and 20s.0¼d. in 'summer'.[33] The MBA offered 4½d. and 4d. Those rates and the hours proposed would have meant 20s.3d. and 18s. weekly in 'summer' and 16s. 10½d. and 15s. in 'winter'.[34] The union had 2,700 members in Dublin. Of 1,700 in the building trades, 1,300 were locked out by 5 May. The MBA refused to discuss their claim.[35] A week later, 1,500 were locked out and funds were exhausted. They had £700 when the dispute commenced. They launched an appeal for funds to 'all trade union bodies in Ireland and the public in general'. Subscriptions, to be acknowledged in the press, were to be sent to the president, Patrick Golden, 26 Long Lane or Daniel Farrell, 12 Francis Street. The same day the UBLI held a procession from the Francis Street office 'and paraded through the city'.[36] By early June, a 'Mansion House Fund' (indicating dire need) was launched for the support of the labourers.

At the Metropolitan House Painters' Trade Union (MHPTU) meeting it was reported that 200 of the 600 members worked in MBA firms. There was no mention of the two small Dublin Amalgamated Painters' branches[37] at any time during the MBA dispute. The newspaper reported that the MHPTU was 'in treaty with the masters, (DGMP) and they believe there is a rather harmonious tendency'. They were still working in DGMP firms as notice expired on 11 May and negotiations were ongoing. They rejected the MBA proposals. On 9 May, agreement was reached with the DGMP.[38] Its terms, a great improvement, created a major problem for the union in its dealings with the MBA. A month later, a conference with the MBA came to no conclusion.[39]

Other unions, with small memberships, were caught up in the dispute even if they were not party to it. These included the Dublin Regular Glass Cutters, Glaziers and Lead Sash Makers, Dublin Whiteners, Electrical Workers, Dublin Marble Polishers, Stonecutters of Stepaside and Locality, Dublin Saw Millers and Wood Machinists, Alliance Cabinet Makers' Association and the Amalgamated Union of

Cabinet Makers. On 11 May, it was reported that 3,000 were 'disemployed' by the dispute, although this was undoubtedly an underestimate as there was no mention of stonecutters, stonelayers, painters, plumbers, electricians, woodcutting machinists or glaziers affected by the closure of yards and sites.

THE ARCHBISHOP INTERVENES

On 18 June, Dublin's Roman Catholic archbishop, William J. Walsh, convened a meeting with the intention of settling the dispute. His intervention was unsuccessful. On 28 July, in a speech at the laying of the foundation stone for a boy's orphanage at Glasnevin, Walsh referred at length to the dispute, stating: 'The fact is I have exhausted every means at my command in my effort to settle it.'[40] He referred to attempts at mediation by William Field MP,[41] whose 'efforts have been fruitless as mine have been'. Walsh expressed his pessimism when he said (concerning the foundation stone): 'Weeks may elapse, and, I think it no exaggeration to add, years may elapse, before a second stone is laid upon the first.'

TABLE 3:
TRADES AND NUMBERS INVOLVED

Trades	Locked out	No of Men	% locked out
Brick/Stone layers	600	820	73
Carpenters/Joiners	900	1,400	64
Labourers	2,000	2,700	74
Painters	200	500	40
Plasterers	76	400	19
Slaters/Tilers	40	130	31
Stonecutters	50	250	20
Totals	3,866	6,200	62

Sources: *Freeman's Journal, Evening Telegraph*

In mid July, new terms were offered to the carpenters. They were 36s. per week or 8d. for the fifty-four 'summer' hours and 8½d. for a 45-hour week over the six weeks before and after Christmas. When the offer was rejected by a vote, the leadership decided to conduct a ballot. On 13 July the offer was again rejected. It was reported that so far the lockout had cost the ASCJ £4,000. If weekly dispute pay was 15s., then

468 men were out for the eleven weeks to date. On 20 and 21 July, the MBA issued what the *Freeman's Journal* deemed to be an 'aggressive ultimatum', when they proposed to employ non-society men 'on Thursday next if meanwhile the Union tradesmen do not make a complete surrender'.[42] DTCLL vice-president, John Fitzpatrick (ASCJ), dismissed the threat as 'braggadocio', while John Keegan (local Cabinetmakers), claimed it was a 'counter blast' to the fact that strike pay had been increased. Apparently an extra 5s. had been given to those locked out. Whether this was a one-off payment or an ongoing increase in dispute pay (or what trades it applied to) is unclear, although it was probably the carpenters. The same day it was reported that over 100 firms were paying the union's terms. There were then forty-three firms in the MBA. It was also reported that 650 carpenters were working whilst 420 were still locked out. At a DTCLL meeting on 20 July, the 'deplorable' plight of the labourers was discussed. A 'visitor', J. Lenehan, PLG, suggested a weekly 3d. levy on '15,000 trade unionists' to support the labourers. The suggestion received no support and some delegates spoke against such a course of action.[43] The employer's threat to use non-union labour spurred the unions into making arrangements for picketing on 23 July, the only day it occurred.[44] The next day there were 'overtures from the men', seemingly the carpenters, and the MBA met to consider them. On Saturday, 25 July, a conference of seven carpenters and seven employers was held at the Grosvenor Hotel. The ASCJ proposed a fifty-hour week at 8d. per hour for the three months of winter and 'offered to close the dispute on those terms'. This MBA rejected this and proposed a 'sliding scale' for winter hours. They offered 8½d. for a winter working week varying from 45½ to 52½ hours 'according to the length of the day'. The carpenters agreed to charge non-MBA firms an extra ½d. per hour.[45]

When put to a meeting of the carpenters the offer was accepted. Rumours that the ASCJ Manchester headquarters had interfered were rejected as unfounded. The carpenters' dispute with the MBA ended on 27 July 1896. As the yards and sites were not being picketed, it can only be assumed they went back to work on 4 August, even though the others were still locked out. One newspaper stated 'the rules ... are mainly identical to those circulated by the Masters' Association at the beginning of the dispute'.[46] On 10 August the entire ASCJ 'Committee of Management' resigned as a test of the members' confidence in them. The resignations were unanimously rejected.

On 8 August, 3,000 workers were still locked out, according to newspaper reports. In mid August, Archbishop Walsh again intervened and he arranged a meeting at 'Archbishop's House' between five bricklayers and five MBA representatives. Within an hour agreement was reached. The archbishop and the two respective secretaries, Michael Ennis and John Good, drew up 'an account of the terms of the settlement' for release to the press.[47] The agreement was published on 22 August. The rate agreed for 'competent' bricklayers and masons was 8½d. and the hours were fifty-four per week from mid February to mid November (38s.3d. per week). Winter hours were to be forty-nine and a half for the second two weeks in November and the last two weeks in January (36s. per week). For the six weeks, 1 December to 15 January, hours were to be forty-five and a half (32s.3d. per week). The rate and hours agreed had been offered to the bricklayers on 21 July.[48] The union retained apprentice registration and a wage scale was set for them.[49] Walsh, at the invitation of Meade, MBA president, turned his attention to the disputes in the other trades. Meade's letter appeared in the papers on 24 August and stated:

> I am empowered to state that we are exceedingly anxious to terminate the strike still existing of the Plasterers, Stonecutters and Slaters, and are willing to have the questions at issue discussed in the same manner as have been so successful with the bricklayers.

To all intents and purposes this was an admission by the MBA (probably not intended for publication) that they could not win the dispute. Knowing Walsh was leaving Dublin on 25 August, Meade asked him to nominate a 'gentleman' to act in his place. Walsh refused and invited the unions to contact him directly.

On Sunday, 23 August, the archbishop was 'waited on' by representatives of the slaters. The labourers, who also sent a deputation, expressed anxiety about MBA 'promises made to them' arising out of the bricklayers' agreement and were concerned as to how it would impact on them. The archbishop assured them of his confidence that the MBA 'would act loyally by what it had undertaken'. By 4. p.m., none of the other unions had contacted the archbishop. Later the same day Walsh called Meade and the MBA committee to a meeting. The unions involved in the dispute were invited, one trade at a time, to meet the MBA committee at the Grosvenor Hotel on 27 August.

SETTLEMENT

The plasterers' four representatives arrived at 12.30 p.m. and an agreement was reached within a short time. The rate agreed was 8d. for a fifty-four-hour week (36s. weekly). Artificial light was to be provided where necessary by the employers, and if not provided, 'the employers to be at the loss of the time'. Three stonecutters' representatives arrived at 1 p.m. and quickly agreed terms providing:

> Eight pence per hour for a certain specified number of hours per week all the year around. This includes the providing of artificial light during the winter months. In places where artificial light cannot be provided when necessary, and where the hours of work shall consequently be less, in winter, the wages is to be 8½d. per hour.

When the four slaters' representatives arrived, 'the deliberations between the deputation and the MBA were equally satisfactory to all parties', although the terms agreed were not reported.

An essential clause in the settlements was the reinstatement of the three months' notice of proposed changes from either side. An important proviso was added in that the recipient of the notice was obliged to reply within one month. The outcome of the MBA lockout created a major problem for painters. In 1893, a breakaway of MHPTU members formed an Amalgamated Union branch in Dublin. In March 1896, the DGMP was established. In early 1896, the rate was 7d. for a fifty-four-hour week in summer (31s.6d.). The MHPTU claim for an extra ½d. was fraught with danger. If a strike occurred, they feared amalgamated members would not observe the strike and gain access to firms from which they had been excluded.[50] The claim was settled on 11 May 1896. The agreement increased the rate to 8d., hours were reduced from fifty-four to fifty in summer (33s.4d.), and from forty-eight and a half (32s.4d.) to forty-seven and a half (31s.8d.) in winter. The combined changes delivered and extra 2s.8d. weekly: from 31s.6d. to 33s.4d. in summer. The MHPTU now had members working under different rules, hours and rates for MBA employers. The MBA offered ½d. extra or 7½d. and a fifty-four-hour week in summer, giving a wage of 33s.9d. or 5d. more than those in DGMP firms. The MBA claim was placed in abeyance. The MHPTU members locked out seem to have found alternative employment, as no great strain was apparent in their funds. In June, they subscribed £12 to the fund in support of the labourers; in mid June they were able to loan the bricklayers £50 'owing to them running short of funds'.[51] In mid August, they loaned £25 to the plasterers 'subject to a receipt being issued'. By 15 September, no agreement had been reached with the MBA, and the DTCLL offered no help 'as the dispute did not involve very many'.[52]

Despite higher than usual unemployment, in November 1896, both painters' unions decided that no member be allowed work 'under the terms offered' by the MBA. They feared the DGMP would renounce the May agreement and impose the MBA terms. Although not recorded, it seems that the MBA were insisting on a clause allowing the employment of non-union labour. Efforts to secure the assistance of other trades and the DTCLL were of no avail. No progress was made with the MBA. It was clear they believed the threat from MBA leaders 'Good, Bolton and Meade', that they would 'employ a competent man to boss any tramps they might employ in the country'. Meade reportedly employed 'eleven Scotchmen painters at 7½d.'.[53] Although rejecting the MBA terms, they felt it would not be improved upon. They decided to stand by the DGMP agreement and counted on the employers doing the same. Discretion, it was hoped, was the better part of valour. A leading member expressed the view, to which there was no dissent, 'for as they crippled the carpenters we should not let them do so to us'. There was no doubt about the predicament and, rather than confront the MBA, they decided to raise a 'winter fund'. They also decided not to propose changes to the DGMP agreement until 1899. When they sought a new agreement in 1899 it led to immediate lockout.

When the ASCJ accepted the MBA terms on 27 July, they settled for little better than was on offer when they went out. They left 3,000 tradesmen and labourers still locked out to fend for themselves. By late August, all concerned were anxious to settle the dispute. What separated the employers and the unions from the beginning was, while undoubtedly important, marginal. The only construction that can be placed on the waging of such a large and drawn-out struggle over marginal issues can be that it was a test of strength and endurance. If the MBA had hoped to overawe or destroy the unions involved, they undoubtedly failed. The outcome, where known, is set out in Table 4. A fifty-four-hour week applied to the trades with large numbers: carpenters, bricklayers, painters, plasterers and stonecutters.

AN UNEVEN OUTCOME

No settlement in respect of the labourers was recorded. They were simply ignored by the MBA and the press. It seems too that the archbishop's verbal assurance regarding the MBA commitments to them 'was not worth the paper it was written on'. Craftsmen's labourers were paid from 16s.6d. to 22s. per week in 1896. By 1903, wages fell to 16s. By 1914, the weekly wage was 21s.6d. or more.[54] However, in 1914, the UBLI cited a labourer's hourly rate at 4½d.or 18s.9d. per week. The first 'general union' member elected to the ITUC executive was re-elected in 1896.[55]

When the socialist James Connolly arrived in Dublin, in May 1896, the lockout was in progress and a 'James Connolly Esq' is recorded as subscribing 7s.6d. to the public fund for the support of the labourers.[56] He joined the union[57] and when he was an Irish Socialist Republican Party candidate for election to the City Council in 1902, one of his nominators was UBLI president, Patrick Golden. He was also supported by the union (the only one to do so) and had the use of their office.[58]

A major advance had been made in that a higher rate had been achieved for the shorter 'winter' hours in respect of carpenters, bricklayers and plasterers. In respect of bricklayers and stonemasons for two two-week periods, wages were calculated on a weekly rather than an hourly basis. However, a higher hourly rate for the 'winter' hours may have been an illusory gain and may have had little practical application. Higher winter rates may have acted as an incentive to employers to lay-off workers. It may have been a disincentive to undertake work in 'winter', to employ workers or to keep those already engaged in employment. The undertaking on the part of the employers to provide electric lighting in 'winter' months may have had the same effect also.

The employers suffered few if any hardships other than loss of profits. The workers and their families endured hardships in resisting the employers. The tradesmen received almost half of their usual income during the dispute. Whatever hardships they suffered they were less than those endured by the labourers and their families. Craft union dispute pay, in most cases, was about 80 per cent of the pay of a building labourer when working.

Few lessons or lasting effects seem to have resulted from the dispute, although it did affect some of the organizations involved.[59] If the MBA lost the three members who broke ranks at the beginning of the dispute (Crampton, Donovan and Roberts), the loss was made up for by the increase in member firms from twenty to over forty. An attempt to form a 'Federation of Building Trade Societies' in late 1896 failed.[60] No industry-wide solidarity emerged from the experience of 1896. In 1899 the painters were locked out, as were the bricklayers in 1905. In both instances, the lockouts arose from issues that were unresolved in 1896. Both trades were allowed to fend for themselves and, in each case, they were defeated.

The outcome of the lockout of 1896, for craft workers but not the labourers, was an advance. Neither side prevailed and both, especially the MBA, welcomed the face-saving prospect of settlement through the intervention of the archbishop of Dublin. The attempt to dictate conditions, or break the solidarity of workers through the hardships inflicted on them and their families, had failed. One employer wrote: 'The general feeling is that the men have been the gainers, and that the employers and the public will have to bear the loss.' He went on to state: 'Employers will always calculate their profit upon the gross outlay; the advance in wages involves no loss whatsoever to them.'[61] The principal failure was that of the MBA.

NOTES

1. Based on reports in *Freeman's Journal*, *Evening Herald*, *Evening Telegraph* and *Irish Daily Independent* and other sources indicated. None of the major accounts of Irish labour history deal with this lockout. Brendan McDonnell in his 'The Dublin Labour Movement, 1894–1907', unpublished PhD, UCD 1979, also remarked on the paucity of information available.
2. *Reports on Strikes and Lockouts and on Conciliation and Arbitration Boards in the United Kingdom, 1912–1913* (London: 1913), *passim*.
3. *Irish Daily Independent*, 1 May 1896.
4. The Regular Dublin Carpenters merged into the ASCJ in 1891.
5. Joseph V. O'Brien, *Dear Dirty Dublin* (Dublin: 1982), p. 203, citing census figures.
6. British Parliamentary Papers (BPP), *Report of the Royal Commission on Labour* (London: 1892), vol. 30, p. 394.
7. R.W. Postgate, *The Builder's History* (London: 1923).
8. S. Cody, J. O'Dowd and P. Rigney, *The Parliament of Labour: 100 Years Of The DCTU* (Dublin: 1986).
9. See Donal Nevin (ed.), *Trade Union Century* (Cork: 1994).
10. BPP, *Report of the Royal Commission on Labour*, 1892, vol. 30, pp. 49–51, Charles O'Reilly and John Simmons, president and secretary, DTCLL.
11. BPP, *Royal Commission on Labour*, 1892, vol. 36, p. 374, col. 716. The firm S.H. Bolton provided information to the commission, stating it was an MBA member firm.
12. BPP, *Royal Commission on Labour*, 1892, vol. 36, p. 374 (S.H. Bolton and T. & G. Martin).
13. Reports of the progress of the act through parliament appeared during the lockout.
14. Philip S. Bagwell, *Industrial Relations in Nineteenth-Century Britain* (London: 1974), pp. 61–2, 77.
15. John W. Boyle, *The Irish Labor Movement in the Nineteenth Century* (Washington: 1988), p. 144.
16. BPP, *Royal Commission On Labour*, 1892, vol. 36, p. 374, cols 716, 717.
17. John Good, 1865–1941, secretary, MBA, 1896, 1905–11, 1931; president, DBTEA, 1918; councillor and chair Pembroke UDC; secretary, Dublin Chamber Of Commerce; chair of the Federation of Building Trade Employers of Britain and Ireland; Unionist candidate for Pembroke area in 1918; independent TD, County Dublin, 1923–37.
18. *Freeman's Journal*, 2 May 1896 listed thirty-two firms agreeing union terms pending a settlement.
19. *Freeman's Journal*, 1 May 1896.
20. Timothy Charles Harrington (1851–1910), MP for Harbour Division, 1893–1910; lord mayor of Dublin, 1901–04.
21. For details on the National Free Labour Association, see William Collison, *The Apostle of Free Labour* (London: 1913) and, for its Irish activities, see Francis Devine and Peter Rigney, 'Manifesto of the National Free Labour Association to the railway servants of Great Britain and Ireland', *Saothar*, vol. 2 (1975), pp. 33–8.
22. *Freeman's Journal*, 2 May 1896.

23. *Freeman's Journal*, 5, 7, 9 May 1896. In five Newry firms, 50–60 workers were on strike, seeking reduced hours from 61 to 54¼ with wages staying at 30s. They won a 9-hour day and 6½d. per hour. *Evening Telegraph*, 9 May 1896. Dublin hairdressers were also on strike. Wages, with Sunday work, were 25s., 'but under the present system [of charges] receive 13s. at the end of the week'.
24. *Freeman's Journal*, 15 May 1896.
25. *Freeman's Journal*, 7 May 1896. A strike of masons and bricklayers involving forty men started in Dundalk on 4 May. The claim (ignored by the employers) was for hourly rate and winter hours. They claimed 7½d. per hour.
26. *Freeman's Journal*, 5 May 1896.
27. Regular Stucco Plasterers' Trade Union of the City of Dublin, the forerunner of the Operative Plasterers' and Allied Trades Society of Ireland (OPATSI).
28. National Amalgamated Plasterers Granolithic and Cement Workers, which went into the ATGWU in 1968.
29. Although the title did not appear in the papers, the Amalgamated Slaters', Tilers' and Roofing Operatives' Society (ASTRO) had a Dublin branch from the 1890s.
30. *Freeman's Journal*, 5 May 1896.
31. Probably the City of Dublin Stonecutters, which merged with AGIBSLTU in 1966.
32. The ULITU title dated from 1891, having emerged from the 'Dublin United Labourers'.
33. *Evening Telegraph*, 1 May 1896. Henry Carroll, Labourers' Hall, claimed London hours were 50 and rates were: scaffolders 7d. (29s.2d.), hodsmen 6½d. (27s.1d.), groundsmen 5½d. (22s.11d.).
34. *Freeman's Journal*, 4 May 1896.
35. *Evening Telegraph*, 5 May 1896. The UBLI delegates were Patrick Golden (president), Daniel Farrell (general secretary), Nicholas Tyrell (assistant secretary), John Nelson, John Butler, Patrick Cahill and James Neall.
36. Funds for the labourers noted in the press: Metropolitan House Painters £12, Wm. J. Walsh £10, Tailors' Society £10, Brush Makers' Society £5, Amalgamated Upholsterers £5, Operative Butchers' TU £2, Dublin Whiteners' TU £2, Amalgamated Litho Printers £2, A. Grennell, Camden St £1, Newspaper Machinists 10s.
37. NASOHSPD (National Amalgamated Society of House and Ship Painters and Decorators).
38. *Freeman's Journal*, 11 May 1896.
39. *Freeman's Journal*, 5 June 1896.
40. Archbishop William J. Walsh, 1841–1921, involved himself in virtually every aspect of Dublin life, including acting as a one-man 'labour court'.
41. William Field (1843–1935) unseated William Martin Murphy in 1892. He was a Parnellite MP 1892–1900, Nationalist 1900–1918; ITUC delegate (Knights of The Plough) 1894; and major cattle and meat trade businessman. A flamboyant character with long hair and cowboy hat, he was highly regarded by Dublin's trade unions; he was a guarantor for the DTCLL Trades Hall.
42. *Freeman's Journal*, 20, 21 July 1896.
43. *Freeman's Journal*, 21 July 1896, *Evening Herald*, 21 July 1896.
44. *Evening Herald*, 23 July 1896.
45. *The Irish Builder*, 15 August 1896. Agreed carpenter/joiner apprentice hourly rates were: second half of first year 1d., second year 1½d., third 2½d., fourth 3d., fifth 4d. and sixth 5d.
46. *Evening Herald*, 4 August 1896.
47. *Freeman's Journal*, 22 August 1896.
48. *Evening Herald*, 21 July 1896.
49. *Freeman's Journal*, 22 August 1896. Agreed brick and stonelayers apprentice hourly rates were: second half of first year 1½d., second year 2d., third 3d., fourth 4d., fifth 4½d., sixth 5½d. and seventh 6½d.
50. National Archives (NA), MHPTU minutes, 25 February 1896.
51. NA, MHPTU minutes, 18 June 1896.
52. *Irish Daily Independent*, 1 September 1896.

53. *Irish Daily Independent*, 1 September 1896.
54. Fergus A. D'Arcy, 'Wages of labourers in the Dublin building industry, 1667–1918', *Saothar*, vol. 14 (1989), p. 26; and his 'Wages of skilled workers in the Dublin building industry, 1667–1918', *Saothar*, vol. 15 (1990) p. 33.
55. Boyle, *Irish Labor Movement*, p. 351.
56. *Irish Times*, 12 June 1896.
57. Samuel Levenson, *James Connolly: A Biography* (London: 1973), pp. 80, 98.
58. Donal Nevin, *James Connolly: 'A Full Life'* (Dublin: 2005), pp. 167, 171, 192.
59. A builders' labourers' union, known, confusingly, as the Dublin Builders' Labourers' Trade Union, was established in 1896 (Reg. 178T) and dissolved in 1906. The existing union, the DUBL (Reg. 85T), also known as the UBLI, survived.
60. NA MHPTU minutes, November–December 1896.
61. *The Irish Builder*, 1 September 1896. L. Moore, Master Builder, Harrington Street.

7

Outwork, Truck and the Lady Inspector: Lucy Deane in Londonderry and Donegal, 1897

KEVIN J. JAMES

Since Elizabeth Boyle's ground-breaking study of female textile labour in Ireland[1] – identified by historians of gender and the Irish economy as a foundation for the detailed, scholarly analysis of women's industrial work[2] – research into the social, legal, economic and cultural regimes that governed female labour has expanded. In documenting these workers, Boyle aimed to place them within wider accounts of Irish economic and social history; in subsequent research, discourses which surrounded female labour and Irish 'craft' have also been analyzed and situated within broader theories of gender, labour and industrialization.[3] The integration of material and cultural analyses of women's industrial labour – especially manufacture by hand and small machine in dispersed rural settings – continues to develop as historians respond to the provocative synthetic narrative of the decline of females' paid labour in rural Ireland proposed by Joanna Bourke.[4] To test this claim, historians have engaged systems of rural labour and ideologies of gender that shaped them, but in undertaking such research they face daunting challenges. One is the relative paucity of records that offer insight into experiences of rural industrial work, beyond the proceedings and reports of parliamentary committees and commissions at that workers seldom appeared, their experiences instead being represented by other parties. Even in these records, rural outworkers are not documented to the same extent as their urban counterparts: the historian of urban outwork in Belfast has the Medical Officer of Health's reports, which are replete with details on outworkers in the early twentieth century; similar records do not exist for workers in most rural districts. They were, however, the subject of several social investigations – parliamentary enquiries and reports by labour investigators in particular. Historians can use these records to examine how outwork was represented and incorporated within wider narratives of women's industrial labour. These narratives need to be approached as artefacts of institutions for which they were created and products of complex political and bureaucratic processes.[5] They offer multi-layered representations of workers, structures of production and systems of labour imbued with the values of all those who participated in 'giving voice' to female outworkers.

This chapter explores accounts of an 1897 investigation into petitions against the application of Truck Acts and their amendments to the rural shirt industry. It explores modes of public representation attributed to workers and employees, and the role of the state, through the factory inspectorate, in evaluating the content of petitions and the process of petitioning. The factory inspector, Lucy Deane, played a critical role in mediating the relationship between industrial workers and the state, adjudicating on both whether the petitions expressed the views of rural outworkers and whether they accurately represented the conditions of their labour. She also evaluated whether the process of petition-drafting and circulation was susceptible to manipulation and interference, and whether the voice of rural outworkers was constructed by other parties to advance their own ends. If this was the case, then the factory inspectorate asserted its right to correct the imbalance, and establish through empirical inquiry the conditions of labour. This chapter explores two narratives of the inquiry written by Deane, a Home Office factory inspector since 1894 who became closely associated with the campaign against the 'truck system' in Ireland. One is her personal diary, written during the summer of 1897;[6] the second is her official report to the Home Office, submitted in early October that year.[7] Together, these accounts, each constructed for markedly different purposes and audiences and employing distinctive narrative strategies, plot Deane's evaluation of the 'problem' of outwork – and reveal how the plight of rural outworkers was produced through her narratives.

HOUSEHOLD LABOUR AND RURAL INDUSTRIAL WORK

The analysis of outwork as a form of industrial labour presents challenges to the historian, as it did to investigators such as Deane. To what extent did the elevation of 'home industries' to an ideal of industrial organization obscure conditions of paid female labour in rural manufacture? Cottage industry gained purchase in Ireland, appealing to people who imagined it was an alternative to degrading and anonymous mass manufacture. Trades such as lace and tweed-making became discursive foils for routinized factory production. They evoked possibilities for Irish rural prosperity, inspired by continental European models, and achieved through an industrial avenue that promoted rural families, space and culture. Indeed, rural industry allowed proponents of the union to adopt an idiom commonly associated with the cultural politics of Irish nationalism, and affirm that Ireland could be both prosperous and profoundly attached to the land and 'rural values' – even in districts of the west that were often characterized as hopelessly congested. The *Irish Textile Journal*, for instance, the key trade organ and a stalwart advocate of Irish 'industrial interests' within the union, rhapsodized in 1896 about the invigorating effects of rural industry on the people of Donegal:

> It is a great pleasure to be able to report on the cheerful prospect of employment in parts of Co. Donegal. The light railways enable the firms engaged in the shirt trade to push along the lines; and while women may be met in all sorts of new and unexpected places carrying bundles of this work, there seems to be just as many as ever employed by the knitting agents; and the white embroidery has revived in the districts which have a reputation for good workers. Along the shore the smell of kelp burning turns attention to men and women in busy groups working at the seaweed which brings in an advanced price this year. And it is noticeable that this new spurt of industry has extended to the potato patches, which instead of being a mass of weeds, show that some care has been given, with the natural result that the crop is more promising. Hand-made underclothing holds its own and employs those who are capable of attaining skill in it. The unskilled fall back on knitting and machine work.[8]

In a similar vein, a Congested Districts Board inspector, F.G.T. Gahan, found shirt-making widespread throughout north Inishowen, and expressed confidence in the *Baseline Reports* that if the industry, with its footings in the northern districts of Donegal and in the Fanad and Rosguill districts, could be brought to areas such as Lough Eask, 'it would be a great matter'.[9] While the early analysis of rural industry focused on such areas of 'congestion' – districts where observers believed that social, cultural and tenurial factors sustained uniquely dense rural populations and militated against the evolution of a more 'natural' equilibrium between people and resources – recent scholarship has regarded home industries as having a less corrosive influence on rural society.[10] Certainly, there is ample evidence the rural industrial manufacture was intertwined with a range of other paid and unpaid work, and formed part of multifaceted income strategies that included the sale of farm produce, adult migratory labour, and children's participation in agricultural labour markets as farm servants. In November 1894, terms that could be obtained for half-yearly service at the Londonderry Hiring Fair ranged between £2 10s. to £3 for small boys who were hired for herding and 'little' girls for nursing, up to £10 for ploughmen and 'useful experienced men' in the field.[11] Table 1 shows how households incorporated these activities, as well as knitting, sewing and other manufacture, within repertoires of work. The *Baseline Reports* illustrate these strategies, and also testify to state efforts to calculate, evaluate and represent the economic activity of the peasant household.

TABLE 1
RECEIPTS AND EXPENDITURES OF A FAMILY IN 'ORDINARY CIRCUMSTANCES', THE RECEIPTS BEING DERIVED FROM AGRICULTURE, MIGRATORY LABOUR, AND HOME INDUSTRIES, 1891

Receipts	£	s.	d.	*Expenditure*	£	s.	d.
Sale of cattle	6	0	0	Flour or baker's bread	9	2	0
Sale of sheep	2	10	0	Tea	6	1	4
Sale of pigs	3	0	0	Indian meal	3	18	
Sale of eggs	4	0	0	Sugar	2	3	4
Migratory earnings of men	10	0	0	Fish and bacon	2	0	0
Children's earnings as servants	6	0	0	Salt and soap	0	10	0
Knitting, sewing, etc.	7	10	0	Oil and candles	0	15	0
Miscellaneous sales of kelp, butter, fish, fowl, etc.	2	0	0	Clothing[1]	6	0	0
				Rent	1	10	0
				County Cess	0	5	0
				Church dues, etc.	1	0	0
				Tobacco	3	0	0
				Furniture, etc.	1	0	0
				For replacing or exchanging cattle	2	0	0
				Young pig	1	0	0
				Bran	1	0	0
				Carts, implements, etc.	1	0	0
				Artificial manures	1	0	0
Total	£41	0	0		£42	15	0

[1]Exclusive of purchases by migratory labourers while absent from home.
Source: See Appendix C of the *First Report of the Congested Districts Board for Ireland* [C.6908], HC 1893-4, vol. lxxi, p. 33.

In examining industrial manufacture in Donegal, observers of the expansive rural shirt industry detected an aversion amongst women to the proposition that they could come to the city for factory jobs. Instead, thanks to the abundance of cottage industries, they were said to prefer to remain at home.[12] For some, the income offered by shirt-making and other trades represented a source of stability and prosperity for rural families. But inquiries into, and campaigns against, rural outwork in the shirt sector sometimes presented a contrasting representation of industrial manufacture premised on the contention that rural female outworkers were weak and subdued. They asserted that the factory inspectorate had a duty to publicize outworkers' exploitation and pursue policies to end their exploitation. The inspectors' inquiries were represented as formal and systematic investigations of workers that documented the conditions of their labour; their conclusions also influenced bureaucratic formulations, and public representations, of Irish outwork.

TRUCK TRADE IN THE IRISH SHIRT-MAKING INDUSTRY

Rural industrial manufacture was widespread in Ireland – especially in western districts – and shirt-making was the premier industrial activity in the north-west in the last decades of the nineteenth century. Centred on the city of Londonderry, it employed thousands of urban workers, and more in the city's rural environs. Most women were engaged in the stitching of garments in cottages and small farms throughout a large swathe of land stretching into Donegal.[13] The chief factory inspector's report for the year ending 31 October 1888 described a flourishing industry employing over 3,000 people within the city, and many more in rural areas, where, 'all over the adjacent districts, at smaller workshops and from "stations" – i.e. centres for the giving out and receiving back work – many thousands of women find a permanent source of livelihood'.[14] There, the industry was reported to have effected physical, social and mental 'improvement'. Allusions to the 'permanent character' of their labour were not to be construed as indicating 'year-round' work. In spring, females often turned to assist in farm work, 'and consequently,' *the Irish Textile Journal* reported in 1895, 'there is greater difficulty in getting orders completed promptly.'[15] Four years later, it reported on a scarcity of labour linked to the cycle of demand for workers in local agriculture:

> The trouble is, and has been for some time past, not so much the getting of orders, as the getting of them executed. It is a difficulty

more than usually intensified about Derry at this time of the year, and it exists in an especial manner this year. The harvest always interferes with the cottage workers, so many hundreds of whom are scattered over the neighbourhood. Even when the girls do not go into the harvest fields themselves, they have to look after the farm duties at home. The source of the particular difficulty this autumn is the fact that at present light railways are being made on all sides of Londonderry, and afford male employment, which, in turn, takes the female workers from the machines to the farm.[16]

Amid a widespread shortage of labour in the industry in 1899, one shirt-making firm opened an agency in Fannet, Donegal, and another firm established a training school at Carrigart to instruct labourers in machine-work.[17] Messrs Hogg and Mitchell, one of the leading shirt-making companies, pushed into County Antrim in a quest for more workers, opening an agency in Ballycastle.[18] The industry encountered fluctuating demand for its articles; as firms expanded into more remote rural regions, they drew on large and flexible pools of female labour. 'The drawback about these distant agencies,' the *Irish Textile Journal* noted, 'is the infrequency of communication. Special orders, for instance, being needed in a hurry cannot go to a distant cottage worker, nor can any laundry work be executed in the cottages.'[19] Even if a dispersed rural workforce posed such problems, outwork persisted as a component of industrial apparel manufacture on a substantial, if diminishing, scale until the First World War.

As members of a large industrial workforce, incorporated within a sector that spanned urban and rural settings, outworkers also attracted the attention of state agencies and their employees. To some commentators – such as those assessing the degree to which the state should set minimum rates of pay through trade boards, or to more closely regulate systems of remuneration through truck legislation – their condition was part of a wider narrative of the exploitation of female industrial labour throughout the United Kingdom. To other observers, the Irish workers faced specific problems associated with historical practices of credit and remuneration in rural Ireland, and with their status as members of a dispersed industrial workforce in 'congested' rural districts. Formal inquiries into rural industrial labour in later nineteenth-century Ireland focused on specific features of work: (1) the extent to which rural Irish female workers were engaged in 'by-employment', as opposed to 'breadwinning' labour; and (2) systems of industrial remuneration in rural Ireland.[20] These related questions were addressed by Lucy Deane in 1897. That summer – which saw protracted dullness in the sector amid intensifying competition from German and Austrian rivals and the imposition of protective tariffs in other markets such as the Australian colonies[21] – Deane set out to investigate petitions against the truck prohibitions. Putatively instigated and signed by both employees and employers, they had circulated in the district and then had been forwarded to Whitehall. The petitioners contended that the shirt trade should be exempted from the provisions of 1896 legislation that expanded the scope of previous acts requiring employers to pay workers in cash. An 1887 Amendment Act had introduced a much more expansive definition of 'workman' to encompass 'any person other than a domestic or menial servant' engaged in contracted labour, including outworkers.[22] The petitions protested the extension of truck prohibitions to the shirt industry, and Deane was sent out to investigate. Deane's inquiry serves as a focus for exploring the contested voice of the rural outworker. It illuminates how the Irish rural outworker was constructed as a category of industrial labour and how various investigative methods and claims to systematic inquiry and empirical accuracy underpinned Deane's official report.

'LOVELY' VIEWS AND 'BOGUS' PETITIONS: LUCY DEANE IN LONDONDERRY AND DONEGAL

Rural outwork in Ireland became a focus of inquiry for Whitehall in 1897, amid reports that provisions of anti-truck legislation were not being enforced in remote regions of the country and suggestions that both employers and workers were agitating for exemption. The investigation of these claims fell to several women who gained increasing prominence in the factory inspectorate, and influence over discourses of gender and sweating, in the 1890s and subsequent decades. Lucy Deane, Rose Squire and, later, Hilda Martindale became key public articulators of the 'problem' of rural Irish outwork, linking it to wider discourses on labour exploitation, femininity and industrialization. Yet their relationship with the Irish subjects of these discourses was markedly ambivalent.[23] Their narrative of the 'outworker' was plotted against institutional resistance on the part of rural employers and coloured by the belief – expressed in Deane's diary and her report – that the plight of thousands of women was worsened by their complicity in a conspiracy of silence. This theme was also prominent in the published memoirs of several key women connected with the inspectorate. Their retrospective constructions of their struggles in the countryside – paralleled by strenuous efforts to win greater support at Whitehall – highlight the deep-seated suspicion and veils of silence which they believed that they had encountered in rural Ireland – even amongst the women they pledged to aid – and illuminate complex relationships between inspectors and workers in the Irish countryside.[24]

The daunting task of investigating and representing conditions in the shirt industry was aggravated by the diversity of workforces and systems of labour. Encompassing factories, out-stations and cottages as centres of production, the shirt industry promoted economic and social interactions between urban and rural districts, and incorporated a wide range of labour within its workforce. At the turn of 1898, the *Londonderry Sentinel* estimated that the industry employed between five and six thousand factory workers in the city of Londonderry, and that this number represented 'only a limited proportion of those who are dependent upon the industry for their means of livelihood'. Another, much larger, workforce was found in rural farms and cottages, villages and hamlets throughout Counties Londonderry and Donegal:

> The out-workers number upwards of eleven thousand, and the making of this necessary portion of male attire is, as we know, the means of circulating thousands of pounds throughout the neighbouring counties, and bringing happiness and contentment into many a hamlet by providing the women and girls of the household with work, which is at once womanly and fairly remunerative.[25]

This dispersed rural workforce was the principal focus of Deane's inquiries. As she travelled through the countryside and recorded her observations, Deane created parallel public and private narratives of her journeys through the north-west, and produced evocative – and provocative – renderings of the outworkers.

Deane had been instructed by the Factory Department of the Home Office to carry out a local inquiry into the shirt and collar trade in the north of Ireland which, following an application to the secretary of state, sought exemption from the Truck Act. The petitioners purported to be both employers and workers. Deane was despatched to the north-west to investigate their two separate petitions. Her mandate, she reported, was primarily to ascertain from employers the reasons behind the request for exemption, and to determine the authenticity of the workers' petition and assess whether it represented 'the general opinion and desire of those employed in the industry'.[26] Deane's tour took in the factories of the city of Londonderry, where she interviewed managers and workers, and also the country districts where shirt manufacture was widespread. Scrutiny of claims within the workers' petition formed, in Deane's estimation, the 'most important' part of her inquiry, as the petitioners claimed that almost all of the workers had supported the request for exemption. Her first task was the empirical measurement of the 'true' number of workers engaged in the petitioning campaign. She calculated that only 4,308 workers had signed the petition, out of a workforce of 12,281 – or just over one-third of the total. Deane then turned her attention to investigating the processes through which the petition was created, circulated and signed, extending her mandate to assess the processes through which the workers' views were recorded. Closer investigation of the origins of the workers' petition suggested to Deane that the document neither accurately reflected their views nor served their 'interests'. In three firms employing a total of 844 people, for instance, Deane reported that employees were under the mistaken impression that it referred to the question of 'giving out work at night'. She also noted that Richards & Co., one of the 16 firms under question, had 44 employees, but 55 signatories to the workers' petition. These calculations were the means by which Deane constructed a parallel narrative of women's labour – one which she represented as systematic and accurate and which contradicted and undermined the petitioners' claims. In the factories, she established that the workers' petition had been brought to employees by the foreman or forewoman of each department, who were directed to ask the workers if they would add their signatures to it. While Deane could find no evidence of 'direct compulsion', she was sceptical of the means by which workers were apprised of the petition's contents. In most cases, her report concluded, they had not read the petition, and in cases where the petition was read to them, were 'ignorant' of the Truck Act's provisions. Moreover, she was convinced that in two factories the document was understood by workers as an endorsement of their current conditions of work and, in one case, believed that the names of outworkers had been appended by employers to the workers' petitions without their knowledge. Through inquiries in the factories of Londonderry, Deane found that the petitions had been circulated without their contents being made clear to signatories. She detected even more irregular practices in rural districts and expressed surprise that only two of the firms had sent the petition to outworkers for signature. Yet Deane found that workers in both settings were broadly ignorant both of the terms of the petition and the protections that they were offered by truck legislation. She described her inquiries in the countryside, and documented the means by which the document had been circulated there through agents:

I visited every station to which the Petition had been sent for signature.

In most cases, the Workers' 'Petition' had been sent to the agent, accompanied by a typed memorandum – on the trade-paper of the Firm – to the following effect: – 'To the agent at __

The Shirt-Makers of Derry are forwarding a Petition in reference to the Truck Act, and being anxious that their fellow-workers in the country should join with them they will be glad if you get as many signatures to the attached form as you can. Please return this list on __ next addressed to __

Deane alleged that the wording of these instructions had led agents to regard them as 'authoritative' directions from the firm. Consequently, they attempted to fulfil the directions by collecting signatures from country workers. This procedure undermined the petition's claims to represent the independent views of the workers, in Deane's judgement. She contended that the voice that emerged from this process was powerfully shaped by employers and their interests. Deane reported that 'in no instance' when she advised the signatories of its contents did she encounter a worker who understood them. She also reflected on rural outworkers in her diary, in which she dismissed the 'supposed' workers' petition as 'bogus'.[27] Her 'documentation' of the petition's origins and its circulation also reveal Deane's wider evaluation of whether, and why, the voice of the female outworker had been 'suppressed' in rural Ireland. In her diary and official report, she assessed whether fear of the truck masters, 'ignorance' or other factors bound the outworkers to silence; if so, she and other members of the factory inspectorate had an obligation to systematically document, and press to change, the conditions in which these women worked.

Deane's inquiries reveal what she characterized as a significant divergence in practices of remuneration amongst outworkers and shirt factory workers. They lay at the heart of her evaluation of their susceptibility to exploitation within different regimes of industrial production and remuneration. While she heard of no fines levied against workers in city factories, for instance, she did receive complaints of 'heavy charges for "damages"' in country districts and also reported that the agent system through which work and payment was organized had led Londonderry firms to 'disclaim responsibility for the action of their agents'. She reported on deductions which constituted infringements of the Truck Acts in rural allied underclothing trades. Together, they constituted disproportionate charges against the worker, as Deane reported:

> I may cite the case of a Peasant girl in a remote district of Donegal who sent in faultily done work. The Agent was required by the Firm to buy the dozen of spoilt shirts for £1.4.0. He is recovering this deduction from the girl who is now striving to discharge a sum which, in proportion to her wage, (-1/3d. a day, machining shirts) appears enormous. It is a striking instance of a charge which perhaps does not actually exceed the value of goods spoilt, but which appears "immeasurably" heavy for a girl who must work for months to pay off a fine, imposed for a fault made in work which she was learning with difficulty to accomplish.

Underpinning Deane's analysis of the pernicious effects of truck in the countryside was a binary between labour in the factory and that in the countryside, where Deane found a workforce that she characterized as poor and ignorant, and where she detected widespread anxiety surrounding her investigations. The outworkers' disposition to eschew protest, or even to assist in documenting the practice of truck, exercised Deane; she saw it as an index of both their exploitation and their ignorance. In her report she wrote:

> I was impressed by the poverty and ignorance of these women, and where the pay is so low, the damage resulting from the employment of ignorant workers is a risk which it seems perhaps hardly reasonable to charge upon the women ...
>
> I found an excessive nervousness among the Outworkers regarding any complaints made on this subject. They appear terrified that by complaining they should risk the loss of the employment upon which they depend very largely – especially in winter time.

This assessment was also echoed in Deane's diary – a document in which she recorded the minutiae of her official activities, interwoven with a narrative of travel that included remarks on the rural landscapes she encountered on her travels through western districts. In it, Deane recorded that she heard complaints of infringements of the Truck Act, 'but women too frightened to give me any reliable particulars, tho I tried hard to get some'.[28] She concluded in her report to the chief inspector that the workers' petition was a 'worthless document' and in her diary pithily dismissed it as 'bogus'. Buttressed by specific case studies, quotations and calculations, when her report reached Whitehall, it met with the apparent approval of the chief inspector of factories. The memorandum accompanying Deane's report read:

> This is what was to be expected. When the Truck Act was passed

> it was known that the shirt +c industries in the North of Ireland were among those that most needed protection. Now the petition for exemption itself furnishes the strongest additional evidence of how helpless they are. The workers [sic] petition – signed by only about one-third of the workpeople – was in almost every case signed either in absolute ignorance of its content or on entire misunderstandings as to its object and effect.[29]

The chief inspector of factories, Arthur Whitelegge, in a letter to the under-secretary of the Home Department, Kenelm E. Digby, wrote that Deane's report 'places the facts in a very clear light'. Contrary to the claims of the petitioners, Deane had concluded that conditions in the trade required 'special attention' and more active advocacy by factory inspectors on behalf of the female workers.[30]

In advancing such measures, Deane found support from other lady inspectors. The annual report became an instrument with which they publicized their findings within the Home Office and to Westminster; but they were also able to reach a wider audience, with accounts that liberally quoted district inspectors offered extensive data and provided influential commentaries that were widely reported in the press. In her annual report on the work of 'Her Majesty's Women Inspectors' in 1897, for instance, Adelaide Anderson, the principal lady inspector, wrote of the widespread practice of truck that Deane, Rose Squire and Mary Paterson had brought to the attention of the Factory Department through their inquiries that year. She also described efforts to suppress the workers' voices, in a manner signalled by the petition inquiry. Like Deane, she believed that these reports assigned a critical task to the lady inspectors: breaking the silence through which outworkers contributed, unwittingly, to their own exploitation. Indeed, Lucy Deane spent months in the district after drafting and submitting her report, during which she continued to plot her travels and jot observations in her diary. She, Paterson and Anderson came to believe that the outworkers were so enfeebled by truck that one of their foremost duties as inspectors was to articulate the grievances that workers dared not, or could not, voice. The process through which this could be achieved was not the inquiry, which could only help to establish the facts of the case. Aggressive prosecution against truck masters offered a more effective tool for redress, but the inspectors faced daunting challenges in overcoming local resistance to their efforts. In assessing the workers' condition, Deane expressed exasperation to Anderson with the un-cooperative rural workforce, whose behaviour she only partly attributed to the bondage of the agent system:

A serious difficulty lay, however, in officially detecting and proving these infringements of the law. Previous complaints had resulted in strict cautions, given by the Royal Irish Constabulary and by H.M. District Inspector of Factories, to the agents who were, therefore, aware of the illegality of their proceedings and of the danger of detection. The peasants were, I found, completely at their mercy, and, apart from the timidity engendered by their dependent condition, my former experience in these districts proved to me that there is a strong natural inclination on their part to regard with suspicion and dislike any official attempt to enforce the law, even when it is for their own protection.[31]

Deane's comments reflected a view – widely shared by her fellow lady inspectors – that the pernicious silence which enveloped truck in Donegal was partly sustained by a workforce whose quiescence was underlain with distrust of the state. The lady inspectors set themselves the task of establishing a voice for these workers through mechanisms of inquiry, prosecution and advocacy within bureaucratic and public channels. So doing, they constructed the public image of the Irish outworker as a pitiable and obdurate figure and bound their professional remit to advocacy on their behalf.

MUTUAL CREATIONS: THE OUTWORKER AND THE LADY INSPECTOR OF FACTORIES

Lucy Deane's inquiry into the truck petitions in the summer of 1897 illuminates contentious efforts to identify and present the outworkers' 'voice' – a voice which factory inspectors, such as Deane, claimed a key role in constructing and presenting. It was a voice that was continually modified and re-calibrated to the variety of audiences it reached, filtered through the bureaucratic and political channels in which it was expressed. The year 1897 also marked a critical point in the development of what has been characterized as a concerted prosecutorial campaign against truck in the late 1890s[32] – an initiative that was signalled by the famous *Squire v. Sweeney* case. It would continue, intensified, through the first decade of the twentieth century, led by the lady inspectors. While this inquiry also anticipated Deane's further involvement in truck inquiries and prosecutions, it also sketched an enduring portrait of the Irish outworker in two narratives of rural labour: one constructed for an official Whitehall audience, and another contained within private accounts of rural women, work and systems of remuneration. In both accounts, Deane represented the pernicious effects of truck on the social, cultural and economic foundations of Irish rural society through evocative portrayals of workers whose conditions of bondage were condemnable and whose silence was baffling. Plotted in her private diary, the outworker became an even more exotic figure and more silent and exploited than counterparts in the city of Londonderry.

Representations of the conspiracy of silence that enveloped rural Irish industry were also colourful, but compared with the diary observations, Deane's formal report provided a more detailed discussion of the rural industrial systems which, in her view, sustained this silent suffering and also enabled employers to construct the public voice of the female outworker. Filtered through the lens of inspectorate, the outworkers became enshrined in the public consciousness as emblems of the ills of Irish rural society. The processes through which they were 'documented' produced a powerful construct of female industrial labour that was mobilized in debates over womanhood, work, the family and the state. To the bureaucracy at Whitehall, renderings of the outworkers' silence were also mobilized to claim institutional resources that could allow inspectors, such as Deane, to give voice to their suffering and win their release from the pernicious bonds of truck.

NOTES

1. Elizabeth Boyle, *The Irish Flowerers* (Holywood and Belfast: 1971).
2. See Maria Luddy, 'An agenda for women's history in Ireland. Part II: 1800–1900', *Irish Historical Studies*, xxviii, 109 (1992), pp. 19–37.
3. Brenda Collins's work has been especially influential in shaping the direction of research into rural outwork. See her studies, 'The organization of sewing outwork in late nineteenth-century Ulster', in Maxine Berg (ed.), *Markets and Manufacture in Early Industrial Europe* (London: 1991), pp. 139–56 and 'Sewing and social structure: the flowerers of Scotland and Ireland', in Rosalind Mitchison and Peter Roebuck (eds), *Economy and Society in Scotland and Ireland, 1500–1939* (Edinburgh: 1988), pp. 242–54. Margaret Neill has also written on the topic: see 'Homeworkers in Ulster, 1850–1911', in Janice Holmes and Diane Urquhart (eds), *Coming into the Light: The Work, Politics and Religion of Women in Ulster, 1840–1940* (Belfast: 1994), pp. 2–32. A path-breaking book by Joanna Bourke, *Husbandry to Housewifery: Women, Economic Change and Housework in Ireland, 1890–1914* (Oxford: 1993), provided a new theoretical compass to this agenda; see also the subsequent work of James MacPherson, 'Ireland begins in the home': women, Irish national identity, and the domestic sphere in the Irish Homestead, 1896–1912', *Éire-Ireland*, 36, 3–4 (2001), pp. 131–52; and Ciara Breathnach, 'The role of women in the economy of the West of Ireland, 1891–1923', *New Hibernia Review*, 8, 1 (2004), pp. 80–92; Kevin J. James, 'Handicraft, mass manufacture and rural female labour: industrial work in north-west Ireland, 1890–1914', *Rural History*, 17, 1 (2006), pp. 47–63. The study of rural women's paid work is now also incorporated within wider surveys of their labour: see Maria Luddy, 'Women and work in nineteenth- and early twentieth-century Ireland: an overview', in Bernadette Whelan (ed.), *Women and Paid Work in Ireland, 1500–1930* (Dublin: 2000), pp. 44–56.
4. Bourke, *Husbandry to Housewifery*.
5. See David Englander and Rosemary O'Day (eds), *Retrieved Riches: Social Investigation in Britain, 1840–1914* (Aldershot: 1995); Mark Freeman, *Social Investigation and Rural England, 1870–1914* (Woodbridge, Suffolk: 2003).

6. Lucy Deane Streatfeild Diary, Lucy Anne Evelyn Streatfeild Papers, Modern Records Centre, University of Warwick, MSS.69 [hereafter referred to as 'Streatfeild Diary'].
7. Manuscript Report to the Chief Inspector of Factories by Lucy Deane on 'The Petition from Shirt and Collar Workers in Londonderry', 6 October 1897, HO 45/9918/B22738G, National Archives, London [hereafter Deane Report].
8. *Irish Textile Journal*, 15 July 1896.
9. Congested Districts Board, *Baseline Reports*, County of Donegal – Union of Donegal, District of Lough Eask, p. 6.
10. See Anne O'Dowd, *Spalpeens and Tattie Hookers: History and Folklore of the Irish Migratory Agricultural Worker in Ireland and Britain* (Dublin: 1991). Compare two analyses by Cormac Ó Gráda: 'Seasonal migration and post-famine adjustment in the west of Ireland,' *Studia Hibernica*, vol. 12–13 (1972–3), pp. 48–76, and his more recent perspective on Irish migrant workers in *Ireland: A New Economic History, 1780–1939* (Oxford: 1994), pp. 233–5.
11. *Londonderry Sentinel*, 15 November 1894.
12. *Londonderry Sentinel*, 30 December 1890.
13. See Julie Ann Grew, 'The Derry shirt making industry 1831–1913' (Unpublished M.Phil thesis, University of Ulster, 1987).
14. *Irish Textile Journal*, 15 June 1889.
15. *Irish Textile Journal*, 15 May 1895.
16. *Irish Textile Journal*, 15 September 1899.
17. *Irish Textile Journal*, 15 October 1899.
18. *Irish Textile Journal*, 15 December 1899.
19. *Irish Textile Journal*, 15 October 1899.
20. Desmond Greer and James W. Nicolson provide an excellent overview of the truck debate in *The Factory Acts in Ireland, 1802–1914* (Dublin: 2003), pp. 200–6. Greer also discusses the legal history of truck specifically in '"Middling hard on coin": truck in Donegal in the 1890s', an edited version of the presidential address given at the annual general meeting of the Irish Legal History Society on 3 November 2000, kindly supplied to me by Prof. Greer.
21. *Londonderry Sentinel*.
22. Greer, 'Middling Hard on coin', pp. 3–7.
23. See Mary Drake McFeely, *Lady Inspectors: The Campaign for a Better Workplace, 1823–1921* (Oxford: 1988). Chapter 10, 'The gombeen man', pp. 76–86, deals specifically with Deane's role in investigating the practice of truck in rural outwork.
24. See Hilda Martindale, *From One Generation to Another, 1839–1944* (London: 1944), Ch. 3, 'English inspector in Ireland', pp. 91–146 and Rose E. Squire, *Thirty Years in the Public Service: An Industrial Retrospect* (London: 1927), Ch. 6, 'Wage payments', pp. 77–98.
25. *Londonderry Sentinel*, 1 January 1898.
26. Deane Report.
27. Streatfeild Diary, 26 & 27 July 1897.
28. Streatfeild Diary, 5 August 1897.
29. Memorandum attached to documents dated 20 October 1897, HO 45/9918/B22738G, National Archives, London.
30. Arthur Whitelegge to Kenelm E. Digby, 20 October 1897 HO 45/9918/B22738G, National Archives, London.
31. *Annual Report of the Chief Inspector of Factories and Workshops for the Year ending 31 October 1897* [C-8965], HC 1898, vol. xiv, p. 109.
32. McFeely, Ch. 11, 'An army of petticoated inspectors', pp. 87–92.

8

Striking for the Right to be Late at Work: Workers' Resistance to Employers' Time Discipline in Lurgan Power Loom Factories 1899–1914

MATS GREIFF

> I will not stop in your torture shop,
> In the heat and the toil and the roar;
> All weavers I warn, to leave bad yarn,
> I leave, and I'll weaver no more.[1]

The above verse was written by a handloom weaver and published in the *Lurgan Mail* in 1911. It expresses the way he felt about daily work at Lurgan Weaving Company. To him, working in a mill, which contrasted strongly with the more independent weaving at home, was a new experience. After working for a time with bad quality yarn in the 'torture shop', as he calls it, he went to the foreman to give in his notice.

The transition from home-work to factories has been described in some textbooks as an economic development in which industrial production replaced older methods of production. From this point of view, the development towards industrial capitalism, where productivity is higher, is often considered to be a step toward increased prosperity.[2] There were, however, those who had to pay a price for the long-term economic growth; workers used to older methods of production in their own homes or in smaller craft workshops often found it difficult to bear the factory discipline, which employers considered essential. Long days of toil, with working hours and speed governed by the clock, represented a new phenomenon to these workers, one that was decidedly different from the habits of an earlier society. In pre-industrial agrarian society, and in the old urban trades, work hours were determined by the tasks that were to be performed. Moreover, craftsmen asserted their rights to take Mondays off and to decide for themselves when to work. This was directly opposed to the interests of modern industrial capitalists, who set working hours according to the clock.[3]

The introduction, however, of this new time discipline was not without problems for the employers. As has been pointed out by the American historian, Gary Cross, for nineteenth-century capitalism, time was used not only as an instrument for measuring efficiency, but also as a means of social control. Opposing ideas regarding working hours quite often became a breeding ground for conflict between labour and capital.[4] Regular attempts by capitalists to strengthen time discipline among factory workers included the forcing through of new factory rules, division of labour, increased control of the workers, punishments, clocks and steam whistles, sermons and school attendance, and the suppression of popular fair and sports traditions. A completely new rhetoric, bolstering ideas such as 'diligence', was also used in this context.[5]

Despite the varied and many means used by the employers, it took a long time before they succeeded in regulating work hours to the extent that they wished. In England, as in many other countries, they lacked the power to quickly overcome the inherent strength of culture and local customs. Thus, the habit of leaving the workplace on market days survived in certain parts of England until the mid-nineteenth century and, in many districts, the habit of taking Mondays off continued until the end of the 1800s; that is, until long after the factory system had become the dominant method of production.[6] There is, for example, evidence from the Sheffield steel industry in 1874 that the knife smiths continued to celebrate 'Saint Monday'.[7] In most European countries, there is similar evidence of workers' resistance to time discipline. So what of the area – Lurgan in north-east Ireland – from which our introductory poem emanated?

FROM HANDLOOMS TO POWER LOOMS

At the end of the 1820s, flax spinning became mechanized, while power looms were introduced shortly after 1850.[8] Before mechanization, independent spinners and weavers, working in their own homes, carried out a large part of the production. In the Belfast and Lurgan area, a 'putting-out' system had been established in the mid-eighteenth century; linen bleachers purchased yarn at local markets and delivered it to weavers. In this way, the bleachers acquired increased control of the linen production. Thus, the weavers became increasingly dependent on the bleachers, who decided what quantities and qualities the weavers were to produce.[9] This was a first stage in a slow proletarianization process involving the linen producers. Many of these weavers were originally small-scale farmers, weaving when the intensity of farm work was low and selling their linen products at the local market. However, households now involved in the putting-out system were increasingly dependent on the income provided by weaving.

Even though the weaving process underwent no direct change due to the mechanization of spinning, there are reasons to believe that a change in the relationship between workers and capital took place. The swift growth in the amount of linen yarn, created a need for an increased weaving capacity. To secure that, the putting-out system was intensified and higher demands were made on the productive capacity of the households. Weaving and related tasks, once a spare-time job, now became the main occupation. In this way, the whole household became systematically involved in the weaving. Labour division based on gender and generation probably became more and more systematic; household hierarchies were increasingly based on the different roles in the weaving process.[10] This development tended to transform more and more households into full-time weaving mills without land, that were dependent on spinning mill owners or bleachers delivering yarn. This was a second stage of proletarianization.

The third stage was the establishment of power loom factories. The decisive impetus for developing and introducing new technology was the shortage of manpower caused by the Great Famine in the 1840s. This shortage meant that the handloom weavers gained pay increases of 20 to 30 per cent. This did not, however, lead to increased production. On the contrary, higher wages made it possible for many weavers to shorten their working hours and increase their free time. Needless to say, this way of thinking was dramatically different from that of the capitalist businessmen. For the weavers, the most important thing was not to get wealthier, but to maintain their standard of living. When the wages they were paid for each woven yard increased, the average weaver shortened his working hours and maintained the income he was used to receiving. In this way, instead of getting higher pay, the weaver got more time off. The businessmen, however, considered this a problem because the result was a reduction of the total quantity of cloth produced. This was probably the reason why power looms were introduced.

Lurgan and its hinterland became one of the most important centres of handloom weaving in Ireland at an early stage. Already in the early nineteenth century, manufacturing centres with handlooms had been established, which at that time was unusual in Ireland, and it brought exploitation in its wake.[11] In addition to this, mechanisation often allowed greater flexibility for capitalists when it came to changing the composition of the labour force. In the English cotton industry, there was a connection between mechanization and the replacement of men by women. Indeed, because of the opposition of male workers to the new technology and employers' concomitant wish to have obedient and cheap labour, the companies not infrequently took to hiring women workers.[12] Before 1850, the majority of handloom weavers in Ireland were men, but, when power loom factories were established in Belfast, women were employed both as weavers and winders, soon forming a large majority in these establishments. In Lurgan, however, the distribution according to sex among the weavers did not change as a result of mechanization and, consequently, there was still a distinct male majority among weavers in that area through the nineteenth century.[13]

Since men constituted a large majority of the first generation of machine weavers in Lurgan, a good number of them almost certainly had direct experience of weaving at home. However, we must remember that power looms did not immediately supersede handlooms. This was actually a slow process, with both methods existing side by side until the 1890s at least. As late as 1878, 1,000 handloom weavers working in their homes were exploited by the manufacturers James Johnston and Joseph Allen, who supplied them with yarn.[14] In the twentieth century, there were scarcely any active handloom weavers in Lurgan. In the 1901 census, only four persons are counted as handloom weavers. Of course, some may be hidden behind the general title of 'weaver', while others would have lived in the countryside outside the town. Nonetheless, it is clear that numbers had diminished to the point of extinction. There is evidence showing that some handloom weavers emigrated to North America; the majority, however, probably ended up in the power loom factories.[15]

OPPOSITION TO FACTORY DISCIPLINE

Mechanization and its consequences impelled the handloom weavers to consider their position, leading to various strategies of resistance to the new technology. To the handloom weavers, the new methods meant a wage cut, since they were unable to compete with the higher productivity of the factories. The wage issue was not, however, the only important thing. Francis X. McCorry has considered the change from a wider perspective:

> Much more was at stake than a reduced weekly wage. There is little doubt that the weavers and their families foresaw the disappearance of a traditional way of life centred around the hearth, field and loom, and while their lifestyle could only be precarious and poverty-stricken, it tended to reflect the last vestiges of freedom that was age-old.[16]

Workers in Lurgan protested against the introduction of power looms. One of the more important capitalists in Lurgan was James Malcolm, who in the 1850s started one of the first power loom factories in Ireland; shortly after the factory opened, it was attacked by between 2,000 and 3,000 handloom weavers. Those participating in the protest gathered at a location loaded with symbolic value, a place where people used to meet for political protests. After the meeting, the weavers marched towards the town, shouting 'Down with steam!' When they arrived at the town, they marched towards Malcolm's new factory, where a veritable battle took place between the protesters, armed with paving stones, and policemen equipped with bayonets. Shots were also fired. Once the police had been forced to retire, Malcolm's new factory building was attacked and about 200 windows were smashed. However, Malcolm and some assistants, through the use of firearms, were able to prevent the protesters from entering the building itself.[17]

Attacks, such as that on Malcolm's premises, were vigorous, but these protests against using power looms did not force the employers into retreat. This was a lucrative industry and the new technology spread widely during the following decades. Concurrently, with the emergence of mechanized factories, the pay of the handloom weavers decreased; in 1872, they made an attempt to form a union and two years later they went on strike.[18] Nonetheless, efforts by the handloom weavers to halt the ever more far-reaching mechanization were fruitless and there was no way they could resist the slow decline of their occupational group. It does, however, take time to destroy cultural ideas, and the establishment of power loom factories created another kind of long-term opposition, which was not purely economic. Many of those men who became power loom weavers in the Lurgan mills had personal experience of handloom weaving: they had either been weavers themselves, or they had grown up in families where the father had been a handloom weaver. Growing up in such a home created an awareness of the habits and ideas common among handloom weavers, and this culture contained certain notions of freedom. To be sure, most families probably had members working industriously, but, nonetheless, the home-based weavers had the right to decide for themselves when to start and end their work and also to take a day off if they felt the need. This degree of freedom was stressed by the chief inspector of factories and workshops in 1885, when he reported that, compared to the power loom weavers, the lifestyle of handloom weavers was much more independent. The former were subjected to a certain restraint, and, according to the report, they were forced to keep the work hours determined by the factory owners.[19] The workers, regardless, did try to maintain their time-honoured rights. 'Many of them,' it was reported in 1899, 'are habited to work such hours as they pleased.'[20] The employers tried to break the old habits of the workers, using new means and methods. They developed systems for waking the workers, so that they could be at work on time. One way was to let a horn or a steam whistle sound in the residential quarters. Another was to hire guards to walk around and wake the workers by knocking at their doors. An old ballad reminds us of the blowing of a horn:

> At half past five the horn will blow.
> Six o'clock we all must go.
> And if you be a minute late,
> Robert McCabe will shut the gate.[21]

Moreover, to control the time-keeping, the employers erected fences with only one or two gates around the mill area; this made it easier to monitor the workers' attendance and it was also considered an efficient way of maintaining time discipline. When it was time to begin work, the gates were closed and those who were late could not get in until breakfast hour.[22] Thus, a few minutes of extra sleep, or some trouble with the children, could mean a deduction of several hours from their pay.

The workers did, however, create different strategies to undermine factory discipline. One such strategy, aimed at avoiding the hard work in the mill during the summer, was enlisting in the army. This was common among Lurgan power loom weavers. Military training would certainly have implied a high degree of disciplinary submission, similar to factory work, but at least the workers were able to spend hot summer days outdoors without losing any pay, instead of attending looms in factory buildings that – due to the continuous discharging of steam – were almost unbearably hot.[23] Weavers who did not enlist in the army used other strategies to escape the heat in the factories; it was not uncommon for workers to simply absent themselves on a hot summer's day and, instead of going to work, head to Lough Neagh for a swim or to find some other recreation. Correspondingly, it was common in winter for the workers not to arrive at the mill until breakfast hour. In this way, they avoided the cold of the morning in the factory premises. Once the steam engines had been going for some hours, the temperature in the premises would be acceptable.[24]

As has already been mentioned, these strategies – aimed at creating free time and avoiding the worst problems of the work environment – clashed with the employers' demand for time discipline. Disciplining the labour force was no easy task. As late as the early 1890s, almost forty years after the introduction of power looms in the town, antagonism in Lurgan was still evident. Indeed, in 1893 the factory inspector, reporting on the difficulties of recruiting new workers, remarked that these included problems with 'regularity, punctuality and discipline required in factories, without which industries could not exist'.[25]

THE 1899 STRIKE FOR THE RIGHT TO BE LATE AT WORK

Workers considered 'time', and how it was understood, to be important. In their view, it was about freedom and their right to make decisions about their own lives. This was actually a cultural struggle between, on the one hand, earlier ideas about time and the use of it, and the right of independent workers to decide for themselves when to work and when not to work, and, on the other hand, a new conception based on the need for time discipline, which had been introduced through the factory system.[26]

Besides the attack on the factory in 1857 and the limited strike for higher pay in 1874, the antagonism between weavers and factory owners manifested itself on a particularly significant occasion in nineteenth-century Lurgan. The background to the major Lurgan industrial dispute of 1899 was an unexpected and extremely swift increase in the demand for linen cloth. A large number of workers having left the town during the preceding depression, the employers had difficulty in recruiting workers in numbers large enough to maintain a production capacity sufficient to deal with the heightened demand.[27] A few months were needed to train a worker to become a weaver. This meant that the employers had acute and immediate problems. Their solution was not to raise wages and recruit weavers from Belfast or other towns; had they done this, they would have risked ending up with a rising pay spiral and reduced profits. Instead, the employers attempted to exact additional work from the existing labour force and, to facilitate this, they moved to strengthen time discipline. They believed that this could be achieved by introducing a fine for absence without a valid reason and for workers who were late in the morning. Having arrived at a collective decision in this matter, the three power loom factories in Lurgan tried to impose these measures on the workers.[28]

When, on Friday, 3 November, in accordance with contemporary law, the new rules were introduced through notices in the factories, the workers reacted immediately. At Lurgan Weaving Co. they went on strike, apparently spontaneously, though in the afternoon they returned to work. However, after lunch-hour on the following day, they again refused to resume work. Exactly the same pattern was repeated at Johnston, Allen & Co.[29] The short return to work during the Friday afternoon was probably designed to enable the workers to finish the cuts, so that they could get a full week's pay. On the following Monday, however, the strike extended, now including the workers at James Malcolm's factory. This meant that about 1,400 workers in total were on strike, which was more or less the entire labour force in the town's weaving business. None of the workers belonged to a union; a weavers' union was not founded in the town until 1907. Despite this apparent lack of organization, pickets were quickly posted at the factory gates and these stopped the few who wished to work. On the Tuesday, the workers held a mass meeting by the Jubilee fountain in the town centre, where a number of speeches on behalf of the strikers were made and a negotiation deputation was chosen.

This deputation and the employers met by midday the same day. The latter refused to withdraw the new rules but offered the workers a compromise: the right to be late one day a week without being fined. At a renewed strike meeting in the afternoon, the workers rejected the offer and unanimously agreed to continue fighting for their demands. This was described by the *Irish News*: 'The strikers (men and women) are determined to make a bold stand to gain redress of what they consider their grievances, and the granting of their just demands.'[30] The employers' reaction was the same as it used to be when disputes broke out in the Belfast textile industry: they closed the factory gates, thus locking out all the workers. On Thursday, a new strike meeting was arranged in the town hall. To give the employers a chance to listen to the views of the workers and to their complaints, they were invited to the meeting. Unsurprisingly, the employers declined the invitation, but there are many interesting aspects to this meeting. First, among the speakers were three town councillors: William White, Joshua McNeice and Edward Lunn. This means that the workers had political support for their action. Secondly, the arguments voiced in favour of the strike at the meeting were cultural rather than economic. They did not protest against the fines as such, but against the loss of freedom implied by the insistence that they be at work at a certain time. In his speech, William O'Neill, who later became the leader of the local Weavers' Union, stressed that it was the weaver – and not the factory owner – who suffered an economic loss by not arriving at work in the morning. According to O'Neill, this is why a fine, imposed because one is late at work or absent for some other reason, had to be considered unjust. The issue of freedom returned later in his speech when he claimed that:

> The worker could not possibly attend always, and if he was forced to attend in such circumstances under a scheme of fines, then he became a slave.[31]

The comparison made by O'Neill between time discipline and conditions resembling slavery indicates a certain attitude, namely a belief in the right of workers to decide how to use their own time and an assumption that their labour was sold in order to perform certain tasks; in short, it is the worker who has the free use of all his time and who decides to what extent this time should be placed at the employer's disposal. Another worker, Samuel Creaney, also stressed that the workers, and not the factory owners, should decide how much they ought to work, since:

> They were piece-workers and not weekly workers, and, as usual, were not entitled to be fined for remaining out. Each would have to finish his piece of cloth before being paid, and if he had not finished on Saturday he would have to go home to his wife and children without a copper in his pocket.[32]

After the speeches, a new deputation of workers was chosen to negotiate with the owners and the meeting then ended with everybody agreeing to stand firm.[33]

The deputation tried to bring about negotiations with the owners, who refused to take part in such talks and collectively bargain. As a result, they instead went to see each factory owner individually. By doing this, the men in the deputation may have hoped to play off the employers against each other. At Malcolm's, the workers were bluntly told that 'you are only wasting your time'. MacGeagh, chairman of Lurgan Weaving Co., refused to see the deputation at all. However, when they came to the third owner, Johnston, he received them and listened to their concerns.[34] He appears to have considered the issue carefully, understanding that these were not economic complaints but primarily a question of perceived rights, but, at the same time, he felt compelled to strengthen discipline in his factory in order to increase production. The following day, he suggested a modification of the new rules. The system of fines was to be introduced, but each worker would have the right to be absent four mornings a month without being punished. The fines were to be funded and used in a bonus system, giving a reward to those workers who showed up at work most regularly. The company was to help by paying 20 per cent into the fund. Married women were to be exempted from the fine system.

The workers immediately accepted the suggestion and, later the same day, the two other owners offered similar compromises. At Malcolm's, the money was to be used for a health insurance fund instead. The workers at these factories accepted this and work was resumed again on Monday, 13 November.[35] There was an obvious driving force motivating the factory owners to accept this compromise: the conditions of trade were better than ever but their ability to increase profits was compromised by a genuine shortage of experienced weavers and winders. A long strike would have meant a severe setback for the employers. Where the workers were concerned, several had a background in handloom weaving and a large number of the younger factory weavers were the children of handloom weavers. With future prospects for handloom weavers having been poor for several decades, these younger weavers had neither been trained in handloom weaving nor in winding in their homes.[36] Instead, they started to work in the power-loom mills at an early age.

Since the number of power looms had doubled in the 1890s, many workers did not have a very long experience of working in a factory – they were the first generation of factory workers. This meant that a culture where workers were used to deciding for themselves when to work was still vigorous at the end of the nineteenth century. Naturally, we must not make the working conditions of the handloom weavers seem too idyllic; handloom weavers were also used to hard work and long hours, but, crucially, with a certain degree of independence regarding working hours.[37] It is also important to point out that the free-time culture often facilitated the consumption of large quantities of alcohol, a phenomenon that can definitely be associated with irregular working hours. However, it would be a mistake to overstate the link between alcohol and the desire for free time. Douglas A. Reid has shown, using examples from England, that free time was used for non-recreational purposes as well. Thus, with the expansion of factory life, it happened that many people ended up getting married during working hours – there being a law stating that marriage should take place in the mornings.[38] It should also be noted that it was not only workers from a handloom weaving background who were used to so-called task-orientated working hours. To a high degree, this was also true for workers with a background in agrarian production or other craft jobs. This work culture, stressing the carrying out of the task without necessarily allowing the clock to decide the working hours, collided with the factory owners' ambition to establish a new kind of factory discipline.

The new technology in factories, with a central source powering the looms, created an economic incentive for strengthening time discipline, making it financial common sense to have all workers begin and end work at fixed points of time. Otherwise, many of the economic advantages of the new economies of scale would be lost to the factory owners. In a parliamentary inquiry at the beginning of the twentieth century, textile factory owners complained that often the steam engine was warmed up and started without there being enough workers present; in this way, the production per ton of coal used became too low.[39] As we have seen, the contradiction between the weavers' culturally determined ideas on working hours and the economic interests of the employers was brought to a head in Lurgan in November 1899, when the shortage of labour was considered very serious indeed.

The question whether to include women in the new time discipline rules appears to have been of particular interest to the workers, as was demonstrated by exemption of married women from the fines in Lurgan. It is likely that the assumption may have been that, often being mothers, they would suffer more than men from the proposed fines. Women carried the main responsibility for tasks in the home connected with reproduction and care. In particular, their responsibility for the children created extra difficulties with regard to being on time in the mornings. The concern shown in this matter by the male workers could imply a particular solidarity with women, though it is true that a majority of the weavers had neither wives nor daughters working as winders, and thus there existed no close family ties between the groups. Nonetheless, a majority of those working in the weaving mills lived close together in the same neighbourhood, which probably nurtured mutuality and community solidarity.[40] It is debatable, however, whether concern for the particular difficulties of women was a major factor in the 1899 industrial dispute because the outcome was not necessarily to their advantage. The men's action could also be construed as maintaining a gender pattern, where it was considered natural that the primary tasks of women were those connected with reproduction and care. There are examples from England indicating such a view. Factory work prevented women from performing the domestic tasks that were considered central to their social role and this is why people thought that it was acceptable to turn a blind eye to women's working hours being more irregular than those of men.[41] This sentiment was expressed in a statement by the English factory worker, Mary Anne Field: 'Coming late in the morning suits me best, because of getting the children's breakfast.' Other women said that they would prefer having Mondays off because they would be able to spend a whole day washing or cleaning, for example.[42] The same way of thinking positioned the man as the main breadwinner, and his contributions as a wage-earner were considered to be more important to the family, which is why it was necessary for him to show up more regularly at work. Thus, women's regular wage-earning was not considered to be of equal importance.[43] Another aspect of the issue of the exemption of married women from the fines is that, since the mid-1880s, women workers in the Lurgan making-up trade had shown an unusually strong determination in the trade union struggle to maintain good wage levels.[44] The winders may not have been less determined than their sisters living in the same neighbourhood but working in another kind of factories. Thus, we cannot exclude the possibility that it may have been the winders themselves who – with their experience of reproduction and care work – in female solidarity pushed for the exemption of married women.

In certain respects, the strike must be considered a success for the workers. To be sure, they were forced to accept a fine for being absent during the morning hours, but they retained the 'right' to be absent one morning a week. In addition to this, the money from the fines was to be used for the benefit of the workers themselves. Thus, the new regulation did not imply a total loss of freedom where working hours were concerned, but rather a redistribution of money within the group of workers. Even though the result of the 1899 dispute meant that the employers were able to strengthen their demands for time discipline and attendance, their problems had still not been solved. Workers continued enlisting in the army to do military training, rather than factory work, during the summer months. Thus, it was reported in July 1900, for example, that hundreds of looms were standing idle, with demand surpassing supply.[45] Workers also continued the habit of taking hot afternoons off during the summer in order to escape the heat of the factory. Likewise, many workers also continued the deeply rooted habit of not coming to work at six o'clock in the winter, waiting instead until after the breakfast hour in order to avoid the icy cold that could reign in the factories during early morning hours. This meant that hundreds of looms might be unmanned during part of the working day, causing the factory owners to discuss seriously in 1909 whether to start work at nine instead during the winter months.[46]

THE ETERNAL ISSUE OF ULSTER AND CREED: PRESBYTERIANS, ANGLICANS AND CATHOLICS

According to the 1901 census, 11,782 persons lived in Lurgan proper. As can be seen in Table 1, there was a Protestant majority, while Catholics made up about one third of the population. As in other Ulster towns, housing was strongly segregated according to creed.[47]

TABLE 1.
RELIGIOUS COMPOSITION IN LURGAN, 1901

Denomination	Percentage
Episcopalian	42.2
Roman Catholic	34.8
Presbyterian	13.4
Methodist	5.1

Source: Census of Ireland 1901, County Armagh.

However, among those working in the weaving factories, the demographics were different. Here, Catholics constituted a narrow majority.

TABLE 2.
RELIGIOUS COMPOSITION IN THE WEAVING INDUSTRY IN LURGAN, 1901: PERCENTAGES

Denomination	Male weavers	All male workers	Female weavers	Female winders
Episcopalian	33.4	38.6	24.8	35.3
Roman Catholic	53	43.8	59.5	50.1
Presbyterian	7.6	10.7	11	6.9
Methodist	3.7	4.7	2.4	3.9

Source: National Archives, Dublin, Returns of Census, 1901, County Armagh, Lurgan.

Of 994 weavers listed in the 1901 census, 54 per cent were Catholics and, out of 334 winders, 50 per cent were Catholics (see Table 2).[48]

Interestingly, however, even though only a minority of weavers and winders were Presbyterians or Methodists (much less than their percentage of the town population), they constituted a rather important part of the workforce in the weaving sheds, in real numbers about 220 workers. In his article, 'Time, work-discipline and industrial capitalism', E.P. Thompson has highlighted the importance of Puritanism to the breakthrough of capitalist time discipline. Because of Puritanism, Thompson claims, an inner compulsion rather than an external one now maintained time discipline. Puritan ethics praised conscientiousness and criticized laziness or free time from a moral point of view; to use every minute as if it were the most precious treasure and devote it entirely to the road of duty was the message in Puritan texts.[49] This kind of Puritanism was often considered to be in accordance with Presbyterian views on industry, dedication and hard work.[50] This view is obvious in the way Protestant workers in Belfast – mainly Presbyterians – used to look upon themselves: they were industrious, disciplined and hard working. It appears very clearly in the former shipyard hand Harry Fletcher's characterization of himself and his fellow Protestant workers:

> I have always found that the Ulsterman is a very determined sort of person. And I found it very noticeable when I first came to work in the shipyard. Whenever I met the different types of people who were given the different tasks I found that their one theme in life was to do as good a job as it was humanly possible for them to do. They were dedicated men and they had one thing in common – they were shipyard workers. They took a pride in the job and they made sure that the shipyard came first, second and third in their lives. Their whole life and their family's life were built round the fact that they worked in the shipyard.[51]

In this way, part of the Presbyterian exegesis – success in working life was God's reward for the devotion shown in one's work[52] – actually legitimized the condescension with which Catholics were regarded: their poverty could be interpreted as a sign of moral laxity and lack of conscientiousness, reactionary views and an excessive use of alcohol. Such stereotypes were vivid elements in the conception of the world of large Protestant – especially Presbyterian – groups in Ulster. Thus, the exegesis significantly contributed to the creation of 'us' and 'them' groups that were built on commonplace stereotypes.

However, Presbyterians were not the only ones to raise the issue of industry and conscientiousness. Methodists and Episcopalians discussed the topic, advocating careful economizing with time.[53] In this context, it seems remarkable that Protestants and Catholics united together in opposition to the Lurgan factory owners on the question of time discipline. First, by going on strike, the workers showed a belief in common identity, going beyond ethnicity and also gender, which could, on certain occasions, have a uniting function for the whole working class. In terms of the industrial action, there was total unity between the different groups of workers. It is also important to remember that, first and foremost, the strike had cultural origins, thus indicating that the groups could have common values with regard to the conception of time and liberty. Where the right to free time and, accordingly, a weaker time discipline were concerned,

Presbyterians, Methodists and other Protestants were in apparent agreement with Catholic workers. Thus, the assumed importance of Puritanism to the internalized motivation of workers to accept time discipline can be questioned. At the very least, it demands a problematized nuancing.

EPILOGUE

In 1899, the Lurgan weaving workers went on strike, literally, for the right to be late for work. Connected to this perceived right, moreover, was the custom of taking off an especially hot afternoon. This custom, regarded 100 years later through the sources, may seem almost improbable. Today, time discipline appears normal and few people would make such strong protests against something that is considered natural – the employer's insistence that one be on time for work. In that context, it is worth looking briefly at the reasons why views of time discipline changed so radically during the twentieth century.

As late as the winter of 1913, there is evidence that the employers were displeased with the attendance of the weavers and winders in Lurgan. In connection with an all-embracing strike for higher pay, the employers pointed out that the workers' wages could have risen, had they only been present during the prescribed working hours. Average attendance was forty-nine hours a week, out of the fifty-four decreed.[54] It indicates that the habit of arriving late, or taking some afternoons off, still existed during the 1910s. In 1914, in the wake of a major wages dispute, the employers acted with determination to strengthen discipline, introducing high fines for unlawful absence.[55] On that occasion, it appears that the employers were determined to teach the workers a lesson and show them who was really in charge of the workplace. This purposefulness must also be considered against the background of the workers having formed unions and shown strong unity during the strike, which lasted for five weeks. In this way, they had seriously challenged the factory owners, who felt the need to reassert their power. Ultimately, time discipline came to be accepted by the workers and was seen as normative. But what explains why and how the workers accepted the new time discipline? Gary Cross has pointed to the importance of Fordism and the way that workers' culture changed, stressing consumerism instead of free time. In addition, he singles out the trade union movement as an important actor in the changing process. According to Cross, the unions stressed the issue of higher pay above all and allowed questions about 'laziness', shorter working hours and free time to fall down the agenda; socio-cultural concerns were not pursued by the trade unions. He also points to the recessions in the 1920s and 1930s and their key importance in bringing about the change. During this time, the primary concern of workers was to protect their jobs. In such circumstances, it became increasingly difficult to fight for the right to flexible working hours.[56]

I have already questioned the role of religion as a kind of inner motivating power impelling workers to accept the new time discipline. Cross chooses instead to point to the introduction of a consumption culture into working-class life and to how a changing conception of need acted as a decisive motivating factor.[57] Today's consumption culture has caused a large number of people to connect economic growth with a higher material standard of living, unlike the nineteenth-century weavers who saw economic growth as a possibility to increase their free time. It is clear that the idea of time discipline as both necessary and natural has survived into the twenty-first century. E.P. Thompson has aptly described these developments and their impact on workers: 'They had learned their lesson, that time is money, only too well.'[58]

NOTES

1. *Lurgan Mail*, 4 February 1911.
2. This view is prolematicized by, for example, Eric J. Hobsbawm, *Labouring Men: Studies in the History of Labour* (New York: 1964) and John Belchem, *Industrialisation and the Working Class: the English Experience, 1750–1900* (Aldershot: 1990), pp. 13–36.
3. For a discussion, see E.P. Thompson, 'Time, work-discipline and industrial capitalism', in *Customs in Common: Studies in Traditional Popular Culture* (New York: 1993).
4. Gary Cross, 'Time, money, and labor history's encounter with consumer culture', *International Labor and Working-Class History*, vol. 43 (1993), p. 5.
5. Thompson, 'Time', p. 375; Lars Berggren, *Ångvisslans och brickornas värld. Om arbete och facklig organisering vid Kockums Mekaniska Verkstad och Carl Lunds fabrik i Malmö 1840–1905* (Malmö: 1991), pp. 303–15.
6. F. M.L. Thompson, *The Rise of Respectable Society: A Social History of Victorian Britain, 1830–1900* (London: 1988), pp. 273–4.
7. Thompson, 'Time', p. 375; Douglas A Reid, 'The decline of Saint Monday, 1766–1876', *Past and Present*, vol. 71 (1976), p. 91.
8. This process is described by W.H. Crawford, *The Handloom Weavers and the Ulster Linen Industry* (Belfast: 1994); Jane Gray, 'Working-class formation in the Irish linen Industry', in Laura L. Frader and Sonya O. Rose (eds), *Class and Gender in Modern Europe* (Ithaca: 1996); Brenda Collins, 'Die Heimarbeiterschaft im Leinengewerbe Ulsters während des 19. und 20. Jahrhunderts', in Karl Ditt and Sidney Pollard (eds), *Von der Heimarbeit in die Fabrik. Industrialisierung und Arbeiterschaft in Leinen- und Baumwollregionen Westeuropas während des 18. und 19. Jahrhunderts* (Paderborn: 1992). Regarding changing living conditions among English weavers, see E.P. Thompson, *The Making of the English Working Class* (Hammondsworth: 1982), Chapter 9.
9. W.H. Crawford, 'The evolution of Ulster towns', in Peter Roebuck (ed.), *From Plantation to Partition: Essays in Ulster History in Honour of J.L. McCracken* (Belfast: 1981), p. 147.
10. Gray, 'Working-class formation', p. 38.
11. Francis X. McCorry, *Lurgan: An Irish Provincial Town, 1610–1970* (Lurgan: 1993), p. 68.
12. Thompson, *Rise of Respectable Society*, p. 215.
13. British Parliamentary Papers (BPP), 1887, *Labour Statistics. Returns of Wages. Published between 1830 and 1886*, p. 75.
14. McCorry, *Lurgan*, p. 78.
15. BPP, *Report of the Chief Inspector of Factories and Workshops for the Year ending 31st October 1886* (1887).
16. McCorry, *Lurgan*, p. 81.

17. *Northern Whig*, 14 November and 17 November 1857. On luddism and machine-breakers, see Eric J. Hobsbawm, 'The machine breakers', in *Labouring Men*; Thompson, *The Making of the English Working Class*, Chapter 14.
18. Mats Greiff, *Kvinnorna marscherade demonstrativt iväg. Strejker och facklig organisering bland kvinnliga textilarbetare i Ulster 1870–1914* (Ystad: 1996), p. 36.
19. BPP, *Report of the Chief Inspector of Factories and Workshops for the year ending 31st October 1885* (1886), p. 9.
20. *Irish Textile Journal*, November 1899.
21. Alfie Tallon, *Memories of Old Lurgan* (Lurgan: 1987), p. 27.
22. This was widespread in Ulster. See, for example, BPP, *Annual Report of the Chief Inspector of Factories and Workshops for the Year 1906* (1907), pp. 240–50.
23. *Lurgan Mail*, 25 June 1910. The heat is described in BPP, *Report of the Departemental Committee on Humidity and Ventilation in Flax Mills and Linen Factories* (1914).
24. BPP, *Report of the Departmental Committee on Humidity and Ventilation in Flax Mills and Linen Factories. Minutes of Evidence* (1914), pp. 17, 81.
25. BPP, *Report of the Chief Inspector of Factories and Workshops for the year ending 31st October 1892* (1893–4), p. 113.
26. See Thompson, 'Time', *passim*.
27. *Irish Textile Journal*, October 1899.
28. *Irish Textile Journal*, November 1899.
29. *Irish News*, 7 November 1899; *Lurgan Mail*, 10 November 1899.
30. *Irish Textile Journal*, November 1899; *Irish News*, 8 and 9 November 1899.
31. *Lurgan Mail*, 11 November 1899.
32. Ibid.
33. *Irish News*, 10 November 1899; *Lurgan Mail*, 11 November 1899.
34. *Irish News*, 11 November 1899.
35. *Belfast Newsletter*, 11 November 1899; *Irish News*, 11 November 1899; *Irish Textile Journal*, November 1899.
36. BPP, *Report of the Chief Inspector of Factories and Workshops for the Year ending 31st October 1886* (1887).
37. Gray, 'Working-class formation', pp. 52ff.
38. Douglas A. Reid, 'Weddings, weekdays, work and leisure in urban England, 1791–1911: the decline of Saint Monday revisited', *Past and Present*, vol. 153 (1996).
39. BPP, *Report of the Departmental Committee on Humidity and Ventilation in Flax Mills and Linen Factories. Minutes of Evidence* (1914).
40. National Archives, Dublin, Census returns, County Armagh, Lurgan 1901.
41. Reid, 'Weddings', pp. 87–9.
42. Ibid.
43. On the male breadwinner ideology, see, for example, Laura L. Frader, 'Engendering work and wages: the French labour movement and the family wage', in Frader and Rose, *Class and Gender in Modern Europe*.
44. Mats Greiff, '"Marching through the streets singing and shouting": industrial struggle and trade unions among female linen workers in Belfast and Lurgan, 1872–1910', *Saothar*, vol. 22 (1997), p. 36.
45. *Irish Textile Journal*, July 1900.
46. *Irish Textile Journal*, October 1909.
47. BPP, *Lurgan Riots Inquiry Commissioners 1880* (1881), p. 2. Regarding Belfast, see Catherine Hirst, *Religion, Politics and Violence in Nineteenth-Century Belfast: the Pound and Sandy Row* (Dublin: 2002).
48. National Archives, Dublin. Census returns, County Armagh, Lurgan 1901.
49. Thompson, 'Time', *passim*.
50. Max Weber, *The Sociology of Religion* (Boston: 1993), pp. 248–60.
51. David Hammond, *Steelchest, Nail in the Boot and the Barking Dog: the Belfast Shipyard* (Belfast: 1986), p. 20.
52. Dale Cannon, *Six Ways of Being Religious: a Framework for Comparative Studies of Religion* (Belmont: 1996), p. 209.
53. Thompson, 'Time'.
54. *Lurgan Mail*, 18 January 1913.
55. *Lurgan Mail*, 21 March 1914.
56. Cross, 'Time, money, and labor history's encounter with consumer culture', pp. 6–9.
57. Christer Sanne, *Arbetets tid. Om arbetstidsreformer och konsumtion i välfärdsstaten* (Stockholm: 1995), Chapters 3 and 4; Gary Cross, *An All-Consuming Century: Why Commercialism Won in Modern America* (New York: 2000), pp.13–14.
58. Thompson, 'Time', p. 390.

9

The Belfast Shipyards and the Industrial Working Class

JOHN LYNCH

By the end of the nineteenth century, Belfast could not only claim to be the industrial heartland of Ireland but also one of the major manufacturing centres of Britain. If the proportion of the total labour force engaged in manufacturing is accepted as a reliable measurement of how 'industrialized' a city became, then Belfast was clearly an important centre (see Table 1). In addition, an ever growing proportion of those Irish workers classified by the census enumerators as engaged in the manufacture of 'ships and boats' were to be found in Belfast. The shipyards of the Lagan contained the greatest concentration of unionized skilled labour in Ireland and were amongst the most important in Britain.

TABLE 1.
PROPORTION OF LABOUR FORCE IN MANUFACTURING SECTOR[1]

	1881	1891	1911
United Kingdom Total	22.6%	23.1%	23.8%
England and Wales	24.3%	24.5%	25.0%
Scotland	28.2%	28.1%	28.6%
Ireland	9.9%	10.5%	10.2%
Belfast	37.3%	42.2%	39.8%
% Total Irish in Belfast	21.5%	26.1%	32.9%
% Irish workers in 'Ships & Boats' in Belfast	59.7%	67.5%	82.4%

As I have previously pointed out, sources on the composition of the labour force of Harland and Wolff are limited, and those of Workman Clark almost non-existent.[2] However, these firms shaped the industrial economy of Belfast in its years of growth. In 1902 Workman Clark noted that 5,000 men were 'usually employed' in their yards and by 1909 this had increased to 9,000;[3] in March 1915 one of the few complete listings for Harland and Wolff show that they had 10,504 workers in their Belfast yard.[4] At the end of the First World War employment in the yards reached a peak. Workman Clark employed 10,000 men[5] and a return for Harland and Wolff shows them employing 20,057 in August 1919.[6] However, this return makes no reference to boilermakers and so clearly does not include the engine works, which had employed 6,245 men in May,[7] or the 'office' workers who numbered 1,261 in December.[8] On the basis of these figures, Harland and Wolff were employing a peak figure of 27–28,000 men and women and the industry over 36,000. Clearly the Belfast shipyards were significant employers, and within the limitations of the material available I intend to examine the composition of their labour force and industrial relations until the early 1920s.

THE LABOUR FORCE IN THE BELFAST SHIPBUILDING INDUSTRY

The construction of large steel ships and their engines represented a highly complex industrial process which required a wide range of skills. As a result, British shipyards of this period were characterized by large and diverse labour forces. The workers in the shipyards were not a single coherent body but rather a heavily stratified social organization, and relationships between workers and employers or between groups within the labour force were often complex. To try and make sense of these relationships, I have divided the shipyard workers into five broad groups: skilled, apprentices, semi-skilled, unskilled and white-collar. Moss and Hume in their history of Harland and Wolff claim that the attitude of the management in that firm was, to say the least, positive:

> The company's industrial relations had been remarkably good since the 1895 strike. There had only been a handful of trivial disputes since the formation of the Committee of Managing Directors in 1907. Pirrie had gone out of his way to win the confidence of the representatives of the numerous trades employed at Queen's Island and at the new works on the mainland.[9]

The most striking example of this policy was the agreement reached with the unions in July 1914 which allowed for the settling of demarcation disputes without recourse to industrial action.[10] However, this agreement did not apply to Workman Clark and, as I shall discuss later, this picture of paternalistic harmony within Harland and Wolff is not quite complete.

SKILLED MANUAL WORKERS

The skilled workers were the backbone of a shipyard's labour force. As a group, they were united by shared skills, social origin (insofar as their fathers had usually been skilled workers) and the experience of apprenticeship. If the lists of 'hands employed' by Harland and Wolff are taken as a guide, there existed twenty-three trades within the yard in which apprentices were employed, but this probably represents a serious underestimate, as others suggest up to ninety trades in a shipyard.[11] If the employment data for Harland and Wolff is examined, then skilled men represented 8,733 out of the 20,057 employed in the yard in August 1919 (43.5 per cent) and 1,739 out of the 6,245 in the engine works in May (27.8 per cent).[12] Given the nature of their output, the proportion of skilled men employed by Workman Clark was probably slightly lower. Pollard and Robertson argue that shipbuilding wages were low in Belfast,[13] but their conclusion was distorted by low wages paid to unskilled labour in the city. Skilled wages were amongst the highest in the shipbuilding industry (Table 2).

TABLE 2.
WEEKLY WAGES OF ENGINEERING WORKERS (OCTOBER 1905)[14]

	Belfast	Range in ten other shipbuilding areas	Average of other areas
Fitter	37s.	35–36s.	35s. 1d.
Turner	38s.	35–36s.	35s. 2d.
Smith	37s.	34–38s.	35s. 6d.
Patternmaker	39s.	37–39s. 6d.	38s.
Labourer	15-18s.	18–23s. 6d.	c. 20s.

The wages of skilled men increased dramatically during the war. A patternmaker who was earning 44s. a week in 1914 saw his wages increase by eight stages to 73s. 6d., a 67 per cent increase. Other groups fared even better: fitters got 72 per cent (41s. to 70s. 6d.), shipwrights 79 per cent (40s. 6d. to 72s. 6d.) and sailmakers almost 82 per cent (36s. to 65s. 6d.).[15] Although some prices, notably foodstuffs, increased by 150 per cent, other critical expenses, notably rents, were controlled and the standard of living of the skilled shipyard worker was probably not seriously eroded.

As a group, their scarce skills were difficult, if not impossible, to replace and the employers had to recognize and co-operate with the unions representing their interests. They formed a largely self-perpetuating elite within Belfast's labour force; it was their sons who tended to enter 'trades' through apprenticeships to create the next generation of skilled workers.

However, they also faced certain problems, notably the desire of all such workers to protect their 'craft' from new technological processes or other groups of skilled workers. Demarcation disputes were a feature of the British shipbuilding industry in these years and, although these were/are often presented as petty and pointless, it should be remembered that the main reason for such action was to safeguard the employment of groups of skilled workers in a rapidly changing industry. John Beattie, an official of the Associated Blacksmiths and Ironworkers' Society, worked in Harland's just after the war and his workload was probably fairly typical; his trade union work included trying to sort out a dispute between engine-smiths and ship-smiths within his own union, arguing with the plumbers about who installed hydraulic pipes on cranes and flange connections on ships' engines, discussions with Harland's about the introduction of the 'air oliver' for making bolts and training apprentice smiths in acetylene welding.[16]

As certain trades declined in importance, their members were forced to fight to retain employment in the yards, while, conversely, other crafts aggressively tried to create monopolies at the expense of their less powerful 'brothers'. An example of this in Belfast's shipyards were the shipwrights, who had dominated shipbuilding while wood was the main material but who had refused to adapt to working in iron. The significance of this soon became clear. In 1850, 90 per cent of new tonnage was built in wood but by 1880 this had declined to only 4 per cent.[17] Within a generation, the shipwrights were reduced from being the dominant trade in shipyards to desperately trying to protect what remained of their work from encroachment by joiners/carpenters. Friction between these trades was a major problem in the Belfast yards, as the Belfast shipbuilder John McIlwaine told a Royal Commission in 1893:

> There has always been a certain amount of jealousy between the shipwrights and joiners, but the demarcation of work was formerly left entirely in the hands of the employers, and, on the whole, so managed that the division of work never led to more than a passing suspension of work by either class, when their members felt themselves aggrieved. Within the last five years the feeling of jealousy has increased so much that it has been impossible in some cases to avoid stopping of work. The dispute in this district is much aggravated by the amount of personal ill-feeling indulged in by the workmen towards each other.[18]

Demarcation disputes between these trades led to major strikes in Belfast in 1890, 1891, 1911 and 1913 with, in each case, the joiners gaining work at the expense of the shipwrights.[19]

There were also problems when competing unions recruited the same craftsmen and tried to ensure their employment of their members at the expense of their rival. In 1892 Belfast witnessed an example of such confrontation between the United Kingdom Pattern Makers' Association (UKPA) and the Amalgamated Society of Engineers (ASE) when the former planned strike action in the city. An appeal by UKPA to the local ASE members to support their action, or at least undertake not to break the strike, was met with hostility, and assurances were only given after a direct appeal to the general secretary of the ASE.[20] UKPA then called its members out on strike but after a few days the ASE wrote to employers offering to supply tradesmen; the strike collapsed and a number of UKPA members lost their jobs.[21] The National Executive of the ASE assumed full responsibility, claiming UKPA members had stated they would not end their strike until ASE members who had remained at work were dismissed; this was denied by UKPA. It is impossible to discover what really happened, although the history of UKPA offers a plausible explanation:

> It was made quite clear that our members never made such a threat, although it might have been true that some individual, probably in his cups, said something which aroused the indignation of someone else, probably in a similar condition.[22]

Sometimes difficulties could be sparked by the aggressiveness of a union, as is illustrated by the experience of the Tin Plate Workers' Union in the shipyards. As a body, by the end of the nineteenth century the Tin Plate Workers were facing competition from the Boilermakers, who had begun admitting light plate workers with a view to ultimately claiming all such work in shipyards. In 1898, this potential confrontation was averted when the Tin Plate Workers' surrendered all sheet metal work over one-eighth of an inch to the Boilermakers, establishing a demarcation line.[23] However, the Glasgow branch of the Tin Plate Workers' succeeded in protest and formed the Sheet Iron and Light Platers' Society in 1900 which, although it initially had only sixty-eight members, began to recruit in the shipyards with the declared aim of driving out their old colleagues.[24] In the north-east yards of the Tyne, Tees and Wear, relations between the two bodies deteriorated to the point that the Federation of Engineering and Shipbuilding Trades initiated an enquiry which publicly rebuked the Light Platers methods as 'wanting in the spirit of fair play and recognized trade union principles'.[25] Such criticism did not change the Platers' policy and they and the Tinplate Workers' remained bitter rivals in the yards. Both were active in Belfast and both signed the memorandum of agreement with Harland and Wolff in 1914, although one can imagine the Platers' keeping their fingers crossed while doing it.

However, it would be wrong to present inter-trade union relations in the shipyards as constantly fratricidal. Co-operation was possible and indeed the Belfast shipyards offer a good example of local tradesmen working together despite the national disagreements of their unions. One of the eighteen bodies that signed the agreement with Harland and Wolff in July 1914 was the 'Amalgamated and General Society of Carpenters'.[26] This body never existed! It appears to be a joint committee representing members of the General Union of Carpenters and Joiners and the Amalgamated Society of Carpenters and Joiners, two independent and somewhat hostile bodies. The General Union rejected amalgamation with the newer and larger Amalgamated Society in 1902, 1904 and 1907, and they were not to combine until 1921 when they came together in the Amalgamated Society of Woodworkers.[27] This committee was not a temporary negotiating body; as early as 1911 it had written to Harland and Wolff concerning employment of non-union labour.[28] Whatever the feelings at national level, the carpenters in Belfast's shipyards seemed capable of uniting for their common interests.

Although the skilled workers formed an 'elite' within the shipyards, their working conditions remained harsh and dangerous. Although seldom affected by seasonal unemployment and enjoying higher than average wages, they faced, as did all groups of shipyard workers in this period, high rates of industrial injury. In 1907, forty-eight foundry workers in every thousand were subject to industrial injury and their average life expectancy was about fifty-nine years.[29] The average life expectancy of engineers was under thirty-eight years in the 1860s and only forty-eight years by the end of the 1880s.[30] In many of the shipyard trades, physical injury and disablement was a common, and accepted, feature of working life.

> It may be taken as a fact based upon experience that artisans who are exposed to such loud noises as are made in hammering rivets suffer from deafness. Boilermakers and riveters become deaf at an early age, while their comrades engaged in other kinds of work in the shipyard do not suffer.[31]

In 1912, in the shipyards of Belfast, the Clyde and the Tyne 1,448 workers were injured and 62 killed in falls while 1,400 were injured and 15 killed by objects falling on them.[32] James Connolly knew and described the conditions in the yards:

> Our shipyards offer up a daily sacrifice of life and limb on the altar of capitalism. The clang of the ambulance bell is one of the most familiar daily sounds on the streets between our shipyards and our hospitals.
>
> It has been computed that some seventeen lives were lost on the *Titanic* before she left the Lagan; a list of maimed and hurt and of those suffering from minor injuries, as a result of the accidents at any one of these big ships would read like a roster of the wounded after a battle upon the Indian frontier.[33]

Although it might be assumed that relations between employers and unions were confrontational, there is evidence of co-operation and indeed the unions could even be called upon by the employers to maintain discipline amongst their members. On 23 February 1917, Harland and Wolff wrote to the Amalgamated Engineering Workers (AEW) accusing eighteen fitters of poor timekeeping. Two days later, the AEW official replied:

> I have gone over the names submitted to me. With regards to the last name (George Moore) I regret to say he is not responsible for his absence having only a few days ago found his last resting place.

However, on the 27th, a further letter was received by Harland's from the same official that read:

> The District Committee have decided to have the members concerned brought before them and give them a final warning. If such is needed a course will be recommended and backed up by the committee which will have the desired effect.[34]

Clearly, the Engineers had very definite views about what constituted 'proper' behaviour from their members and saw no problem in disciplining them if a legitimate complaint was received from the employer.

APPRENTICES

As a group of workers, apprentices can be seen as related to, or even part of, the skilled working class as almost every craftsman learned his trade by this process and, as previously mentioned, the major source of recruits were the sons of skilled workers. An apprenticeship usually began at the age of sixteen and in most cases lasted for five years, although carpenters, joiners and painters served six and plumbers seven years in Belfast before the war.[35] Compared to the Clyde, where opportunities for training were more plentiful, apprenticeships in Belfast often lasted longer and rates of pay were usually lower (see Table 3). Parents also had to pay a deposit to ensure their son's good behaviour of between two and five pounds, a practice abandoned on the Clyde.[36] In addition parents had to purchase the boy's tool kit which represented a considerable outlay. A shipwright's tools lost in transit in 1915 was valued by the owner at £6 11s. 4d., almost three weeks' wages.[37]

TABLE 3.
APPRENTICE PAY RATES HARLAND AND WOLFF: AUGUST 1912[38]
(Figures in brackets indicate payments/period of apprenticeship at H&W Goven yard on Clyde)

Trade	Payment in Shillings							Deposit for good behaviour
	1st	2nd	3rd	4th	5th	6th	7th	
Carpenter	5 (8)	6 (9)	8 (10)	10 (12)	12 (14)	14		£2
Joiner	4 (6)	5 (7)	6 (8)	7 (10)	8 (12)	10		£5
Polisher	4 (6)	5 (7)	6 (8)	7 (10)	8 (12)	10		£2
Patternmakers	5 (6)	6 (7)	7 (8)	8 (10)	10 (12)			£5
Angle Smiths Platers Caulkers Rivetters	8 (6)	9 (7)	10 (8)	11 (9)	12 (10)			£5
Drillers	7 (12)	8 (14)	10 (16)	12	14			£2
Plumbers	5 (6)	6 (7)	7 (8)	8 (10)	9 (12)	10 (14)	12 (16)	£2
Electricians	4 (8)	5 (9)	6 (10)	8 (12)	10 (14)			£5
Smiths	5 (7)	6 (8)	7 (10)	8 (12)	10 (14)			£2
Painters	6 (6)	7 (7)	8 (8)	9 (10)	10 (12)	15		£2

At the end of August 1919, there were 1,780 apprentices employed in the Belfast yard of Harland and Wolff, 8.9 per cent of the labour force.[39] Their status was ill-defined – on one level they were acquiring an increasing level of skill and so could be seen as moving into the elite but they were legally bound to their employers by their articles of apprenticeship. They could, and indeed were expected to, join the trade unions representing their respective skills but they were treated very much as second-class members. Apprentice electricians, for example, could only enrol in a special section, full membership being reserved for qualified craftsmen and the Boilermakers' only allowed apprentices to join for benefit purposes.[40] There were occasional revolts against such treatment, notably a major strike in 1913 that involved 1,300 apprentices from both yards,[41] but in the main the combination of employer and craftsman control kept them under a fairly rigid discipline.

SEMI-SKILLED WORKERS

Throughout British industry, there were workers who, while not undergoing a formal process of apprenticeship, had acquired 'skills' that made them difficult to replace and who as a consequence enjoyed considerable industrial power – railwaymen, miners and dockers being conspicuous examples. In the shipyards there existed a wide range of jobs, often critical to the shipbuilding process, which were in the same way 'semi-skilled'. Pollard and Robinson suggest that 60–65 per cent of the labour force in the British shipbuilding industry was skilled;[42] however, if the limited detailed information available in the Harland and Wolff papers is typical, the Belfast figure is lower at about 44 per cent. Why did this difference exist? I would suggest it is largely because a number of significant groups of semi-skilled workers have been counted with the skilled. How can we separate them? In the Harland and Wolff papers there is a letter to the city clerk of Belfast which makes it clear that skilled and semi-skilled workers were viewed as separate groups, and this with the list of 'hands employed' produced at the same time allows us to identify which groups were semi-skilled.[43] This included important groups of shipyard workers such as crane drivers, smiths' strikers, holders-up, stagers and riggers whose specialist knowledge and experience was vital to the industry. According to the August 1919 list of 'hands employed', there were 2,122 men employed in jobs that can be seen as 'semi-skilled' (10.6 per cent of the labour force); the less detailed figures for the boilershop suggest they formed 14.6 per cent of the labour force.[44] In Harland and Wolff, it is probable that about one worker in eight was 'semi-skilled' while at Workman Clark, given their more limited requirement for skilled trades, the proportion was probably slightly higher.

What was the status of such workers compared with the 'skilled' group? Clearly neither the tradesmen nor the employers considered them equal but the 'semi-skilled' performed a range of critical tasks in the yards. There is evidence that some categories of semi-skilled workers were in short supply in the Belfast shipyards. In 1919, according to figures produced by Clyde shipbuilders, holders-up in Belfast were the best paid in Britain at 31s. a week; conversely, smiths' strikers in the city received the worst wages in the industry.[45] One far from perfect indicator of social status is comparative wage rates. By late 1918, a semi-skilled rigger in Belfast earned as much as a sailmaker, a declining skilled trade. In contrast the rigger would have been earning 8.5 per cent less than a fitter, 11.5 per cent less than a shipwright and 13 per cent less than a patternmaker, although the gap had closed during the war years.⁴⁶ Stagers, another 'semi-skilled' group, were clearly less valued and earned only 54.4 per cent of a patternmaker's weekly wage in 1913.⁴⁷ If the wage rates at Harland and Wolff are examined it is clear that the hierarchy of skills within the yard can be seen in terms of pay. The patternmakers, the elite of the skilled trades in a shipyard, were paid more than essential groups such as fitters, who, in turn, were paid more than declining trades such as shipwrights and sailmakers, while the 'semi-skilled' riggers were clearly more highly valued than the stagers (see Table 4). The effects of labour shortages and dilution during the First World War appear to have greatly benefited the 'semi-skilled' and in comparative terms their wages increased dramatically. The nine groups of workers in this category were paid between 59s. 6d. (the same rate as a general labourer) and 78s. 3d. for a standard forty-seven-hour week in April 1920 and it was noted that all were receiving an additional 12.5 per cent for working seventy-two hours at that time.⁴⁸ The 'semi-skilled' represent a very diverse group of workers within the labour force whose status varied from those seen, and paid, as little better than labourers to others such as stagers and irondressers whose wages approached those of skilled workers. Some categories such as cranemen and machinemen were clearly very broad as they included both individuals being paid as labourers and others earning rates comparable with skilled workers.

The 'intermediate' nature of the semi-skilled within the shipyards can be seen by looking at their trade union affiliations. Some groups were admitted by the craft unions; the Boilermakers', for example, always recruited holders-up whose work was critical in the riveting process, while the Electricians' organized the temporary light men.⁴⁹ Other groups formed local unions, such as the Belfast Ship Riggers Protective Society, but by the early twentieth century there was a tendency for these groups to amalgamate into national bodies or be absorbed by craft unions.⁵⁰

By the First World War, the main union representing the 'semi-skilled', and indeed the unskilled, in the shipyards of Belfast was the National Amalgamated Union of Labour (NAUL), a body established in the Tyneside shipyards to protect platers' helpers and others who were directly employed by craftsmen belonging to the Boilermakers' Union rather than the shipyards.⁵² These tensions between skilled craftsmen and their 'semi-skilled' helpers were also to be found in the shipyards of the Lagan. In the same year as the NAUL was established on the Tyne over 200 platers' helpers and rivet heaters struck in Belfast against the platers, with the strikers insisting they had no grievance against the

TABLE 4.
WAGE RATES OF SKILLED/SEMI-SKILLED WORKERS IN HARLAND AND WOLFF[51]

Date	Patternmaker	Fitter	Shipwright	Sailmaker	Rigger	Stager
1897	38s.	36s.	37s. 1.5d.	32s.	30s.	
1898	39s.	37s.	38s. 3d.	32s.	30s. 6d.	19s.
1903	39s.	36s.	37s. 1.5d.	32s.	30s. 6d.	19s. 6d. (1899)
1906	39s.	37s.				
1908	40s.	37s.				
1911	41s.(Mar)	38s.	40s. 6d.	33s.	31s. 6d.	20s.
	42s.(Oct)	39s.				
1912	43s.	40s.	40s. 6d.	36s.	33s. 6d.	21s.
						22s.
1913	44s.	41s.	40s. 6d.	36s.	33s. 6d.	24s.
1915	47s. (Feb)	44s.	46s.	39s.	38s. 6d.	
	49s. (Sept)	46s.	47s.	41s.	40s. 6d.	
1916	52s.	49s.	50s.	44s.	43s. 6d.	
1917	57s. (Apr)	54s.	55s.	49s.	48s. 6d.	
	60s. (Aug)	57s.	58s.	52s.	51s. 6d.	
	65s. (Dec)	62s.	63s.	57s.	56s. 6d.	
1918	68s. 6d. (Aug)	65s.6d.	66s. 6d.	60s. 6d.	60s.	

employers.[53] There were similar outbreaks of industrial unrest between craftsmen and helpers in 1892, 1893, 1894, 1897 and 1900 in the Belfast shipyards.[54] Given the *raison d'être* of the NAUL and its record of confrontation with craft bodies, it was hardly surprising that the latter were rather slow and begrudging in accepting that the semi-skilled had the right to unionize. The NAUL was not admitted to the Federation of Engineering and Shipbuilding Trades until 1908 and the even more 'labourer'-focused National Union of Gasworkers and General Labourers was not permitted to join until 1910. Even when they were admitted it was expected that they should 'know their place', and the refusal of the Workers Union to 'give assurances' to the Engineers resulted in their expulsion from the Federation.[55] The NAUL was not amongst those who signed the Articles of Agreement with Harland and Wolff in 1914. Did the craft unions object, was demarcation not seen as an issue or did the employers see the semi-skilled as easily replaceable?

The relationship with the employers was complex; the NAUL had successfully unionized a large proportion of the non-craft labour force and, even if it did not represent craftsmen, it had to be treated with respect. In 1911, the union wrote to the management of Harland and Wolff enclosing a copy of a resolution which had been passed by their members working in the firm's foundry:

> After the 4th of October, we, the individual members of the National Amalgamated Union of Labour, employed as labourers, iron dressers, cranemen, etc., employed in Messrs Harland and Wolff's foundry department, will cease to work with any person employed in said department who is eligible to become a member but who on the aforesaid date has not joined the National Amalgamated Union of Labour.[56]

The response of the company to this uncompromising demand for the imposition of a closed shop amongst semi-skilled and unskilled workers in a critical area was both moderate and conciliatory.

> As you are aware, the firm have always fully recognized the various trade and labour unions, and have endeavoured to work amicably with them, and we are somewhat surprised that your members should take this step. We hope, however, that on further consideration they will see some other way out of the difficulty.[57]

Harland's clearly distinguished between 'trade' and 'labour' unions but emphasized that they tried to work with both groups, an indication perhaps that the NAUL was strong enough in the yard to present a threat? Certainly, the relationship between Harland's and the NAUL was reasonably positive and, as with the skilled bodies, co-operation was extended by both sides. In 1913 the company wrote to the union.

> We regret having to complain of the bad timekeeping of the platers' helpers and the angle iron smiths' helpers. From one fourth to one third of the platers' helpers are absent every morning, and quite a number absent every day. The angle smiths' helpers are even worse. We should be glad if you can do anything to effect an improvement.[58]

The union's reply, while making the point that members of another union (the smiths' helpers) had a worse record than their own (the platers' helpers), was not in any way antagonistic or defensive. Enclosed was a copy of a notice which the union had sent to every platers' helper in the yard.

For some time past, the firm has strongly complained about bad time keeping on the part of a large section of our helper members. So bad has this become of late that they have decided on taking drastic action to deal with this evil unless there is a marked change in the immediate future. No union can defend bad timekeeping and we therefore hope this warning will have the desired effect.[59]

UNSKILLED LABOUR IN THE BELFAST SHIPYARDS

As an industrial process, iron and steel shipbuilding was dependent on skilled labour, but over a third of the labour force was classified as unskilled. General and specialist labourers, craftsmens' assistants, cleaners, storemen and watchmen formed a vital element in the yards. As a group many of them were casually employed and, unlike the semi-skilled, they had little skill or knowledge that was not easily, or cheaply, replaceable. Indeed, unlike some shipbuilding regions, Belfast always enjoyed a surplus of unskilled labour with the result that, in contrast to the skilled workers who were in scarce supply, the wages of the city's shipyard labourers were amongst the lowest in the industry.[60] If we are looking for the classic exploited proletariat in the shipyards of Belfast, it is amongst the ranks of the unskilled that we will find them.

On the morning of 28 March 1911, a member of the office staff of Harland and Wolff passed a note to William Pirrie, the firm's managing director:

> Mr Strachan rang up this morning to speak to me, and when I got to the phone I found it was Mr Clark. He referred to the question of shipyard labourers wages, and said they proposed if we have no objection, to give some of their men a 1/- and others a 6d. rise, and he thought that if H&W gave only 6d. it would make the rates more level.[61]

As well as giving an interesting insight into the working relationship between Harland and Wolff and Workman Clark, who were often presented as bitter rivals, this note also provides an example of the management technique of the time. Pirrie wrote his reply/decision on the bottom of the note.

> If Messers Workman Clark & Co grant an advance of 6d. per week I am disposed to advocate our doing the same rather than that there should be any feeling of discontent on the part of our men.[62]

The matter then appeared to be passed to Samuel Bartlett in the pay office, who offered the following warning about potential costs.

> We have at the present time 589 labourers, watchmen, sweepers and storemen, leading rate 18/6 per week; if they got an advance the following would also be looking for the same.

Shipyard
363 Scrapers
202 Fitters' Assistants
238 Plumbers' Assistants
206 Wood Labourers
15 Carters' Assistants
4 Sailmakers' Assistants
111 Labourers' in the Electrical Department

Engine Works
Boilermakers' Assistants
739 Fitters' Assistants
76 Coppersmiths' Assistants
116 Labourers
29 Wood Labourers

What Bartlett was saying was that if Harland and Wolff gave its 3,324 unskilled workers an increase of 6d. a week, this would add just over £83 a week to the firm's wages bill! Of course, we must remember that the 'leading rate' of 18s. 6d. was paid for a full fifty-four-hour week, but short-time or absence could drastically reduce the wages of the unskilled worker in the yard. On 30 June 1911 Samuel Bartlett made a note of payments made to 216 plumbers' assistants; two of them had received over the leading rate (20s. 6d. and 19s. 6d.), 141 had received between 15s. and 18s., sixty-five had 10s. to 14s. and eight less than 10s.[63]

On the basis of Bartlett's unusually complete list, it appears likely that something under 40 per cent of the labour force in Harland and Wolff were unskilled. In 1920, when more complete figures are available, we know that employment in the shipyard had increased to 7,423 unskilled, including 641 boys, and they formed 37 per cent of the labour force.[64] In the engine works, the figure is more difficult to assess, due to the way the figures were compiled, but it seems likely that, as in 1911, the proportion of unskilled labour was higher, perhaps up to 50 per cent of those employed there. Workman Clark once again may have had a slightly higher proportion of unskilled due to their production pattern but, taken overall, a figure of 40–45 per cent of the total shipyard labour force seems likely. The labour shortages and dilution during the First World War appear to have benefited unskilled even more than the 'semi-skilled'; the letter to the council discussed earlier showed that labourers' wages had increased to 59s. 6d. for a standard forty-seven-hour week in April 1920 and it was noted that all were receiving an additional 12.5 per cent for working seventy-two hours at that time.[65] By this stage the shipyards were so desperate for labour and the wages being paid had reached such a level that many 'non-shipyard' workers were drawn into the labour force, as Beattie found when he interviewed an elderly barber in the 1990s:

> After the war Arthur Pollock put the barber's shop up for sale, he was moving to the shipyard. That's how good the work was in those days in the shipyard. Men would leave a business to go work in it. I took the shop over.[66]

The difference between the skilled and unskilled labour forces in the shipyards was not simply economic, barriers of status ensured that the two groups remained divided. This division was often marked by ill-feeling, as illustrated by a series of interviews conducted by Sam Hanna-Bell for a radio programme on the Belfast dock strike, 'Neither Wheel nor Hand', transmitted in February 1959.[67] Bob Getgood was a union official who offered some very telling comments on the relationship between skilled and unskilled workers in the shipyards:

> And there was craft pride – I must give him credit for his craft pride. But he hadn't the broad human touch of the other fellow who carried the mud for him, carried the mortar to him, carried the machine – so I have found in the shipyard – got into the hole and with the seat of his pants cleaned the part of the boat and got thruppence for cleaning it. And when the skilled man went in after it was cleaned he got a shilling for working in a dirty corner.
>
> There was no association. The labourers herded together, went off together. But an odd one would have curried favour with a foreman but much more likely to be currying favour with his skilled employee or his fellow employee. He was anxious to be on good terms with him because his job was more secure. He felt that if he could be on good terms with the craftsmen then his value to the craftsmen was seen and if a choice had to be made, he was likely to be retained in preference to the fellow who was probably a better man but harder to work with.[68]

The resentment could have deeper reasons than this, as William Hunter, who had worked as a carter in 1907, recalled:

> There was an antagonism between craft and unskilled ... The craftsman he had something the other unfortunate soul didn't have. Now that came about due to the fact that the parents could afford to put their child to a trade they were all human-they were equal in every other way-but their parents could not afford to put them to a trade.[69]

The control of employment by skilled workers could sometimes result in abuses, as a letter to the manager of Hartland and Wolff's engineering works by the Transport and General Workers Union in July 1924 highlights:

> I am instructed to bring to your notice a practice which is being adopted by the department you control, i.e. tradesmen are being given labourers' work. You will realize that it is not quite fair treatment for these labourers, who are members of our union, to have to stand looking for employment whilst tradesmen belonging to another union are engaged to do their work.[70]

Two weeks later, the firm replied that the T&G must have been 'misinformed' and claimed that there were no skilled men employed as labourers, although they were hardly going to antagonize craftsmen by attempting to stop a practice which also benefited the firm by allowing it to retain its skilled labour at a time of reduced demand.

WHITE COLLAR WORKERS

If timekeepers, pay office staff, the drawing office, foremen and such staff as messengers and porters are included, the 'office' at Harland and Wolff in late 1919 contained about 5 per cent of the total workforce.[71] Many of these workers came from the middle or upper-working class and, in many cases, were highly trained and experienced supervisors and technicians. It was considered a 'step-up' if an apprentice on completing his training was taken 'upstairs' into the office. Certainly, in terms of status, the office staff perceived themselves as being above those employed in the yards and works. The comparative status of some groups of office workers can be seen by their rates of pay; draughtsmen in Harland and Wolff earned average wages of between £5 3s. and £5 9s. in August 1919, depending on the department in which they worked.[72] Two years later the same firm paid its clerks, who served a five-year apprenticeship, between £6 11s. (one individual) and £3 6s. (sixteen individuals) with an average payment of £4 2s. 2d. a week.[73] In August 1914 the seventy-five timekeepers employed by Harland and Wolff earned between 22s. 6d. and 55s. but by August 1918 the ninety-five employed there earned between 54s. and 89s., with an average of 67s., having received seven increments totalling 27s. during the war.[74]

There was a definite hierarchy within the 'office' with the top echelon being formed by the managers who actually ran the yard; in Harland and Wolff this group numbered fifty-four in late 1919. Below them came the supervisory grades, head and assistant foremen and storekeepers, highly trained and experienced individuals who effectively ran the works and yards on a day-to-day basis and in late 1919 Harland and Wolff employed 136 in these grades. The drawing office and pay office were critical to the shipbuilding process and the running of the yard, and in late 1919 Harland's had 330 in the drawing office and 161 in the pay office. Clerical support was necessary and in 1919 Harland's employed 453 individuals in this grade (including typists), a modest 1.6 per cent of the total labour force. To such a compact administrative organization can be added the twenty-two staff in the dining room, six hall porters and 101 porters and messengers.[75]

As a group, the 'office' workers in the Belfast shipyards were slow to unionize; comparatively good conditions combined with vulnerability to victimization made union membership less attractive than for other groups of workers. However, during the war some progress was made. By late 1918, Harland and Wolff were discussing war bonus payments with the National Union of Clerks, and meetings continued to be held with this body after the war.[76] In 1920 this union appointed a full-time official in Belfast, where it was noted 'there was a substantial membership in the shipbuilding industry'.[77] The Association of Shipbuilding and Engineering Draughtsmen was active in Belfast from late 1916 and by the following year was strong enough to claim two members at national meetings rather than the usual one.[78] There were various unions formed to represent foremen and other supervisory staff during the war years, but none of these were ever to be recognized by the Shipbuilders' Federation.[79] There certainly appears to have been at least one local body representing staff in Harland and Wolff in the form of the Foreman's Mutual Aid and Social Society. A letter to the management during the 1919 strike, however, would indicate that this was not a particularly militant body.

> I am instructed by a number of foremen and assistants in your employ to inform you that they were turned back by pickets on the Queen's Road this morning and informed that this was the only

warning they would receive and if they persisted on going, it would be at their own risk. Hoping this will be a satisfactory explanation of our absence from work.[80]

WOMEN

A final group of workers within the Belfast shipbuilding industry are frequently forgotten. Although employment in the yards was predominantly male, it was by no means exclusively so and women formed part of the labour force. As conscription was never introduced in Ireland there was never the need to introduce female labour in the shipbuilding and engineering industries in Belfast on the scale seen in other regions. However, a report dated July 1916 shows that 163 women were working in the yard (1.7 per cent of the labour force). No detail is given as to the nature of their employment but they are clearly not 'office' workers. They might have been unskilled cleaners or workers from skilled groups such as upholsterers or French polishers which contained a large proportion of women. The only groups for which details are given are waitresses (nineteen) and charwomen (twenty-two) who presumably worked in the offices rather than the yard.[81]

The employment of women within the yards and works may have been a temporary response to wartime labour shortages, but the 'office' of the shipyards had always contained women. In the drawing offices, tracers were often women, typists were another group increasingly, but by no means exclusively, female and female clerical workers became more common during the war. Moss and Hume note that the last workers in Harland and Wolff to suffer during the 'expulsions' were female, four waitresses in the staff dining room who were driven out on 27 August 1920.[82]

INDUSTRIAL RELATIONS IN THE BELFAST SHIPYARDS

The picture of industrial peace and harmony presented by Moss and Hume in their history of Harland and Wolff as being typical of the pre-war era was shattered by the engineering strike of January to February 1919.[83] Was this a new departure in industrial relations in the Belfast shipyards, the end of the pre-war golden era and the start of more troubled times? There were pressures within the industry for good industrial relations, skilled labour was in short supply and any disruption in work due to industrial disputes could result in delays and penalties on contracts. Against this there existed, as I have already described, a range of internal frictions and conflicts which were beyond the companies' direct control, such as the inter-union demarcation disputes for which Harland and Wolff negotiated the Articles of Agreement to try and control. I would argue that Hume and Moss go too far in presenting the pre-war era as trouble-free: industrial relations were indeed comparatively good but there was more industrial action than they admit.

The statement that 'the Company's industrial relations had been remarkably good since the 1895 strike' is, to say the least, open to question. The 1895 dispute itself suggests that relations were not as harmonious as the official history of the firm suggests. The origin of the dispute lay in a carefully co-ordinated campaign by the shipyard owners of the Clyde and Lagan to force the unions to accept bargaining procedures covering both areas.[84] The strike collapsed in the face of determined management action, but resistance was slow to crumble in the Belfast yards. There the workers refused to return to work and accused the Clyde members of betrayal, and only the union's withdrawal of strike benefit finally forced the Belfast shipyard workers to accept the union's decision.[85]

Prior to the 1895 strike, Moss and Hume mention only two major strikes in the period since 1880: in 1884 on the question of wage reductions and in 1886 in response to the Home Rule Bill.[86] This appears a very creditable record but is it complete? Given the tensions within the labour force this seems unlikely. There was certainly a one-month stoppage which affected the shipyards in 1887 in protest against the introduction of fortnightly pay amongst engineers and boilermakers.[87] The history of the boilermakers, confirmed by the Board of Trade reports, shows another strike involving 5,000 men in 1888.[88] The Board of Trade reports contain at least seventeen industrial disputes which affected the Belfast shipyards between 1888 and 1894, many of them being highly disruptive demarcation disputes. In addition, there was another dispute which was not noted by the Board of Trade but which was mentioned in the Report of the Factory Inspector as part of a general description of conditions in Belfast in 1892.[89] After 1895, there continued to be disputes in the shipyards, some of which are difficult to dismiss as 'trivial'. After 1901, only 'major' disputes were reported by the Board of Trade and yet there were still eight disputes in the shipyards worthy of record.[90]

The labour force in the shipyards of Belfast represents a highly complex social organization as well as an industrial one, with many divisions and antagonisms within it. Although the firms' historians have attempted to show industrial relations within Harland and Wolff were good, the company was certainly not free of problems, notably demarcation disputes, within the workforce. This pattern of relationships was not unique to Belfast, but rather was typical of British industry as a whole at this time. In the shipyards of the Lagan sectarianism may, on occasion, have sharpened the ill-feelings between individuals, but religious belief did not create these divisions. It was the perceived status of differing groups and the social chasms between 'office' and 'yard' or between skilled and unskilled workers that created the web of often antagonistic relationships in the yards, to a far greater degree than religious affiliation. Industrial relations were shaped by these internal tensions. Management, for pragmatic reasons, sought to avoid industrial disputes which might delay completion of vessels and incur penalty charges. Harland and Wolff's 'Articles of Agreement' of 1914 make perfect sense in this context, an attempt to defuse disputes between groups of skilled workers rather than between employer and labour. Industrial relations in the Belfast shipyards were surprisingly good and the employers made great efforts to stay on good terms with their workers and the unions that represented them. However, the picture of paternalistic harmony offered by Moss and Hume overstates this as there were situations that the company was simply unable to control, as when the shipwrights and carpenters fought about work! As with all major industrial concerns, employment practices and industrial relations within the shipyards were highly complex, and while it may be tempting to present the story in terms of employers versus workers, this would be both unjust and misleading.

NOTES

1. UK, Scottish, English and Irish data taken from *1901 Census General Report, Table 55*; Belfast Data from *Census, Ireland 1881, 1891, 1901*.
2. John Lynch, 'Harland and Wolff: its labour force and industrial relations, autumn 1919', *Saothar*, vol. 22 (1997), p. 47; John Lynch, *Forgotten Shipbuilders of Belfast: Workman Clark, 1880–1935* (Belfast: 2004), p. vi.
3. *Belfast Trade Directory* (Belfast: 1904 and 1914).
4. Harland and Wolff (H&W) Papers, Public Record Office of Northern Ireland (PRONI) D2805/TUR/13-15 – Statement of Timekeeping, w/e 10 March 1915.
5. Workman Clark (1928) Ltd, *Shipbuilding at Belfast* (Belfast: 1933), p. 10.
6. Harland and Wolff Papers (PRONI) D2805/TUR/29-30 – Hands Employed w/e 27/8/1919.
7. Ibid., Hands Employed in Engine Works, 28 June 1919.
8. Ibid., Administrative Workers in Belfast, 22 December 1919.
9. J.R. Hume and M.S. Moss, *Shipbuilders to the World: 125 Years of Harland and Wolff, Belfast, 1861–1986* (Belfast: 1986), p. 168. The 1895 strike was provoked by a management attempt to force joint bargaining procedures on shipbuilding unions on the Lagan and Clyde. When the Belfast workers struck, the Clyde yards began a progressive lock-out of their workers in support of the Belfast employers.
10. Ibid., pp. 170–7. This agreement represented an almost unique attempt within the industry to improve industrial relations by compulsory negotiations prior to industrial action.
11. S. Pollard and P. Robertson, *The British Shipbuilding Industry, 1870–1914* (Cambridge, Mass: 1979), p. 154.

12. H&W Papers (PRONI) 27/8/1919, 28/6/1919.
13. Pollard and Robertson, *British Shipbuilding*, p. 55.
14. British Parliamentary Papers (BPP) *Working class rents, housing and Retail Prices* [3864] cvii 1908, pp. 62–9, 75–80, 239–44, 311–17, 318–25, 421–7, 436–9, 446–52, 531–7, 539–42, 546–70.
15. H&W Papers (PRONI) 1/9/1919.
16. A. Tuckett, *The Blacksmiths' History* (London: 1974), p. 212.
17. J.B. Jefferys, *The Story of the Engineers, 1800–1945* (London: 1946), p. 45.
18. BPP, *Royal Commission on Labour: Third Report Shipbuilding* [6894] cccii 1893–4, Question 24.
19. BPP, *Board of Trade Reports on Strikes and Lockouts*.
20. J.O. Mosses, *The History of the Pattern Makers' Association* (London: 1927), pp. 99–100.
21. BPP, *Board of Trade Report of Strikes and Lockouts* (1892).
22. Mosses, *Pattern Makers*, p.100.
23. A.T. Kidd (comp.), *History of the Tin Plate Workers and Sheet Metal Workers and Braziers Societies* (London: 1949), p. 169.
24. A. Marsh and V. Ryan, *Historical Directory of Trades Unions*, vol. 2 (Aldershot: 1984), pp. 122–3.
25. Kidd, *Tin Plate Workers*, p. 179.
26. Hume and Moss, *Shipbuilders*, pp. 170–2.
27. Marsh and Ryan, *Directory of Trade Unions*, vol. 3 (Aldershot: 1987), pp. 21–2, 24–5.
28. H&W Papers (PRONI), April 1911.
29. H.J. Fyrth and H. Collins, *The Foundry Workers* (Manchester: 1959), pp. 114–15.
30. Jefferys, *Engineers*, pp. 66–7.
31. T. Oliver, 'Effects of concussion on air', in T. Oliver (ed.), *Dangerous Trades* (London: 1902), p. 752.
32. BPP, *Report of the Secretary of State for the Home Department on Accidents Occurring in Shipbuilding Yards* [7046] LX, 1913, p. 3.
33. James Connolly, 'Belfast and its problems', in James Connolly, *Collected Works*, vol. 1 (Dublin: 1987), p. 233.
34. H&W Papers (PRONI), February 1917, correspondence with AEW.
35. Ibid., 17 August 1912, letter from Govan shipyard.
36. Ibid.
37. Ibid., early 1915.
38. H&W Papers (PRONI), 17 August 1912.

1 box	12s. 0d.	1 Saw	6s. 6d.	1 Jack Saw	4s. 6d.	1 Hand Plane	3s .6d.
1 Pap Plane	1s. 9d.	1 Maul	3s. 6d.	1 Foot Edge	4s. 0d.	1 Screw Augre	10s.0d.
Ratchet Brace	7s. 6d.	1 Set of Bits	16s. 0d.	2 Augre bits	2s. 9d.	1 Square	2s. 6d.
1 Hammer	2s. 0d.	Caulking Mallet	3s.6d.	Caulking Irons (9)	9s. 0d.	Opening Iron	2s. 0d.
Set of Gouges	12s. 0d.	Set of Chisels	14s.0d.	Dooling Bit	1s. 6d.	Expanding Bit	9s.10d.
2 Cutters		Spokeshave	3s. 0d.	Total Cost of Outfit = £6 11s. 4d.			

39. Ibid., 27 August 1919.
40. W.C. Stevens, *The Story of the Electrical Trades' Union* (London: 1952), p. 60; J.E. Mortimer, *History of the Boilermakers' Society*, vol. 1 (London: 1973), p. 122.
41. BPP, *Board of Trade: Strikes and Lock Outs* (1913).
42. Pollard and Robertson, *British Shipbuilding*, p. 153.
43. H&W Papers (PRONI), 'Letter to Town Clerk of Belfast', 19 April 1920.
44. Ibid., 28 June 1919, 20 June 1919.
45. Ibid., 29 August 1911.
46. Ibid., September 1919.
47. Ibid., 28 February 1919.
48. Ibid., 19 April 1920.

Cranemen	59s. 6d. – 72s.	Iron Dressers	68s. 6d.
Smiths' Strikers	63s. 6d.	Temporary Lightmen	62s.
Firemen	63s.	Drillers (semi skilled)	69s. 3d.
Donkey Boilermen	63s.	Machinemen	59s. 6d. – 78s.
Stagers	66s. 6d.		

49. Stevens, *Electrical Trades Union*, p. 60; Mortimer, *Boilermakers' Society*, p. 122.
50. Sarah Ward-Perkins (ed.), *Select Guide to Trade Union Records in Dublin* (Dublin: 1996), p. 241. Belfast Riggers' Protective Society was founded in 1890 and dissolved in 1904.
51. H&W Papers (PRONI), 28 February 1913, September 1919.
52. H.A. Clegg and A.F. Thompson, *History of British Trade Unions since 1889* (Oxford: 1964), p. 66.
53. BPP, *Board of Trade Strikes and Lock Outs* (1889).
54. Ibid.
55. K. Coates and T. Topham, *The History of the Transport and General Workers Union*, vol. 1 (Oxford: 1991), pt. 2, p. 513.
56. H&W Papers (PRONI), 2 December 1911.
57. Ibid., 3 December 1911.
58. Ibid., 21 June 1913.
59. Ibid., 26 June 1913.
60. Ibid., 29 August 1911.
61. Ibid., 11 March 1911.
62. Ibid.
63. Ibid., 30 June 1911.
64. Ibid., 27 April 1920.
65. Ibid., 19 April 1920.
66. G. Beattie, *We are the People* (London: 1993), p. 113.
67. Sam Hanna-Bell Papers (PRONI), D3358/1.
68. Ibid., interview with Bob Getgood.
69. Ibid., interview with William Hunter.
70. H&W Papers (PRONI), 10 July 1924.
71. Ibid., 22 December 1911.
72. Ibid., 19 December 1919.
73. Ibid., 18 August 1921.
    Payments to apprentice clerks in Harland and Wolff:
    1st year 8s.
    2nd year 10s.
    3rd year 12s.
    4th year 15s.
    5th year 20s.
74. Ibid., letter to NUC, late 1918.
75. Ibid., 22 December 1919.
76. Ibid., undated but late 1918; 15 October 1921.
77. F. Hughes, *By Hand and Brain: The Story of the Clerical and Administrative Workers' Union* (London: 1953), p. 64.
78. J. E. Mortimer, *A History of the Association of Shipbuilding and Engineering Draughtsmen* (London: 1960), pp. 28, 39.
79. A. Marsh and V. Ryan, *Directory of Trade Unions*, vol. 1 (Aldershot: 1980): Amalgamated Managers' and Foreman's Society, pp. 4–5; National Foreman's Association, pp. 40–1; Association of Supervisory Staffs, Executives and Technicians, p. 151.
80. H&W Papers (PRONI), 28 January 1919.
81. Ibid., 31 July 1916.
82. Hume and Moss, *Shipbuilders*, p. 225. Although Catholic workers were the main focus of attention, it should be remembered that left-wing activists and other 'rotten-prods' formed almost a quarter of those expelled. The response of the labour movement to these events did them little credit; only the Amalgamated Society of Carpenters and Joiners attempted to use strike action to get their members reinstated but this call was largely ignored in Belfast.
83. For an account of this strike in Belfast, see Austen Morgan, *Labour and Partition* (London: 1991), pp. 229–49.
84. J. Dougan, *The Shipwrights* (Newcastle, 1958), p. 94.
85. Jefferys, *Engineers*, p. 141.
86. Hume and Moss, *Shipbuilders*, pp. 49, 55.
87. Henry Patterson, *Class, Conflict and Sectarianism: the Protestant Working Class and the Belfast Labour Movement, 1868–1920* (Belfast: 1980), p. 26.
88. Mortimer, *History*, p. 112; BPP, *Board of Trade Report on Strikes and Lockouts*, 1888.
89. BPP, *Report of the Factories and Workshops Inspector*, 1832.
90. BPP, *Board of Trade Reports of Strikes and Lockouts*.

10

The IRA and Trade Unionism, 1922–72

BRIAN HANLEY

During July 1922, with the Civil War between republican and pro-Treaty forces a month old, the assistant chief of staff of the anti-Treaty IRA, Ernie O'Malley, contacted his Dublin adjutant with a request relating to organized labour. He suggested making some arrangement with the Irish Citizen Army (ICA) or 'Roddy Connolly's men', the small communist group, for the purpose of effecting 'something' with regard to the trade unions.[1] He argued that it was 'essential' workers be 'prevented' from aiding the Free State in any way, such as through the movement of troops and munitions by rail and that the ICA and 'Connolly's bunch' might also be useful in gathering intelligence for the anti-Treatyites. Eventually a section of the Citizen's Army agreed to co-operate and supplied the IRA with lists of sympathetic men working on ships, railways and in the printing trade.[2] That the IRA felt that it needed to approach two small and effectively marginal organizations for a link to organized workers illustrates a long-standing difficulty in the organization's relationship with trade unionism. That the IRA leadership considered that if persuasion failed that force might be utilized illustrates another problem in the organization's relationship with labour.

How does a military body, with a defined aim – the overthrow of the Free State and/or the ending of partition – interact with organizations containing workers of a variety of political views who are essentially organized in defence of their immediate working conditions? How does a secret organization that demands military discipline from its members interact with broader democratic, if flawed, organizations? These problems would dog the IRA's attempts to become involved in trade union struggle. Not surprisingly, the organization's greatest efforts to engage with trade unionism have come in periods when the left within the IRA was in the ascendant – the late 1920s/early 1930s and the 1960s. In both eras there was a tendency towards using military methods in support of industrial struggle. During the 1960s, however, the organization began to map out a more coherent plan towards gaining influence within the labour movement.

'IRISH LABOUR FOR THE REPUBLIC'

Writing from Mountjoy gaol during August 1922, Liam Mellows expressed the desire that republicans should make a determined effort to reach the ranks of organized workers. Famously, he argued that 'we should certainly keep Irish labour for the Republic: it will possibly be the biggest factor on our side. Anything that will prevent Irish labour becoming Imperialist and 'respectable' will help the Republic.'[3]Mellows also contended that 'the official labour movement has deserted the people for the fleshpots of the empire'.[4] Mellows' belief that the Irish working class was predisposed towards support for republicanism and only held back by a treacherous leadership would continue to inform IRA thinking. However, it was only after both Mellows' death and defeat in the Civil War that some in the IRA tried to put his words into practice. As the organization sought to rebuild itself during the 1920s it increasingly reflected on the reasons for its defeat. When the IRA took control of *An Phoblacht* during 1926 it was decided that the paper should take a 'very friendly attitude' to labour from then on.[5]

The thinking behind the IRA's attitude to recent trade union history was outlined in two Army Council documents written during 1927. In the first, *Notes on the Irish Labour Movement*, the author argued that, prior to 1914, outside of James Connolly and the ICA there was 'little revolutionary thinking in Irish workers as such'. However, after Connolly's martyrdom in 1916 his teaching became a feature of the rising tide of national feeling. The Irish Transport and General Workers Union (ITGWU), because of its association with Connolly, came to be seen as a 'special arm' of 'Ireland's fight against England'. As a result the union grew rapidly, recruiting in both rural and urban areas. Initially many small farmers, 'admirers of Connolly', had joined the ITGWU, but the hostility of urban workers had eventually forced them out of the union. Small farmers found themselves at meetings where the overwhelming opinion was behind resolutions debarring farmers or farmers' sons from getting work in the towns until the unemployed had first been looked after. Within unions which were British-based, 'Connollyites' forged an alliance with the republican movement, but cross-channel control held them back from greater involvement. The labour movement failed to knit itself closely with the national revolutionary movement and was unable to define its direction. The blame for this was primarily laid at the feet of Thomas Johnson, who had aligned the trade unions with the 'middle-class outlook' which 'passes for Labour in England'. The Labour leadership remained obsessed with its finances and organizational strength at the expense of the national revolution. However, when the War of Independence began, the 'most rebellious spirits' in the unions, both rank and file and officials, joined the IRA, while the 'nervous' and 'weak' collected around Johnson, whose 'anemic liberalism' dominated Labour politics. After 1921 Johnson and his allies supported the Treaty, and organized trade union meetings advocating pacifism. This not merely alienated republicans but enraged the workers who formed the 'great mass' of the IRA. In 1922, Johnston associated the Labour Party with the Free State government and, in 1923, in 'an impassioned outburst' actually encouraged them to persist in their policy of executions.[6]

These views were echoed in a second army council document, *General Outline of the Present Movement*, written in August 1927. This argued that Johnson and his colleague, William O'Brien, were not only 'anything but revolutionary' but also active supporters of Free State repression. They had, the author conceded, uttered some 'very mild protests' about coercion, but even though many of the victims of the 'wayside murders' and executions were trade unionists, Labour remained solidly behind the Free State. This was because the supporters of the Labour Party were mainly 'those people who were afraid of another war' while being not necessarily wholeheartedly pro-Treaty. Labour's supporters were for the most part the 'small shopkeepers, small farmers and the well to do working class'. The IRA, however, was 'almost solely composed of workers and peasants' and that section of the population 'for the most part' continued to support the republican movement. Labour's position on the Treaty could not be said to reflect the views of most workers.[7] Both documents claimed that the IRA had high hopes for the return of Jim Larkin from the United States during 1923; 'every republican looked to him for help, expecting he would assist in the revolutionary movement.' In the internment camps, prisoners came up with 'comprehensive schemes' to collect volunteers behind Larkin. This 'wonderful opportunity' was squandered when Larkin arrived in Ireland in a 'maudlin, sentimental mood' and urged the IRA to surrender their arms 'into Mrs Pearse's lap'. Indeed Larkin had, on arrival in Ireland, called for a truce and then for the IRA to give up its weapons.[8] The IRA claimed that this had 'finished Larkin in the eyes of republicans'. Having failed to secure his old position of leadership, Larkin formed a rival union to the ITGWU and engaged the two bodies in a war with each other, leading to the formation of the Workers Union of Ireland (WUI). The IRA concluded that Larkin's power was dead – 'he has got as far as any man with his weapons could hope to reach' – and that his personality rendered him incapable of revolutionary leadership.[9]

This meant that the IRA's task was now to collect 'the broken industrial movement' around a nuclei of their units around Ireland. The IRA rejected 'the old trade union idea' that urban workers were sufficient to rescue the country from imperialism. In fact the Irish rural masses, the 'peasantry', were the potentially decisive force. It was they who comprised the vast majority of the IRA and the organization must organize them, eventually establishing a close-knit peasant union. The basis for this organization would be found in resistance to land annuities collected annually for England. A militant campaign by farmers of refusing to pay the annuities would lead to clashes with bailiffs and the police. The IRA would intervene militarily on the side of the defaulters and make it impossible for annuities to be collected. The government would have to attempt to use the Free State army to maintain order and the IRA would appeal to this force's essentially 'peasant' rank and file to refuse these orders. Confiscated cattle and other animals might be brought to the towns for export, but here the IRA would appeal to workers to refuse to transport livestock. Dockers would be asked to refuse to handle herds that include any of the seized animals.

This ambitious plan would be furthered by the IRA using its 'leverage' within the transport union to 'seize it'. They would then take back to that union the elements that had followed Larkin into the WUI. The IRA would 'stiffen the resolve' of the ITGWU by placing its members in pivotal positions as officials. Armed groups would be formed inside the union's structures. Fusion between workers and rural organizations was a long-term aim but was not to be attempted until the trade unions had first shown real solidarity with the farmers and rural labour. A revolutionary situation might then be brought about by 'district committees of workers and peasants' under the control of the IRA that would be a step on the road to a revolutionary government.[10]

These documents reflected the thinking of army council member Peadar O'Donnell in particular, hence the rural focus and suspicion of both the trades unions and the Labour Party. They were possibly written in order to win support from the Comintern, with which the IRA was developing links and, therefore, consciously played down both the importance of Larkin and the mainstream Labour leaders. Certainly, the growth of the ITGWU after 1918 was linked to the national revolution but it was not solely a product of it.[11] There was little indication that the vote for the Labour Party in 1922 had been taken seriously by the IRA. This was despite the fact that Labour had topped the poll in several constituencies and narrowly outpolled the anti-Treatyites overall.[12] Liam Mellows had actually lost his seat to a Labour candidate in Galway.[13] Some Labour successes had come in areas where conflict between farm labourers and farmers was raw, while many urban workers probably voted Labour out of a desire for peace. Undoubtedly, the IRA rank and file was mainly made up of industrial workers and poor rural labourers. But the mass of the Irish poor clearly did not support the IRA in the late 1920s. Whether they could have been won over is, of course, another question. Many workers, both rural and urban, supported Fianna Fáil after 1927, but substantial numbers continued to support the Labour Party as well. There was evidence that, independently, IRA members had been supporting Larkin in Dublin during his dispute with the Irish Transport Union and clashing with strike-breakers.[14] But the suggestion that huge hopes had been placed in his return by the IRA was probably exaggerated in order to emphasize Larkin's unreliability to the Soviets.

While O'Donnell did succeed in pushing his organization into endorsing a campaign against the payment of land annuities, the IRA's contact with trade unions remained largely external.[15] Most of the IRA leaders, such as Moss Twomey, Jim Killeen and Seán MacBride, had limited experience of trade union struggle and several of them had not been in any employment, except the IRA itself, since the revolutionary period. An exception was O'Donnell himself, who had been the 'stormy petrel' of the transport workers during a period as an ITGWU organizer from 1917 to 1920.[16] The other major exception was Mick Fitzpatrick. From Wexford, Fitzpatrick had been active in the War of Independence and was briefly the commander of the anti-Treaty IRA in Dublin during the Civil War. Considered by Free State intelligence to be one of the 'driving forces' behind the anti-Treatyite campaign in Dublin, he was interned during 1923. In that year he became involved with the fledgling Communist Party for a brief period. By the late 1920s he was a member of the army council and central to every one of the IRA's organizational links to radical labour. In 1927 he was part of the Trade Union International Relations Committee delegation to the USSR. In 1928, he helped found the Irish section of Friends of the Soviet Union. In 1929, he was involved with the Dublin Trade Union Unity League and the Irish Labour Defence League, an affiliate of the Communist International's Class War Prisoner's Aid. But Fitzpatrick was also involved in mainstream trade unionism. He was assistant secretary of the Irish National Union of Vintners', Grocers' and Allied Trades Assistants, better known as the 'Grocer's Union'. He later became an official of the Commerical Employees Union (CEU). Fitzpatrick was secretary of the Grocer's Union social club based in the Banba Hall in Dublin's Parnell Square, where he also ran the Balalaika Ballroom.[17]

LABOUR INTERVENTIONS

During June 1929, Fitzpatrick and fellow IRA officer Thomas Merrigan met with communists to discuss the setting up of a workers' defence corps. The IRA was to form the nucleus of this group, which would be active militarily during strikes and lockouts. The communists argued that membership of the corps should only be open to trade unionists, but the IRA succeeded in ensuring that 'persons whose social position does not admit membership of trade unions' would also be allowed join. This was agreed to only as long as the IRA agreed to instruct all of its members to join trade unions.[18] The proposed defence corps was only one of a number of potential armed labour groups being mooted at the time. Roddy Connolly and others were talking about reviving the ICA or a similar body because they did not believe the IRA should have a monopoly on armed force.[19] The result of these discussions was inconclusive. However, during June 1930, a strike by workers at the Irish Omnibus Company gave the IRA the opportunity to illustrate its concern for organized labour.

The IRA attacked strike-breaking buses with sniper fire in Wexford, Galway and Clare. In Granard, County Longford, a driver was held up by armed men, both he and his conducter beaten up, and the bus driven into a bog. These activities were seen by many within the IRA as a useful application of military training. In Galway, the IRA claimed that its proficiency had improved since the policy of attacking buses commenced. During the strike, *An Phoblacht* defended the National Union of Railwaymen from charges of being a foreign union, although it argued that 'Irish labour, organized in Ireland' was the preferable option. However, by the strike's unsatisfactory conclusion *An Phoblacht* was arguing that the NUR's British headquarters had contributed to its inability to secure a victory for its members.[20] Aside from military action, the IRA's concern for labour was also expressed in symbolic gestures. Strikers from the Greenmount Mills in Dublin took part in the IRA's Easter commemoration in April 1931 and the IRA's Dublin brigade staff made a small donation to their strike fund.[21]

The IRA's next major intervention concerned a public transport dispute north of the border. During November 1932 the six Irish railway companies announced wage cuts of up to 15 per cent. In the South the government stepped in and subsidized the rail workers' wages. However, in the North five of the companies went ahead with the cuts and on 31 January 1933 the strike began. The railway companies utilized Queen's University students and office staff as strike breakers. On the first day of the strike a train operated by strike breakers was derailed at Dromiskin, County Louth and two workers from Dublin killed. There was widespread use of sabotage and militant tactics during the strike. Strike breakers were refused service in pubs and shops in many towns along the border. Buses and trains were stoned in Dundalk and Dublin, and scabs physically attacked on several occasions. The IRA began sniping at trains and tried to blow up a railway bridge at Dunmurray. In Newry they carried out grenade and bomb attacks on the railway line. The RUC set up a special guard of 100 men to patrol the railway tracks.[22]

In Belfast, the organization carried out two bomb attacks on the GNR and Midland railway depots on the night of 26 February 1933. Bombs were thrown into each, though there were no injuries.[23] These attacks were significant because they were carried out by striking Protestant railwaymen; B-Specials no less, supplied with explosives by the IRA. Seán Russell, the IRA's quartermaster general, was in Belfast directing these operations. He wrote about what a change it was 'to find one group of 'Specials' searching the houses of our men, whilst another can be found collaborating with them!' Russell noted that the striking Specials had actually sought out the IRA's assistance.[24] Another attack on a railway depot in Belfast led to the death of an RUC constable in a shootout, the first member of that force to be killed by the IRA. The IRA saw the strike as highly significant, believing that there had been a 'realignment within the ranks of the Orange population upon a class basis ... this tendency has even, in some cases, brought the Catholic and Protestant workers into joint armed conflict with the six-county Government on issues of mutual interest.' IRA chief of staff, Moss Twomey, felt that there was 'an amazing change up there ... this railway strike is doing great damage to the Craigavon gang.'[25] But when the strike ended with a resolution condemned by the IRA as unsatisfactory, it was unclear what exactly the organization had gained from its actions.²⁶ Their co-operation with striking B-Specials was hidden from history, from both Catholics and Protestants. For obvious reasons, Protestant strikers did not reveal their involvement with the IRA. However, the IRA did not make its co-operation with striking B-Specials public either. Many nationalists would presumably have taken a dim view of the IRA providing explosives to the hated 'B-men'. Part of the motivation behind the IRA's efforts was the realization that it had missed out on the Outdoor Relief strike of October 1932. But this militant intervention was not universally approved of within the IRA itself.

The IRA's general army convention was held in March 1933 and a motion was put forward which stated that 'in order to make clear our stand to the "Workers' Republic" and as a means of keeping the Volunteers constantly engaged in the various phases of the struggle leading up to the final one, Óglaigh na hÉireann participate in every working-class struggle, strike, lockout, eviction ... where sanction is received from GHQ for such action.' A counter-amendment was proposed which demanded that the 'Army take no action in connection with strikes or trade disputes'. J.J. Murray from Armagh argued that the IRA had 'no right to take life in a labour dispute. I personally could not agree to it.' His unit had decided at their battalion convention not to take part in the railway strike. These arguments reflected wider divisions within the organization on its social policies. Tadgh Lynch from Cork asked should the IRA 'decide on the killing in active service ... whether one man has a shilling more or less than another man ... is it wise for us to inflict our opinions on those who differ from us socially?' In Lynch's view, the IRA was not out to 'free the country for the capitalist or the worker ... we are out for the freedom of all.' He argued that there were many examples of 'monied people who are as nationally minded as any other part of the community'. Tom Barry agreed with his colleague, stating that 'I maintain that I am entitled to take life only for the people as a whole.' When O'Donnell and others suggested that they were merely following the arguments put forward by Liam Mellows in 1922, Barry countered that 'Mellows was not infallible in these important matters. It was simply his opinion. We in 1922 would not accept his suggestions.' However, despite this opposition, the leadership motion was passed overwhelmingly. There were also those, like Seán Russell, who were not socially radical but did not object to IRA intervention in strikes simply because it was useful military activity.²⁷

Tensions over the extent of the IRA's embracing of social radicalism, and especially after 1932 of its association with communism, contributed to the split in 1934 that saw the formation of the Republican Congress. O'Donnell and his ally, George Gilmore, were among those who left to from the new group. However, several IRA officers who had been closely involved in its radical phase, including Fitzpatrick, Seán McCool and Donal O'Donoghue, remained within the organization. The departure of many of its leading leftists did not prevent the IRA continuing to intervene in industrial disputes. *An Phoblacht* maintained its extensive labour coverage, giving support to the mainly women strikers at Somax shirt makers and the workers at the Erne soap factory during the summer of 1934.[28] During September that year, the paper highlighted the campaign by the Commercial Employees Union (CEU), of which Fitzpatrick was now an official, for shorter hours for shop workers. When the strike had a successful conclusion that paper announced that 'Lord Long Hours is Dead'. Fitzpatrick was very visible on picket lines and in visiting shop workers during the dispute but the Garda Special Branch concluded that on this occasion the IRA's armed muscle was not being utilized.[29]

During the autumn of 1934, there was a strike by the printers employed by newspapers in Dublin. There were no Irish national daily papers printed, but the IRA sought and gained the permission of the strike committee to publish *An Phoblacht*. As well as the normal weekly, special editions appeared three times a week bearing the masthead 'by consent of the strike committee'.[30] It meant that, effectively, the strikers had access to a national mouthpiece. IRA Adjutant General Donal O'Donoghue boasted that at last *An Phoblacht* was 'Ireland's only national paper!'[31] During the strike, the IRA clashed with newspaper boys who were affiliated to Dublin's notorious animal gangs, who it accused of strike breaking.[32] During December that year, workers at O'Mara's bacon shops, a chain of stores owned by a prominent Limerick Fianna Fáil family, struck over union recognition. They wanted to join Fitzpatrick's CEU rather than the Shop Employees' Society, which was described as a company union. A few days before Christmas, armed IRA men held up Gardai on duty outside four of the shops in central Dublin and groups of men entered, smashing windows and machinery. In one case, the shop's management alleged that the raiders made off with a 'handsome turkey'.[33]

The ability to intervene in strikes militarily could be problematic. For individual IRA members, the temptation to use their arms was sometimes irresistible. An IRA member involved in a strike at a bakery in Dublin's Donnycarney blew up the premises. In Belfast, a sacked worker appealed to his comrades, who fired shots into his former employer's home, forcing him to live in 'constant dread'. After the sacking of one of their officers, Michael O'Donnell, a stationmaster and member of the Irish Road and Rail Federation at Fenit in County Kerry, the IRA retaliated by burning the station house. In Kilrush, County Clare, the IRA intervened in a strike involving a local merchant by raiding the home of a farmer and ordering him to stop dealing with the business. The local IRA officer informed headquarters that he found the circumstances and course of the dispute so 'complicated and interwoven' that he could not write an adequate report on them.[34]

These IRA interventions were increasingly subject to a belief that the Fianna Fáil government was embarking on a dictatorial policy in regard to labour relations.[35] Rhetoric accusing the government of fascist intentions was increasingly common in *An Phoblacht*, which saw Fianna Fáil introducing corporate-type legislation to shackle the unions. During March 1935 a strike took place on Dublin's trams and buses and after three weeks the government announced that army trucks would be brought onto streets to facilitate passengers. *An Phoblacht* called for a general strike in protest at 'Fianna Fáil's fascist step'. The IRA then issued a statement arguing that 'the action of the government in using the Free State Army for strike-breaking purposes' constituted a 'definite challenge to all workers'. They offered their military backing to 'assist in mobilizing the maximum support for the Dublin transport workers'.[36] The IRA also offered to meet the strike committee to discuss their support. In fact, the Gardaí had information that meetings had already taken place. While the trade union leadership disclaimed any knowledge of the IRA's plans, at least one member of the strike committee was also in the IRA.[37] The organization planned to set fire to trucks and to mine tram depots. On 26 March, the day after the IRA's statement, forty-four men – members of the IRA, Congress and ICA supporters – were arrested. The IRA leadership was forced to go on the run for the first time since Fianna Fáil came to power.[38] Moreover, de Valera's denunciation of the organization for abandoning its former national goals in favour of sectional strife and becoming like a 'racketeering' organization also hit home.[39] The IRA's former comrades in congress rather sourly described the IRA's efforts as 'terrorist adventures'.[40] This did reflect some rethinking on the part of O'Donnell and his colleagues on the desirability of clandestine intervention in labour disputes. However, armed members of their own organization had also taken action during a dispute at de Selby quarries in Bray the previous year. By 1935, congress and the small Citizens Army were emphasizing the need for open agitation within the unions as opposed to dramatic intervention from outside.[41] Over the next year, the IRA would limp from crisis to crisis until it was banned. They would then undergo several leadership changes, with Fitzpatrick briefly becoming chief of staff, before embarking on a bombing campaign in England during 1939. Despite the involvement of individual trade unionists, the focus for the IRA over the next twenty years would be on armed campaigns against partition. It was not until the failure of one such campaign in 1962 that trade union agitation began to be taken seriously again.

LEFTISM IN THE IRA IN THE 1960s

The new interest in the labour movement occurred in the context of a slow and halting move to the left by the IRA. Much of the IRA's initial interaction with the unions was through organizations such as Sceim na gCeardchumann. Founded in Cork during 1960, Sceim was a trade union-based Irish language organization.[42] Among those involved from an early stage were Packie Early, a 1930s IRA veteran and communist, and former Fianna boy Des Geraghty, who would eventually become chair of Sceim. It became an important forum for some of the debates within republicanism. Sceim organized céilis and lectures with speakers such as Seán Cronin, Desmond Ryan, Donal Nevin and Breandan Ó hEithir.[43] It published Seán Cronin's pamphlet *Jemmy Hope* during 1964, which told the story of the Presbyterian weaver and United Irishman, offering a working-class perspective on the 1798–1803 period. This pamphlet was an important influence on republicans looking for a left-wing interpretation of the 1798 events.[44] Indeed it was explicitly recommended as reading to IRA volunteers.[45] The move to the left was framed in language attractive to those who joined the IRA to engage in military activity. Prior to the organisations Convention in 1965, Chief of Staff Cathal Goulding made clear in the IRA's 'official organ' *An t-Oglac* that that he intended that their 'next military campaign will be the final one. I work for that now ... our new and vital orientation in the fields of co-operation and land [are] laying the basis for our future effort in the north.' However as part of this effort IRA units had to take on board the 'responsibility of local leadership on all occasions where the people require a lead.' This might involve 'having a pier rebuilt so that fishermen can land their fish to getting a University for Derry rather than Coleraine, or from preventing a town being sold up to assuming the leadership in a builders strike.' It would be necessary for volunteers to learn `how to resist evictions (or) how to run a trade union branch.' Goulding stressed that `those who doubt the value of this social work ... read of Cuba, of Algeria, of Cyprus.' The IRA would continue to 'depend on an armed people for success' but this would not occur without a 'solid and real basis in and among the people' part of which was building up experience of the labour movement.[46]

The first indication of this shift in terms of trade unionism was positive coverage in the *United Irishman* newspaper for organizations such as the Itinerant's Action Group who were cultivating trade union support. The year 1964 saw a major dispute in the building industry for a reduction in working hours; the strike movement spread and featured widespread militancy. During September, the largest labour demonstration since the war took place in Dublin.[47] The *United Irishman* established a relief fund for the strikers, a few of whom were republicans. Republicans also began to intervene more practically in disputes. From April until July 1965, a strike took place at the Dundalk engineering works in which local IRA O/C Peter Duffy played a prominent role. Republicans also became involved in agitation at Castlecomer and Ballingarry mines.[48] Of national significance was a strike by mainly women telephone operators for union recognition during November 1965. Republicans offered their support to the Irish Telephonists Association (ITA) whose pickets faced both arrest and jailing under the Offences Against the State Act. The ITA was also condemned by other trade unions.[49] At one point, roughly eighty-five phone boxes were vandalized during one night in a co-ordinated effort. Sinn Féin president and IRA army council member Tomás MacGiolla attacked the major unions for their desire to appear 'ultra-respectable' and for sacrificing their members' interests as a result. Republican support for the ITA was portrayed in the *Evening Herald* as part of a subversive plot, an interpretation backed up by Minister for Justice Brian Lenihan. Lenihan warned that 'physical force' elements were 'cashing in' on the dispute.[50] Republicans argued that the ultimate 'shameful defeat' of the ITA was because of the failure both of other unions to support them and an 'unholy alliance' between the trade unions and the government.[51]

During 1965 more serious efforts were made to co-ordinate intervention in the labour movement. The IRA leadership agreed that it was of 'fundamental importance that the movement assume an organizational form that will attract back people of national outlook in the trade union movement so that their efforts can be co-ordinated'. It was felt that there should be 'an organization of representatives in the trade union movement whose function it would be to examine trade union law and structure with a view to making trade unions more revolutionary, and to draw up directives for Volunteers on the subject of trade unionism. This organization should be in the form of a "staff" not necessarily a branch of GHQ, but under the control and direction of the Chief of Staff.'

Realizing that the majority of Sinn Féin members were unlikely to be supportive of this idea, the IRA would 'be the backbone' of the effort and would see that the 'push' towards union activity in Sinn Féin came 'from the bottom or from local area level'. It was even suggested that, where possible, 'factory cumann' be set up, meeting monthly, and to set up within its membership specialist groups of activists devoted to giving leadership to the factory workers on issues affecting their interests. 'A factory cumann would have groups oriented towards the shop-floor, the administrative staff (and) technical staff.' The IRA would remain the 'backbone' of this intervention.[52]

The IRA considered its 'most successful venture' in the industrial field to have been the Dundalk Engineering Works strike. It claimed that the 'strikers called upon us for our assistance. We worked with them behind the scenes and can take complete credit for their total victory.' The strikers themselves were said to be still in touch with the IRA's Dundalk O/C and 'at his disposal for activity in the trade union field'. An educational conference on trade unionism was held in December 1965 at which forty IRA members were present. The volunteers invited were those who already had a 'known practical interest in social and economic problems'.[53] In January 1966, the IRA organized a Dublin trade unionists conference. The speakers were 'active trade unionists' and the discussions concerned the history of trade unionism and the problems of breakaway unions. During February, the IRA organized another conference on trade unionism in the six counties. The two main areas of discussion were (a) how to organize industrial workers in small towns and (b) if it was possible to get non-sectarian trade union support for the Belfast Easter commemoration. They optimistically felt that if their links with trade unions could be solidified in the North then it would represent a 'major national victory' that would make the unionist government 'shiver'.[54]

In Belfast, during Easter 1966, the Trades Council was invited to take part in the republican movement's fiftieth anniversary celebrations. Trades Council and Communist Party member, Betty Sinclair, was to speak at the event in Casement Park but withdrew at the last moment because of objections from the GAA.[55] However, a delegation from the Belfast Trades Council did take part in the Bodenstown commemoration during June.[56] During that year, there was more regular industrial coverage in the *United Irishman* and Sinn Féin condemned the Electricity (Special Provisions) Bill as an 'anti-worker' law designed to limit the ability of workers to defend their conditions.[57]

Nevertheless, there were problems in that much of the republican effort was coming from outside the ranks of the labour movement. Of the IRA leadership, Chief of Staff Cathal Goulding ran his own painting and decorating business, Mick Ryan was an insurance agent, Seán Garland, essentially full time, Seamus Costello, a car salesman, Tomás MacGiolla, a clerk in the ESB, Ruairi Ó Brádaigh, a vocational school teacher, Malachy McGurran, a former meat factory worker and Seán MacStiofáin worked for Gael Linn, though he had been in a union when he worked as a railwayman in Britain.[58] Roy Johnston had been a member of Acton Trades Council in London but the IRA leadership's collective experience of trade unionism was generally limited.[59]

There were individual republicans active in the unions, such as ITGWU official Francie O'Donoghue in Monaghan, Donnchadh Mac Raghnaill, a member of Drogheda Trades Council, clerk and ITGWU member Lar Malone and the Whelan brothers, active in the bricklayers' union in Dublin. Despite this, there was no network of rank and file republican trade unionists. During late 1967, the IRA bemoaned how this had meant that it had been unable to respond effectively to the closure of two factories, Rawsons in Dundalk and Electra in Dublin. *An t-Oglac*, in December complained that with Rawsons 'we let the grass grow under our feet. It was some weeks before we convened a meeting of workers; by then the machinery had been removed and the organising of a productive sit-in was not practicable'. In Dublin their weakness had been 'lack of advance information [and] any feeling of urgency or responsibility among the members of the local unit of Movement'. The IRA admitted lacking 'influence with the Dublin T.U. leadership. We were looking at the situation from the outside.' The first step to remedying this was 'building a central register of Trade Union members and their organizing into conscious pressure groups'.[60]

This partially explains the attraction of the communists, north and south of the border, to the IRA leadership. The Irish Workers Party (IWP) in the South and the Communist Party of Northern Ireland both had significant influence in the unions. Many within the IRA leadership felt a closer arrangement with them would open up the labour movement to republican influence. For their part, the communists were also attracted to aspects of the IRA's potential. It was a national organization, with a powerful historical appeal and deep roots in Ireland. Unlike the communist groups, it possessed a rural base with some influence in farmers' organizations. The IRA was also armed and had the ability to carry out types of activities beyond the communists' aptitude.

Roy Johnston prepared an educational document which was distributed throughout the republican movement in late 1967. In it, he placed the movement's leftism within the Irish radical tradition of Tone, Lalor, Mellows and Connolly. He argued that republicans could no longer 'insulate' themselves from international politics and theoretical debates. Thus, an effort was made to explain concepts such as 'Stalinism' and 'Trotskyism'. Johnston argued that the 'negative tradition of Stalinism' had been a major flaw in the Communist Parties, particularly with reference to their dependence on Moscow. However, the 'wealth of trade union experience' of the Irish communists and their 'considerable influence' in the labour movement could not be ignored by republicans. Johnston hoped that the initiation of dialogue between the Vatican and the USSR had ended the 'state of cold war' between the two and made it possible for Catholic radicals to find common ground with Marxists. The Trotskyites, however, were 'basically anti-national' in their philosophy and unlikely to have any significant influence in Ireland due to their ultra-leftism.[61]

The growth of industrial militancy and increasing trade union membership offered opportunities for republicans to win influence. The tendency of the *United Irishman* was to heavily criticize the union leaderships for not being militant enough in defence of their members' interests. The Belfast IRA O/C Liam McMillen not only explicitly described the aim of republicans as being a 'workers' republic' but criticized the trade unions for having 'abdicated their role as leaders of organized labour'.[62] How the IRA should respond to issues such as factory closures was a matter of debate. When Rawson's factory announced its closure, MacStiofáin argued for burning the company's headquarters in England. English IRA members prepared to carry out the burning but the army council called off the operation. However, in early 1968 workers had struck at the American multinational EI in Shannon, County Clare. The IRA considered the EI strike 'the most important dispute since 1913'. The *United Irishman* again criticized the trade union leadership for not upping the ante and concluded that the EI strikers faced employers, Leinster House *and* their trade union leaders.[63] A decision was taken to intervene and on 29 May the IRA destroyed six buses carrying strike-breakers to the factory in Limerick and attacked property in Kildare, Dublin and Louth belonging to companies facilitating the strike-breaking. At Bodenstown a few weeks later, Garland made clear that the EI attacks were 'no isolated incidents' and that the 'day is past' when workers would have to fight alone.[64] However, republicans did not argue that the IRA's support could win the strike. Instead, 'Larkinite tactics' were needed, crucially solidarity action from other unions. The IRA made clear that it was not a substitute for broader action and that only 'workers drugged by too much *Batman* on television might think this'.⁶⁵ The IRA's military actions in support of the strike were noted by the *Washington Post*, which informed its readers that the IRA had decided 'to soft pedal its old demands for unification ... in favour of agitating, via trade unions ... for a socialist workers' republic. [It] claimed responsibility for the recent burning of six buses used by an American firm in Shannon to transport non-union workers to its strike-bound factory. And an IRA spokesman said more of the same was possible if American companies, who come for tax benefits, do not conform to practices in this most unionized country in Western Europe.'⁶⁶

The fact that the Labour Party was openly adopting socialist policies also impacted on the IRA. Firstly it made it more acceptable to talk about socialism and to declare itself in favour of a democratic socialist republic, as it did during 1967. But the success of Labour in the 1967 local elections, especially in Dublin where it outpolled Fine Gael, also had an important effect.⁶⁷ The WUI affiliated to the Labour Party in 1965, followed by the ITGWU and ATGWU in 1968. Republicans feared that their involvement in social agitation would pay dividends for Labour rather than themselves: 'Campaigns ... are only of limited value if the political advantages are going to be picked up by Labour.' They noted that 'Labour has a readymade broad base in the trade union movement. It is the lack of a corresponding base that is Sinn Féin's major problem.'⁶⁸ Republican activity in the unions was necessary to win support away from Labour.

In a document called *Ireland Today*, produced in March 1969, the IRA leadership set out a new strategy. In the South, despite the 'moribund ... bureaucracy' of the trade union leadership, there was a new radical mood being expressed through support for the Labour Party and by social agitation. But the Labour Party, 'despite its apparent radicalism', had 'a basically opportunist leadership', and its supporters would be disillusioned in time. The republican movement then had an opportunity to significantly influence events. It represented the 'great mainstream of the national and social revolutionary tradition' in contrast to Labour, which represented 'national and social compromise'. The republican movement had an all-Ireland newspaper and a base in both urban and rural Ireland. It had 'physical defence experience', which would be necessary in future to defend itself from 'counter-revolutionary attack'. Therefore agitation on housing and trade union activity must be kept up, and organized to involve all existing radical political groups, as well as 'trade unionists and homeless people'. The republicans could become the driving force in a new alliance, a 'National Liberation Front'. The

NLF would include republicans, elements from Labour, cultural activists and communists embodying the radical alliance originally envisaged in the republican education programme of 1967.[69] During 1968, a 'secret mechanism' for contact between Goulding and Mick O'Riordan of the IWP had already been opened up. However, contacts between the two organizations remained clandestine.[70] It was also the case that radical thinking within the IRA encompassed a variety of strands, including some that were highly critical of the IWP and international communism from both left-wing and traditionalist perspectives.

However, trade union strategy was only one facet of contemporary republican agitation and not necessarily the most important one. The Northern Ireland Civil Rights Association, the 'fish-ins' on privately owned rivers and lakes and especially housing protest in Dublin, were the subject of intense activity. The rhetoric of rank and file protest continued, usually from a distance. The *United Irishman* attacked the ITGWU for not taking strike action in protest at the dismissal of a shop steward at Gortdrum mines in County Tipperary. The paper stressed that what was 'needed is for trade unions to be real fighting organizations of the working people, democratic not bureaucratic, not watered down house associations under the thumb of the Federated Union of Employers'.[71] However, the growing general agitation had seen a number of trade union activists among those attracted into the republican movement, with Des Geraghty joining in 1968.[72]

THE IMPACT OF THE 'TROUBLES'

Republican activity in the labour movement was still in its infancy when the events of the summer of 1969 in Northern Ireland transformed priorities utterly. There was a broad labour movement response to the August events. The National Solidarity Committee was set up with Michael Mullen of the ITGWU and the Dublin Trades Council involved in relief work for northern nationalists. However, the split in the IRA, and the rush to regain influence and control, meant the republican leadership was preoccupied. Nevertheless, in Britain, the republican movement's 'exiles' organization, Clann na h-Éireann, was able to mobilize several thousand Irish workers in a one-day strike in Birmingham during August 1969.[73] Despite opposition from the Connolly Association and the Communist Party, who considered the strike call 'adventurist', it was the largest Irish demonstration in Birmingham in generations. Clann activists such as Séamus Collins were threatened with dismissal from Murphy's building firm as a result. The strike laid the foundation for the building of a rank and file network of Irish construction workers.[74] Clann activist Pádraig Yeates edited *Site Action Press*, 'for workers' control of the building industry', which raised issues of safety, health and wages on construction sites.[75] It was published in co-operation with members of the International Socialists, who were influential in Birmingham and pursuing a rank and file industrial perspective.

In contrast, the early Provisionals expressed little interest in trade unionism. In May 1970, their newspaper *An Phoblacht* applauded the attitude of Leo Collins, a County Meath businessman, who encouraged his employees to join trade unions. The 'friendly atmosphere and good relations' in his workplace were in 'stark contrast to the class warfare propagated by extreme and doctrinaire socialists'.[76] At that stage, the Provisionals were still claming that the influence of 'Marx, Mao and Castro' on Goulding and his supporters had been responsible for the disaster of August 1969.[77] There were exceptions, such as Peter Duffy in Dundalk, but it would be the late 1970s before a resurgent left within Provisional Sinn Féin would seek to revitalize its trade union base.

The Official IRA continued to give military backing to strike action. In early 1970, a long strike took place at Irish Cement. The company's two factories in Drogheda and Mungret, County Limerick, were closed but cement continued to be imported from abroad. On several occasions, strikers attacked trucks carrying imported cement from across the border with Northern Ireland. In Dublin, the Official IRA burned premises, machinery and vehicles belonging to two building companies importing cement.[78] There was also an OIRA arson attack on a Ballyfermot haulage firm during a strike in July 1971.[79] In Belfast, the Officials blew up premises used by a building company in Dunville Park during a strike by tunnellers.[80] Intervention in a dispute at the Silvermines in Tipperary that year had tragic consequences, however. A miner had been dismissed for allegedly stealing a packet of cigarettes and 400 men walked out in his support. However, production at the mines was continued by a skeleton workforce. The Official IRA held up security staff and planted bombs on the electricity transformers. These exploded, causing £1 million worth of damage, but 20-year-old Corkman Martin O'Leary was electrocuted and badly burnt, dying a few days later. At O'Leary's funeral, Cathal Goulding praised him as the 'prototype' of a 'modern revolutionary' and warned that a 'new phase' of IRA activity was beginning in the South. Famously, he stated that if 'the forces of imperialism ... repress, coerce, and deny ordinary people their God-given rights ... then it is our duty to reply ... in the language that brings these vultures to their senses most effectively – the language of the bomb and the bullet.'[81] There was some sympathy for the IRA's action, as a delegation of miners at the funeral showed.[82] In February 1972, the Official IRA in Newry destroyed lorries carrying Polish coal into the North from the Republic in support of the British miners' strike. In March, they shot and wounded the owner of an Armagh haulage firm whose company was involved in strike-breaking in Kilkenny and blew up his premises.[83]

The Official IRA's actions led British Prime Minister Ted Heath to enquire if that organization had 'schemes to promote industrial action' along the 'lines of the recent miners strike' in Northern Ireland. He was reassured that the sectarian divisions among workers in the north made republican inspired strike action of that scale at least, unlikely.[84]

However, the Official IRA ceasefire in May 1972 and longer term rethinking on the role of the IRA and its relationship to the party saw the end of these tactics. In late 1971, Seamus Costello and Mick Ryan had suggested that the movement establish an industrial sub-committee to co-ordinate work within the unions.[85] A loose republican trade union group was established, which, in 1972, formally became an industrial department. This grouping, later known as the Republican Industrial Development Division (RIDD), was to play an important part in the development of Official republican strategy over the next decade.[86]

NOTES

1. A C/S to Adjt. Dublin Brigade, 22 July 1922, in Sighle Humphries Papers, University College Dublin Archives (UCDA), P106/1954 (2).
2. Adjt, Dub. Bdge to A. C/S, 26 July 1922, in Humphries Papers, UCDA, P106/1954 (8).
3. C. Desmond Greaves, *Liam Mellows and the Irish Revolution* (London: 1971), pp. 364–5.
4. Michael Gallagher, *The Irish Labour Party in Transition, 1957–82* (Manchester: 1982), p. 125.
5. 'Lines on which paper is to be run', Army Council meeting, 29 April 1926, in Moss Twomey Papers, UCDA, (MTUCDA), P69/181 (41).
6. *Notes on the Irish Labour Movement*, 1927, in MTUCDA, P69/72 (15–18).
7. *General Outline of the Present Movement*, August 1927, in MTUCDA, P69/72 (3–11).
8. Emmet O'Connor, *James Larkin* (Cork: 2002), pp. 72–3.
9. *Notes & General Outline*, MTUCDA, P69/72.
10. Ibid., (15–18).
11. See Emmet O'Connor, *Syndicalism in Ireland, 1917–1923* (Cork: 1988).
12. Michael Gallagher, *Irish Elections: Results and Analysis, 1922–1944* (Limerick: 1993), pp. 3–20.
13. Gallagher, *Labour*, p. 125.
14. Military Intelligence report, 22 October 1925 in Desmond FitzGerald Papers, UCDA, P80/847 (117).
15. D. Ó Drisceoil, *Peadar O'Donnell* (Cork: 2001), p. 44-50.
16. See Anton McCabe, '"The stormy petrel of the Transport Workers": Peadar O'Donnell, trade unionist, 1917–1920', *Saothar*, vol. 19 (1994).

17. Brian Hanley, *The IRA, 1926–1936* (Dublin: 2002), p. 192.
18. Garda intelligence report, 19 June 1929, in FitzGerald Papers, UCDA P80/851 (20).
19. Garda Intelligence report, 1 July 1929, in FitzGerald Papers, UCDA P80/851 (20).
20. Hanley, *The IRA*, p. 55.
21. *An Phoblacht*, 11 April 1931; and IRA, 5 May 1931 in MTUCDA, P69/151 (4–5).
22. *Irish News*, 2–20 February 1933.
23. *Irish News*, 27 February 1933.
24. 'Q' to C/S IRA, 28 February 1933, in MTUCDA, P69/53 (296-98).
25. Hanley, *The IRA*, pp. 151–3
26. *An Phoblacht*, 15 April 1933.
27. Notes of 1933 General Army Convention, MTUCDA, P69/187 (90-117).
28. *An Phoblacht*, 21 July 1934.
29. Garda report, 26 September 1934, in National Archives of Ireland (NAI), Jus 8/365.
30. *An Phoblacht*, 11 August 1934.
31. D. O'Donoghue to S. Humphries, 30 August 1934, in Humphries Papers, UCDA, P106/1644 (1–4).
32. *An Phoblacht*, 29 September 1934. Garda report, 12 September 1934, NAI, Jus 8/67.
33. *Irish Times*, 22 December 1934.
34. Hanley, *The IRA*, p. 56.
35. *An Phoblacht*, 21 July 1934.
36. *Irish Times*, 25 March 1935.
37. Garda report, 27 March 1935, NAI Jus 8/405.
38. *An Phoblacht*, March 1935.
39. Hanley, *The IRA*, p.143.
40. *Republican Congress*, 30 March 1935.
41. See Brian Hanley, 'The Irish Citizens Army after 1916', *Saothar*, vol. 28 (2003).
42. *United Irishman*, June 1966.
43. *United Irishman*, January 1966.
44. Tomás MacGiolla, interview with author.
45. *An t-Oglac*, May 1945, PRONI, HA/32/2/13.
46. Ibid.
47. S. Cody, J. O'Dowd and P. Rigney, *The Parliament of Labour: 100 years of the Dublin Council of Trade Unions* (Dublin: 1986).
48. *United Irishman*, September and October 1965.
49. *United Irishman*, November 1965.
50. *Evening Herald*, 1–4 November 1965.
51. *United Irishman*, January 1966.
52. Captured IRA Economic and Social Plan, (1965) in Department of Justice 98/6/495 NAI.
53. Department of Justice, review of unlawful and allied organizations, 1 December 1964 to 21 November 1966, Jus 98/6/495 NAI.
54. *Republican Educational Bulletin*, January 1966.
55. *Irish Democrat*, June 1966.
56. *United Irishman*, July 1966.
57. Ibid.
58. Seán MacStiofáin, *Memoirs of a Revolutionary* (London: 1975), p. 51.
59. Roy Johnston, *A Century of Endeavour* (Dublin: 2006), p.168.
60. *An t-Oglac*, December 1967 (author's possession).
61. *Republican Educational Manual*, vol. III (October 1967).
62. *Irish News*, 15 April 1968.
63. *United Irishman*, March and April 1968.
64. *United Irishman*, July 1968.
65. *United Irishman*, August 1968.
66. *Washington Post*, 8 August 1968.
67. Gallagher, *Labour*, pp. 49–62.
68. *United Irishman*, November 1968.
69. *Ireland Today*, March 1969.
70. C. Andrew and V. Mitrokhin, *The Mitrokhin Archive: the KGB in Europe and the West* (London: 2000), p. 492.
71. *United Irishman*, July 1969.
72. Des Geraghty, interview with author.

73. *Irish Times*, 21 August 1969.
74. Pádraig Yeates, interview with author.
75. *Site Action Press*, 2, 1, 1970.
76. *An Phoblacht*, May 1970.
77. *An Phoblacht*, June 1970.
78. *United Irishman*, April 1970.
79. *Irish Times*, 7 July 1971.
80. Belfast Official IRA members, interview with author.
81. *Hibernia*, 16 July 1971.
82. *Irish Press*, 9 July 1971.
83. *United Irishman*, March and April 1972.
84. Prime Minister, 13 March 1972, in Home Office and Northern Ireland Office 88.Registered Files, National Archives, CJ4/193.
85. Official Sinn Féin Coiste Seasta minutes, 29 November 1971 (Courtesy Workers Party of Ireland).
86. Official Sinn Féin Coiste Seasta minutes, 14 February 1972 (Courtesy Workers Party of Ireland).

11

Catholic Stakhanovites? Religion and the Irish Labour Party, 1922–73

NIAMH PUIRSÉIL

The modern Labour Party in Ireland prides itself on its support for the 'liberal agenda' over recent decades. Speaking in 2007, the Labour leader, Eamon Gilmore, claimed that its support for socially progressive causes was one of the party's core values and argued that 'more than any other political movement, it was Labour and its allies which drove the modernisation of this State.'[1] Nevertheless, while it is undoubtedly the case that since the 1980s, Labour has often taken a courageous stance on social issues and was in the vanguard of change on issues such as contraception, divorce and secular education at a time when such views were profoundly controversial, it would be wrong to suggest that support for liberalism was always a 'core value'.

In fact, for much of the party's history, the opposite was the case. Not only did Labour shy away from anything that could have been construed as liberal (to be fair, so too did every other major political party[2]) but it tailored its policies and its language in such a way as to avoid criticism by the Catholic Church, which led to the somewhat unkind description of the party as the 'political wing of St Vincent de Paul'. Of course, it is only natural that political parties should reflect the culture from which they originate and the people they aim to represent. That Labour was influenced by Catholicism is neither unusual in the Irish context (clearly both Fine Gael and Fianna Fáil are also products of this predominantly Catholic society) nor more generally – after all, it is often said of the British Labour Party that it owes more to Methodism than Marx.[3] This essay explores some of the ways religion has influenced Labour in Ireland.

POLITICS AND THE CATHOLIC CHURCH BEFORE 1922

The impact of the Roman Catholic Church on Irish politics has been immense ever since the early nineteenth century when clerical engagement and popular mobilization spurred the campaign for Catholic emancipation to victory. As Patrick Murray has noted, 'having thus acquired a taste and talent for political activity, and for the exercise of political power, priests soon came to regard these as their right, and even their duty'.[4] The Catholic Church remained active in politics, lending its support to land agitation, home rule and, in the twentieth century, the pro-treaty side during and after the civil war.

Where Ireland differed from other predominantly Catholic countries of the time was in that the Church was not identified with the ruling class or regime but with those working against them, which meant that the Catholic Church enjoyed both spiritual and political authority among the Catholic population, and was intrinsically identified with the nationalist cause. There were occasions when some nationalists were prepared to ignore the Church's stance on particular issues – most notably in the case of the Fenians, the Parnell split and the civil war – but while there may have been ambivalence and occasionally hostility towards the Church among some nationalists and republicans, these views were seldom expressed publicly, and certainly not by anyone trying to succeed in politics. In effect, there was a high level of support for the Church on political matters, and among those who opposed the Church, there was a propensity to keep quiet. Across the political spectrum, there was consensus that crossing the Church did not pay at the ballot box.

This caused particular problems for the Irish left. The Catholic Church's teaching on socialism outlined in the papal encyclical *Rerum Novarum* (1891) was unequivocally hostile, and following the arrival of James Larkin in Dublin many churchmen there had become especially preoccupied with the dangers of the socialist menace. Several socialist campaigners, most notably James Connolly in his pamphlet *Labour, Nationality and Religion* (1910), tried to spread the word that it was possible to be a socialist and a good Catholic[5] (indeed, as far as Christian socialists were concerned, it was impossible to be a good Christian if one was not a socialist); as far as the hierarchy and religious were concerned the two were mutually exclusive. Churchmen might occasionally intervene in industrial disputes and the like, but notions such as common ownership and state welfare were anathema and became all the more so with the rise of the welfare state and later during the cold war. Until the advent of the second Vatican Council, the Catholic Church's attitude towards labour's forward march was one of 'thus far shall thou go and no further'. Labour more often than not circumscribed its policies accordingly, which tended to render the party a pale imitation of itself.

LABOUR IN THE NEW STATE, 1922–27

While elements within the Catholic Church had been worried about the labour movement's threat to faith and morals, by the early 1920s the outbreak of civil war meant that Labour was left relatively unmolested as the Church focused on condemning republicans. After contesting its first general election in 1922, and with republican deputies abstaining from the Dáil, Labour found itself the main opposition to a government which was self-consciously Catholic and inclined to legislate accordingly. It was a priggish administration, of which the Minister for Justice, Kevin O'Higgins, was probably the worst offender as he crusaded against the evils of drink and literature and preached to the Catholic Truth Society on the decline of morality among the Catholic laity.[6] Both inside and outside the Dáil, Labour stood somewhat aloof from the ostentatious piety that had become the order of the day. That is not to say it opposed Cumann na nGaedheal's moral legislation – it supported the 1925 ban on divorce, for instance – but it did so without Catholic grandstanding.

In fact, much of Labour's rhetoric and ethos during the 1920s might best be described as Christian socialist. The ILP&TUC was informed by its roots in the Independent Labour Party (ILP) in Britain which had a strong Christian socialist tradition.[7] Thomas Johnson, leader of the parliamentary Labour Party, was one of those to have come through the ILP, having been brought up in the Unitarian church. Johnson's right-hand man in Congress, R.J.P. (Ronald) Mortished, was also from a Protestant background, although he listed himself as an atheist in the census of 1911.[8] Their religious backgrounds, combined with the fact that both men were English-born, left them open to attack. Several other senior members of the parliamentary party and/or trade union movement, such as William O'Brien and Cathal O'Shannon, were atheists. Naturally, there were others who were Catholics of varying degrees of observance, but in a small party the relatively high proportion of non-Catholics was noted with suspicion. For instance, the future of the Irish labour movement was called into question by a number of speakers at the Catholic Truth Society annual conference in 1923 because of the presence of non-Catholics in its leadership.[9] O'Shannon used the pages of the *Voice of Labour* to point out the beam in the eyes of these critics, arguing that 'in the struggles of the Irish workers against the inhuman and unchristian forces of Mammon it is an incontrovertible fact that the clergy of all denominations have been conspicuous by their absences.'[10] His uncompromising, almost aggressive, stance against the Catholic clergy's criticism was by no means unique at this time. If anything, it was the norm, with the labour movement's newspapers regularly highlighting attacks on Labour by the Church, and responding with the unambiguous message that not only was the Church wrong, but it had no business expressing an opinion in the first place. As O'Shannon put it in one editorial, 'the general feeling is certainly that the less the Church has to do with party politics the better both for the Church and for politics.'[11]

This anti-clericalism was echoed elsewhere. Following the September 1927 general election, for instance, Labour's paper, the *Irishman*, noted that there had been an effort by the clergy to intimidate the electorate against voting Labour. In one case a 'clerical school manager let it be known that any teacher who supported Labour "would be dealt with" – the result being that teachers who had been somewhat lukewarm promptly became very active in the west.'[12] In another incident, the Galway Labour deputy, Gilbert Lynch, recalled coming home one evening to find the local curate departing from his flat, leaving Lynch's wife in tears. It seems the curate had expressed surprise at the presence of a Sacred Heart, on account of Mr Lynch being a 'Godless socialist'. Whether because of his wife's distress or because of the aspersions cast on his own faith, Lynch claimed that he became enraged to the point where he threw the curate down the stairs.[13] Assault was, nevertheless, unusual.

While the party was always prepared to put up a robust defence against clerical attacks, its ethos and often its language was profoundly Christian, for it was still possible to be anti-clerical without being anti-Catholic. Parallels were drawn between Labour's lack of success and Fianna Fáil's popularity, noting: 'after all, it was Jacob, the cheat and liar, who was multiplied and not Esam, the honest man, whose first consideration was bread and butter.'[14] The Free State government was criticized for administering over a jurisdiction 'free from any "taint" of "socialism" or Christianity',[15] and W.T. Cosgrave was pointed in the direction of *Rerum Novarum*.[16] Significantly, when Æ (George Russell) wrote that Labour was a Marxist party, Tom Johnson responded that:

> For the original inspiration of the Labour Party you should look to

the medieval denunciations of usury, to Fintan Lalor and John Mitchel, Robert Owen and John Ruskin, Edward Carpenter and Walt Whitman, James Connolly and George W Russell, Bernard Shaw and A.R. Orage, Pope Leo XIII, the Book of the Prophet Isaiah and the Epistle of St James rather than to Karl Marx and *Das Kapital* or the 'Communist Manifesto'.[17]

This emphasis on Christian socialism was not without its critics. When a visit to Dublin by the general secretary of the International Confederation of Christian Trade Unions garnered several pages of coverage in the *Irishman*, for instance, the ITGWU official and Citizen Army veteran, Frank Robbins, complained that there should be no place in the working-class movement for religiously based unions.[18] Equally, there was resistance to making Labour a religiously based party, even by implication. In 1930, the Irish Labour Party and Irish Trade Union Congress separated into two individual organizations, which meant each had to formulate a new constitution, but while earlier drafts of Labour's new constitution referred to the responsibilities of the 'Christian state', these had all been removed by the time the constitution was put before the new party's conference for approval.[19]

LABOUR AND 'INTELLECTUAL TERRORISM' IN THE 1930s

Notwithstanding the absence of references to religion or Christianity in the party's new constitution, Labour's religious character had begun to change. This was due to a change in personnel since Ronald Mortished had left Congress to work in the International Labour Organisation in Geneva and Thomas Johnson had lost his Dáil seat in 1927 (although he remained active and was a senator). T.J. O'Connell, general secretary of the Irish National Teachers' Organisation (INTO) became leader of the parliamentary Labour Party. Not only was he a practising Catholic, but he enjoyed 'a close relationship with a number of prominent clerical figures', and was especially close to John Charles McQuaid,[20] the future archbishop of Dublin who was then headmaster of Blackrock College. Any change in the party's ethos was largely imperceptible but Johnson, at least, was conscious of a shift. When, in 1930, two members of the parliamentary party were expelled after breaking the whip to support Cumann na nGaedheal's draconian security legislation, Johnson warned against the party taking such a strong line against conscientious dissidents, telling Mortished: 'Gently as possible I referred to possible religious issues – thinking of myself!'[21]

Evidence that Johnson's concern was justified was soon forthcoming. That same year, controversy arose over Mayo County Council's refusal to appoint Letitia Dunbar-Harrison, a Trinity graduate, as county librarian after she had been awarded the post by the Local Appointments Commission.[22] Ostensibly, Dunbar-Harrison's lack of proficiency in Irish rendered her unsuitable for the post, but the reality was that her Trinity education and the fact she was Protestant rendered her unappointable in the eyes of the Mayo County Library Committee, a view shared by all too many local politicians and clergy, among them the dean and archbishop of Tuam.[23] The Cumann na nGaedheal government reacted by dissolving the council, but Fianna Fáil, noting the level of popular approval for the county council's stance, not to mention the opportunity to curry favour with the Church, seized upon the issue and rounded on the government's efforts to have Dunbar-Harrison appointed. It was a crass piece of sectarian populism in which Labour proved happy to join. It was a decision, no doubt, influenced by T.J. O'Connell's position as a Mayo deputy, but it is inconceivable that Labour would have taken such a stand only a few years earlier.

By the 1930s, the Free State had gone from self-conscious Catholicism to a full-scale devotional revival, with the Eucharistic Congress of 1932 representing a celebration of nationhood as well as faith. An important part of this Catholic revival was the establishment and rapid growth of lay organizations,[24] and their popularity was bolstered significantly by the sense of crisis and instability at home and on the continent, the latter the driving force behind the thinking in *Quadragissimo Anno* which updated Leo XIII's *Rerum Novarum* in the context of the Great Depression. With the emphasis on Catholicism and orthodoxy, the cultural climate soon became one of 'intellectual terrorism', in John Swift's phrase,[25] in which religious or political dissent was tolerated by neither state nor society.

The year 1932 was a hugely significant one for Labour as a general election saw its parliamentary party halved to a paltry seven deputies. Party leader, T.J. O'Connell was one of those to lose his seat and his successor was William Norton, the 32-year-old general secretary of the Post Office Workers' Union. Taking on this role at Labour's lowest ebb, Norton was determined to arrest Labour's decline and was prepared to take the party in whatever direction he felt would pay electoral dividends. Norton abandoned the pretence of equidistance between Labour and Fianna Fáil and Cumann na nGaedheal, not only through external support for the government but also by shifting his party's rhetoric towards a more republican and Catholic stance. This was especially evident in his maiden speech as

Labour leader in which he spoke of how the new government's task was to work towards 'that life of frugal comfort which Pope Leo XIII laid down as the God given right of every man and woman'.[26] Norton was a member of the Knights of St Columbanus, the Catholic lay organization devoted to furthering Catholic social teaching (especially that of Leo XIII), but he was never regarded as particularly devout and it seems likely that his membership owed more to political expediency than faith; certainly, Norton was a consummate opportunist, and was willing to move the party in whatever direction he felt would benefit it most. In Archbishop John Charles McQuaid's eyes, Norton's sole criterion was 'votes from anywhere and how to get them'.[27]

Norton's reorientation of Labour towards a more friendly relationship with Fianna Fáil soon proved problematic as it became increasingly clear that it was losing votes to the larger party as a result rather than vice versa, and in an effort to put clear red water between the two parties, Labour began to shift rather sharply to the left. This culminated in 1936 when the party conference adopted a new constitution which called for the setting up of a Workers' Republic.[28] Although the Workers' Republic constitution amounted to little more than window dressing, it did not take long before it began to raise alarm bells within Church circles. The timing of the new departure had been inauspicious, since the outbreak of war in Spain in the summer of 1936 saw the political climate turn. Encouraged by sensationalist headlines in the *Irish Independent* and the *Catholic Standard* which told of republican church burnings and the mass murder of religious, public opinion saw the war in Spain as a battle between Christianity and atheistic communism, a view which was also common within Labour. Though many others within the party's ranks supported the republicans, the leadership felt – probably correctly – that any identification between Labour and the Spanish government's cause was bound to damage the party. As Fearghal McGarry has noted, this meant Labour's attitude towards Spain became one of 'don't mention the war'.[29]

Nonetheless, the Catholic hierarchy began to display a preoccupation with the dangers of communism in Ireland, notably in Lenten pastorals, and various newspapers including the *Limerick Leader*, the *Catholic Standard*, the *Irish Rosary* and the *Irish Catholic* all expressed concern that, with its new constitution, Labour had placed itself on a slippery slope towards communism.[30] Norton and his colleagues were perturbed about calumnies at home but the news that these accusations had been re-printed in the Vatican's own newspaper, *Osservatoro Romano*, caused even greater alarm and prompted the Labour leader to write to the papal secretary of state,

Cardinal Pacelli, in protest and to reassure him that his party 'strongly opposed any attempt to introduce anti-Christian doctrines into the movement'.[31] The Vatican newspaper published a retraction, but closer to home, where it mattered the most, the press campaign against Labour continued apace. Norton's behaviour was a let-down to many in his party, however, not least his predecessor, Thomas Johnson. Norton's letter, he complained to the party secretary, represented an unreasonable blurring of the boundary between politics and personal morality and he was particularly upset that Norton had suggested to Cardinal Pacelli that he (Pacelli) ought consult a 'recognised Catholic authority qualified to interpret authoritatively such tendencies' among the Irish labour force, rather than Congress or the Labour Party. 'If the party adopts the position that this question is one concerning faith and morals and in consequence is a matter for the Hierarchy to pronounce authoritatively upon,' Johnson warned, 'I for one will have to reconsider my position as a member.'[32]

An indication of the degree of sensitivity within the Labour leadership about the party's relationship with the Church can be gleaned from the fate of its weekly paper, *Labour News*, which was published from 1936 to 1938. Unlike its predecessors, *Labour News* was edited by a professional journalist, Christopher O'Sullivan. This made the paper easily the most lively and most readable Labour publication yet, but posed its own problems as the editor's eye for a good story or memorable headline saw him skirt a little close to the edge for the Labour leadership's liking. O'Sullivan was able to avoid mention of Spain readily enough but he proved less successful at avoiding taboo areas closer to home. At a time when Labour was being subjected to regular criticism from Catholic sources, *Labour News* editorials were frequently belligerent, as was its reportage. Far from avoiding controversy, its editor displayed a propensity to throw fuel on the fire – not satisfied with engaging in a week-by-week spat with the *Limerick Leader* over Labour's alleged communist leanings, the editor produced a poster proclaiming 'CHURCH HAS NO SOLUTION FOR LABOUR' to advertise a subsequent issue of the paper.[33] A week later, *Labour News* ran an article relating how Catholic clergy in Youghal had issued an edict that no women would be admitted to church if they were bare legged, *Labour News* arguing that they were only likely to be bare legged if they could not afford stockings and so the issue was not one of modesty but low pay.[34]

The editor was warned to pay more heed to the party's particular sensitivities after a number of such incidents, but he paid scant notice to these entreaties. In the end, a seemingly innocuous verse entitled 'Poem by a Negro boy to God' proved to be the final straw. It was no worse than a lot of the poems that had graced the pages of the paper, but one line, 'You must have a great laugh up there in your big sky, Lord!', proved too much.[35] One associate of Norton's wrote to him to complain about the issue, asserting: 'I am not a "crawthumper" or a mass of religion but one must take exception to *tripe* of the nature as frequently published by *Labour News*.'[36] Norton agreed, and expressed his displeasure at this 'piece of blasphemy'.[37] After countless warnings about this type of content, he and his fellow directors had had enough. O'Sullivan's services were dispensed with immediately and publication suspended until a replacement editor could be found. It seems astonishing that a paper could be wound up on such a flimsy basis, but Norton was convinced, as he told the liquidation meeting that, useful as the paper had been, the party would have 'lost more seats if they had kept the paper on'.[38] As he conceded privately, 'certain individuals – who are non-Catholic – will probably disagree with our attitude but we cannot help that and must meet any criticism they make.'[39] No doubt by design rather than accident, the lead story in the final edition of *Labour News* suggested that there was to be 'a theological censor for Dublin'. It was the last time that the Labour leadership allowed itself to be put in such a position. No other newspaper was ever allowed sail as close to the edge as *Labour News*. A year later, the Dublin Regional Council began to publish a weekly paper called *Torch* – significantly, while it was more radical than *Labour News* in its politics, it never criticized the Church.

More significantly, the Workers' Republic constitution had been abandoned at Labour's 1939 conference after the INTO had secured the hierarchy's opinion that it ran contrary to Catholic social teaching. Clearly, holding on to it was more trouble than it was worth, although several voices were raised in complaint at the Church's interference in the party's business.[40] It is important to remember in this case, however, that the hierarchy had interfered at the instigation of laymen. Norton had proved that if he could be opportunistically radical, he could be opportunistically conservative too, and he had no interest in sticking to a position that might lose his party votes and seats.

DEVILS CITING SCRIPTURE: SCHISM AND RELIGION, 1943–50

Norton's willingness to abandon ship when it came to the Workers' Republic paid off in the short term, but the party's respite from criticism proved short lived. In 1944, the ITGWU disaffiliated from Labour and the majority of its deputies left to form the National Labour Party, ostensibly because Labour had been 'infested by communists', although this was merely a smoke screen for the personality disputes (notably William O'Brien and James Larkin) and inter-union rivalry (the Irish unions, especially the ITGWU, and the British-based amalgamateds and the WUI) that were really behind the move.[41] Regardless of the genuine reason for the split, Labour was subjected to a barrage of accusations about the activities of communists within the party from National Labour itself and in weekly exposés in the Catholic *Standard* penned by Alfred O'Rahilly, professor of ethics in UCC and a committed Catholic Actionist with close links to the labour movement. Perhaps more so than any other occasion in Irish politics, religion became a stick with which the cynical could hit their opponents. National Labour painted itself as the Irish ultra-Catholic party despite the fact that several senior members, such as Cathal O'Shannon and Frank Robbins, had been vocally anti-clerical in the past, not to mention the long-time atheist William O'Brien. Notwithstanding their secular pedigree of old, however, these men proved the maxim that the devil can cite scripture for his purpose as they proved only too happy to paint their former comrades as an anti-God, anti-national party. Other enemies of Labour, such as Seán MacEntee, enthusiastically copied their example. More than ever, Norton and his colleagues became determined that no ammunition should be given to the opponents of the party. Before long, no Labour speech was complete without at least one reference to an encyclical.

When Bishop Dignan of Clonfert's *Social Security: Outlines of a Scheme of National Health Insurance* was published in 1944, Labour became vocal proponents of the scheme, which proposed the organization of social insurance along vocational lines, a suggestion which one commentator described as neo-fascist.[42] It was evidence of a certain à la carte attitude towards Catholic social teaching: the fact was, while Labour opposed vocationalism (as seen throughout the 1930s and on the publication of the report of the Commission on Vocational Organisation in 1944) it was unable to pass up a social welfare scheme written by a bishop, even if it fell far short of the type of state-organized universal scheme that the party actually favoured. The opportunist nature of Labour's support became clear some four years later when Norton became Minister for Social Welfare. Not only did he ignore the suggestions of the Dignan scheme but he dissolved the National Health Insurance Society of which Dignan was chairman and the organization on which the bishop's plan had been based.[43]

With Labour competing with National Labour for the mantle of most holy, it was vital that would-be heretics were kept silent. Brian

Inglis, a (Protestant) journalist in Labour's weekly, the *Irish People*, remembered how the writers and editors were under strict instructions to 'avoid writing about any subject in which criticism, even if justified, could be construed as criticism of the Church',[44] but if its Dublin writers endured the paper's limitations with stoicism, outsiders were not always as understanding. When Seán O'Casey submitted an article which contained criticism of the Roman Catholic archbishop of Westminster, Cardinal Griffin, its editor, Sheila Greene, had to write to him and explain that she could not print it as it stood, as 'without putting a tooth in it, it would be harmful to the Labour Party ... I think if you lived here you would understand what I mean'.[45] Greene asked O'Casey to resubmit the article without reference to the cardinal, but O'Casey was unsympathetic. 'Goethe's last words were, "More light. More light",' he wrote. 'Mine will probably be "More courage. More courage".' His conclusion was damning: 'I am not out to force the Labour Party of Ireland. Their ways rest with their own conscience. Please let me have the article back. No wonder Bill O'Brien has had his way.'[46]

O'Casey's distain was very well, but the fact remained that even though Labour assiduously avoided anything which might leave it open to attack for the rest of the 1940s, it remained suspect in the eyes of both the state and the Church. It was regarded by the Knights of Columbanus, for instance, as a 'tentacle of Communism',[47] while a confidential dossier drawn up by the Department of Justice on communism in Ireland identified almost every senior member of the Labour Party in Dublin as a communist, or fellow traveller at the very least.[48] Significantly, it devoted a whole page to Trinity College Dublin's affiliations with communist and left-wing groups. As, effectively, a Protestant university, Trinity became home to many 'political queers' (as one Fianna Fáil Minister for Justice later put it)[49] at a time when clerical dominance in UCD, UCC and UCG meant that politically suspect lecturers were not hired and political radicalism on the part of the students was actively discouraged as late as the end of the 1960s.[50] The Justice dossier noted people's religious affiliations where known, with *Irish People* editor, Sheila Greene, for instance, identified as a Trinity graduate and a lapsed Quaker. It is interesting that although many of those active in the Labour Party in Dublin at this time were Protestant or non-Catholic, almost none was prepared to stand for election. Among the reasons given by one activist at the time for not going forward for election was that she felt she was 'too vulnerable in certain respects (not being a practising Catholic etc.)'.[51]

In the end, far from showing 'more courage', Labour's pronouncements became more sectarian and more reactionary as the decade wore on, not least when it tried to effect a *rapprochement* with National Labour in 1947. Unable to put their differences aside, the two parties went head to head at the 1948 general election, with candidates from both factions outdoing themselves in their citation of papal encyclicals.

IN GOVERNMENT, 1948–51

The end result of the general election was the formation of the first inter-party government which comprised of Labour, National Labour, Fine Gael, the farmers' party Clann na Talmhan, the new republican party Clann na Poblachta as well as various independents. Described by Fianna Fáil's Seán Lemass as a 'makeshift majority', the first inter-party government spanned the full spectrum of Irish politics from Commonwealth to republican and from right to left, but on one issue it was united, as the government went out of its way to emphasize its Catholic allegiance.[52] One of the government's first actions was to send a message of homage to the pope through the Taoiseach in which the pontiff was assured not only of the cabinet's filial loyalty and devotion but of its 'firm resolve to be guided in all our work by the teaching of Christ, and to strive for the attainment of a social order in Ireland based on Christian principles'.[53] The letter represents the most obsequious correspondence by an Irish government to another power, but it is likely that the various parties had very different reasons for supporting it. Fine Gael, for instance, was an orthodox Catholic party which supported vocationalism and had a tradition of clerical support, Clann na Talmhan was a conservative rural party, its ministerial representative Joe Blowick's brother being a parish priest in Mayo, while James Dillon, the independent minister, was a member of the Ancient Order of Hibernians. The other parties' ministers' motives are more ambiguous. All were nominally Catholic, and most were practising Catholics – but certain in the cases of Labour's William Norton and Clann na Poblachta's Seán MacBride, it does seem as though they lent their support to this type of ostentatious Catholicism in an effort to inoculate themselves from external criticism since both men's parties had been subjected to accusations of communism during the election, with Clann na Poblachta especially having been subjected to a smear campaign by the clergy.[54]

Labour's priority going into government was to establish a new social welfare system, and as Minister for Social Welfare, Norton was determined that no-one should do anything which might endanger his plans. It was a very sensitive issue since the Catholic Church was opposed to increasing the state's role in welfare provision which it viewed as contrary to Catholic social teaching, a view shared within the government by the Fine Gael ministers and James Dillon. Norton knew he would have to act with great sensitivity if he was going to succeed on the issue, a view confirmed on the first occasion his scheme was put before cabinet, when the Fine Gael Minister for Finance, Patrick McGilligan, responded to the plans by suggesting that the views of Reverend Dr Peter McKevitt, the chair of Catholic Sociology and Catholic Action in Maynooth, be taken on the matter before it went any further.[55] Norton's social welfare bill is a classic example of the gap between Labour's rhetoric and reality, for while the party had given its full backing to bishop Dignan's plan for social insurance after 1944, once in government the bishop's plan was dropped immediately. In an effort to avoid conflict on the subject, Norton worked behind the scenes to assuage the hierarchy's concerns and bring them onside. At the same time, it was made quite clear to members of his own party that it should avoid saying anything which might make Norton's task more difficult in this regard. Brian Inglis recalled that they were told:

> Don't forget, Norton's drafting a new social security Bill. It can't go far, because Fine Gael won't vote for it if the Bishops don't like it, and if they won't vote for it we can't get it through; if you go rocking the boat and get people scared that we're all a lot of fellow travellers, we'll get nowhere. People have got to realise we're an Irish party, not taking our orders from Moscow.[56]

How, it would be reasonable to ask, might the leap be made from not identifying with the British Labour government to looking like a puppet of the Soviets, but there was a deliberate blurring of the boundaries between the two by Irish conservatives. Certainly, in the context of the escalation of the Cold War, socialism was identified as a stalking horse for communism. As the archbishop of Dublin, John Charles McQuaid, explained in 1948:

> Atheistic Communism has not yet attempted violence in this land. It has not openly pronounced its brutal sentence on all the principles of our Catholic Faith and culture. Its agents have been content to disguise their aims under the mask of Socialism, which seems to look only for fair conditions of a decent livelihood.[57]

As such socialism was portrayed as being, to all intents, the same as communism, except a more insidious variant of the latter – as one Catholic newspaper later remarked, 'the Welfare State is diluted Socialism and socialism is disguised communism.'[58] For the purposes of Irish Catholicism, Clement Attlee was placed on an ideological par with Joe Stalin.

Having worked diligently to get the hierarchy onside, Norton managed to escape the Church's full-scale wrath when he put forward his scheme, although he fell far short of securing its support.[59] If it seems distasteful that a government minister should devote so much time to garnering the support of the Catholic hierarchy, it is worth looking at the result of an alternative approach. Noël Browne, Clann na Poblachta Minister for Health, ignored the Catholic hierarchy to his cost when he tried to put in place the Mother and Child Scheme which had been formulated by his Fianna Fáil predecessor. Had Browne shown more of Norton's diplomacy things might have worked out very differently, but he did not, and rather than succeeding in putting in place free health care for children under sixteen he merely provoked a furore. In the end, neither man managed to see in his scheme, but while one became a popular left-wing martyr, the other's reputation was tarnished irreparably. All the same, regardless of whether members of the first inter-party government kow-towed to the Church for reasons of devotion or opportunism, they had succeeded in winning the approval of the archbishop of Dublin, John Charles McQuaid. A year after the government's collapse, McQuaid reflected on his experiences in dealing with it and with Fianna Fáil administrations, particularly on the question of health. 'To deal with Mr Costello's Cabinet was, with the exception of Dr Browne ... and Mr McBride ... a very pleasant experience,' McQuaid opined to the nuncio. 'To deal with Mr de Valera and his Ministers is indeed a different matter.'[60]

COLD WAR CATHOLICISM

The Mother and Child Scheme marked the zenith of Church power in independent Ireland but it was a Pyrrhic victory. Although impossible to measure, its role in preventing the Mother and Child Scheme engendered a backlash of sorts among ordinary people. Many shared Labour minister Michael Keyes' belief that 'they shouldn't be allowed to do this',[61] and that on this occasion the bishops had gone too far.[62] In response, the hierarchy pulled in its horns and removed itself from so overtly political interference but, behind the scenes, it was as active and as influential as ever. There may have been occasional examples of resistance to Church edicts – the most famous being the mass attendance at the Ireland versus Yugoslavia football match in 1954 in defiance of a Church-led boycott – but, for the most part, Irish society remained intrinsically Catholic and profoundly hostile to the left. Throughout the 1950s, the heavy weight of peer pressure was brought to bear on individuals, unions and Labour to be seen to be acting in an orthodox Catholic fashion. There were fewer Catholic spectaculars, such as McQuaid's massive collection for the Italian Christian Democrats in 1948, or the enormous street protests against the imprisonment by communist regimes of Cardinal Stepinac of Zagreb in 1946 and of Cardinal Mindzenty of Hungary in 1949 on which occasion an estimated 150,000 people marched through the streets of Dublin led by their lord mayor, John Breen, himself a former member of the CPI,[63] but at a practical level little had changed. Groups such as the Irish Housewives' Association remained under surveillance and subject to accusations of communism, while the case of the Church-orchestrated boycott of the Ballyfermot and Inchicore co-operative due to the involvement of a number of communists proved the clergy's ability to use the pulpit to bully was undiminished.[64] Where the men and women of the labour movement held views that were either too left wing, too liberal or too secular for the time, they simply kept their own counsel. When they did not they faced ignominy or assault.[65] The pressure to conform was unrelenting, as Mina Carney explained to Seán O'Casey in 1955:

> Young Jim is having a hard time resisting the invasion of the union by the Church. There is a move to try and have all Irish Unions to each have their own chaplain. Many unions now have the crucifix over their doors which means every member entering the headquarters must genuflect.[66]

Similarly, one Labour man from the North Strand wrote to O'Casey some months later, lamenting that 'the ole place has changed for no good. A few months ago Larkin's Union took over Vaughans Hotel as H.Q. and at a formal opening in it last week, half the clergy in Dublin were in it. "Hail Queen of Heaven" has now replaced the Watchword of Labour as the anthem of the union.'[67] Nor was this caution restricted to the Labour movement. During discussions about establishing a left-wing paper in 1956, Noël Browne's political partner, Jack McQuillan, was adamant that it should not take an openly socialist line because 'such a policy would not get the support of the people [and] his parish priest would be on his trail if he became publicly identified with socialism.'[68] It was an unedifying state of affairs, prompting a typically cynical Seán O'Casey to muse: 'I should be surprised if there were not competitions soon of endurance and speed in the recital of rosary and litany. Catholic Stakhanovites. The Campaign of Emulation. 150 percent over quota in prayer and penance.'[69]

A RETURN TO CHRISTIAN SOCIALISM?

This climate of stifling conformism was more than many Labour activists on the left could take, and many of those who had been active during the 1940s and 1950s had dropped out by the following decade when finally the atmosphere had begun to change. It was a long time coming, however, and even though the change was significant, it was by no means as profound as it appeared. In 1960 William Norton resigned as Labour leader after twenty-eight years in the role and was succeeded by Brendan Corish. Corish was generally well liked but there was concern in some circles over the shape his leadership would take. Known as a devout Catholic (and a Knight of Columbanus, as Norton was before him), he had firmly aligned himself with the Church on several controversial occasions. He had declared himself a 'bishops' man' on the Mother and Child Scheme and later told the Dáil: 'I am an Irishman second; I am a Catholic first ... if the hierarchy give me any direction with regard to Catholic social teaching or Catholic moral teaching, I accept without qualification in all respects the teaching of the Hierarchy and the Church to which I belong,'[70] a comment which bore remarkable similarities to his father's proclamation two decades earlier when he told the 1936 Labour conference: 'I am neither socialist, syndicalist nor communist. I am a Catholic, thank God, and am prepared to take my teaching from the Church.'[71] Sometimes this alignment manifested itself in a kind of unthinking conservatism. For instance, when the left-wing newspaper *Plough* complained on one occasion that the 'lengths to which [Labour] will go in seeking to identify themselves with reactionary policies is almost terrifying', Corish was singled out for attack because of his support for 'bigger and better censorship' of everything from children's matinees to British television.[72] More alarming, however, was his behaviour during the Fethard-on-Sea boycott in 1958. It was an extremely bitter episode, made all the worse because it involved the break up of a family, and its resolution required a combination of diplomacy and moral leadership, which then Taoiseach de Valera showed in spades. Corish, on the other hand, was happy to stoke the bigotry that was fuelling the boycott, and called on de Valera to ensure that 'certain people will not conspire ... to kidnap Catholic children',[73] a stance which led

Noël Browne, in typically jaundiced fashion, to refer to him subsequently as the 'Bastard of Fethard'.[74]

In the event, however, Corish's conduct as leader was never as reactionary as some had feared. In fact, Labour shifted leftward under his leadership and declared itself to be a socialist party for the first time in its history. How could Corish's Catholicism be reconciled with the course his party took under his watch? This might be attributed in part to his kitchen cabinet or circle of advisors and speech writers who were more liberal than he, including Labour's parliamentary officer and Corish's chief speech writer, Catherine McGuinness, who was an active member of the Church of Ireland. Corish was deeply influenced by the changes brought about by Pope John XXIII, and became arguably the first Labour leader to quote from papal pronouncements and actually mean it. It was the middle of the 1960s before the fear of socialism began to wane, as the pontificate of John XXIII ushered in an age of détente after the Cold War Catholicism of Pius XII. Not only did Pope John move away from Pius XII's aggressively anti-communist outlook in international relations (the latter having issued 123 anti-communist proclamations during his nineteen years as pontiff[75]), but perhaps equally significantly, he managed to reconcile Catholic social teaching to the positive aspects of the more interventionist nature of the contemporary state in his 1961 encyclical, *Mater et Magistra*, and further enunciated his teaching on social justice in his 1963 encyclical, *Pacem in Terris*. For some on the left, this profound shift in Church thinking allowed them to reconcile themselves back to the Church, the late historian and socialist Miriam Daly being one such example.[76] For others, it allowed them to reconcile their politics to their faith. Arguably, Brendan Corish was among these. In an article published in 1969, Corish described Pope John as 'one of the greatest contributors of all to changing Irish attitudes', and taken at one level he was probably correct. It is difficult to exaggerate the ubiquity of *Mater et Magistra* in so many Irish publications in the months, and even years, after it was published. There were summer schools devoted to it for both religious and laity, and articles in the many Catholic periodicals and such like. So much might be expected, but it also received heavy coverage in everything from trade union publications to the *Irish Socialist*. In fact, the *Irish Socialist*[77] regularly referred to *Mater et Magistra* to back up Irish Workers Party policy on the economy. Even more bizarre was the occasion of the *Irish Socialist* denouncing the government because 'its whole line ... runs contrary to the doctrines of *Pacem in terres*'![78]

There was, it must be said, a certain amount of resistance within the

Irish Church to the movement towards a greater emphasis on social justice and a more cuddly form of Catholicism, but the new teaching did trickle down nonetheless, not least among younger, more educated Catholics who were involved in organizations such as the Catholic sociology group, *Christus Rex*, the Dublin Institute for Catholic Sociology, or even, as the decade wore on, students of politics in UCD who were being taught by Rev. Fergal O'Connor, lecturer in political philosophy in the Department of Ethics and Politics.[79] On balance, however, the influence of Pope John was profound, but very uneven, and if delegates at *Christus Rex* conferences could quote chapter and verse of *Mater et Magistra*, the same might not be said for the average reader of the *Messenger*. The shallow impact of Pope John in Ireland became abundantly evident at the 1969 general election. Labour had adopted some very left-wing policies and had declared that the 1970s would be socialist. The party had expected to come under attack for its socialist policies but was taken aback by the ferocity of Fianna Fáil's campaign against it, which included telling voters that Labour planned to nationalize family farms and Guinnesses. Before long, Labour's general secretary Brendan Halligan began making speeches across the country stressing Pope John's influence on Labour Party policy. Soon the *Irish Times*' political commentator, John Healy, was laughing at how 'Pope Halligan' (described elsewhere as the 'cleric in mufti') planned to take the 'stars from the plough and the stars to fashion a new version of the miraculous medal'.[80] None of this was enough to prevent Labour being called off the altar from one end of the country to another. It certainly could not hope to compete with Jack Lynch's infamous convent tour which he undertook the week before the poll. As Conor Cruise O'Brien later recalled:

> The press and media were not present for that series of convent chats, but the word came through all the same. A Labour colleague from Munster told me ruefully of a mothers' meeting convened in his constituency by a Reverend Mother on the day before polling day. It was not, said the Reverend Mother to the other mothers, for her to advise them on a political matter. Certainly not! She only wished to remind them of their duty, as Catholic mothers, both to vote and to be very prudent about how to vote ... Whatever party they voted for, however, they should be sure ... was free from any tendency to communism. If there was doubt as to whether there might be communists in a certain party, it would be better not to vote for that party.[81]

Not all nuns were as circumspect as their Munster sisters, however. One Roscommon remembered:

> A nun in our local convent told fifth class primary to tell their parents not to vote Labour as they were all communists in the Labour Party. Now this spread like wild fire to every home, and even though I don't know what effect it had, I know enough to know it had its effect. I heard one mother saying, 'The two parties are much of a muchness, but I won't vote Labour because O'Brien and Thornley are communists and should be shot.'[82]

As the British ambassador, Andrew Gilchrist, noted at the time, 'the priests in Ireland may no longer tell their parishioners who to vote *for* but are quite capable of telling them who to vote *against*.'[83] Far from making the advance it had expected, Labour suffered a net loss of seats. This was due to a variety of factors of which Church condemnation during the campaign was only one. It is impossible, especially at this remove, to assess how influential the Church's opposition to Labour was on people's voting behaviour, but it certainly cannot have helped, not least when political opponents are willing and able to capitalize on this distrust, as Fianna Fáil was on this occasion.

CONCLUSION

The Church rarely mobilized against Labour, but this is because Labour was assiduous in making sure that it was given no cause to do so. The degree of self-censorship was enormous in both policy and language, be it Labour's amendment of the Workers' Republic constitution, its silence over the Spanish Civil War, or its failure to support social reforms such as non-means-tested social welfare benefits or health reforms which would have, in the eyes of the Church in Ireland, been contrary to Catholic social teaching. Had Labour heeded O'Casey's call for 'More courage!', would this have won it more votes? It is impossible to tell. The truth is that, until very recently, it would *seem* that parties whose policies or doctrine went against that of the Catholic Church would suffer at the hands of the electorate. Anecdotal evidence tends to indicate that the Church was influential and for a politician or party to be called off the altar would be profoundly damaging, but we can never know just how important it was because each time Labour came close to getting a belt of the crosier they pulled back. At the 1969 general election when Labour stood under an avowedly socialist banner, the only occasion (during the timeframe being looked at here) that the party showed 'more courage', it lost seats. Yes, some of this was due to other more mundane factors like constituency boundary changes and candidate rivalries,[84] but there was a belief nonetheless that the Church had played an important role in halting Labour's hoped-for advance. On the other hand, there are occasions, such as following the Mother and Child Scheme, when more courage would almost certainly have benefited Labour in a most practical way. Despite the hierarchy's opposition to the scheme, it remained popular, and the election not only of Noël Browne himself, but other Browneite candidates gives a reasonably clear indication that people would vote against the bishops and the bishops' men when their health and welfare were so clearly at stake. Ultimately, Labour had to walk a tightrope when it came to matters religious. Ecclesiastical condemnation was a constant threat which, if realized, could prove hugely damaging, but we can never know how damaging because Labour so assiduously avoided doing anything which might bring it into effect.

NOTES

My thanks to Susannah Riordan for her suggestions on an earlier draft of this chapter.

1. *Irish Times*, 27 August 2007.
2. The only party in Dáil Éireann to deviate from this until the 1970s was the National Progressive Democrats which was less a party than an umbrella for Noël Browne and Jack McQuillan.
3. See for example Graham Dale, *God's Politicians: the Christian Contribution to 100 Years of Labour* (London: 2000).
4. Patrick Murray, *Oracles of God: The Roman Catholic Church and Irish Politics, 1922-37* (Dublin: 2000), p. 1.
5. See Donal Nevin, *James Connolly: 'A full life'* (Dublin: 2005), pp. 327-33; 673-90 for a review of the writings on Connolly and religion.
6. *Irish Times*, 13 October 1923.
7. James Larkin and James Connolly were the most notable of these.
8. This was asterisked by the enumerator who wrote at the foot of the household schedule, 'further information refused'. Mortished's sister, Kathleen, put herself down as an 'Agnostic'. Thanks to Fintan Lane for bringing this to my attention.
9. *Voice of Labour*, 20 October 1923.
10. *Voice of Labour*, 20 October 1923.
11. *Irishman*, 25 June 1927.
12. *Irishman*, 1 October 1927.
13. Gilbert Lynch, unpublished memoir.
14. *Irishman*, 19 July 1930.
15. *Voice of Labour*, 13 December 1924.
16. *Irishman*, 1 October 1927.
17. *Irishman*, 26 March 1927.
18. *Irishman*, 28 April 1928.
19. See Provisional Draft of the National Labour Party (Confidential) 4 Dec. 1929 ILHM&A POWU.
20. Noel Ward, 'The INTO and the Catholic Church, 1930-1955' (MA, UCD, 1987).
21. J.A. Gaughan, *Thomas Johnson* (Dublin: 1980), p. 474.

22. See J.J. Lee, *Ireland 1912-1985* p.162.
23. Ibid.
24. O'Connor, *Reds and the Green* p.186.
25. John P. Swift, *John Swift: An Irish Dissident* (Dublin: 1991), p. 83.
26. DD 29 April 1932.
27. John Cooney, *John Charles McQuaid: Ruler of Catholic Ireland* (Dublin: 1999), p. 224.
28. See *Labour Party Annual Report* 1933–4, p. 70; Fearghal McGarry, '"Catholics first and politicians afterwards": the Labour Party and the Workers' Republic, 1936–39', *Saothar*, vol. 25 (2000), pp. 57–66. Niamh Puirséil, *The Irish Labour Party, 1922–73* (Dublin: 2007).
29. Fearghal McGarry, *Irish Politics and the Spanish Civil War* (Cork: 1999), p. 188.
30. *Irish Rosary*, February 1937; *Labour News*, 27 February 1937; McGarry, 'Catholics first', p. 60.
31. The letter was reprinted in full in *Labour News*, 6 March 1937 and *Labour Party Annual Report* 1937–8, pp. 14–16.
32. Johnson to Luke Duffy, 6 March 1937, NLI Ms 17231.
33. *Labour News*, 31 July 1937.
34. *Labour News*, 7 August 1937.
35. *Labour News*, 26 March 1938.
36. T. Kehoe to Norton, 9 April 1938, ILHM&A POWU.
37. Norton to T. Kehoe, 11 April 1938, ILHM&A POWU.
38. Owen Sheehy Skeffington, 'What is wrong with the Labour Party?' in *Workers' Action*, May 1942.
39. Norton to T. Kehoe 11 April 1938, ILHM&A POWU.
40. See Annual Report.
41. See Puirséil, *Irish Labour Party*, pp. 91–103.
42. *Irish Times*, 26–8 October 1944 quoted in Susannah Riordan, '"A Political Blackthorn": Seán MacEntee, the Dignan plan and the principle of ministerial responsibility', in *Irish Economic and Social History*, xxvii, p. 49.
43. See Riordan, '"A Political Blackthorn"'.
44. Brian Inglis, *West Briton* (London: 1962), p. 107.
45. Sheila Greene to Seán O'Casey, 7 October 1946. NLI O'Casey papers. Ms 38,005.
46. Seán O'Casey to Sheila Greene, 12 October 1946. NLI O'Casey papers. Ms 38,005.
47. Evelyn Bolster, *Knights of St Columbanus*, p.105.
48. Communism in Ireland. Department of Justice typescript, 31 December 1947. UCDAD P67/548 (1).
49. *Irish Times*, 7 June 1969.
50. See for instance C.S. Andrews, *Man of No Property* (Dublin: 2001), p. 59 on the attitudes towards socialism held by UCD's Commerce faculty in the 1920s.
51. 'Peggy R' [Patricia Rushton] to John de Courcy Ireland, 14 May 1953, UCDAD P29/I/156. One exception was Arnold Marsh, the headmaster of Drogheda grammar school and author of *Full Employment in Ireland*, who took 5 per cent of the poll in Dun Laoghaire-Rathdown in 1948. Outside Dublin, R.M. (Bobby) Burke came close to taking a seat in Galway where he won 14 per cent of the poll on his second outing in 1943. Burke, a professed Christian socialist, ran a co-operative farm in Tuam and was appointed to the Seanad when Labour entered government in 1948.
52. J.H. Whyte, *Church and State in Modern Ireland*, pp. 157–8.
53. Ibid.
54. MacBride, *That Day's Struggle* (Dublin: 2005), p. 141.
55. Minute of meeting of the cabinet committee, 30 August 1949. UCDAD P190/554 (10).
56. Inglis, *West Briton*, p. 135.
57. Address on Radio Éireann, 11 April 1948, quoted in Cooney, *McQuaid*, p. 218. See also McQuaid's Lenten pastoral earlier that year in *Irish Times*, 9 February 1948.
58. *Hibernia*, February 1952.
59. For Norton's efforts on social welfare see, Whyte, *Church and State*, pp. 179–83.
60. McQuaid to apostolic nuncio, Most Reverend Gerald P. O'Hara, DD 7 November 1952. DDA McQuaid papers.
61. Browne, *Against the Tide*, p. 175. Keyes was well liked and respected but by no means regarded as a radical, having attracted criticism from the left over a decade earlier when he had attended a meeting of the Irish Christian Front during the Spanish Civil War.
62. Tom Garvin, 'A quiet revolution: the remaking of Irish political culture', in Ray Ryan (ed.),

Writing in the Irish Republic: Literature, Culture, Politics 1949–1999 (London: 2000), p. 193. Apart from anecdotal evidence, this is backed up by the electoral successes of candidates at the subsequent general election who took a Browneite position either during the crisis or during the contest.
63. Young Jim Larkin did likewise. As one of his supporters later explained, 'he dared not do otherwise; if he hadn't it would have split the union.' Private source.
64. Hilda Tweedy, *A link in the chain. The story of the Irish Housewives' Association* (Dublin: 1992); interview with Joe Deasy, 2001; Puirséil, *Irish Labour Party*, pp. 146–9.
65. For example, during the local election campaign in the summer of 1955, one Labour candidate in Mayo was denounced as a communist by the local parish priest (who was the brother of the Minister for Lands, Joe Blowick) while a former Blueshirt tried to pull him from his platform. The candidate abandoned his meeting in order to prevent further trouble. Thomas Kilroy to Jim Larkin, 6 June 1955, ILHM&A JLJ/3 1953–7 (LP).
66. Mina Carney to O'Casey, 10 April 1955. NLI MS 37.989.
67. Pat McDonnell to O'Casey, 2 October 1955, NLI MS 37.995.
68. Memorandum on recent meeting of new political group, 16 October 1956. UCDAD P7b/120.
69. O'Casey to Carney, 22 February 1945. David Krause (ed.), *Letters of Séan O'Casey Vol. 2, 1942–54* (New York: 1980), p. 217.
70. DD Volume 138, Column 839, 29 April 1953.
71. Labour Party annual report 1936.
72. *Plough*, June 1958. See for example DD 17 April 1958 vol. 167, col. 330.
73. Quoted in Michael Gallagher, *The Irish Labour Party in Transition, 1957–82* (Dublin: 1982), p. 42.
74. Information from Owen Dudley Edwards and Justin Keating.
75. Mike Milotte, *Communism in Modern Ireland: The Pursuit of the Workers' Reepublic Since 1916* (Dublin: 1984), p. 247.
76. Miriam Daly, 'Believing today', *The Furrow*, 18, 10, (October 1967), p. 555.
77. July 1964. The vogue for citing papal pronouncements often resulted in quite ludicrous pronouncements. For instance, in August 1967 the *United Irishman* featured an article examining 'papal and republican parallels'. Comparing quotes from Paul VI's 'On the development of Peoples' with passages by Pearse, Lalor, Seamus Costello and Muintir Wolfe Tone's pamphlet 'The case against the Common Market', the pope was found to be in full agreement with all those on this particular pantheon.
78. Milotte, *Communism*, pp. 247–8. See also *Irish Socialist*, July, August, September 1964; September, December 1965; January 1966; November 1967.
79. See, for example, Denis McCullough, 'Protest and the Student' *UCD News* magazine, no.1 no date (NLI); interview with Brendan Halligan, 8 February 2002. It is also worth noting the appearance in Ireland of left-wing Christian groups at the end of the 1960s. These included the Student Christian Movement, eventually founded in UCD after a great deal of resistance from college authorities, an Irish branch of Slant and a short-lived magazine, *Grille*.
80. *Irish Times*, 31 May 1969.
81. *Conor Cruise O'Brien, Memoir: My Life and Themes* (Dublin: 1988), pp. 321–2.
82. *Sunday Independent*, 29 June 1969.
83. Gilchrist to Stewart, forthcoming election in Irish Republic, 29 May 1969. TNA FCO33/1753.
84. For example, see Puirséil, *Irish Labour Party*, p.269.

12

Writers of the Left: Politics and Culture in Ireland during the 1930s

PAUL O'BRIEN

THE LITERARY CLASS WAR

The cultural history of the 1930s in Ireland has received relatively little attention or has been dealt with in a general manner. Much of the existing work has concentrated on 'political institutions and developments, dominated by the changes and tensions in the constitutional relationship between Ireland and Britain'.[1] Domestically, the key element was a sense of post-revolutionary disillusionment, as first the Cumann na nGaedheal and then the Fianna Fáil governments failed to deliver on the radical social programme that the independence movement had promised. Internationally, this was a period of global economic crisis, allied to the rise of fascism and the threat of war.[2]

The Fianna Fáil government of Éamon de Valera came to power in 1932 at the beginning of a decade that was dominated by economic stagnation, isolationism, censorship, Church control of hospitals and education, and the imposition of a narrow Catholic social morality. Terence Brown has sketched a gloomy portrait of a nation struggling in two different directions. On the one hand, de Valera believed that Ireland's destiny 'lay in cultivating her national distinctiveness as assiduously as possible'.[3] On the other, many intellectuals and those on the left argued that Ireland's economic and cultural provincialism could only be redeemed if this was combined with a proper concern for and acceptance of the riches of European culture and politics.[4] Culture in the Irish Free State was 'dominated by a sense of disenchantment with the romantic vision of Ireland cultivated by the Literary Revival and later institutionalized by the

State'.[5] A new generation of writers and artists was forced to discover freedom in a history dominated by colonialism and nationalism. Many were brave enough to shatter the Irish literary stereotype, which the revival had created, and alter their style in response to the changing world around them.

Internationally and in Ireland, in different ways, and at a different pace, the economic and political imperatives of the decade demanded that writers be engaged and committed. Many on the left argued that literature could not remain neutral and claimed that literature itself was on the barricades. This prevailing sense of impending disaster seemed to be realized with the outbreak of the Spanish Civil War in 1936, and the most important writing of the period can be seen as an effort to respond to this crisis. Elements of the 1930s cultural movement saw themselves as genuine revolutionaries deriving inspiration from the urban working class and political movements that populated the decade. Writing itself became a vehicle for social criticism and revolt. However, a cultural movement that wanted to relate to the larger social movement needed to alter its own attitudes, its habitual metropolitan bias, its disdain for the working class and its reverence for the insights of university-educated social elites. The best took up the challenge; inspired by the war in Spain and the fight against fascism, they tried to transform the cultural radicalism of the period into a political force. George Orwell put the case for political commitment: 'If fascism triumphs, I am finished as a writer.'[6] British publications such as *New Writing* and *Poetry and the People* attempted to combine aesthetic ideas with social attitudes. *New Writing*, edited by John Lehman, introduced European writers to British and Irish audiences. *Left Review*, which was founded in 1934, provided space for many Irish left-wing writers and became the vehicle for many of the young writers who had become personally and directly involved in radical politics.

Alick West, a former student at Trinity College Dublin, wrote of the tension between culture and propaganda that dominated much of the debate on the international left in the 1930s:

> In this sense, it was true that culture is a weapon in the fight for socialism. But the truth depended on recognition of the greater truth that socialism is a weapon in the fight for culture. For our final aim was not the establishment of a political and economic structure, but the heightening of human life. Without this recognition, the slogan becomes a perversion of the truth, since it degraded culture into a means to a political end.[7]

These young revolutionaries attempted to fuse politics and aesthetics into a movement whose triumph seemed historically inevitable. However, there was an unresolved tension at the heart of the dream that art could be political, appreciated by the masses, yet produced to the highest aesthetic standards. Unfortunately, this debate happened at a time when the Communist Party at an international level was squeezing the life out of cultural production. Socialist realism, a combination of elements from the proletarian cultural movement in the 1920s allied to traditional realism, became the theoretical basis for Soviet culture in 1934. The party line was imposed, experimentation was discouraged, and movements in art and literature were denounced as counter-revolutionary if they did not conform to the schema demanded by the party. Despite the most generous impulses of humanity, the movement was torn apart by those who believed 'it is better to be waiting for Lefty, than to be waiting for Godot'.[8] Even before the imposition of socialist realism, activists were unsure how to relate to the modernist movement because of its apparent detachment from the reality to which it alluded. The Marxist philosopher Georg Lukács' attack on modernism, as embodying the decadent world of late capitalism, found a resonance among many of the writers and artists who were influenced by Soviet cultural theorists.

These were the parameters within which socially conscious Irish writers and artists had to operate. John Hewitt, Peadar O'Donnell and Sean O'Casey understood more than most how art in itself could be part of the attempt to change the course of history without descending into determinism or abstract propaganda. Other artists and writers, influenced by the Communist Party, simply desired to dramatize the struggles of the labour movement. Their conceptions were practical, not aesthetic, with little formal interest in literature and art. In recent years, much of this work has been dismissed as simplistic or merely propagandistic. But any extended examination of the original work reveals this judgement to be inadequate. Unfortunately, such an examination is not easy to do because so much of the material was ephemeral, is out of print, or buried in obscure publications and archives. What sets them apart, however, and makes it worth retrieving is that a significant minority of the 1930s output was beautifully written or produced.

IRELAND

The cultural popular front in Ireland was forced to plough a lonely furrow. Despite the fact that literature in Ireland is closely linked to the immediate reality of politics, there was no tradition of a left-wing or

Marxist cultural movement in Ireland. Writers and artists who wished to engage with social reality had to rely on British publications such as *Left Review* or the Left Book Club, described by Edna Longley as 'literary food parcels' arriving from abroad. Neither the Communist Party of Ireland nor the Irish left-wing intelligentsia could command the support of an Auden or Spender, Malraux or Lorca, Brecht or Piscator. Unlike Britain or Europe, Irish Marxism was a fringe working-class movement, with little intellectual support from writers, artists or historians.

Those 'outside the gate' were not totally isolated from cultural life, but few Irish cultural activists made any attempt to engage with the experience of working-class life or the factory. Writers such as Daniel Corkery and Seán Ó Faoláin challenged the Anglo-Irish domination of culture but almost no one developed a critique of working-class culture. While the revival had an anti-capitalist dimension to it, this resistance was usually posed in terms of an opposition to the 'modern' or an idealization of the Gaelic pastoral past. What was missing was 'any real assimilation of the rich heritage of Marxist critical theory'.[9] The 'grocer's republic' was already taking shape. However, Seamus Deane is only partially correct in his description of Ireland in the thirties and forties as 'a provincial backwater'.[10] A more sympathetic reading of the 1930s reveals a submerged working-class political and intellectual response allied to an artistic activity that was much more European in its outlook than the 'gombeen republic' portrayed by many modern cultural historians.

Daniel Corkery's book *The Hidden Ireland* published in 1924 tried to restate the ideals of the Gaelic League for a new generation and introduce contemporary Irish-language writers to modern literature. Corkery's volume was at the centre of the 'Irish Ireland' debate and the uncompromising brand of cultural nationalism promoted by the Gaelic League. Concern for Irish culture often manifested itself as antagonistic to modernism and cosmopolitan values. Brian Hanley suggests that the republican movement's attitude to popular culture 'reflected both the bias of nationalist critics towards "foreign" influences and the organization's ambivalent but more open attitude to modern trends'.[11] They did not take broader cultural issues seriously; the overriding concern was the establishment of the Irish language and Gaelic culture as the everyday experience of the Irish people, and discussion of wider cultural matters was mainly left to individual taste. But there was another hidden Ireland, which has seldom been acknowledged, that reached out to the European experience of modernism and political radicalism. Europe played an important, but largely unacknowledged, role in the formation of the Irish literary revival. Paris had always provided the possibility of intellectual freedom and artistic experimentation that was not possible in Ireland. In the 1930s, many young writers and artists, inspired by the presence of James Joyce, gravitated towards Paris. Of course, this was not one-way traffic; many returned and European modernism gained currency with a small but influential strand in Irish culture. Poets such as Dennis Devlin and Brian Coffey produced work that was urban, experimental and avant-garde, though they received little critical attention at the time.

THE NOVEL AND THE SHORT STORY

The novel was the weak point of the Irish literary revival. The novel was more at home in the 'complete societies' of late nineteenth-century Europe and America than the fragmented and impoverished Irish communities where individualism and tradition were dominant. Benedict Kiely described the revival as 'mainly a matter for poets and playwrights'.[12] The brilliance of James Joyce cast a shadow over the novelists of the subsequent generation. Seán Ó Faoláin considered the Irish novel in the 1930s an honourable failure that could never measure up to the work of Joyce. The 'big house' literature of the Anglo-Irish gave way to a narrative that depicted the squabbles of the petty bourgeois in small-town Ireland that had little appeal for audiences abroad. The realist novels of the 1930s by writers such as Liam O'Flaherty and Seán Ó Faoláin sought to expose the reactionary and puritanical tendencies of post-revolutionary Ireland, while Flann O'Brien and Eimar O'Duffy used satire and caricature to attack the narrow sexual and social mores of Irish society. Flann O'Brien blended fantasy and farce in *At Swim Two Birds*, an experimental novel that showed how the Gaelic past could be co-opted into a modernist satire that laid bare the hypocrisy of Irish society. First published in 1939, which was hardly a time for literary experimentation, the book disappeared without trace. It was re-issued in 1960 and immediately recognized as a modern classic.

The great literary innovation of the period was the short story, which became an 'enactment of humanist faith in Irish society'.[13] Seamus Deane makes the point that while 'much of the literature of the period registers alienation it is not in itself the literature of alienation'.[14] The best of the genre managed to avoid the 'miserablism' popularized by the likes of Frank McCourt sixty years later. At its best, the short story registered a social reality that flew in the face of nationalist self-congratulation. The short story should have been the ideal vehicle for workers who had literary ambitions. However, there were few outlets for their work other than occasional pieces in the trade union or socialist press. The short story format was either too long for the impoverished left-wing press, or not literary enough for the mainstream press. Frank O'Connor was virtually the only acclaimed writer from a working-class background who used the life of the streets and quays of his own city as the subject matter for his fiction. Writers who had already established their reputations, such as Seán Ó Faoláin and Liam O'Flaherty, developed their sparse and bitter stories to wage a protracted intellectual struggle against the isolationist and right-wing drift in Irish political life.

Left-wing writers, such as Peadar O'Donnell, who was born in Donegal in 1893, had a distinctive tale to tell.[15] A republican, he fought in the War of Independence and in the Civil War. His youthful experience of the emigrant potato pickers in Scotland transformed his life. As he picked his way through the sleeping harvesters on the steps of Glasgow Central station, he resolved to do something for them. For the rest of his life, he wielded his pen and his sword on their behalf. O'Donnell is best known for his novels about rural Donegal in which his portrayal of the poverty and struggles of small rural communities provide the most unsentimental and honest account of Irish life written in the last century. A supporter of socialist causes, he was an advocate for the co-operative movement as a way of 'checking the rampant gombeenisn ushered in during the grab-bag early days of the Free State'.[16] O'Donnell's work, never fashionable, is now beginning to receive the attention it deserves. However, two of his lesser-known works, written in response to the political imperatives of the time, have never been re-printed.

On the Edge of the Stream (1934) is set in Donegal and focuses on a group of small farmers who wish to set up a co-operative in opposition to the local shopkeepers and businessmen. This was a theme that was to find reality in the unsuccessful fight to establish a co-operative in the working-class Dublin suburb of Ballyfermot in 1950. O'Donnell's voice seldom intrudes; he lets the characters speak for themselves. His occasional interventions pose questions or express the collective consciousness of the local farmers and workers. Powerful women are at the centre of his work: the wonderful figure of Nelly McFadden Joyce, the victim of an arranged marriage, dominates the book. O'Donnell carefully explores the misery of women forced into a loveless marriage. On the day of her wedding, her childhood sweetheart, Phil Timony, left for Scotland. The years have passed and Phil returns, a corduroy tramp, and casually announces that he has 'got out of the habit of going to

Mass'. The local farmers are hesitant about opening a co-operative store, but Phil steps forward to lead it. The establishment attempt to intimidate the men by calling on 'the holy Fathers' to preach a mission against the godless co-op, but Nelly's heartfelt speech at the end of the book rallies support and the project is saved. It is unclear whether Nelly leaves her husband and her loveless marriage, but she is lost to him and, for the first time in her life, she is free to make her own decisions. O'Donnell, as in all his work, offers a hopeful view of the future. This important work, full of subtlety, humour and contradiction, is more than a period piece and deserves an audience today.

In 1936 O'Donnell went to Spain hoping to find an environment that was free of the oppressive nature of the Irish Catholic Church and write the novel that was 'crumbling in his mind from neglect'. A few months later he found himself in the midst of a civil war and his novel was thrown aside. The war had a terrible similarity with the events in Ireland just fifteen years earlier. He found the idealism and sacrifice of ordinary people caught up in great events, the same self-organization and sometimes the excesses that are inherent in any civil war. *Salud!* (1937), his record of events in Spain, was hastily composed and, as a consequence, is uneven and episodic. The political comment and analysis that dominates much of the book is not sustained in any consistent form. *Salud!* lacks the political cohesion and objectivity of George Orwell's *Homage to Catalonia*, which was written by an active participant and is without equal in its analysis of the political complexities of the war. However, O'Donnell's account shares with Orwell the advantage of the novelist's eye and feel for the collective emotions of the participants:

> Girls walked hurriedly through the streets carrying rifles at short trail, with the air of people bent on everyday tasks. And now a rumour went through the city that a column was being assembled for service on the Aragon front, and a new excitement became evident. Youths with arms attracted new attention. Here and there goodbyes were being said. The lad who was going was bursting with pride and impatience, and the father was aglow with pride for his boy.[17]

O'Donnell's book was written to influence public opinion in Ireland and Britain. He describes his return to Ireland in 1937 and the anti-communist hysteria that gripped the country. The Christian Front, led by Paddy Belton, organized mass rallies in support of Franco with grotesque stories of burning churches, nuns systematically abused and priests crucified. O'Donnell went to great lengths to tell the truth about these events, which helped to dispel the image of the war as a contest between Christianity and a godless communism. Always an honest writer, O'Donnell was one of the first to hint at the possibility of Franco's victory. When an Irish brigade under the command of Frank Ryan was proposed, O'Donnell helped to procure arms, but he was reluctant to send young men out to fight for a cause that already seemed lost. He believed that Irish revolutionaries should stay at home in readiness to take up the fight for a socialist republic in Ireland.

THE PRESS

Over the past 200 years, the 'little magazines' have played a part in Western cultural history quite out of proportion to their circulation. The *Edinburgh Review*, the *Quarterly Review* and *The Bell*, most of whom sold only a few thousand copies, helped shape the consciousness of generations. The decade opened with the closure of the *Irish Statesman*. After seven years of weekly publication that interrogated Irish society with a constant and passionate criticism, it disappeared due to a lack of interest among the Irish reading public. With its collapse came a sense of isolation. Of the rest, the *Dublin Magazine*, the most European of the Irish periodicals, was well past its best and represented a continuity of the Irish revival rather than a challenge to it.

The left-wing press struggled to sustain itself, through sheer dedication and personal sacrifice. Many of the best activists and leading intellectuals, such as Leslie Daiken and Charlie Donnelly, were forced into exile by political or economic considerations. Newspapers such as the *Irish Front* (1934), *Irish Freedom* and the *Irish Democrat* (both 1937) were published in London and provided a political and intellectual link between the Irish and British socialist movements. Socialist newspapers published in Ireland, such as *Irish Workers' Voice* (1930) and *Irish Workers' Weekly* (1939), valiantly tried to sustain regular publication. Titles changed in quick succession without making any impact on the wider political movement. Despite this, they managed to find space for film, drama, literature, architecture and a good deal of radical verse. This included work by Peadar O'Donnell, Tom O'Brien, Ewart Milne, Charlie Donnelly and the satirical ballads of Somhairle Macalastair. The *Workers' Republic* published 'Red Envoy' by Brendan Behan, a 16-year-old painter's apprentice, in 1938:

> I bring no songs of rolling drums,
> Of pennons flying gaily,
> I sing of filth and dirty slums,

> Gaunt men, with hunger crazy,
> Canticles, not of virtue bright, nor wholly austere lives.[18]

Ireland To-Day, launched in 1936, just one month before the outbreak of the Spanish Civil War, was one of the few Irish mainstream magazines that put politics at the centre of their editorial policy. It concentrated on literature, cinema, art and politics and promoted itself as an all-Ireland magazine with a number of contributors from the northern Protestant community. The magazine was one of the first to have a regular film column; Liam Ó Laoghaire, a founder member of the Irish Film Society, tried to introduce his readers to the best of European film in order to break the grip of Hollywood on Irish audiences. However, the supporters of *Ireland To-Day* were hopelessly split over the role of the magazine. Seán Ó Faoláin, in a private letter to the editor, set out what he felt its role should be: 'that of finding the future intelligentsia of a new Ireland, nursing them, getting their brains to work for them ... I feel, in a sense out of it ... how far is it left propaganda, how far it is an open forum, what's its picture of the ideal Ireland?'[19] He suggested that they try to sell the concept of the magazine to businessmen in the hope of financial support. Ó Faoláin's call for a sharper ideological position was disingenuous. The magazine at this time was under attack for its outspoken left-wing republicanism. Owen Sheehy Skeffington, the foreign affairs editor, faced constant opposition from the Catholic Church because of his support for republican Spain. In reality, Ó Faoláin wanted to change the ideological outlook of the magazine and redirect it towards the Irish intellectual middle classes. Ó Faoláin was, at this stage, moving towards a European-style liberalism that would come to fruition with the launch of *The Bell* in 1940. Some of the contributors and supporters wanted the magazine to reflect the popular front politics that were gaining support across Europe. Others, including Peadar O'Donnell, hoped that *Ireland To-Day* would provide a platform to revive republicanism and wanted to orientate the magazine towards that layer of republicans close to Fianna Fáil. The failure to resolve these differences would eventually lead to the magazine's demise in 1938.

This unresolved ambiguity surfaced in a special issue, 'A Symposium on Spain', in September 1936. A favourable report on the Spanish popular front government ended with a tersely worded criticism of the Catholic Church's role. However, it distanced itself from outright support for the popular front government or any charge of partisanship: 'In presenting our readers with a symposium on the position in Spain, we are not to be taken as concurring in all the viewpoints expressed.'[20] Owen Sheehy Skeffington wrote the foreign commentary, which featured in every issue, between June 1936 and March 1937. He used his column to subvert the right-wing interpretation of the war as Catholic versus heathen, pointing out that Catholics were fighting on both sides. Sheehy Skeffington's support for the popular front government in Spain, and his left-wing commentaries, attracted intense criticism from the Catholic hierarchy. The editor, Jim O'Donovan, worried that this anticlerical line was affecting sales, asked him to tone down his commentary. But Sheehy Skeffington was not prepared to alter his position; following further criticisms in February and March 1937 of the Church's position on Spain, he was asked to resign. His valedictory column never appeared:

> Some time ago the Editor suggested that I might temporarily 'tone down' my observations, and avoid Communism, and avoid Fascism, and avoid Russia, and avoid Spain ... As a socialist, I considered it futile and undesirable to try to write without a good healthy socialist bias. It is unfortunate that none of my critics has been willing to put his point of view beside mine, and let the two stand on their merits.[21]

O'Donovan decided that this was too provocative to publish and the 'Skeffington controversy' spilled over into a public meeting in March 1937. Peadar O'Donnell claimed: 'O'Donovan was giving the bishops Skeffington's head on a plate.'[22] Sheehy Skeffington's article was eventually published in the socialist newspaper the *Irish Weekly Democrat* in April 1937.

O'Donovan, the editor of *Ireland To-Day*, leaned towards Christian socialism. He commissioned articles by Eric Gill, the left-wing English artist, who had converted to Catholicism in 1913. Gill, along with Chesterton and Belloc, was Britain's leading apologist for Catholic social teaching. In a grovelling reply to the Reverend Martindale, about alleged Communist advances in Ireland, O'Donovan insisted that 'our Editorial Committee of eight, are, with one exception, practising Catholics ... Although priests have visited newsagents and ordered the withdrawal of our magazine from their shops, yet her conscience can be quite clear.'[23] There were many reasons why *Ireland To-Day* failed, despite a healthy print run, in Irish terms, of 3,500. Church opposition made it exceedingly difficult to sustain the magazine, but, ultimately, it failed to connect to the large minority of politicized working-class readers or to offer political leadership to a potential audience that were responding to the great events of the 1930s.

The war in 1939 left Ireland isolated from the rest of the world and the fears and cautions of the middle classes were consolidated into a conservative post-revolutionary stagnation. The establishment in 1940 of a new literary magazine, *The Bell*, under the editorship of Seán Ó Faoláin was an instance of hope. Ó Faoláin sought to fill the gap left in the market by the demise of *Ireland To-Day* two and a half years previously. *The Bell* was based on the best of the British left-wing journals such as *Left Review*, but, unlike its British counterparts, *The Bell* was not interested in bringing about socialist transformation. It was launched at a time when Catholic morality was deeply entrenched in the ruling ideology of the country. The war had cut Ireland off from progressive movements abroad and de Valera's government had little to fear from liberal opinion. *The Bell* set itself the task of exposing actual conditions in Ireland through a documentary empirical exploration of Irish society. Ó Faoláin, and Peadar O'Donnell who succeeded him as editor in 1946, carried on an incessant challenge to the narrow censorship of the Irish Free State. Despite the isolation of the war period, *The Bell* opened Ireland's eyes to the world beyond its shore.

Belfast followed suit with the launch of *Lagan* in 1943 by John Boyd and Sam Hanna Bell. Ulster regionalism, the ideological core of the magazine, never 'involved a declaration of literary separatism', but it inevitably 'diverted political aims and energies into cultural channels'.[24] *Lagan* provided the space for young writers to make up their minds on the question of Ulster regionalism, but this unsettling exclusivism led to divisions and closure in 1945. Former members of the Communist Party in the twenty-six counties, which had suspended its activities in 1941 because of wartime restrictions imposed by the government, sponsored the launch of the *Review* in 1945, a monthly review of 'politics, letters and art' in a courageous attempt to provide a literary and political magazine in the style of *Ireland To-Day*, but the stagnation and paralysis of post-war Ireland proved barren soil for such a venture. Nevertheless, thanks to *The Bell*, *Lagan* and to a lesser extent the *Review*, the modernist impulse gained some ground and, as Patrick Kavanagh noted, there was now in Ireland a 'public of connoisseurs in embryo', but they would have to wait many years to gain recognition and influence.[25]

THEATRE

The rejection by the Abbey Theatre in 1928 of two remarkable plays – Sean O'Casey's experimental play *The Silver Tassie* and Dennis Johnston's *The Old Lady Says 'No!'* – dealt a serious blow to the Abbey's future. The experimental second act of *The Silver Tassie*, influenced by

German political theatre and the expressionist techniques of Ernst Toller, was beyond Yeats's taste or understanding. As a result, O'Casey was lost to Irish theatre and the one Irish dramatist of world standing spent the rest of his life in exile sending his 'blasts and benedictions' across the world.

In 1934, O'Casey set out his dramatic manifesto: 'The polished dramas of today have sucked the life and soul out of the drama ... true to life on the stage, as far as drama is concerned, really means true to death. So to hell with the so-called realism, for it leads nowhere ... realism died years ago, and the sooner we buried the body the better.'[26] Realism, the traditional staple of Irish theatre, could no longer describe the reality of the world torn between war and revolution. Theatre had something new to say and the old techniques were not able to say it. Modernism, with its clash of values, set out to surprise and shock its audience. But, for many on the left, modernism was associated with middle-class intellectualism. Socialist realism, which by 1934 had become the official cultural policy of the Soviet Union, seemed to offer a way in which working-class writers could take on the world in a manner that reflected their own experience. The Workers' Theatre Movement, which emerged at the end of the 1920s, became an effective weapon for the promotion of working-class values and propaganda. At its best, it was imaginative, revolutionary in form and content and brought theatre to workers on street corners and factory canteens. However, it also harboured the worst type of workerist ideas: this was class against class theatre with little interest in aesthetics or in raising the cultural awareness of workers. Conventional realism was rejected as bourgeois, and even left-wing dramatists such as Shaw, O'Neill or O'Casey found little favour with the movement because of their association with mainstream theatre.

The Workers' Theatre Movement made little impact in Ireland. The Belfast shipyard worker Thomas Carnduff wrote a number of plays between 1932 and 1935 that were produced by the Abbey Theatre in Dublin and the Belfast Repertory Theatre that were part of a general artistic response to the crisis of the interwar years.[27] However, his political position was much less clearly defined than the radical politics and form adopted by the Workers' Theatre Movement. His work is often compared to the Dublin plays of Sean O'Casey and the realist melodrama of the pre-First World War British socialist theatre. Nevertheless, Carnduff managed to express the emerging sense of class-consciousness in the Protestant working class in Northern Ireland.

In the mid thirties the political shift by the Communist International from class confrontation to popular front politics was followed by a reconciliation between agit-prop and conventional theatre forms. The politics of theatre were transformed and, in this new atmosphere, the Group Theatre in the United States and Unity Theatre in London produced some of the most dynamic and interesting theatre of the period. This was the political and artistic background that inspired the formation of the New Theatre Group in Dublin and the Left Book Club Dramatic Group in Belfast in 1937. This coincided with the Spanish Civil War and the extension of the Left Book Club (LBC) to Ireland; the LBC was launched in Britain in 1936 and, by the end of that year, had over 40,000 members. It quickly became an umbrella group for left-wing activists, writers and artists. Within a few months, radical book clubs, and poetry and theatre groups were formed across Britain. The LBC had about 500 subscribers in Ireland and, within this milieu, a left-wing literary conscience was emerging. In Belfast, Davy McLean's Progressive Bookshop, a distribution centre for the LBC in Northern Ireland, was the hub for a circle of left-wing intellectuals who were trying to stir things up. There was a considerable overlap between the 300 members of the LBC in Belfast and the files of known agitators held by the RUC special branch. Sam Hanna Bell, Louis MacNeice, John Hewitt and John Boyd were part of a movement that for a while managed to unite orange and green around progressive demands.

The New Theatre Group (NTG) in Dublin was an offshoot of the Left Book Club.[28] The Unity Club at 14 Sackville Place, a well-known left-wing centre in the 1930s, was used as a venue for the Left Book Club meetings and as the administrative centre by the NTG. The founding members were mostly committed socialists or members of the Communist Party of Ireland; Roddy Connolly, Bill Clare, Rosie Burke, Alex Digges, Tom O'Brien, Barney McGinn and Sean MacColum all believed that there was an audience in Dublin for serious political theatre and the NTG had the talent and skill to provide it. The NTG opened in April 1937 with Clifford Odet's *Waiting for Lefty*, an experimental production that owed some of its inspiration to the techniques of Bertolt Brecht and the Group Theatre in New York. They were certainly ambitious; the *Irish Workers' Weekly*, which regularly reported on their productions, compared them to the Moscow Art Theatre and said that they were:

> ... exactly in the same position as was the Moscow Arts Theatre, before it adopted the name ... composed of a few enthusiastic hard workers who scrounged the use of a theatre and put on plays far beyond their ability. But they kept at it and it was the same people who put the Moscow Arts Theatre in the forefront of world theatre.[29]

By 1939, the NTG was strong enough to present a season of plays written by members of the group that explored key moments in Ireland's own recent history. Thomas O'Brien, who had been a volunteer in Spain, was the prime mover in this development. In September 1939, the NTG presented *The Last Hill* by Tom O'Brien, a one-act verse play about a last-ditch resistance by republican soldiers during the civil war in Spain. The cast included the best of the NTG actors, Seán Ó hEidirsceoil, Ruaidhrí Roberts and Desmond McNamara. This was followed by *Lock-Out*, a verse play about the 1913 events by Seán Ó hEidirsceoil. Tom O'Brien contributed two other plays, *Strange Dew* and *Decent Citizens* (which never received a production), a witty and ironic play that satirizes the obsession of the Church and state with communist influence. The most innovative play produced by the NTG was Bill Clare and Tom O'Brien's *Partition*, which was the first play in Ireland to make use of the 'living newspaper' format developed by the Federal Theatre Project in the United States.[30] This new dramatic form abandoned the traditional plot and tried to inform the audience of current social or political issues by means of documentary, megaphone commentary, music, verse and audience participation.

The demise of the NTG in 1946 happened for a number of reasons. The tensions in the wider socialist movement over the political response to the Second World War meant that many of the founder members had left the group by 1940. In an article in *Surge*, the magazine of the NTG in 1943, Tom O'Brien outlined the problems facing the NTG and recommended that they attempt to develop a renewed artistic and aesthetic response to Ireland's needs:

> The membership, its spirit, its audience have altered. It has completely lost its *Waiting for Lefty* audience. The term 'workers' theatre' is no longer used … it must become the National Theatre of Ireland … it must find its own national playwrights and it must produce their plays in a theatre which is capable of paying royalties and wages.[31]

The obstacles facing left-wing theatre groups such as the NTG, the LBC Drama Group in Belfast or even Unity in Britain are put into perspective by a comparison with the methodology and dramatic innovations made by Bertolt Brecht and the Berliner Theatre in stage and scenic design and their use of film as an integral part of the setting a decade earlier. Some of the experiments that they undertook alone cost more than £100,000. However, lack of technique and finance were not the only problems that prevented Irish or British theatre groups from implementing Brecht's vision. Britain, and even more so Ireland, lacked a mass social movement that could have provided the resources and an audience for such a theatre. Without it, Unity and the NTG could only produce a shallow imitation of what Brecht and Piscator had achieved in Berlin. The other factor was political. After the Nazis came to power, Brecht's work was practically unobtainable in published form and the adoption of socialist realism by the Soviet Union in 1934 made his theatre unfashionable and politically suspect for many on the left.

THE POETS

Great claims were made in the 1930s for poets as a social force; they were 'the trumpets that see men to battle, the unacknowledged legislators of the world'. The civil war in Spain caught the poets' imagination; Stephen Spender called it the 'poets' war'. Writers joined the International Brigade in 'a rush to the barricades and the printing presses'. This sense of purpose gave rise to a new type of poet who tried to change the patterns of injustice by influencing men's actions rather than their emotions. A new voice was heard: 'the voice of the worker, of the small farmer, the middle-class man of the town, articulating his right to beauty, blue skies, peace, and above all else security in daily life'.[32] The new poetry was chiefly declamatory, a rhetorical shout expressed in free verse.

Unfortunately, *Goodbye, Twilight*, an anthology of Irish poetry published in 1936, represents the worst of that tradition. In his introduction, the editor, Leslie Daiken, created an unnecessary cleavage between socialism and aesthetics, with a crude representation of modernism as an 'inconsequential groping in the dark for a new bourgeois aesthetic ... that fostered pessimism'.[33] However, this tendency was resisted by those who understood that the relationship between literature and politics was much more varied and complex than the simplistic theories of socialist realism. John Hewitt in his review of *Goodbye, Twilight* yearned for 'a real sharp and singing contribution ... from the workers and peasants' but he refused to 'submit to the crying down' of the great poets of the past.[34] A minority resisted the temptation offered by those blunted weapons; Ewart Milne, Charlie Donnelly, John Hewitt and Louis MacNeice all wrote poetry that was redolent of the time, yet had implications, which continue to be felt.

Charlie Donnelly was an extraordinary young man and one of the most exciting poets to come out of Ireland in the 1930s. He was born in 1914 in County Tyrone. He grew up in a middle-class family and entered University College Dublin in 1931. He was part of a remarkable generation of writers and poets at UCD – Dennis Devlin, Brian Coffey, Niall Montgomery, Flann O'Brien and Donagh MacDonagh. Donnelly was active in student politics and a member of the left-wing Student Vanguard group. The young poet, by now a convinced Marxist, was increasingly drawn to the life of a political activist: 'His mind was already turning to the humanizing role of poetry in a heartless and impoverished world.'[35] He came under the political influence of Frank Ryan and George Gilmore of the Republican Congress and was active in the Congress campaign against slum housing in Dublin, which eventually led to his arrest and imprisonment in 1934. Worn out and depressed, he left for London after his release from jail in 1935. He wrote for a variety of left-wing magazines and inevitably made his way to Spain, arriving in early January 1937. During those few months, he wrote at a furious pace, and some of his best poems date from that time:

> Death comes in quantity from solved
> Problems on maps, well ordered dispositions,
> Angles of elevation and direction;
>
> Comes innocent from tools children might
> love, retaining under pillows,
> Innocently impaled on any flesh.[36]

Donnelly's literary internationalism set him apart from many of the Irish writers who sometimes allowed the consequences of the 'unfinished revolution' to overshadow their work. He had nothing but contempt for the 'Celtic twilight' writers, who purveyed an image of post-revolutionary Ireland that was at odds with reality. European modernism, particularly as expressed in the work of Brian Coffey and Dennis Devlin, was his first real poetic influence. At its best, his work bridges the gap between responsibility towards society and responsibility towards poetic form. George Gilmore described a letter he received from Donnelly during 1936, in which he spoke about uniting politics and poetry. He was 'reading Shelley in the political context and Connolly in the literary one'.[37] Inherent in his poetry was the possibility of bringing to maturity the aesthetic possibilities implicit in much of the 1930s poetry.

Charles Donnelly never realized that possibility; he died, aged 22, in February 1937 at the battle of Jarama. His small body of poems are a testament to his potential and can stand comparison with the finest of the decade. The pressure to take sides led many into propaganda and compromise. Donnelly was a dedicated communist and, to his credit, he never allowed his poetry to be compromised by party demands. Donnelly defended the writer's creative freedom against political expediency. He avoided the clichéd outbursts of left-wing rhetoric that damaged much of the 1930s poetry. His work is a fusion of the personal and the political, modern, tight and sparse in style, with all the commitment, precision and passion of a Shelley or Neruda. He was a poet and an activist who managed, better than most, to resolve this apparent contradiction:

> And with flesh falls apart the mind
> That trails thought from the mind the cuts
> Thought clearly for a waiting purpose.
>
> Progress of poison in the nerves and
> Discipline's collapse is halted.
> Body awaits the tolerance of crows.[38]

Many poets and writers died at the front in Spain – Charles Donnelly, Ralph Fox, John Cornford, Julian Bell, Federico Lorca and many others – but, for all of that, it was hardly a poet's war. Such claims merely romanticize the war and do a disservice to the tens of thousands of working-class volunteers who fought and died there. In Spain, many learned that 'one can be right and yet be beaten, that force can vanquish spirit'.[39] Charles Donnelly's final words, 'even the olives are bleeding', summarized for many the despair of fascism's victory in Spain. However, the poets translated their faith in the future into words. Franco may have won the war, but he lost the literary battle.

CONCLUSION

It is rare for a decade to be so self-conscious, though, viewed from our perspective, the 1930s looks more dazzling than it really was. By the end of the thirties, the dogmatism of the Communist Party internationally was presenting its bill and many were not prepared to pay it. The real tragedy of the period was the complete identification of socialism with the Soviet Union. Stripped of their illusions, many abandoned socialism altogether. In those circumstances, it was not surprising that several of that generation either drifted away from left-wing politics or became Cold War warriors on behalf of American imperialism.

Sean O'Casey, like John Hewitt, Peadar O'Donnell, Ewart Milne, and Louis MacNeice understood that the crucial political issues of the decade went beyond whether or not to join the Communist Party and that these issues had not gone away with the outbreak of the Second World War. They, and many others, whose names are now forgotten, produced some of their best work during an era of ideological poverty in Ireland. But their work, scattered and uncollected as it is, was part of an emancipatory process; they created a dissenting space where the social possibilities of art and literature could be explored.

Little remains of the progressive Irish literary and artistic movements from the 1930s. Not all of it was good, though all of it, I believe, was sincere and some of it deserves to be remembered. Not all renounced their past and remained 'exiles from a future time'. Some managed to achieve the aim of every working-class or progressive writer: 'to create characters whom readers of any class will find as fully human as themselves'.[40] Fifty years later, a new generation swept away the confessional state and vindicated the enthusiasm and sacrifice of those who never gave up hope. Charlie Donnelly summed up both the optimism and isolation of the period and the way in which the private and public were fused together. It was that unmistakable quality that made this intensely troubled and creative decade unique:

> Your flag is public over granite. Gulls fly above it.
> Whatever the issue of the battle is, your memory
> Is public, for them to pull awry with crooked hands,
> Moist eyes. And village reputations will be built on
> Inaccurate accounts of your campaign. You're name for orators,
> Figure stone-struck beneath damp Dublin sky.[41]

NOTES

1. Joost Augusteijn (ed.), *Ireland in the 1930s* (Dublin: 1999), p. 7.
2. On this aspect of the 1930s, see Joe Cleary, 'This thing of darkness', in *Outrageous Fortune* (Dublin: 2007), pp. 140–54.
3. Terence Brown, *Ireland: A Social and Cultural History* (London: 1985), p. 146.
4. Ibid., pp. 141–70.
5. Joe Cleary, 'Modernisation and aesthetic ideology', in Ray Ryan (ed.), *Writing in the Irish Republic* (London: 2000), p. 111.
6. Patrick Deane, *History in Our Hands* (London: 1998), p. 384.
7. Alick West, *One Man in his Time* (London: 1969), p. 132.
8. Julian Symons, *The 30s and the 90s* (Manchester: 1990), p. 48.
9. Cleary, 'Modernisation', p. 127.
10. Seamus Deane, 'Irish poetry and Irish Nationalism', in Douglas Dunn (ed.), *Two Decades of Irish Writing* (Cheadle: 1975), p. 11.
11. Brian Handley, *The IRA, 1926–1936* (Dublin: 2002), p. 61.

12. Benedict Kiely, *Modern Irish Fiction* (Dublin:1950), p. 374.
13. Brown, *Ireland*, p. 160.
14. Ibid., p. 159.
15. For biographical details see Michael McInerney, *Peadar O'Donnell: Irish Social Rebel* (Dublin: 1974).
16. Alexander G. Gonzalez, *Peadar O'Donnell: A Reader's Guide* (Chester Springs: 1997), p. 15.
17. Peadar O'Donnell, *Salud!* (London: 1937), p. 102.
18. Brendan Behan 'Red Envoy', *Workers' Republic*, August 1938.
19. Frank Shovlin, *The Irish Literary Periodical: 1923–1958* (Oxford: 2003), p. 77.
20. *Ireland To-Day*, 14 (September 1936), p. 1.
21. Shovlin, *The Irish Literary Periodical*, p. 85.
22. Ibid., p. 86.
23. Ibid., p. 91.
24. Edna Longley, *The Living Stream* (Newcastle: 1994), p. 123.
25. Charles Sidney, 'Art Criticism in Dublin', *The Bell*, 9, 2, p. 110.
26. *New York Times*, 21 October 1934.
27. *Workers* 1932, *Machinery* 1933, *Traitors* 1934, *Castlereagh*, 1935.
28. For further details of the NTG see Joe Deasy, 'Reviving the Memory', *Labour History News*, no. 3, Spring 1987.
29. *Irish Workers' Weekly*, 2 December 1939.
30. The scripts for *The Last Hill*, *Lock-Out* and *Decent Citizens* as well as a comprehensive history of the NTG are reproduced in Gustav Klaus (ed.), *Strong Words, Brave Deeds* (Dublin: 1994). Unfortunately, the script for *Partition* cannot be found.
31. *Surge*, March 1943.
32. 'Introduction' in Leslie Daiken (ed.), *Goodbye, Twilight* (London: 1936), p. xvii.
33. Ibid., p. xvii.
34. John Hewitt in *Forum* supplement to *Irish Jewry*, January 1937.
35. Joseph O'Connor, *Even the Olives are Bleeding* (Dublin: 1992), p. 28.
36. Ibid., p. 126.
37. Ibid., p. 83.
38. Ibid., p. 126.
39. Albert Camus, quoted in *The Nation* (New York), 11 December 2000.
40. Ruth Sherry, 'Working-class fiction of Cork', *Threshold*, no. 35 (Winter 1984–5), p. 10.
41. O'Connor, *Even the Olives are Bleeding*, p. 127.

13

Money Matters in the Lives of Working Women in Ireland in the 1940s and 1950s

ELIZABETH KIELY AND MÁIRE LEANE

Research into money and related issues of power and control is fraught with difficulty. There is a natural reticence from the researcher about prying into private financial affairs and a corresponding reluctance among individuals to make public what is, in many respects, a very intimate area of life. It is thus not surprising that the subject of money and practices surrounding its control and use, particularly in the context of family or household relationships, is a subject that has received little attention in the Irish context.[1] Oral history, however, provides a technique for the collection of data, which is often missing from the historical record.[2] This essay, which considers the topic of money and its significance in the lives of Irish women in the 1940s and 1950s, is based on material generated by an oral history project, examining 42 women's experiences of waged work in the Irish Republic between 1936 and 1960.[4] The narratives were not collected from a random or representative sample of women who worked in this period, yet they provide deeply layered ethnographic accounts of women's experiences of diverse kinds of waged work and associated issues.[4] For the purpose of this essay, we analyzed the women's narratives to identify stories which related to money and its significance in their lives. In particular, we considered how the women perceived their earnings and how these earnings were perceived by others. The women's decision-making power in relation to their own earnings and in relation to the family or household wage provided by husbands or other relatives was also analyzed. This analysis highlighted the significance of gender, class and marital status in shaping women's personal experiences of money and revealed that, for many women, money was considered a family, as distinct from an individual, resource. Furthermore, it revealed a widespread cultural attitude of frugality, which permeated all classes and gave rise to many resourceful strategies for saving and managing money.

EARNING A LIVING: WOMEN'S PERCEPTIONS OF WORK AND EARNINGS

Women's relationships to money in the Ireland of the 1940s and 1950s were circumscribed by the economic and cultural climate of the time. The period was characterized by high rates of unemployment, emigration, poverty and war rationing.[5] Living conditions, particularly in rural areas and in working class urban settings, were poor.[6] In the narratives of the women interviewed, recollections of these depressed economic conditions feature frequently. The scarcity of employment opportunities for young women, particularly those with no formal vocational or educational training is also clearly evidenced in the women's stories. Ireland at the time was a predominantly agricultural economy and census returns for 1946 indicate that of the 30.9 per cent of the adult female population gainfully occupied, the largest category, 7.5 per cent, were working in agriculture.[7] The second highest category of employment for women in 1946 was domestic service (7.2 per cent), followed by the professions (3.4 per cent), industry (3.2 per cent), white-collar/secretarial work (3.0 per cent) and shop service (1.9 per cent).[8] Women's access to the limited range of occupations available in the 1940s and 1950s was further circumscribed by factors such as poverty in family of origin, the prevalence of large families, the cost of second- and third-level education and the expectation that women would leave the workforce upon marriage or if required to provide care for sick, elderly or younger family members.[9] It is therefore not surprising that the work histories of the women interviewed are, for the most part, characterized by involvement in a narrow range of occupations, short-lived and disjointed career trajectories and limited access to independent income throughout their lives.

Few of the women interviewed recalled having any clear career aspirations as young girls and most noted that, even when they began working, they had few expectations where career progression and job satisfaction were concerned. Indeed, most recollected that they believed their working lives would not extend beyond marriage and motherhood.[10] Rose Smyth*,[11] who was born in the early 1930s, was conscious of the low cultural expectations of women:

> They [women] weren't encouraged to go away and make anything of their lives you know. 'Twas just ... Well, most people got married anyway. Two out of three got married and if you didn't get married like, you just had to keep working.

For most of the women interviewed, securing employment and accessing a wage, however small, was the priority. Our narratives suggest that leaving school at the age of 14 to take up employment was a common pattern among women from working-class backgrounds and was prompted by the difficult financial situation at home and the cost of participating in second-level education.[12] Joan Fitzgerald, who started work in Mill Industries in Cork in the 1940s at the age of 14, observed:

> 'Well they [parents] didn't have the money then to send us to secondary school ... most of our kind, our generation, well ... working class ... went to work at fourteen ...'

Joan Noonan also finished her schooling at 14 and entered into domestic service. She was keenly aware that continuing her education was out of the question:

> I had no choice because it was, you know now, when a father would be earning maybe five shillings a week, do you know, and trying to feed us all and work hard, work day and night and all this. Like, you had to live by that then, you had to do what you're told like.

Limited job opportunities and the dire need to access an income, however small, meant that many women had little choice about what employment they would take. Maura Canty, a telephonist in the 1940s, summarized the attitude of many female workers at the time:

> I mean when you got a job long ago, you didn't say there's not enough money in that, like they do nowadays and go on to something else. Bottom line is money in your pocket. They [women] had no higher thoughts than that.

However, notwithstanding the limited opportunities available, women did exercise agency in their selection of work and made conscious choices about whether to prioritize earnings or work status and conditions. The lure of higher wages was identified by a number of interviewees as their reason for taking up factory work, which had low social status and frequently involved dirty and physically demanding work conditions. Alice Delea noted:

> Eileen and Anne [sisters] worked with me in the dry-cleaners and then Mary [sister] worked in the sack factory and they'd great wages in the sack factory – there'd be an awful smell off ya. Goodbody's sack factory. And they used to clean out the bags you know. Brush them and clean them out – oh, you'd be stinking. They [sisters] left me to go to work with her because the wages were brilliant. A terribly smelly job but the wages were brilliant.

Margaret Twomey was very conscious of the decline in status she suffered when she resigned from her office job to take up a job in Dunlop's factory in Cork city. She was enticed into such work, however, by the prospect of her salary being doubled:

> Well, the money was great. Eight pounds a week. I changed from the four pounds a week job ... you had what you called 'rough diamonds' working in factories that you wouldn't get, say, in an office ... all I can say is you had all classes of people working in the factory.

Though it was definitely more unusual, a few women did sacrifice higher earnings for status when making career choices. Elizabeth Shorten, who joined the Irish army as a nursing sister in the mid-1950s, acknowledged the pay differential between army and hospital nurses, but felt that the status of being in the army made up for this. 'We were paid less, I can't remember exactly what the difference was, but it was quite a social sort of cache to be a sister in the Irish army, so for some reason or other, because of that you were paid less.' Joan Daly, who was also a nurse with the Irish army, identified the availability of job 'perks' as a factor motivating her to join the army: 'You had a lot of perks, you know. We travelled first class for third-class fares and you got reduced fares in the planes and all that sort of thing. And, of course, the uniform ... the uniform was a great attraction.'

Other professional women such as poultry instructresses, cheese makers and engineers enjoyed relatively good salaries and high status, but due to the existence of the marriage bar[13], this lasted only up until the time they married. Mary Taaffe, a poultry instructress, commented on her good salary relative to those earned by many other women in the 1940s:

> And I do remember my first month's wages, which were very, very, good, considering the circumstances at the time ... £23. 5s and 8 pence. A year into the job there, when I bought a car, it was a very expensive car too. What, it cost me a hundred and thirteen pounds. A doctor, the teacher and myself had a car, so a car gave you great status plus it made you very popular.

Given the economic climate of the time, it is not surprising that job security, particularly that provided by a permanent and pensionable job in the public sector, was highly coveted. As Joan Griffin recalled, when she was completing her secondary schooling in 1948: 'They [parents] wanted me to get a permanent and pensionable job. That was the way to live that time. You'd get a permanent pensionable job and that's it like.'

Our findings suggest that for working-class and lower middle-class women in Ireland in the 1940s and 1950s, decisions about employment were influenced primarily, though not exclusively, by earning potential and job security. For many women, however, securing employment did not guarantee access to an income over which they had control. On the contrary, it seemed that, for single women, parental control of earnings was commonplace.

POWER AND RESPONSIBILITY: WOMEN, MONEY AND DECISION-MAKING IN IRISH FAMILIES

The women interviewed who commenced work very early in their lives invariably reported that they gave their earnings directly to their parents, most usually their mother, who then granted them pocket money to spend as they wished. The money Joan Noonan earned in her first live-in domestic position in 1937 was paid directly to her father, who came to collect it at Christmas time. As she explained: 'If you were under age like, if you were young your father would collect it. They wouldn't give it to you for fear you'd spend it.' What is significant in the women's accounts is their lack of a sense of entitlement to ownership of their earnings. They appeared to perceive their earnings as a family, as distinct from an individual, resource, with the majority expressing a strong sense of obligation to contribute to their families of origin. The women's accounts suggest that the amount of pocket money they received from parents out of their wages varied between families. Catherine O'Driscoll, who worked as a dispatcher in a sweet factory in 1931, earned ten shillings a week but she received so little in pocket money that buying a pair of stockings required saving. In contrast, Margaret Twomey, who was working in R and D Cleaners in Cork city in 1957, commented on her good fortune in comparison to others:

> My mother handed me back fifteen shillings, which was half, which was very good at that point in time. I had heard of people maybe only getting five shillings, you know ... that they'd have got less than that you know? Whereas I thought that was kind of a fair return, more than fair.

Parental control of their earnings did not appear to be a source of resentment among the women interviewed. Indeed, women who began work in clerical positions, usually at the somewhat older age of 16, or those who had professional qualifications, e.g. teaching, and were over eighteen when commencing employment, appeared to share the view that their income was a family resource. Joan Harold, who worked in a clerical post in the labour exchange in Newcastlewest in Co. Limerick during the 1940s, recalled what happened when she brought home her pay packet: 'I'd give it to my parents and I'd be happy to have four pence on a Sunday night to go to a local dance.' Chris Nolan, who commenced working in an office in 1939, clearly accepted her obligation to supplement the family finances with her earnings and viewed the practice as customary at the time:

> When you left school to get a job, you got a job so you could contribute at home. Give so much, pay so much at home, you know. There was no such a thing as you kind of getting your salary and putting it in your pocket ... It happened a lot that you handed over your salary and you got back pocket money ... It would be more or less that kind of thinking in my day. They [parents] supported me and fed me and educated me so now what I must do is pay them back.

Similarly, interviews with professional women reveal that they too were accepting of the practice of handing over a substantial amount of their earnings for family use. Kathleen Cranitch, who began working as a national school teacher in the mid 1930s, was aware of her obligations to supplement the family wage.

> I knew that a lot depended on me. My father being a carpenter got a fair share of idleness at that time. My mother was teaching all the time and there were six younger than me. And I knew well that I had to put my shoulder to the wheel.

Catherine Walshe, whose parents were small business owners, qualified as a civil engineer in 1949 and earned a very substantial salary of £8.10 a week. She was obliged, however, to send three pounds home every week to contribute towards her brother's boarding school education. This would suggest that the practice of parental control of earnings prevailed even in families who could be classed as lower middle class and were not in dire financial need.

Increasing age, or changing family or personal circumstances such as a marital engagement, resulted in most parents or, more commonly, mothers gradually granting daughters more control over their own earnings. Referring to her wage from her first job as an office clerk in 1950, Mary O'Sullivan Greene explained that she:

> ... handed it up at home and my mother gave me back my bus fare and whatever other expenses I would have and then if I wanted something she gave me money to buy it. As time went on then and other members of the family moved out and got married or were in a different position, I kept my money myself then.

According to Mary, being able to manage her own money as she got older was considered to be 'a good preparation for life'. Engagement and the decision to marry appear to have been significant in influencing single women's financial practices. Saving for getting married features in many women's accounts and suggests that single women's obligation to contribute significantly to their family of origin was dissolved by the prospect of their establishing households themselves. However, Maura Canty, who described her family as financially comfortable relative to others, recounted that 'up to the day I left the telephone exchange, my wage packet was handed up. To my mother. The controller of programmes ... Oh, I gave it as I got it, up to the time I got married.' It is noteworthy, however, that while Maura's mother retained control over her earnings, they were not used to bolster the family finances; rather, Maura believes that her mother saved most of the money and used it to provide her with the deposit for a house when she married in 1951.

Our findings indicate that the practice of parental control of their single daughters' earnings was common among working- and middle-class families and was generally accepted by the young women concerned. When viewed in the context of the time, this finding is not remarkable. Most of the women we interviewed began working at a young age and lived at home. As such, it is not unreasonable that they would be expected to make some contribution to family resources. Furthermore, there is a long-standing cultural expectation in Ireland that unmarried children would supplement the finances of parents and other dependent siblings; indeed, this cultural practice was evident even when an employed son or daughter went to work overseas. What our findings do not reveal is whether the practice of parental control of earnings was prevalent among the upper classes and whether it was common for parents to exercise similar control over the earnings of sons. A personal testimony provided to Caitriona Clear as part of her investigation of issues of money and authority in Irish households between 1922 and 1961 recounted the practice of the sons on a farm in east Galway in the 1920s and 1930s handing up any earnings they made to their mother, who then granted them pocket money. In the absence of more extensive research, it is not possible to determine if, or to what extent, the practice of unmarried children contributing their income to the family of origin was a gendered practice. What the research presented in this article does reveal is that mothers, in the vast majority of households, held the responsibility for managing monetary affairs.

During the 1940s and 1950s, marriage brought an end to full-employment for most Irish women and placed them in a position of economic dependence on their husbands.[14] However, as our research and that of others has indicated, women, particularly in working-class and small farming families, were responsible for managing the household on whatever money was provided by their husbands.[15] At the same time, husbands typically retained decision-making power in relation to how much of their earnings they provided to their wives for household management. Kathleen Fitzgibbon commented on this, when interviewed:

> I know lots of them [wives] didn't know how much their husbands earned ... I know my father only gave up a certain amount always. They didn't argue so much about getting more money because I think women just took it that time. It was the norm, if you know what I mean. They [husbands] didn't want to know. It wasn't that they didn't understand at all, but they didn't want to know. You got that and do with it and what you like with it. The men were top dogs then I think.

Previous research indicates that practices varied among husbands, with some giving their wives their unopened pay packet while others retained a part of their wage for their personal consumption, regardless of the struggle many wives endured to make ends meet.[16] Alice Delea's father emigrated to England during the war years and she commented on the fact that her father did not send much of his earnings home:

> I didn't even know what a father was, but we had a brilliant mother. She was mother and father! ... She worked all hours of the day because my father sent very small money. My father used to send about five pounds a week to keep five of us. According to him, he had two homes to keep. He worked in Ford's in Dagenham, which had very good money, but he just didn't send it like.

Eileen Dolan, describing her childhood on a farm in Cork in the 1930s, recalled her father's practice of retaining money for personal consumption:

> My father used to go to Coachford fair and he'd come home in the evening and a calf would have made seven pound and he'd give that to my mother with a few pounds kept for himself ... The men always kept their own bit of money but the women only got the house money.

Our findings suggest that the limited earnings of some husbands, or the limited amount of earnings accorded to their wives to run the household, prompted many married women to seek ways of generating additional income, over which they could exercise complete control. Kathleen O'Regan, who grew up in Cork city in the 1940s, recalled her mother's struggle to combine her household work with paid employment as a domestic worker for another family:

> Our mothers worked very hard you know, my mother did anyway ... It was kind of ... well, my father was working then, but he might not have been great like, he was fond of his drink and she had to work you know. But she liked always to keep her little bit of independence too like.

Engagement in paid employment in the formal labour market was more difficult for married women who lived in rural areas. However, women living on farms frequently made money through the sale of butter or eggs or through rearing animals or poultry for sale. Sr Paul O'Flynn described the money made by her mother in the 1920s through the sale of butter and eggs, as her mother's 'dowry for the year'. Similarly, Eileen Dolan witnessed her mother's savings arrangement with the huckster who came to collect eggs from many farming families in her locality in Co. Cork in the 1930s:

> Every week the huckster would come ... come for the eggs ... and my mother wouldn't take the money. She'd have a book and write down a dozen eggs at seven pence or five pence and when she'd want money she'd ask him for a cheque against the eggs. We'd say when a bill would be coming. The rent or the rates. She'd ask him for ten or fifteen pounds and it was a lot together.

Other methods used by women to generate home-based incomes included renting spare rooms, taking in washing, knitting Aran jumpers and doing book-keeping at home. In most of the instances recounted by our interviewees, the money earned by married women was used to meet family and household needs. Bridie Dunne, who always generated additional income rearing animals and selling eggs and milk in Co. Limerick in the 1950s, explained how she spent her earnings:

> Well, I spent it on the house for the food and the clothes. And when they'd be getting confirmation or communion, I always had a pig or a calf, an animal to sell ... I had that money then ... I had it hid under the mattress ... and another time there was one of them getting confirmation and I sold a heifer that was two years old and the price of her dressed every one of us in the house and we had lovely style.

Some women reported that men often felt threatened by the increased independence their wives would attain as earners.[17] Mary Taaffe, a poultry instructress who worked in different parts of rural Ireland during the 1940s, was acutely aware of the resentment she encountered from some farming men when she visited their wives, who kept poultry:

> You had many instances in Ireland, of course, where men were notoriously mean ... There are many women who never saw any money ... That was the only money they had [poultry money]. Most of them educated their children with their poultry money ... They would have improved things in their houses, you know. This was during the time when rural electrification came in ... They [farming men] resented any kind of intrusion in their lives ... the fact that you [poultry instructress] were going in there and helping her, perhaps to become more independent.

The power gained by a married woman who had an independent income, no matter how small, was emphasized by Margaret Twomey, who described how she used her earnings from the part-time work she undertook:

> I really kept it for myself as a source of independence ... My mother used to say, every woman should have her own money. And I am a strong believer in that, and I am still a believer in that today and I tell my daughter ... she should always have her own little bit of independence. And I would have opened an account for myself and my right hand wouldn't leave my left hand know what I had, and now if there was something needed then in the household and I could subsidize it, I would do so, but I had my own few bob, I had the choice to use it.

Our research suggests, however, that in the main married women did not use their earnings for personal consumption but rather to improve the living conditions of the entire family and particularly children. Our findings revealed only two situations where married women took lowly paid part-time work, not out of financial necessity but out of a desire for the stimulation and companionship provided by employment and for the extra financial independence, which the 'pin money' they earned provided.

Our research also revealed that it was not uncommon for single women to leave paid employment at different stages of their lives so as to care for next of kin. Most accepted it as their duty at the time, but they were conscious of the impact on their independence and some expressed feelings of resentment about their lack of choice in the matter. Mary Godfrey, who qualified as a secondary school teacher in the late 1930s, only worked for one year before she had to return home to care for her widowed father, who was ill. She explained:

> I loved it, I loved teaching and I had to give it up – broke my heart. I had to go home and stay you see. I could see offers of jobs but I couldn't take them. There was no one there to look after him. I could not leave him to the mercy of, you know, a housekeeper ... There was no such thing as a carer in those days. I mean, no, I didn't regret it. Of course, I did when I was young. It was very tough, you know, when you're young and, you know, tied down like. I took seventeen years like that. 'Twasn't easy.

Mary's awareness of the significance of her lack of a personal income during the time she was caring for her father was evident when she commented: 'It's very important for women to have independent financial security even if it is only to buy a small present.'

Achieving financial security was particularly challenging for married women who became sole family breadwinners due to early widowhood. Social attitudes to working mothers and statutory discrimination in relation to pay and work conditions were recounted by some of the respondents. Catherine Walshe, a civil engineer who was widowed when her five children were young, was interviewed for the same post on two occasions in the 1960s but never received any correspondence as to her suitability or otherwise for the position. As she explained:

> I applied again ... And I had my interview. They [interview panel] were very nice, very courteous and again asked the problem of the five kids and the driving up and down, and I came out and I didn't get any regrets yet for either of those jobs.

Similarly, Mary Taaffe, who returned to work as a poultry instructress due to early widowhood, remarked that 'There was a lot of discrimination against me because I was a widow ... that I look back on with some bitterness.'

It would thus appear that, for most women, accessing an independent income following marriage was somewhat challenging, and while there is evidence that some women met this challenge in resourceful ways, the money they generated was used primarily to bolster the family finances rather than for personal consumption. This suggests that, unlike their husbands, many married women, particularly working or lower middle-class women, had little sense of an entitlement to use either their own or their husband's earnings for their personal gratification. This gendered consumption of financial resources was mirrored in the consumption of food within the household. Many of our interviewees noted that fathers got served first and got the best of the food available, followed by male children, female children and lastly the mother. Indeed, many women recalled that they rarely saw their mother sitting down to eat a dinner with the rest of the family. It is likely that this practice of denying themselves a proportionate share of available food was another of the many strategies that working-class mothers employed to eke out meagre resources.

FRUGALITY AND THRIFT: WOMEN AND MONEY MANAGEMENT IN IRISH FAMILIES

Considering the difficult financial climate that prevailed in the 1940s and 1950s, it is hardly surprising that good financial management was part of the cultural fabric of the time. An ethos of thrift was very evident during the period under investigation and it was characterized by the emphasis women put on saving throughout their lives. Many women recounted that although wages were generally small, most saved whatever they could, encouraged by parents who placed a huge value on money. The very few women who recounted stories of being wasteful or less careful with their earnings tended to be living independently of their parents and in well-paid professional positions. The importance of saving was impressed on women from an early age. Joan Harold, who worked in the labour exchange and was very conscious of the serious unemployment problem at the time, remembered opening her first savings account during the 1940s:

> When I got the increase in my pay – thirty eight and six pence – and we all decided this evening – girls now – to start a post office account and I started off my account with two shillings. 1938 ... ah well, 'tis a long time. Could you imagine going into a post office now with two shillings a week savings?

Joan Griffin's parents also encouraged her to save the extra money she earned when she entered a permanent post in Kerry County Council in 1951. In factories, the large number of employees facilitated the development of informal savings schemes such as the Christmas club and what was called the 'diddlum' or the 'manage'. Rose Smyth explained how the 'diddlum/manage' operated in the Sunbeam factory in Cork:

> A 'manage' is where you, you save so much and there would be some one of your colleagues minding it or putting it in the bank. And you'd have to pick a number say one to twelve then and every month then like, someone of the twelve would get the money ... you might get your money, it might be twelve pound at the end of the year ... if I picked number one then, might pick in February, I'd have only just started. I'd have a pound paid in ... I'd love if 'twas number, say ten.' Twould be two weeks before Christmas ...

The 'manage' enabled Joan Fitzgerald to get her hair done, when she worked at the Irish Optical Company in the 1940s:

> And we had a 'manage', we used to call it. We'd pay a shilling every week in and they'd pick out your number then and you might be number seven. Well, after the seventh week, you'd get the seven shillings to get your hair done and you'd keep paying it then until the twelve had their hair done.

The women's saving practices took place in a depressed economy, where a strong consumer culture did not exist. The women frequently referred to the fact that few luxury goods were available in Ireland at the time, even for those who could afford them. When the women were single and had some disposable pocket money, the items they most commonly spent it on were: sweets, cigarettes, the cinema, dancing, public transport, clothes and bicycles. However, scarcity of money and lack of commodities meant that shopping was not the leisure activity it is today. As Mary O'Sullivan Greene, who grew up near Cork city, explained:

> At that time, shops were different. Woolworths was the only place you could walk in like they do now. All the other shops, Munster Arcade, Dowdens, Grants and all of those, you only went in there if you wanted to buy something.

Maura Duffy remembered the colour and excitement prompted by the visit of the dolly man to her house in Limerick city. His suitcase was full of the kind of luxury goods that were so unusual at the time:

> That time in Fish Lane, there use to be a dolly man come around ... He used to come around and he used to be dressed in all silks and a turban on his head and a big thing up through it and he'd have a suitcase, a large suitcase ... And on Friday or whatever day you had your pension or wages, my mother would open the door ... He'd open his suitcase, he'd have all silk scarves, silk stockings that we never could buy and lovely dresses, beautiful clothing and for a shilling you could get maybe a scarf, you could get maybe silk and you'd get a lot of stuff for a shilling and that's the way he earned his living.

The women's recollections also reveal that the purchase of new clothes was a rare occurrence for many and that clothing was often made or remodelled by women. Joan Noonan, who worked hard as a domestic servant/farm labourer throughout her life and reared 14 children, remembered her resourcefulness in this regard:

> I hadn't the price of a pair of laces one Sunday morning. The shops were shut. Oh my God above tonight, I polished two white cords and polished them black and they were fine. They passed as laces anyhow, you know ... the Confirmation frock I had, my children had it for their First Communion, because there were these lace flounces and you could take them off for First Communion and put them on for Confirmation, do you know. That kind of a way ... You always had to be economical about everything like.

Similarly, Rita O'Donovan recalled her early working life in the 1940s and commented:

> 'Twas little coats or shoes we had! We used to get our coats turned and when they'd get faded again, we'd dye them. There was no, they was hardly any such thing as buying a coat ... It was really tough and that's the truth.

The practice of making clothes at home also appeared to have been widespread, with many of the respondents commenting on women's skills in that regard. Rena McCarthy explained: 'My sister used actually make our clothes. She's a very good sewer, she used make our clothes for us.' Similarly, Alice Delea recollected:

> Myself and a friend ... she lived up the road from me, we could dress well now. Beautiful skirt going down to the Arcadia [ballroom] at night. 'Aw, they're beautiful! Where did you buy them?' We made them. We'd make them in a day. I got an old second-hand

machine then. She'd come down to my house, then she got a new one and do all fancy stitches. I'd go up to her for the fancy stitches. We'd buy a bit of stuff inside in Hickey's [fabric shop].

Due to the lack of a disposable income, many women could rarely pay large bills or make significant purchases instantly and so they entered into credit arrangements, which afforded them the opportunity to pay over an extended period. Localized credit arrangements with shopkeepers or drapers to pay what was owed at the end of the week or the month were also common.[18] Just like many of the women we interviewed, Joan Fitzgerald required a bike when she started work in the Irish Optical Company in Cork in the 1940s, but as she explained:

> You got the bike on hire purchase, that was the only way. You'd never have the fourteen pounds now to buy the bicycle you know ... the stronger the bike the better. You weren't going for fancy ones at all. And I paid it off by the week then, out of my wages.

Joan Noonan depended on the children's allowance[19] to pay for furniture she bought for the house:

> Thirty shillings a month of my allowance and that was paying for a table ... When I'd that paid for, I bought a wardrobe and four chairs. We had old chairs and they were falling over the place with age ... I never drew my allowance, only take my allowance over to Michael Smith [furniture shop owner] over in Charleville. And I was happy then, when everything was paid.

When credit arrangements were not an option, neighbours were called upon to provide money, food or other assistance. Maura Duffy, who lived in Limerick city in the 1940s, explained:

> There was a family next door to us ... and they were very badly off. So this Wednesday the lady of the house came to my mother, and she said 'Mary, would you lend me six shillings for the day, I'm caught out for the rent and to get food for the table?' So my mother was after getting her pension, ten shillings, and she didn't want to give that six shillings, but she didn't at the same time want to fall out with her neighbour so she gave her the six shillings.

It is clear from the women's narratives that being in serious debt generated fear and possibly stigma. Maureen O'Mahoney explained the thinking at the time: 'We had to work on a strict budget and we owed nothing and that was the done thing. You just didn't owe money you know.' Bridie Dunne's recollection of her husband's reaction to her practice of buying household goods on hire purchase clearly indicates that she was responsible for managing family resources. However, it also highlights a trend discernible in the narratives, namely that women had greater aspirations around home improvement than had their husbands:

> And he was saying, 'Aw, we'll go into the debtor's court!' And I said, 'Hey, did anyone knock at the door and say your wife owes money?' And if it was the rent money, the mortgage, or anything, 'twas upstairs in the big black purse as we called it.

During desperate times, some mothers would have had to resort to the services offered by local moneylenders and, indeed, the 'Jewman' featured in some women's recollections of growing up in Limerick city. Maura Duffy recounted the kindness shown by a moneylender on one occasion when her mother could not afford the interest she owed him on her loan. She had already been refused charitable help on the grounds that she was 'too well dressed'.

> So, she heard of Jewmen and she went up to one of them and she got a loan of the money and she paid it back every week until the last week when she had nothing ... We walked up along O'Connell Street, we knocked at the Jewman's house. She went in and he was sitting down at his desk and he had his skull cap on ... them caps ... He was in ordinary clothes, I don't know, a black kind of a suit. She said 'I haven't your last, I haven't your interest, your last interest.' 'I've no money,' she said. 'I'll tell you what I'll do, I'll clean your office. I'll clean your house. I'll do anything for you to pay my way because I worked with Jews in America.' Before I knew where I was, he took out an envelope out of the drawer and he put something into it and he said 'Here, forget about the interest. There's a little something to tide you over for a rainy day.' 'And come back child,' says he to me. And I don't remember was it six pence or three pence he put into my hand. 'Twas like a million pounds and I went down the street, I don't know what I got, but my mother had enough to tide her over.

CONCLUSION

In this chapter, oral history research on women's working lives in Munster between 1936 and 1960 was used as original source material, through which aspects of women's relationships to money could be illuminated and interrogated. Our analysis reveals that women's experiences of money and its meanings in their lives were shaped by the prevailing economic and social climate of the day and by the changing contexts of their life cycles. An ethos of monetary thrift and caution was induced by economic stagnation, high unemployment and rampant emigration. The prioritization of the family rather than the individual as the key economic and consumption unit was significant in shaping women's expectations around employment and money. The widespread practice of young single women ceding control of income to parents was described without expressions of resentment by the majority of the narrators, who appeared satisfied with being granted a portion of their earnings for personal use. Nonetheless, class differences were detected when we analyzed the use made of young single women's earnings. In working-class households, earnings tended to be consumed by the family unit, whereas in middle-class families, single women's wages were usually saved until such time as they were getting married. A culture of prudence in relation to the use of money permeated narrators' stories, and frequent reference is made to a variety of informal and formal workplace saving schemes in which they became involved as they got older and assumed greater control over their own earnings.

Our research indicates that upon marriage women typically assumed responsibility for the household budget but rarely accorded themselves a portion of the family wage for their own personal consumption. The management of family finances was an onerous responsibility, particularly in families where income was inadequate. Furthermore, men retained control over the allocation of earnings, and the narrators' accounts reveal that while some husbands put their entire wage at the disposal of the family, others did not. Financial need occasioned by the limited earnings of husbands, their retention of too high a proportion of their earnings for personal consumption, their illnesses or their deaths obliged many married women to seek ways of generating additional earnings to improve their families' physical and material lives. The women's life stories reveal the range of strategies they deployed to make extra money. Thus, they complicate notions that women's lives at that time were very strictly circumscribed. Married women who combined motherhood and homemaking with paid employment or with other income-generating work blurred the traditional boundaries of public and private. Their experiences challenge traditional, narrow representations of married women of the time as financially dependent homemakers.

While married women's earnings were generally small, they were significant in making ends meet in many cases and they afforded women a greater sense of entitlement to decide how these earnings should be spent. Stories of resourcefulness and inventiveness were frequently recounted by our narrators, who remembered the challenges they and their mothers experienced as managers of family finances. These accounts reveal that household management occurred in the context of a community financial network managed by women. In the absence of disposable income and limited consumer goods, the spending of money was carefully planned, and purchasing was regulated through credit arrangements such as hire purchase or buying goods 'on tick' from local suppliers. When they were desperate, women turned to neighbours for help or sought out charitable aid or loans provided by moneylenders.

In conclusion, it would appear that any comprehensive account of women's relationship to money in the Ireland of the 1940s and 1950s must recognize the multi-dimensional nature of women's lived realities. Their relationships to work and money were complex and contradict simplistic accounts of women as insignificant workers or financial managers.

NOTES

1. Irish work which has considered aspects of household decision-making and control in relation to finances includes Alexander J. Humphreys, *New Dubliners: Urbanisation and Irish Family* (London: 1966); Charles Clancy Gore, 'Nutritional standards of some working-class families in Dublin, 1943', *Journal of the Statistical and Social Inquiry Society of Ireland*, vol. XVII, no.1 (1943–4), pp. 241–53; Jeremiah McNabb, *The Limerick Rural Survey 1958–64* (Tipperary: 1964), pp. 215–16; Caitriona Clear, *Women of the House: Women's Household Work in Ireland, 1922–1961* (Dublin: 2000), pp. 171–201.
2. For a discussion of oral history and its use in this project see www.ucc.ie/wisp/ohp
3. The project was funded by the HEA Programme for Third Level Institutions Cycle 1.
4. The oral history project participants self-selected, in that they responded to a public call for project participants.
5. For a more detailed discussion of the social and economic conditions of the 1940s and 1950s, see J.J. Lee, *Ireland 1912–85: Politics and Society* (Cambridge: 1989) and Dermot Keogh, Finbarr O'Shea and Carmel Quinlan (Eds), *Ireland: The Lost Decade in the 1950s* (Cork: 2004).
6. By 1946, the majority of urban homes had electricity and almost 92 per cent had access to piped water. However, over 91 per cent of rural householders were still reliant on pumps or wells for domestic water supply and the rural electrification programme only began in 1946. See Aileen Heverin, *ICA: The Irish Countrywomen's Association – A History 1910–2000* (Dublin: 2000), pp. 106–14.
7. The 1946 census also identifies 54.5 per cent of the adult female population as 'engaged in home duties', i.e. married women working in households and farms. See Chapter 1 of Clear, *Women of the House*, p. 18.
8. Clear, *Women of the House*, pp. 13–26.
9. Legislative barriers to the employment of women, in particular married women, also limited women's employment opportunities. By 1933, white-collar public service work including national school teaching was precluded by a marriage bar for women. The Conditions of Employment Act, 1935 also limited women's employment in certain areas of industry; see Liam O'Dowd, 'Church, state and women: The aftermath of partition', in Chris Curtin, Pauline Jackson and Barbara O'Connor (eds), *Gender in Irish Society* (Galway: 1987), pp. 3–36.
10. The Limerick rural survey revealed similar attitudes among the daughters in farming families. However, the survey also indicated that secondary education was desired by the young

women as a means of entry into work and social situations where they might meet potential non-farming marriage partners. See Jeremiah McNabb, *The Limerick Rural Survey, 1958–64* (Tipperary: 1964), pp. 215–16.
11. Where there is an asterisk beside a woman's name, it indicates the use of a pseudonym in order to protect the interviewee's identity.
12. Employment at a young age would appear to have been common as the Census of Population included anyone over the age of 14 as an adult for the purposes of calculation in 1936. Prior to that, anyone over the age of 12 was viewed as a potential worker. See Clear, *Women of the House*, p. 14.
13. The marriage bar, which prohibited women from engaging in employment after marriage, was introduced in 1933. It operated until 1958 for primary school teachers and until 1973 for all other categories of jobs in the civil service. A similar bar operated in many other spheres of employment such as in Aer Lingus and the banks up until 1974. See Eoin O'Leary 'The Irish National Teachers' Organisation and the marriage bar for women national teachers, 1933–1958', *Saothar*, vol. 12 (1987), pp. 47–52.
14. The 1946 census records only 5 per cent of married women as gainfully occupied. The figure remained the same in the 1961 census; see Clear, *Women of the House*, p. 23. The 42 oral histories of women interviewed for this study suggest that many married women engaged in income-generating work outside of the formal labour market. For more discussion, see Elizabeth Kiely and Máire Leane, '"But you know, times were not too great for women then": Oral narratives of Irish married women's working lives, 1936–1960', *Womens' History Review* (Special Edition: Earning and Learning), 13, 3, pp. 427–45.
15. Clear, *Women of the House*, pp. 184–93; McNabb, *Limerick Rural Survey*, pp. 215–16; Noel Magnier, *Is That You Boy?* (Cork: 2000), p. 47.
16. See Clear, *Women of the House*, pp. 184–90, for a discussion of her own and others' findings on this topic.
17. Similar reports of husbands' resistance to their wives taking employment in this period was noted by Clear, *Women of the House*, p. 191. A working wife suggested that a husband was a poor provider and some husbands were opposed to their wives working because they felt threatened by the possible slight on their reputations as breadwinners.
18. Noel Magnier, in his memoir of growing up in a working-class area of Cork in the 1940s and 1950s, refers to his mother's practice of paying a few pence into the Christmas Club in a local toy shop on a weekly basis; see Magnier, *Is That You Boy?*, p. 19.
19. The Children's Allowance, introduced in 1944, was a universal state payment for third and subsequent children. The debate about whether the allowance should be paid to fathers or mothers provides some interesting insights into views about fathers' and mothers' relationships to money; see Clear, *Women of the House*, pp. 51–6.

14

The Decline of the Collaborators: The Ulster Unionist Labour Association and Post-War Unionist Politics

HENRY PATTERSON

ORIGINS

Most of what has been written about the Ulster Unionist Labour Association (UULA) has been confined to the period of its foundation and the early years of the Northern Ireland state. In the most serious treatment of it by a labour historian, Austen Morgan claims that 'the labour unionists were redundant, following the establishment of the state. The UULA was a failure though it lingered on as a member of the unionist family.'[1] While agreeing that the organization never attained the influence which its founders had hoped for, this chapter will focus on attempts to reinvigorate it to meet the challenges to Ulster unionism brought by the Second World War and argue that its trajectory reveals much about class divisions in the unionist bloc.

The organization had been created in 1918 largely at the instigation of the unionist leader, Sir Edward Carson, to counteract what was seen as socialist and liberal misrepresentation of the interests and opinions of working-class Protestants. Carson was concerned to counter the claim that Ulster unionism was a project of the landlord class and the bourgeoisie and prevent any seepage of working-class support to Labour in the 1918 Westminster election. Its core support came from trade unionists in the Belfast shipyards. To burnish unionism's pan-class image three of the party's candidates for the election were trade union members of the UULA, and in the elections for the Northern Ireland parliament in 1921 it had five members returned, including its president, John M. Andrews, a company director in his family's flax spinning firm, who became Minister of Labour. In the 1930s, Sir James Craig referred to the UULA as the 'most wonderful organization in Ulster' and claimed it had won the 'cream' of the working class and many influential trade union leaders to the unionist cause. There was, he claimed, nothing like it anywhere in the world.[2]

In fact, this estimate of the UULA's influence was exaggerated. Despite the purges of socialist trade unionists from shipyards and factories during the violence associated with the creation of the northern state,[3] the UULA's influence on the trade union movement was limited because of the widespread perception that it was supported and sponsored by the employers.[4] The fact that its president was a prominent local industrialist did little to dispel such perceptions. In the 1920s, it had branches in Belfast, Londonderry and a number of other towns in the province. It ran adult education classes and provided social facilities, including two workingmen's clubs in Belfast.[5] However, the economic depression of the early and mid-1930s led to a contraction of activities, and when an attempt was made to revive it towards the end of the war it was down to three branches in Belfast. Although the organization was claiming 600 members in its negotiations for funding with party headquarters, its own records give a membership of less than 100.[6] When this is compared to the twenty-one members of its executive, the picture is of a declining and sclerotic organization whose main function seems to have been to support the political ambitions of its small band of MPs and senators. By this time it had no social clubs and its main activities were an annual wreath-laying ceremony at the statue of Lord Carson at Stormont and lectures by members of the government. It ran a Welfare Bureau based in Glengall Street, which in 1945 dealt with around 800 cases. Significantly, the largest number of enquiries was from Protestants from the Free State who wanted help in obtaining a residence permit.[7]

THE THREAT FROM THE LEFT

Widespread popular dissatisfaction with the government's failure to respond effectively to the challenges of war-time mobilization had been apparent before the death of the prime minister, Lord Craigavon, in 1940, and was not assuaged by the accession of the UULA president, John Andrews, to the premiership. In February 1941 the Unionists lost Craigavon's North Down seat to an Independent Unionist. Then, in what Graham Walker has described as 'the biggest electoral upset in Northern Ireland's political history',[8] Harry Midgley of the Northern

Ireland Labour Party (NILP) won the hitherto solidly Unionist constituency of Willowfield in East Belfast in a by-election in December 1941.

Unionist leaders were particularly worried about the position in Belfast, which it believed was threatened by a mixture of socialist and communist agitation and apathy amongst traditional unionist voters. There was increasing concern that, faced with an unprecedented radical surge, the party was structurally and materially unprepared. This was a major concern of a business committee created during the war with the aim of modernizing party structures.[9] At one of its meetings the MP for Ormeau, Fred Thompson, claimed that the Communist Party was very active: 'they had issued pamphlets and leaflets and also held many meetings. The Unionist Party were far too slack and unless they wakened up they would lose seats in the City.' Maurice May, a North Down company director, agreed, bemoaning the fact that 'little or nothing' had been done on the propaganda front by party headquarters at Glengall Street while the opposition were displaying great activity. He highlighted the fact that Unionists lacked an authoritative statement of government policy. How could Unionist speakers counteract the communist paper *Unity*, which was 'poisoning the minds of the workers'?

May raised the possibility of a unionist paper for working-class loyalists to counteract communist and NILP propaganda.[10] By the beginning of 1945, such a paper had been created by the UULA. Its paper, a monthly duplicated news-sheet, *Unionist–Labour*, folded after eleven issues. According to its irate editor, this was because of lack of support from the party.[11] However, the briefest consideration of the content provides a better clue to its lack of appeal to ordinary trade unionists. The main article in its fifth edition was entitled *Men of Vision*, and it was a eulogy to the heroic entrepreneurs who had transformed a backward province into the 'present position where prior to the war Belfast contained four of the largest industries in the world'. The 'greatness of Belfast and Ulster came into being through the toil and sweat of independent men – private enterprise – who built our state of Ulster and its capital city'.

Not only was the working class excluded from any role in this story of economic success; as far as the UULA appeared to be concerned it was not required to play much of a role in its current governance, which could be left to the 'sons and grandsons' of the industrial pioneers 'who today sit in high places in Ulster's councils and its government'.[12] Deference to the local bourgeoisie and the unionist elite was combined with a defence of free enterprise which ignored the effect of the

Beveridge Report on popular attitudes to the role of the state and even the commitment of the previous Unionist premier to a major post-war reconstruction programme. There was an implicit recognition of the shift to the left in popular expectations that the war had produced: 'There's a general feeling that things must be made better for everyone and that things can't be allowed to slip back into the old muddle.' But those who might be tempted by radical politics were warned that they should not be 'in too much of a hurry to make drastic changes in government. Let things settle down a bit. Let the employers do the worrying for a while ... Let them find the trade, we'll do the job. They have the experience in markets and management, and they have the connections. If we took over all that, green as we are, we might do more harm than good.'[13]

The paper clearly identified Unionism with the British Conservative Party, quoting from denunciations of the British Labour Party's proposals as amounting to 'bureaucratic government controls that cannot be trusted to run an industry, a business or for that matter a whelk stall'. Strikes were denounced: 'It is the Socialist and Communist agitators, paid by results, who alone benefit by strikes.' Maynard Sinclair, the minister of finance, was quoted approvingly when he attacked demands for more public expenditure: 'He said the State has no bottomless purse, in fact of itself it has no money at all, it is only the money of the people – your money.'[14]

The Unionist Party fought the Stormont elections in 1945 on a strong anti-socialist and pro-private enterprise platform although it also stated that it would introduce whatever social reforms were brought in in the rest of the UK. This contradictory message contributed to the defection of a substantial minority of the Protestant working class to the NILP and other left-of-centre parties. Labour parties of various shades won 32 per cent of the vote in Northern Ireland and five Stormont seats, while in the Belfast constituencies the 'non-nationalist left', which included the NILP, the Commonwealth Labour Party and the Communist Party, won 40 per cent of the vote to the Unionist Party's 50 per cent.[15] The Unionist Party won thirty-three seats, six less than in the previous election in 1938, and its vote was down by 6 per cent.[16] The labourist upsurge, though not on the same scale as in the rest of the UK, helped to convince Brooke that his government had to embrace the welfare state no matter how much this enraged many party members.

THE UULA AND THE UNIONIST PARTY

After the 1945 general election, when its secretary, Sir Wilson Hungerford, who had had a junior governmental position, lost his seat in North Belfast, the UULA's Stormont representation was reduced to one MP, the Minister for Health and Local Government, William Grant. Grant, who was chairman of the organization, had been active in Conservative and Unionist politics since the time of the Ulster Unionist mobilization against the Third Home Rule Bill. At that time he was president of the Shipwrights' Society employed at Harland and Wolff's shipyard.[17] An active member of the UVF, he had played a central role in organizing a mass meeting of trade unionists opposed to home rule in the Ulster Hall in April 1914.[18] Elected to parliament for the Duncairn constituency in North Belfast in 1921, he was the only working-class UULA MP to hold on to his seat through the inter-war period and was eventually rewarded with a junior ministerial position in 1938 and promoted to minister of labour in 1943. The other UULA MPs at the outbreak of the war had been Hungerford, MP for Oldpark in North Belfast, and John F. Gordon, MP for Carrick. Neither had much claim to be working class. Hungerford had held the full-time position of secretary to the Ulster Unionist Council from 1921 and continued to hold that position when he became an MP, going on to hold a number of junior ministerial positions and ending up as chief whip of the Unionist Parliamentary Party at Westminster. Gordon, although he claimed to be a member of the Amalgamated Engineering Union (AEU), had been a manager in the linen trade and although he ended up during the war as parliamentary secretary to the minister of labour, resigned his seat in 1943 to become chairman of the Assistance Board although continuing to play an active role in the UULA, replacing Hungerford as secretary in 1946.[19]

The UULA was also represented in the Senate, the second chamber of the Northern Ireland parliament. This twenty-six-member body had few powers, and as it was elected by the members of the House of Commons most of its members were there because of their record of unquestioning party loyalty.[20] Of its three senators, the only significant figure was Joseph Cunningham. Cunningham was one of the founding members of the organization and, like Grant, had been active in Conservative and orange politics since the Edwardian period when he had been an engineering worker in Harland and Wolff. At that time he had been one of a number of Unionist trade unionists who had gone to England to propagate the Ulster cause to English trade unionists.[21] In 1922 he became the salaried secretary of Duncairn Unionist Association and was also a councillor for the Dock ward. He played an important role in the Orange Order where he was a member of the County Grand Lodge of Belfast from the 1920s and became deputy grand master of the

Grand Orange Lodge of Ireland in 1940. Craig made him a senator, and he and two or three other UULA members were members of the Executive Committee of the Unionist Party throughout the post-war period.[22]

THE UULA AND SECTARIANISM

There was little evidence that the UULA used its influence in the party to push it in the direction of policies more reflective of working-class interests. It contented itself with echoing the mainstream unionist claim that voting Labour was as bad as voting for the traditional nationalist enemy:

> When a loyalist hears the enemies of his cause raising their voices in condemnation he knows where he stands ... but a much more dangerous and hidden campaign is in progress, setting Protestant against Protestant, Loyalist against Loyalist ... This is clearly playing into the hands of our political opponents. Under whatever name they appear these opponents must be opposed and defeated, because the return of any one of them would be broadcast as a defeat for Unionism.[23]

It was in the vanguard of those demanding action against 'peaceful penetration' of Ulster by Catholics from the Free State. When trade union leaders raised the issue of possible post-war redundancies, *Unionist-Labour* attacked them: 'We question their sincerity when they insist on importing more alleged tradesmen from Éire to be trained in our shipyard to do work which could be done by loyal Ulster men.'[24] It demanded that war workers from the Free State return south when hostilities ended: 'These people from another State should not be encouraged to remain in Northern Ireland, increasing the unemployment figures and swelling the demand for houses.'[25]

Cunningham and the other UULA representatives on the party executive could be relied on to promote the most narrowly sectarian of agendas. Thus in February 1952 he raised the issue of Catholic attendance at the memorial service for King George VI at Stormont: 'There were supposed to be six or seven hundred RCs there. He had been asked to enquire into the matter and find out the number of RCs as compared with Protestants.' He and his comrades were oblivious to the arguments of one of the more liberal members of the executive who 'thought it was good propaganda in our favour' to have a high Catholic attendance.[26] Throughout the 1950s, they targeted the granting of employment permits to workers from the Republic.[27] In 1952, the executive decided not to try and get the employment permits of two Catholics from the Republic who had been working for the Great Northern Railway since 1942 cancelled because they were worried about the bad publicity this might attract. The two UULA representatives were aghast, with one, Robert Armstrong, later a Unionist senator, exclaiming: 'The sooner we stand up for our rights the better' and the other, a Mr Megraw, warning: 'The Church of Rome has made greater progress in the past five years than she had done in the last fifty.'[28]'

'NOT REPRESENTATIVE OF WORKERS TODAY'

Unionist-Labour had folded by the end of the war and the party leadership was faced with increasing evidence of the weakness and lack of influence of the UULA. An attempt to hold a series of mass meetings in Belfast to be addressed by government ministers was a miserable failure, with only small attendances and the UULA clearly failing to mobilize any significant support.[29] UULA members bemoaned the organization's lack of influence in the Belfast trade unions, particularly in the crucial sector of shipbuilding and engineering workers. This was all the more galling as it was from this sector that most members of the organization came. The South Belfast branch demanded to know what the UULA leadership was doing 'to counteract and subdue the activities of the Communist Party ... this evil within our Province, particularly in the Belfast shipyard and Aircraft factory'.[30] As one AEU member employed in Harland and Wolff's engine works put it, 'the trade unions are controlled by too many damned Socialists and Communists', while another, a branch official and shop steward in the Boilermakers' Union, referred to the 'stranglehold our opponents are gaining'.[31] In 1948 UULA members in the Electrical Trades Union (ETU) created a group: 'It is our earnest desire that sufficient members will be enrolled and that Romanist, Socialist and Communist influence will be effectively counter-acted.'[32] This development may have reflected the high profile of the ETU activist and anti-partitionist, Brendan Harkin, a particular *bete noir* for UULA members.[33] If so it appears not to have been very effective, for in 1951 one of the UULA representatives on the party executive was looking to employer action, not UULA activity, to counter Harkin's activities: 'Why can our Party not do anything about Mr Harkin. In the electrical department of Short and Harland, Protestants have no chance, the Heads are traitors to our Party.'[34]

Such ineffectuality had led to an increasingly hostile scrutiny from leading members of the party elite who doubted if the organization was worth supporting as a serious anti-socialist force. In 1947, the party executive, at the behest of J.M. Andrews, decided to provide an annual grant of £250 a year to meet the costs of a full-time organizer. The decision was to be reviewed after two years.[35] By 1950, the financial secretary of the UUC, Philip Smiles, was complaining that 'we have not had value for money from the UULA. I am told that the UULA might have been an extremely valuable body but it is not a power in the land today.'[36] The organization had shrunk even by its own inflated estimation, from 800 to 700 over the previous two years, and Smiles contended that 'it was not representative of workers today'. However, support continued to be given. In part this reflected the influence of J.M. Andrews, the former premier, who argued: 'While it may not have large enough numbers, the Union has no stronger supporter than these men.' He put continuance of support for the organization in the context of the two main dangers to the unionist cause: 'First, our young unionists are being influenced to join the Socialist Party and second infiltration from the Free State.'[37] The UULA was also considered to be 'a very useful name to have'[38] because of the strongly felt need of party strategists that the Unionist Party appear to be a pan-class movement and not an Ulster Conservative Party as was constantly alleged by its labour and populist critics.

CLASS TENSIONS IN POST-WAR UNIONISM

One of the most difficult challenges to the party elite was how best to manage the conflicting demands of its middle and working-class supporters. For while the party could rely on the support of a sizeable section of the Protestant working class, much of this support reflected the attitude noted by the anthropologist, Rosemary Harris: 'The basic political problem of the poorer Protestant was that to secure his independence from the Irish Republic he had to support politically those whom he neither liked nor trusted.'[39]

Insofar as the post-war period saw an invigoration of the party, this was largely in terms of it becoming more of a sounding box for the provincial Protestant middle class. Part of the reorganization was the creation of an annual conference where there could be discussion of government policies and the current political concerns of the party members. Up until then, the annual meeting of the UUC had functioned to elect and acclaim the leader. Now the rank and file had been given a notional role in the shaping of policy but it soon became clear that the conference mainly served as a safety valve for the repetitive expression of middle class *angst* over the government's policy of going 'step-by-step' with allegedly 'socialistic' legislation imported from Westminster.

In 1951, the executive discussed the low attendance at the annual conference when out of 1,600 ticket issued, only 330 attended. Blame was placed on the government's ignoring of conference resolutions and the fact that very few cabinet ministers or MPs bothered to attend. Both Sir Clarence Graham, the chairman of the Standing Committee and Colonel Topping, the chief whip, defended the government by criticizing the 'stupid' and 'irresponsible' resolutions that were often passed.[40] Graham pointed to a leading article in the *Belfast Telegraph*, which had criticized the unreflective, right-wing tone of the conference. One resolution demanded greater financial independence from Britain in order to allow cuts in estate duties while another demanded the denationalization of public transport. The article pointed out that social services and the standard of living depended on the principle of equal taxation with the rest of the UK – something which the Minister of Finance had pointed out during the debate 'yet the conference went its own way forgetful of the broad basis of working class men and women on which the party stands'. The transport demand 'loses sight of the ordinary Unionist people who made the 97 million journeys by bus in the past year'.[41]

However, the culture of the party was not such to encourage the articulation of working-class views or interests. Both the UUC annual meeting and the conference took place on weekdays during working hours, as did meetings of the executive and Standing Committee.[42] James O. Bailie, who was appointed as a provincial organizer for the party in 1946, had produced a blueprint for making local unionist associations more active and democratic. He pointed out that some were content to hold only one or two meetings a year and others were dominated by self-perpetuating cliques who actively discouraged new members. Most crucially, he emphasized the importance of widening the class basis of party membership:

> Sometimes attention is confined to only a particular class. This is wrong. Loyalty should be the only test. In one constituency I know, there are a great many factory and mill workers. Strenuous efforts were made by the Socialists to capture those workers, but the loyalists were alive to the danger and formed a workers' branch. There was a monthly meeting for factory lassies and mill workers ... the women came sometimes in their shawls, sometimes with no hats, and even with their babies ... no matter how they came they were assured of a hearty welcome.[43]

Such branches were the exception, as were the voices of working-class delegates in key party bodies like the executive and Standing Committee.[44] If anything, the existence of the UUA exacerbated the problem by encouraging the complacent belief that in it the party had a vehicle for the articulation of Unionist working-class interests despite its strongly deferential and class collaborationist nature.[45]

In times of heightened constitutional uncertainty, the party could rely on working-class Protestants to come out and vote Unionist. This was the case in the Stormont election of February 1949 conducted against the background of the withdrawal of the Irish state from the Commonwealth, the declaration of a republic and the launching of an all-party anti-partition campaign in the Irish Republic. The NILP did disastrously in the inflamed sectarian conditions and Brooke noted in his diary: 'A magnificent victory ... all the socialists knocked out.'[46] However, by the time of the next election in October 1953, the anti-partition campaign had faded and unionists could take comfort in the Ireland Act of 1949 which asserted that there could be no change in the constitutional position of Northern Ireland without the assent of the Stormont parliament. At the same time, the NILP had adopted a clearly unionist position on the border, which made it difficult to question its loyalty. At a time of rising unemployment and with the Conservatives in power in London, the NILP blamed the Unionist government's links with and support for the Tories for Northern Ireland having an unemployment rate four times the national average. A combination of apparent constitutional security and economic grievances contributed powerfully to a sharp fall in the Unionist vote and the loss of two seats.

In its post-election autopsy, party headquarters noted that, 'our party is losing the support of the lower paid income group and the artisans to the NILP', and bemoaned the fact that 'we have no members of parliament drawn from this category and many of the divisional associations are not as representative or democratic as they ought to be.' It noted the fact that with a greater degree of constitutional security the 'Big Drum which had heretofore dominated Unionist politics' was no longer so effective in mobilizing the working-class electorate.[47] It suggested 'an intensive campaign of political education' but was unspecific what the themes of this should be. However, in a subsequent discussion of the analysis it became clear that the party elite was divided over whether such a propaganda campaign should emphasize the party's opposition to socialism. One proposition was that the electorate be educated 'on the evils of socialism and that no more legislation of a socialist nature should be introduced'. The MP for the south Belfast constituency of Windsor,

Alexander Wilson, a company director in the linen industry, complained that 'since I entered Stormont the policy of the Government has been 95 per cent socialistic' and claimed that the administration's policies on health, welfare and transport had all been failures. He was supported by the Westminister MP for East Belfast, Colonel McKibben, another company director with interests in property and the drink industry, who complained that 'the whole policy of the imperial government (by this time a Conservative one) has to do with nationalization. If we don't fight the next election on the evil of socialism, we have nothing to fight it on.'[48] However, the chief whip pointed to the dangerous political implications for the party of a clear identification with the right:

> We have got to have all shades of opinion in our party. If we implement this paragraph we are altering the constitution of the party as there is nothing about challenging socialism in it. Do you suggest that we go out and admit that the attacks on us all these years – that we are not just a Unionist Party, that we are in fact a Conservative, right wing party – were correct?

Topping was supported by Clarence Graham: 'The Unionist Party is on a broad basis, within its ranks there is room for every man. If a man puts the constitution of Ulster first he could belong to the Unionist Party.' Others pointed to the dangers of anti-socialist propaganda backfiring, with the prominent Derry unionist, John Drennan, referring to a meeting at Coleraine 'where a gentleman made an attack on the Labour Party and through that Sir Ronald Ross lost over 3,000 votes … we have got a number of working men and women in Ulster today, who, if they were in England would be socialist.' The UULA representatives supported this line, with Senator Cunningham claiming that making anti-socialist propaganda would not help the UULA to address the situation where 'we have lost control of the trade unions in Belfast and other places'.

So, despite the strong anti-socialist sentiments of many party members, the dominant tendency in the leadership was to try and maintain the pan-class credentials of the movement. Nevertheless, the party faced an increasingly serious challenge from the NILP in the Belfast constituencies. The threat was sharply delineated in a memorandum sent to Glengall Street in 1955 by the Unionist Society, a group of professionals and academics affiliated to the party:

> The recent emergence of a full-blooded Socialist Party in Ulster who claim to be supporters of the Constitution has produced for the first time in Northern Ireland's history a potential opposition, whose chances at the polls in future are excellent especially among

the working class. It is this challenge more than the nationalist challenge that the Unionist Party will have to meet. The party has failed to produce a policy with any appeal to the electorate and the old battle cries are no longer adequate as a platform on which to fight an election. The government must produce a progressive policy statement for the next election.[49]

In fact, the party went into the next Stormont election after the government had introduced a piece of housing legislation, the Rent Act, which was intensely unpopular in working-class areas as it allowed landlords to increase rents for the first time since the war.[50] The government was also plagued throughout the decade by a provincial unemployment rate which was significantly higher than the UK average. The NILP was successful in depicting the Unionists as ineffective 'lap-dogs' of the British Tories who had been unable to get their allies in government at Westminster to take any special measures to create or defend jobs in the province.[51] Labour also accused the government of being an 'amateur' and 'part-time' administration. Down to the early 1960s Stormont was a regime of part-time ministers and a parliament that often met for no more than two afternoons a week when in session. Combined with Lord Brookeborough's semi-detached style of government, which allowed him ample time for running his estate in Fermanagh, it made the government vulnerable to Labour's charge that decades in power had bred complacency and incompetence.

THE TRADE UNION ADVISORY COMMITTEE

In the March 1958 Stormont election the party lost four Belfast seats to the NILP as thousands of working-class Protestants defected to Labour. The Standing Committee set up a committee of inquiry into the losses and it concluded that the three main factors were the Rent Act, unemployment and an ongoing strike in the shipyard. It reported on a delegation of trade unionists from the larger industries in the city:

> They informed that there is a great need for the Unionist Party to demonstrate that it is, in fact, truly representative of all sections of the community and that it is particularly anxious that the loyal trade unionists should play an active role inside the Party. Belfast trade unionists were no longer content to take their politics from the past and these men, particularly the younger element, have to be won over to Unionism by practical means and not sentiment.[52]

These trade unionists had been dismissive of the UULA, which was now 'a shadow of its former self ... it is doubtful if it has a large percentage of active trade unionists amongst its membership of about 200'. In an attempt to stem the tide of working-class disaffection, Billy Douglas, secretary of the Ulster Unionist Council, sent out letters to all party branches asking them to nominate two active trade unionists for a conference in party headquarters at Glengall Street in Belfast. The conference was to discuss 'ways and means to extend the Unionist influence in trade unions in Northern Ireland'.[53] The request was met with an unpromising reaction from many associations outside Belfast, who either claimed not to have any trade union members or denied that they faced any problem of working-class disaffection.[54] However, the first meeting of what became known as the Trade Union Advisory Committee went ahead on 5 December 1959 with thirty-two present, fifteen of them from Belfast. There were prominent members of the UULA, including Senator Cunningham, who listened to the chairman of the meeting, S.J. McMahon, who was also chairman of the party executive, when he informed them that 'It was obvious that some drastic steps must be taken if we are to create again a lively trade union organization within our Party.'[55]

The meeting was addressed by the Minister of Labour, Ivan Neill, who declared 'it was essential that those trade unionists who vote Unionist should be brought within the Party and take a more active interest in it. We could not afford to have a second party like the Socialists in Northern Ireland.'[56] However, Neill also added that the UULA had to be maintained as an organization and it was unclear how successful any new initiative would be as long as the ageing UULA leadership had a significant role in it. More fundamental a problem was Neill's declaration that any such organization should 'make the point that the Unionist Party since its inauguration as a Government in 1921 had done more for workers in Northern Ireland than any other government in the Commonwealth'. But it was precisely the image of the UULA as a governmental and Unionist Party stooge that had ensured its marginality in the workplaces of Belfast. As one irate East Belfast delegate put it: 'It was common knowledge in the shipyards that you are reminded that you could not be a good trade unionist and a member of the Unionist Party.'[57] The fundamental problem facing any attempt to replace or revivify the UULA was set out clearly in a letter from a working-class Derry unionist explaining why he was not going to attend the initial meeting:

> I am convinced that the formation of this organization must come from the wage earners of all walks of life in Ulster ... It is a mistake to ask the Minister of Labour to address the meeting ... he will

be in a position to dictate to those present what he would want done and not what we would like him to do for us.⁵⁸

The only concrete results of the meetings of the committee were a series of lectures on the social history of Ulster since the seventeenth century to be delivered through the Workers' Education Association and a recruitment leaflet. The lectures were considered a unionist victory as they had been opposed by socialists within the WEA.⁵⁹ The draft leaflet was entitled 'Trade Unionists We Need You!' In the first section, 'Political Questions' it appealed to unionist workers to 'take an interest in your trade union branch and see that loyalists control it. Why let Communists and Fellow Travellers use the trade unions to wreck our economy?' It also encouraged them not to contract in to pay the political levy to the Labour Party.⁶⁰ The rest of the leaflet lauded the Unionist government's industrial policy since the war and claimed that it aimed to provide a job 'for every man and woman who is prepared to work'. In the discussion of the draft, Daniel McGladdery, a UULA member who had recently been made a senator, pointed out a problem with the reference to trying to get loyalist control of the unions:

> The people who take an active interest in the trade unions are mainly socialists. There are members of the Catholic Action Society who are out to control the trade union movement but they do not mention the fact. We are in effect out to capture the trade union movement in the long run, but we should be much more diplomatic. To allow this second paragraph to go out would be fatal to our cause from the beginning.⁶¹

The reference to loyalist control was deleted from the leaflet and it was issued with a membership form for the Unionist Trade Union Organisation (UTUO). Apart from the lack of clarity of what was to be the relationship between the UULA and the new organization, the context for the venture was particularly unfavourable as both the aircraft and shipbuilding industries were experiencing large-scale redundancies in the early sixties. The result was further inroads by the NILP. In the 1962 Stormont election, although it did not win any new seats, its share of the vote rose from 16 to 26 per cent and, in the sixteen Belfast constituencies it contested, it won nearly 59,000 votes, just 10,000 less than the Unionist Party.⁶²

In an address to the executive in the run-up to the election, Brookeborough had outlined the depth to the challenge posed to the party:

> Hitherto our principal opposition has derived from those who have been opposed to Northern Ireland's constitution and the issue has been clear-cut. On this occasion, however, particularly in Belfast, the fight has shifted to the economic front and our opponents will be Socialists who profess support for our Constitutional position but are bent on discrediting the economic and industrial achievements of our Government.[63]

The supreme task was to 'break down the apathy of that section of the electors who although Unionist in outlook and sympathy usually neglect to go to the poll'. Traditionally the party could have looked to the Orange Order to mobilize the working-class electorate but that resource was itself increasingly riven with division. As Sir George Clark, Grand Master of the Grand Lodge of Ireland, admitted publicly after the election, the order in Belfast 'contained a great many Labour men who, while wearing a sash, nevertheless had a different political outlook'.[64] Even the sacred events in the Protestant and unionist calendar were affected. A joint committee of the UUC and the Grand Orange Lodge of Ireland had been created to plan for the celebration of the jubilee of the signing of the Ulster Covenant against home rule in 1912. However, William Douglas had to report to the executive that a section of the orangemen on the committee wanted the four NILP MPs to be on the platform.[65]

It was most unlikely that the UULA or the putative UTUO could have compensated for these intra-orange divisions. In fact the UTUO had to be re-launched by Brookeborough's successor, Terence O'Neill, as the Unionist Trade Union Alliance in 1963. This time it was decided to make a clean break with the UULA, and the new organization's secretary was Nelson Elder, a former member of the NILP who had pressed for a new organization because of the UULA's inactivity.[66] The UULA lingered on but was increasingly ignored by the party leadership. In 1966 its secretary, William Clulow, wrote to James Chichester Clark, Unionist chief whip at Stormont, to complain that none of the eight UULA nominations for the Senate had been chosen, while Nelson Elder had been elected to the second chamber.[67] However, there is little evidence that Elder's organization had any more success in winning back Protestant workers to the Unionist cause than the UULA. When the NILP lost two of its seats in 1965 it was because of the adoption, by O'Neill, of a new activist strategy of economic modernization and planning.[68]

CONCLUSION

There was a space for a form of unionist labourism but not of the top-down variety incarnated in the UULA. It was contained within the tradition of independent, populist unionism which combined the UULA's sectarianism with attacks on the unionist establishment. The emergent force of Paisleyism was the dominant form of this tradition in post-war Ulster. Paisley had briefly flirted with the UULA in the late 1940s. He addressed the East Belfast branch in February 1949, and UULA records contain a membership proposal form for him dated 5 November 1949.[69] Paisley had been an admirer of the Independent Unionist MP for Woodvale, J.W. Nixon, and in the fevered conditions of the 1949 election he had worked for the Unionist candidate in the Dock constituency. This was the constituency which Senator Cunningham represented on Belfast Corporation and at this time Paisley, who was a member of the Orange Order, shared orange platforms with the UULA senator.[70] However, Paisley was soon to break with both the Orange Order and the Unionist Party over their alleged indulgence of 'papist' encroachments in Northern Ireland. Although Cunningham and his comrades were just as exercised by the supposed 'RC' infiltration of Ulster, their institutional and personal integration into the unionist regime made them part of the 'appeasing' establishment as far as Paisley and his expanding number of working-class followers were concerned.

In an attempt to explain why 'ethno-national' politics vanquished class politics in Northern Ireland, Colin Coulter has highlighted the role of the UULA in allowing the Unionist Party to be seen to be taking on board the grievances of working-class loyalists: 'The association would appear to have performed the role for which it was designed with considerable success.'[71] This chapter has tried to demonstrate that the UULA was too comfortably ensconced in Parliament Buildings at Stormont or party headquarters at Glengall Street to be taken seriously in the workplaces of Belfast.

NOTES

1. Austen Morgan, *Labour and Partition: The Belfast Working Class 1905–23* (London: 1991), p. 215.
2. Quoted in Paul Bew, Peter Gibbon and Henry Patterson, *Northern Ireland 1921–2002: Political Forces and Social Classes* (London: 2002), p. 61.
3. See Henry Patterson, *Class Conflict and Sectarianism: the Protestant Working Class and the Belfast Labour Movement, 1868–1921* (Belfast: 1980), pp. 115–42.
4. Christopher Norton, 'Creating jobs, manufacturing unity: Ulster Unionism and mass unemployment, 1922–34', *Contemporary British History*, vol. 15 (Summer 2001), pp. 9–10.
5. See Maurice Goldring, *Belfast From Loyalty to Rebellion* (London: 1991), pp. 123–35.
6. Public Record Office of Northern Ireland (PRONI), UUC Papers, D/1327/11/1/15, General Material and Correspondence of UULA and D/1327/11/1/17, list of West Belfast members and letter from J.F. Gordon to William Douglas, 1 May 1947.
7. UUC papers, D/1327/11/1/15, seventh annual report of Welfare Bureau, 31 December 1945.
8. Graham Walker, *A History of the Ulster Unionist Party: Protest, Pragmatism and Pessimism* (Manchester: 2004), p. 91.
9. UUC papers, D/1327/15/9, business committee, 27 August 1943.
10. UUC papers, D/1327/15/9, business committee, 12 January 1945.
11. Ibid., letter from J.M. Andrews to Wilson Hungerford, 1 December 1945. It quoted from a letter to Andrews from the editor, Percy Howe: 'The future is black unless we do something to win back some of the lost ground.'
12. UUC papers, D/1327/11/1/15, *Unionist – Labour: Official Organ of the Unionist Labour Association*, 1, 5 (May 1945).
13. 'Should I become a communist?', by an Ulster Working Man, in *Unionist-Labour*, 1, 3 (March 1945).
14. *Unionist-Labour*, 1, 5 (May 1945).
15. Terry Cradden, *Trade Unionism, Socialism and Partition* (Belfast: 1993), p. 46.
16. Walker, *A History of the Ulster Unionist Party*, p. 100.
17. Morgan, *Labour and Partition*, p. 216.
18. Patterson, *Class Conflict and Sectarianism*, p. 86.
19. Details on Hungerford and Gordon from John F. Harbinson, *The Ulster Unionist Party, 1882–1973* (Belfast: 1973), pp. 190 and 194; and UUC papers, D/1327/11/1/15, UULA, annual report 1943.
20. Harbinson, *The Ulster Unionist Party*, pp. 122–8.
21. PRONI, D/1288/1A, 'Particulars of my life', by Senator Joseph Cunningham..
22. PRONI, D/1288/1B, 'Particulars of my Orange Connections' and D/1288/1A, Interview with Cunningham's widow by Brian Trainor, 6 January 1966.
23. UUC papers, D/1327/11/1/15, *Unionist-Labour*, 1, 3 (March 1945).
24. Ibid.
25. 'Eire Applicants', *Unionist-Labour*, 1, 2 (February 1945).
26. UUC papers, D/1327/6/32, executive committee, February 1952.
27. See resolution from the UULA executive 'expressing growing dissatisfaction of loyalists at granting of employment permits to disloyal people from Éire which is working to the disadvantage of loyalists born in Northern Ireland', UUC papers, D/1327/6/36, executive, 31 October 1952.
28. UUC papers, executive committee, D/1327/6/33, April 1952.
29. UUC papers, D/1327/11/1/17, circular from William Douglas, secretary to UUC, to UULA and other affiliated organizations, 7 July 1947: 'The mass meetings have been held but the attendance was extremely disappointing. For the last meeting the UULA asked for 200 tickets but only used 35.' East Belfast branch of the UULA were issued with 50 but only used 4.
30. UUC papers, D/1327/11/1/18, letter from South Belfast Branch of UULA to William Barclay, secretary, 7 April 1948.
31. UUC papers, D/1327/11/1/18, notes from T. Corkell, 73 Thistle Street, Blacksmith's helper,

and John Turner, Templemore Avenue, Boilermakers', Iron and Steel Shipbuilders' Society.
32. UUC Papers, D/1327/11/1/18, UULA Annual Report 1948.
33. On Harkin see Terry Cradden, *Trade Unionism, Socialism and Partition* (Belfast: 1993), p. 181.
34. UUC papers, executive committee, 5 January 1951, comments by Mr Megaw.
35. UUC papers, D/1327/11/1/17, letter from William Douglas to William Grant MP, 1 September 1947.
36. UUC papers, D/1327/6/18, executive committee, 9 June 1950.
37. UUC papers, D/1327/6/19, executive committee, 29 September 1950.
38. The words are those of Philip Smiles at executive committee, 9 June 1950.
39. Rosemary Harris, *Prejudice and Tolerance in Ulster* (Manchester: 1972), p. 187.
40. UUC papers, D/1327/6/27, executive committee, June 1951.
41. *Belfast Telegraph*, 30 April 1951.
42. UUC papers, D/1327/15/9, minutes of Finance sub-committee, It was noted that UULA members on the executive and standing committee had to leave work to attend and had lost pay because of it.
43. UUC papers, D/1327/12/1, 'How to run a Unionist Association'.
44. UUC papers, D/1327/7/44, 'Reasons for the small Unionist poll at October 1953 general election': 'Many of the divisional associations are not as representative nor as democratic as they should be.'
45. UUC papers, D/1327/15/9, UUC advisory committee: 'On the question of creating a greater interest among the working class in an endeavour to combat Socialism and Communism it was suggested that the executive of the UULA should be consulted.'
46. Brian Barton, 'Relations between Westminster and Stormont during the Atlee premiership', *Irish Political Studies*, vol. 7 (1992), p. 11.
47. UUC papers, D/1327/16/3/51, 'Observations on the 1953 election.'
48. UUC papers, D/1327/6/45, executive committee, 26 March 1954.
49. UUC papers, D/1327/6/54, executive committee, 24 June 1955.
50. Walker, *A History of the Ulster Unionist Party*, p. 124.
51. Jeremy Smith, 'Ever reliable friends? The Conservative Party and Ulster Unionism in the Twentieth Century, *English Historical Review*, CXXI, 490 (February 2006), p. 96.
52. UUC papers, D/1327/6/75, report of committee set up by the standing committee of the UUC to investigate organization and election machinery, 27 February 1959.
53. UUC papers, D/1327/11/6/1, letter from William Douglas to Unionist Associations, 23 October 1959.
54. UUC papers, D 1327/11/6/1, UULA papers, correspondence between William Douglas and various unionist associations. Typical was a letter to Douglas from Charles Cooper, hon. secretary of the Central Armagh Unionist Association, 2 October 1959: 'We feel that all of us in the Party are of one mind, employer and employee and it is unwise to make a distinction. In this area we get the fullest co-operation from the working classes. They are in fact our best supporters when the need arises. It was felt that the problem you are addressing is one for Belfast city.'
55. UUC papers, D/1327/11/6/2, trade union advisory committee, 5 December 1959.
56. Ibid.
57. UUC papers, D/1327/11/6/7, trade union advisory committee, 22 October 1960.
58. UUC papers, D/1327/11/6/7, letter from James Bryan, Londonderry to William Douglas, 28 November 1959.
59. UUC papers, D/1327/11/67.
60. Ibid.
61. Ibid.
62. Henry Patterson, *Ireland since 1939: The Persistence of Conflict* (Dublin: 2006), p. 143.
63. UUC papers, D/1327/6/96, executive committee, 2 February 1962.
64. *Belfast Newsletter*, 6 June 1962.
65. UUC papers, D/1327/6/99, executive committee, June 1962.
66. Marc Mulholland, *Northern Ireland at the Crossroads: Ulster Unionism in the O'Neill Years, 1960–9* (London: 2000), p. 44.

67. UUC papers, D/1327/11/1/25, letter from William Clulow, hon. secretary of UULA, to James Chichester Clark, 12 February 1966.
68. Patterson, *Ireland since 1939*, pp. 185–93.
69. UUC papers, D/1327/11/1/19, letter from Fred Anderson, hon. secretary of East Belfast UULA, 10 October 1949.
70. Ed Moloney and Andy Pollak, *Paisley* (Dublin: 1986), pp. 29–30.
71. Colin Coulter, *Contemporary Northern Irish Society: An Introduction* (London: 1999), p. 97.

Index

1798 rebellion, 167
1916 rising, 15, 18

A

Abbey Theatre (Dublin), 209–10
Accession Declaration (1901), 59
Act of Union (1801), 53, 58
Æ (George Russell), 180–1
agrarian agitation, Catholic, 10, 57
agricultural workers, 11–12, 107–8, 219, 224–5, 226–7, 231
Ahern, Bertie, 22
alcohol and working hours, 127, 131
Alltagsgeschichte ('history of everyday life'), 20
Amalgamated Society of Carpenters and Joiners (ASCJ), 84, 88, 90–1, 94, 95, 98, 140
amalgamated unions, 2, 78, 83, 85–6, 88, 97, 138, 141, 145–7, 171
An Phoblacht, 158, 162, 165, 166, 173
Ancient Guild of Incorporated Brick and Stone Layers' Trade Union (AGIBSL), 91–2
Anderson, Adelaide, 114
Andrews, John M., 239–40, 245, 246
Andrews, Todd, 22
anthropology, 20, 21
Antrim, County, 108
apprentices, 141–2
Armagh, County, 41, 43
armed forces, 123, 129, 221
Association for the Relief of Distressed Protestants (ARDP), 54–5
At Swim Two Birds (Flann O'Brien, 1939), 203
atheism, 179, 186
Auxiliaries, the (British paramilitary forces), 16

B

Ball, Elrington, 58–9
Ballyfermot and Inchicore cooperative, 191, 204
Barrett, Dermot, ix, 6
Baseline Reports, 105, 106
Behan, Brendan, 206–7
Belfast
   dock strike (1907), 50, 74
   economy, 66–8
   electoral politics, 50–1, 65, 67, 69, 71, 72, 73–4
   food crises (early nineteenth-century), 31, 36–7
   Labour Party and, 65–6, 69, 70, 71–80
   loyalism, 49–52, 59–60, 62, 77–80
   Orange Order, 62, 65, 69, 253
   Protestant working class, 49–52, 58, 65–8, 69–71, 74, 77–80
   sectarianism and, 49–52, 54, 244–6
   trade unionism, 51, 66, 67–72, 74, 75–9, 239

see also Harland & Wolff; shipbuilding industry, Belfast
Belfast Corporation, 71, 72, 75, 254
Belfast Labour Chronicle, 73
Belfast Newsletter, 36–7, 39, 65, 71
Belfast Protestant Association (BPA), 50, 51, 58, 73
Belfast Protestant Working Men's Association, 69
Belfast Repertory Theatre, 210
Belfast Socialist Society, 74
Belfast Telegraph, 71, 247
Belfast Trades Council, 3, 50, 68–71, 72–4, 75–6, 77, 78, 79, 169
   home rule and, 74, 76, 77, 79, 80
Bell, Sam Hanna, 209, 211
Bell, The, 206, 207, 209
Belton, Paddy, 205
Bergin, Paddy, vii
Beveridge Report, 241–2
Birmingham one-day strike (August 1969), 173
Black, Boyd, 66
Board of Trade, 87, 153
Boilermakers Union, 139, 142, 144, 145, 245
Bolton, Samuel H., 86, 89, 98
Bourke, Joanna, 103
Bowen, Elizabeth, 62
Bowley, Arthur Lyon, 10
Bowman, Alexander, 69, 70
Boyd, Alex, 50–1, 72, 73
Boyd, John, 209, 211
Boyle, Elizabeth, viii–ix, 1, 3–7, 103
Boyle, John W., viii–ix, 1–3, 11–12, 20
Boyne, Battle of, 53
Braithwaite, Richard, 50, 58
Brecht, Bertolt, 202, 211, 212–13
Breen, John, 191
Britain, 2–3, 11, 16, 67–8, 174
   general elections, 50, 58–9, 73, 239–40
   see also Labour Party, British
Broadhurst, Henry, 69, 70

Brookeborough, Lord, 242, 248, 250, 252–3
Browne, Noël, 190, 191, 193, 196
B-Specials, 163, 164
building trades, 167, 173
   lockout (Dublin 1896), 83, 84, 88–100
   wages and conditions, 84–5, 86–7, 89, 90, 91, 95–6, 97, 99
Burke, Rosie, 211

C

Callan, Charles, vii
Campbell, D.R., 75–6, 77, 78
Canada, viii–ix, 4, 5–6, 7
canal network, 33, 37, 41–2
Carlow, County, 31–2
Carnduff, Thomas, 210
Carson, Sir Edward, 59, 79–80, 239, 240
Catholic Action Society, 186, 252
Catholic emancipation, 55, 178
Catholic Standard, 183
Catholic Truth Society, 179
Catholicism
   cultural tradition, 52
   Irish politics and, 55, 177, 178–80, 181–96, 199
   Labour Party and, 177, 179–80, 181–96
   left wing politics and, 178–80, 183–4, 189–90, 190–2, 194–5, 206
   Lurgan weaving industry, 130, 131–2
   nationalism and, 62, 178
   Protestant hostility and, 10, 55–6, 57, 58–9, 60–1, 244–5
   social class and, 53, 54, 56–7, 59
   social welfare and, 186, 189, 190, 193–4, 195, 196
   Spanish Civil War and, 183, 205–6, 207–8
   trade unions and, 68
charities, Protestant, 54–5

children as farm servants, 106
Christian Socialism, 178, 179, 181, 193–4, 208
Church of England, 58
Church of Ireland, 51, 52, 56, 193
Churchill, Randolph, 56
Civil War, Irish, 157, 158, 178, 179, 204
Clann na h-Éireann, 173
Clann na Poblachta, 188, 190
Clann na Talmhan, 188
Clare, Bill, 211
Clare, County, 32, 40, 44, 170–1
Clark, Sir George, 253
Clarkson, Jessie Dunsmore, 17
Class Conflict and Sectarianism (Henry Patterson, 1980), 66
closed shop demands, 146
Coffey, Brian, 203, 214
Cold War, 178, 189, 190–2
Collins, Peter Gerard, 66
Collins, Séamus, 173
comintern, 161, 162, 210–11
commemoration culture, Protestant, 52–3
Commercial Employees Union (CEU), 162, 165
Commonweal, The (Socialist League newspaper), 10
Commonwealth Labour Party, 242
communism
  Catholicism and, 183–4, 189–90, 190–2, 194–5, 206
  comintern, 161, 162, 210–11
  historiography and, 15–18
  IRA and, 157, 161–2, 164–5, 169–70, 172, 173
  Labour Party and, 186, 187, 189–90, 194–5
  Ulster Unionist Party and, 241
Communist Party, 169, 173, 201, 215, 216
  Ireland, 173, 201, 202, 209, 211
  Northern Ireland, 169, 170, 241, 242, 245

Conciliation (Industrial Disputes) Act (1896), 87
Congested Districts Board, 105
Connolly, James, 16–18, 20, 140–1, 170, 178, 181
  home rule and, 74–5, 76
  nationalism and, 2–3, 13–15, 18, 66, 158
  socialism and, 13–15, 66, 74
  trade unions and, 13, 75, 76, 98–9, 158–9
Connolly, Roddy, 157, 162, 211
Connolly Association, 173
Conservative Party, 51, 53, 58
  in Belfast, 49, 50, 65, 69, 73
  Protestantism and, 53, 59–60, 61
  unionism and, 80, 242, 246, 248, 249, 250
Conservative Working Mens' Club, Dublin (CWC), 56–9, 61
construction industry, 68
Contemporary Club (Dublin), 11
Corish, Brendan, 192–3
Cork, County, 16, 21, 29, 34–5, 38, 45
coronation oath (1901), 59
Cosgrave, W.T., 180
Costello, John A., 190
Costello, Seamus, 169, 174
cottage industry, 103–4, 105, 106–16, 118, 120, 121–2
Coulter, Colin, 254
Country, Class or Craft? The Politicisation of the Skilled Artisan in Nineteenth-Century Cork (Maura Cronin, 1994), 21
craft unions, 2, 68, 77, 88–98, 99, 100, 138–41, 144
  see also trade unions
Craig, Sir James, 240, 243–4
Craigavon, Lord, 240
Crawford, Robert Lindsay, 51, 58, 60–1
credit arrangements (1940s and 50s), 232, 233, 235

Cronin, Seán, 167
Cross, Gary, 119, 132–3
Crowds in Ireland (eds. Peter Jupp and Eoin Magennis, 2000), 29
culture in Ireland (1930s), 199–216
  social class and, 200, 202, 210
  social realism, 201–2, 203–4
Cumann na nGaedheal, 179, 181, 182
Cunningham, Joseph, 78, 79, 243–4, 251, 254
'Curragh mutiny', 78
Cusack, Margaret, 11

D

Daiken, Leslie, 206, 213
Daly, Miriam, 193
Davis, Murray, 70
Davitt, Michael, 10
de Valera, Éamon, 166, 190, 192–3, 196, 199, 209
Deane, Lucy, 104, 108–16
Deane, Seamus, 202, 203
deindustrialization (nineteenth century), 12
demarcation disputes, 136, 138, 153, 154
Devlin, Dennis, 203, 214
Dickson, David, 29
'diddlum' and 'manage', 230
Digby, Kenelm E., 114
Digges, Alex, 211
Dillon, James, 188, 189
divorce, 179
Dixon, Sir Daniel, 73
dolly men, 230–1
Dolly's Brae (1849), 53–4
domestic service, 219, 220, 222, 226, 231
Donald, Thompson, 78
Donaldson, Frank, 60
Donegal, County, 39, 105, 107, 108, 110, 113, 115
Donnelly, Charlie, 206, 213–15, 216

Douglas, William, 251, 253
Dublin, 54–61, 63, 87
  economy, 12, 29, 31, 33, 54, 67
  electoral politics, 58–9, 60–1, 98–9, 171
  labour unrest, 18, 20, 83, 84, 88–100, 163, 165, 166, 212
Dublin Evening Post, 38
Dublin Guild of Master Painters (DGMP), 89, 93, 97, 98
Dublin Magazine, the, 206
Dublin Protestant Operative Association (DPOA), 55–6
Dublin Socialist Society, 13
Dublin Trade Union Unity League, 162
Dublin Trades Council and Labour League (DTCLL), 84, 85, 86, 88, 94, 95, 97, 173
Dublin University Review, 10
Duffy, Peter, 167, 170, 173
Dunbar-Harrison, Letitia, 182

E

Early, Packie, 167
economics, 11–12, 26–46, 54, 55, 66–8, 252
  1940s and 50s, 219, 229, 234
  cottage industry, 103–4, 105, 106–16, 118, 120, 121–2
  industrialization, 12, 118–33
  stagnation (1930s), 199, 240
Edwards, Robert Dudley, 9
Eiríksson, Andres, 39
Elder, Nelson, 253
electoral franchise, 56, 69, 71
electoral politics
  in Belfast, 50–1, 65, 67, 69, 71, 72, 73–4
  British general elections, 50, 58–9, 73, 239–40
  in Dublin, 58–9, 60–1, 98–9, 171
  Irish general elections, 161, 179, 180,

182, 188, 194–6
  municipal, 60–1, 71, 72, 98–9, 171
  Northern Irish elections, 239, 240–1, 242–3, 248, 250, 252–3
  UULA and, 239–40, 242–3
Electrical Trades' Union (ETU), 76, 144, 245
Electricity (Special Provisions) Bill, 169
Eley, Geoff, 16
Ellis, Peter Berresford, 13–14
Engels, Friedrich, 11
engineering industry, 67, 78
engineering unions, 78, 138, 141, 145, 151
engrossing (food-marketing practice), 27
Ennis, Michael, 91, 95
Episcopalianism, 131
Erin's Hope: The End and the Means (James Connolly pamphlet, 1897), 13
Eucharistic Congress (1932), 182
evangelicalism, 51, 53, 54, 55, 57, 59
Evening Herald, 32, 168
export restrictions, food, 27, 28, 29–30, 36, 39
expulsions from employment, 78, 152

F

Factory Acts in Ireland, 1802-1914, The (Desmond Greer and James W. Nicolson, 2003), 21
factory inspectorate, 104, 107, 108–16, 123, 124, 153
factory system, 118–19, 122–9, 130–3
'Fair Wages Clause' (1891), 87
famines, 12, 29
Federation of Engineering and Shipbuilding Trades, 78, 145
female labour *see* women and work
Fethard-on-Sea boycott (1958), 192–3
Fianna Fáil, 161, 166, 177, 182, 188, 190, 199, 207
  Labour Party and, 182–3, 194, 195
Field, William, 94
film, 207
Fianna Fáil and Social Classes, 22
Fine Gael, 171, 177, 188, 189
First World War, 15–16, 17, 67, 68, 136, 144, 149, 152
Fitzpatrick, Mick, 161–2, 165, 167
Five Years in Ireland (Michael J.F. McCarthy, 1901), 60
food crises
  anti-export activities and, 27, 29–30, 36, 39
  early nineteenth-century, 26–7, 28, 29, 31–7, 38–45
  eighteenth century, 29–31
  famines, 12, 29
  food riots, 27, 28, 29–30, 31–7, 38–46
  market interventions, 26–7, 31, 36, 38, 42, 46
football match (Ireland v Yugoslavia, 1954), 191
Foreman, Stephen, 10
forestalling (food-marketing practice), 27, 28, 29–30, 31, 33, 41, 45
Foster, John, 2
Fox, R.M., 18
'Free Labour Association', 90
Freeman's Journal, 31, 94

G

Gaelic League, 202
Gaelic revival, 14–15, 17
Gageby, Robert, 65, 66, 74
Galway, 27, 32, 36, 38–9, 43, 45
Garland, Seán, 169, 171
General Outline of the Present Movement (IRA Army Council document, 1927), 159–61
gentry, Protestant, 62–3
George V, King, 59
George VI, King, 244

Geraghty, Des, 167, 172
Geraghty, Hugh, ix
Germany, 11, 16, 20
Gibbon, Peter, 62
Gill, Eric, 208
Gilmore, George, 165, 214
Gladstone, William, 69–70
Good, John, 87, 89, 95, 98
Goodbye, Twilight (ed. Leslie Daiken, 1936), 213
Gordon, John F., 243
Goulding, Cathal, 169, 172, 173, 174
Gramsci, Antonio, 13
Granard (Co. Longford), 28, 40, 43, 162
Grant, William, 78, 79, 243
Great Famine, 12
Greaves, C.D., 18
'green sash' incident (1893), 71
Greene, Sheila, 187
Greenmount Mills (Dublin) strike, 163
Gregg, Revd. Tresham Dames, 55–6
Greig, George, 75
Griffith, Richard, 33
Group Theatre (New York), 211

H

Halligan, Brendan, 194
Handloom Weavers in Ulster's Linen Industry, 1815-1914 (Kevin James, 2007), 21
Hanna-Bell, Sam, 149
Harkin, Brendan, 245
Harland & Wolff, 78, 135, 243, 245
   Articles of Agreement (1914), 140, 145–6, 153, 154
   employment data, 136, 137, 143, 144, 145, 148, 150–1
   industrial relations, 136, 140, 141, 145–7, 150, 152–4
   management, 136, 146, 147–8, 150, 151, 153, 154
   manual labour force, 137, 138, 140, 141, 142, 143–8
   white collar workers, 150–2
Harrington, Tim, 90
Harris, Rosemary, 246
Harrison, Mark, 30
Haughey, Charles, 22
Healy, John, 194
Henderson, Arthur, 73
Hewitt, John, 201, 211, 213, 215–16
Hidden Ireland, The (Daniel Corkery, 1924), 202
history
   academic, viii, 9, 10, 17, 18–20, 21, 22
   non-academic, 10, 11, 13–14, 17–18, 19–20
   Protestantism and, 52–4
History of the Dublin Bakers and Others (John Swift, 1948), 18
History of the Irish Working Class, A (Peter Berresford Ellis, 1972), 13–14
Homage to Catalonia (George Orwell, 1938), 205
home rule, 67, 69–70, 77–8
   Belfast Trades Council and, 74, 76, 77, 79, 80
   British Labour Party and, 65, 73–4, 78–9, 80
   crises, 57, 69, 71, 77, 80, 153
'Howth set' of unionists, 56
Hume, J.R., 136, 152, 153, 154
Hungerford, Sir Wilson, 242–3

I

Independent Labour Party (ILP), 4, 72, 74, 75, 179
Independent Orange Order (IOO), 51–2, 59–60, 61, 72, 73, 78
Independent Unionists, 240
industrialization, 12, 118–33
Inglis, Brian, 187, 189
Ingram, Thomas Dunbar, 11

injuries, industrial, 140–1
International Labour Organisation, 181
International Socialists, 173
Ireland
   inter-party government (1948–51), 188–90
   Irish Free State, 159, 160, 179–85, 199–216, 240, 244, 246
   Republic of Ireland, 244–5, 246, 248
   southern, 11–12, 62–3, 67, 240
Ireland Act (1949), 248
Ireland Her Own (Thomas A. Jackson, 1946), 18
Ireland Today (IRA document, 1969), 171–2
Ireland To-day (magazine), 207–8, 209
Irish Catholic (newspaper), 183
Irish Church Mission, 59
Irish Citizen Army (ICA), 157, 158, 162, 166
Irish Democrat, 206
Irish Film Society, 207
Irish Flowerers, The (Elizabeth Boyle, 1971), 4, 103
Irish Free State, 159, 160, 179–85, 199–216, 240, 244, 246
Irish Freedom, 206
Irish Front, 206
Irish Historical Studies, 9, 19
Irish Housewives' Association, 191
Irish Independent, 183
Irish Labour Defence League, 162
Irish Labour History Society (ILHS), vii–viii, 1, 6–7, 19
Irish Labour Movement from the Twenties to our own Day, The (W.P. Ryan, 1919), 16–17
Irish Labor Movement in the Nineteenth Century, The (John Boyle, 1988), viii, 2, 20, 49
Irish National Teachers' Organisation (INTO), 181, 185
Irish Nationalism and British Democracy (Erich Strauss, 1951), 18

Irish News, 125
Irish People (weekly paper), 187
Irish Republican Army (IRA)
   communism and, 157, 161–2, 164–5, 169–70, 172, 173
   Labour Party and, 161, 171–2
   labour unrest and, 162–4, 165–6, 167–9, 170–1, 173–4
   leftism (1960s), 167–72, 173
   rural support base, 158, 159, 160, 170
   trade unionism and, 157–66, 167–72, 173–4
   violence, 162, 163, 165, 166, 171, 173–4
Irish Rosary (newspaper), 183
Irish Socialist, 193
Irish Socialist Republican Party, 75, 98
Irish state, 159, 160, 179–85, 199–216, 240, 244–5, 246, 248
Irish Statesman, the, 206
Irish Textile Journal, 105, 107–8
Irish Times, 60, 194
Irish Trade Union Congress (ITUC), ix, 6, 67, 68, 72, 74, 78, 84, 86, 88, 98
   Belfast and, 68, 71, 74, 75, 76, 77
   Clonmel congress (1912, 75, 76
   home rule and, 74, 76
   Labour Party and, 74, 77, 181
   unionism and, 77–8
Irish Transport and General Workers' Union (ITGWU), 2, 68, 158, 160, 161, 172, 173
   IRA and, 158, 160, 169
   Labour Party and, 171, 185–6
Irish Weekly Democrat, 208
Irish Workers Party (IWP), 169–70, 172, 193
Irish Workers Voice, 206
Irish Workers Weekly, 206, 211
Irish Working Class: Explorations in Political Economy and Hegemony, 1800–1950, An (Marilyn

Silverman, 2001), 21
Irishman, the (Labour newspaper), 180, 181
Itinerant's Action Group, 167

J

Jackson, Alvin, 58-9
Jackson, Thomas A., 18
James Connolly Labour College (Dublin), 16
Jemmy Hope (Seán Cronin pamphlet, 1964), 167
Johnson, Tom, 74, 75, 76, 77, 159, 179, 180-2, 184
Johnston, Dennis, 209
Johnston, Roy, 169, 170
Johnston, William, 50, 54, 69
Joyce, James, 203

K

Kavanagh, Patrick, 209
Kelly, James, 29
Keyes, Michael, 190
Kilkenny Moderator, 41, 43-4
Killeen, Jim, 161
Knights of St Columbanus, 183, 187, 192

L

Labour, Nationality and Religion (James Connolly pamphlet, 1910), 178
Labour and Nationalism in Ireland (Jessie Dunsmore Clarkson, 1925), 17
Labour History of Ireland, 1824-1960, A (Emmet O'Connor, 1992), 21
Labour in Irish History (James Connolly, 1910), 14-15, 17, 18
Labour in Irish Politics, 1890-1930 (Arthur Mitchell, 1974), 19
Labour in the West of Ireland: Working Life and Struggle, 1880-1914 (John Cunningham, 1995), 21
Labour News (weekly paper), 184-5
Labour Party, 20, 80
  Catholicism and, 177, 179-80, 181-96
  Clonmel congress (1912, 75, 76
  communism and, 186, 187, 189-90, 194-5
  constitutions (1930s), 181, 183, 185, 195
  elections and, 161, 179, 180, 182, 188, 194-6, 239
  IRA and, 161, 171-2
  Irish State and, 159, 177, 179-96
  social welfare and, 186, 189, 190, 195, 196
  socialism and, 171, 189-90, 193, 194-6
  trade unions and, 74, 159, 171-2, 185-6
Labour Party, British
  Belfast and, 65-6, 68, 69, 70, 71-4, 77-80
  government (1945-51), 189, 190
  unionism and, 65-6, 72-4, 242
Labour Representation Committee (LRC), 72, 73-4
Labour Unionism, 77-80, 239-54
labour unrest
  1960s & 70s, 167, 167-8, 170-1, 173, 174
  Belfast dock strike (1907), 50, 74
  demarcation disputes, 136, 138, 53, 154
  Dublin and, 18, 20, 83, 84, 88-100, 163, 165, 166, 212
  First World War period and, 15, 16, 17
  at Harland & Wolff, 136, 152-4
  IRA and, 162-4, 165-6, 167-9, 170-1, 173-4
  Lurgan textiles industry strike (1899), 124-9, 131-2

non-sectarian activity, 70–1
Protestant militancy, 163, 164
transport strikes (1930s), 162, 163–4, 166
Lagan (magazine), 209
Lalor, James Fintan, 170
land annuities, 160, 161
Land League, 10
language, Irish, 62–3, 202
Larkin, Emmet, 18
Larkin, James, 2, 17, 18, 50, 70, 159–60, 161, 171, 178, 186
Last Hill, The (Tom O'Brien play, 1939), 212
Lecky, W.E.H., 10
Left Book Club, 202, 211, 212
Left Review, 200, 202, 209
Lehman, John, 200
Lemass, Seán, 188
Liberal Party, British, 65, 69–70, 77
Limerick, 44–5
Limerick Leader, 183, 184
Literary Revival, 199–200, 202, 203, 206
literature, 199, 200, 201–2, 203–6, 204
Local Government (Ireland) Act (1898), 60
local studies, 19, 21
Lock-Out (Seán Ó hEidirsceoil play), 212
lock-outs, 70
  1913 lockout, 18, 20, 212
  building trades (Dublin, 1896), 83, 84, 88–100
Londonderry Journal, 26–7, 28, 31, 42
Londonderry Sentinel, 110
Londonderry shirt industry, 107–8, 110, 111, 112, 116
Long, Dr. R.H., 59
Longley, Edna, 202
loyalism, 49–63
  in Belfast, 49–52, 59–60, 62, 77–80
  see also unionism

Luddist movement, 32
Lukács, Georg, 201
Lurgan, 31, 118, 119–33
Lynch, Jack, 194

M

Mac Raghnaill, Donnchadh, 169
Macalastair, Somhairle, 206
MacBride, Seán, 161, 188, 190
MacColl, Malcolm, 16
MacColum, Sean, 211
MacDonagh, Donagh, 214
MacDonald, Ramsay, 73, 74, 78–9
MacDonnell, Elias, 34–5, 37
MacDonnell, Joseph M., 16
MacEntee, Seán, 186
MacGiolla, Tomas, 168, 169
MacNiece, Louis, 62, 211, 213, 216
MacStiofáin, Seán, 169, 170
magazines and newspapers, 206–9
Magennis, Eoin, 29–30
Magheramorne Manifesto, 51–2
Malcolm, James, 122, 125, 126, 127
Malone, Lar, 169
'manage' and 'diddlum', 230
market interventions during food crises, 26–7, 31, 36, 38, 42, 46
market juries, 27–8, 31, 46
Martin, T. & G., 87, 89
Martindale, Hilda, 109
Marxism, 14, 15–16, 18, 170, 180–1, 202, 214
Master Builders' Association (MBA), 84, 85, 87, 89, 90–3, 94–8, 99–100
Mater et Magistra (papal encyclical, 1961), 193, 194
Mayo, County, 40–1
McCabe, Desmond, 41
McCarthy, Charles, 19
McCarthy, Michael J.F., 60–1
McCool, Seán, 165
McCorry, Francis X., 121–2
McCourt, Frank, 203

McDowell, R.B., 62
McGarry, Fearghal, 183
McGinley, Jack, ix
McGinn, Barney, 211
McGuinness, Catherine, 193
McMahon, S.J., 251
McMillen, Liam, 170
McQuaid, John Charles, 181, 183, 189, 190, 191
McQuillan, Jack, 191
Meade, Alderman Michael, 88, 89, 96, 98
Meagher, Thomas Francis, 15
Meath, County, 43
Mellows, Liam, 158, 161, 164, 170
Mercantile Chronicle, 34
mercantilism, 27–8
Merrigan, Thomas, 162
Messenger, the, 194
metal trades, 67, 69, 77
Methodism, 130, 131
Metropolitan House Painters' Trade Union (MHPTU), 93, 97
middle classes
  Catholic, 53, 59
  conservative establishment, 49, 50, 52, 53, 58, 59, 61
  Protestantism, 49, 50, 52, 52–5, 56, 58, 59, 61–3
  socialism and, 10–11, 207
  unionism and, 55, 61, 246–8
  women, 223, 224, 234
Midgley, Harry, 240–1
Milne, Ewart, 206, 213, 215–16
Mindzenty, Cardinal (of Hungary), 191
miners' strike, British (1972), 174
Mitchell, Arthur, 19
modernist movement, 201, 202, 203, 209, 210, 213, 214
monarchy, Protestant, 52–3
moneylenders, 233, 235
Monro, Samuel, 70
Montgomery, Niall, 214
Moody, Theodore William, 9
moral economy thesis (E.P. Thompson), 27–9, 30–1, 39, 45
Morgan, Austen, 66, 239
Morris, William, 11
Mortished, R.J.P., 179, 181
Morwood, Elizabeth (Elizabeth Boyle), viii–ix, 1, 3–7, 103
Morwood, James, 3–4
Moscow Arts Theatre, 211
Moss, M.S., 136, 152, 153, 154
'mother and child' scheme, 190, 192, 196
Mullen, Michael, 173
Municipal Employees' Association, Belfast, 50, 72
municipal politics, 60–1, 71, 72, 98–9, 171
Murphy, John, 68, 71, 74, 79
Murray, Patrick, 178

N

Napoleonic wars, 38
National Amalgamated Union of Labour (NAUL), 145–7
National Labour Party, 186, 188
National Solidarity Committee, 173
National Union of Gasworkers and General Labourers, 71, 145
nationalism, 52
  Catholicism and, 62, 178
  cultural, 10, 13, 202
  James Connolly and, 2–3, 13–15, 18, 66, 158
  Labour Party and, 66
  trade unions and, 2–3, 68
Neill, Ivan, 251
Nevin, Donal, 75, 167
New Democratic Party (NDP, Canada), ix, 4, 5
New Theatre Group, Dublin (NTG), 211–13
New Writing, 200
newspapers and magazines, 206–9

Newtownards to Bangor parade (July 1867), 50, 54
Northern Ireland Civil Rights Association, 172
Northern Ireland Labour Party (NILP), viii, 4, 5, 240–1, 242, 248, 250
  Ulster Unionist Party and, 249–50, 252–3
Northern Ireland parliament, 240–1, 243
  general elections, 239, 242–3, 248, 250, 252–3, 254
Northern Ireland troubles, 19–20, 172–4
Northern Whig, 65
Norton, William, 182–4, 185, 186, 188, 189, 190, 192
Notes on the Irish Labour Movement (IRA Army Council document, 1927), 158, 161
novels and short stories, 203–6

O

Ó Brádaigh, Ruarirí, 169
Ó Cathasaigh, Aindrias, 14
Ó Faoláin, Seán, 202, 203, 204, 207, 209
Ó hEithir, Breandan, 167
O'Brien, Bronterre, 28
O'Brien, Conor Cruise, 194
O'Brien, Flann, 203, 214
O'Brien, Lord Chief Justice, 59
O'Brien, Tom, 206, 211, 212
O'Brien, William, 159, 179, 186, 187
O'Casey, Seán, 187, 191, 192, 201, 209–10, 215–16
O'Connell, T.J., 181, 182
O'Connor, Emmet, 2, 15–16, 21, 30
O'Connor, Frank, 204
Odet, Clifford, 211
O'Donnell, Peadar, 160–1, 165, 201, 204–6, 206, 207, 208, 209, 215–16

O'Donoghue, Donal, 165
O'Donoghue, Frank, 169
O'Donovan, Jim, 208
O'Duffy, Eimar, 203
Offences against the State Act, 168
O'Flaherty, Liam, 203, 204
O'Higgins, Kevin, 179
Old Lady Says 'No!', The (Dennis Johnston play, 1928), 209
Oldham, Charles Hubert, 10
On the Edge of the Stream (Peadar O'Donnell, 1934), 204–5
O'Neill, Terence, 253
O'Rahilly, Alfred, 186
Orange and Protestant Working Men's Association (OPWA), 49–50
Orange Order, 50, 53–4, 58, 67, 243–4, 253, 254
  in Belfast, 62, 65, 69, 253
  in Dublin, 55, 58, 59, 60–1
orangeism, independent, 49, 51–2, 53–4, 59–60, 61, 69, 72
O'Riordan, Mick, 172
Orwell, George, 200, 205
O'Shannon, Cathal, 179–80, 186
Osservatoro Romano (Vatican newspaper), 183–4
O'Sullivan, Christopher, 184–5
Outdoor Relief strike (1932), 164
'overholding system' (food-marketing practice), 35

P

Pacem in Terris (papal encyclical, 1963), 193
Paisley, Ian, 254
partition, 74, 75, 76, 77, 79, 80
Partition (Bill Clare and Tom O'Brien play), 212
Party Processions Act, 50, 52, 69
Paterson, Mary, 114
Patterson, Henry, 51, 60–1, 66
Peelite conservatism, 53

piece-working, 126
Pirrie, William, 136, 147
Plough (periodical), 192
Plunkett, Horace, 58, 59, 60
poetry, 213–15
Poetry of the People, 200
political economists, 26, 28
Politics and the Irish Working Class, 1830–1945 (eds. Lane and Ó Drisceoil, 2005), 20
Pollard, S., 137, 143
Pope John XXIII, 193, 194
Pope Leo XIII, 182, 183
Pope Pius XII, 193
power loom factories, 120, 121, 122–9, 131–2
Presbyterianism, 52, 130, 131
Priests and People in Ireland (Michael J.F. McCarthy, 1902), 60
Progressive Bookshop (Belfast), 211
proletarianization in weaving industry, 120
Protestantism
  conservatism and, 49, 50, 52, 53, 58, 59–60, 61
  employment, 55, 56, 78
  Labour Party and, 179, 187–8
  left-of-centre parties and, 73, 242
  sectarianism and, 49–52, 53–4, 55–62, 66, 67, 79
  social class and, 49–63, 65–6, 239–54
  in southern Ireland, 62–3, 240
  time discipline and, 130, 131–2
  trade unions and, 79, 163, 164
Puirséil, Niamh, 20
Puritanism, 130–1
putting-out system, 119–20

Q

Quadragissimo Anno (papal encyclical, 1932), 182
Queen's University, Belfast, 2, 5
Quinn v. Leatham case, 72

R

railway strike (1933), 163–4
Ralahine co-operative, 15
Redemptorist order, 59
Redmond, John, 78
regional studies, 21
regrating (food-marketing practice), 27, 30, 45
Reid, Douglas A., 127
Rent Act (1957), 250
Republic of Ireland, 244–5, 246, 248
  see also Ireland
Republican Congress, 165, 166, 214
Republican Industrial Development Division (RIDD), 174
republicanism, 52, 66, 74, 158–9, 169, 179, 202
  see also Irish Republican Army (IRA)
Rerum Novarum (papal encyclical, 1891), 178, 180, 182
Review (monthly magazine), 209
Riot Act (1772), 30, 34, 37, 43
Rise of the Irish Trade Unions, 1729-1970, The (Andrew Boyd, 1972), 18
Robbins, Frank, 181, 186
Robertson, P., 137, 143
Rolleston, T.W., 10
Royal Commission on Labour (1892), 85, 86, 87
Royal Ulster Constabulary (RUC), 163, 211
rural outwork, 103–4, 105, 106–16
Russell, George (Æ), 180–1
Russell, Seán, 163, 164
Russian revolution (1917), 16
Ryan, Desmond, 16, 167
Ryan, Frank, 206, 214
Ryan, Mick, 169, 174
Ryan, William Patrick, 16–17

S

Salud! (Peadar O'Donnell, 1937), 205
Saothar (ILHS journal), vii, viii, ix, 6,

19, 22
Saunderson, Edward, 50, 61
Sceim na gCeardchumann, 167
Second World War, 208–9, 212, 216, 239, 240, 241, 244
sectarianism
  in Belfast, 3, 49–52, 54, 244–6
  Catholicism and, 182, 192–3
  expulsions from employment, 78, 152
  Protestant working class, 49–52, 53–4, 55–62, 66, 67, 79
semi-skilled labour, 143–7
shipbuilding industry, Belfast, 67, 68, 71, 78, 135–54
  industrial relations, 136, 140, 141, 145–7, 150, 152–4, 250
  trade unions, 71, 78, 138–42, 144–7, 149–54, 239, 240, 245
  see also Harland & Wolff
Shipwright's Association at Harland and Wolff, 78, 243
shirt industry, rural, 104, 105, 107–9, 110–16
Shop Employees Society, 165
Siege of Derry, 53
Silver Tassie, The (Seán O'Casey play, 1928), 209–10
Silvermines dispute (Tipperary, 1971), 174
Sinclair, Betty, 169
Sinn Féin, 168, 169, 171
Skeffington, Owen Sheehy, 207–8
skilled manual labour, 137–41, 145
Sloan, Thomas, 50–1, 69, 72
Smith, Adam, 26, 27, 29
social class, 2–3, 11–12
  Catholicism and, 53, 54, 56–7, 59
  culture and, 200, 202, 207, 210
  Protestantism and, 49–63, 65–6, 239–54
  women and money, 218, 219, 220–2, 223, 224, 225, 234
  see also middle classes; working classes

Social Security: Outlines of a Scheme of National Health Insurance (Bishop Dignan pamphlet, 1944), 186, 189
social welfare
  Catholicism and, 186, 189, 190, 193–4, 195, 196
  Labour Party and, 186, 189, 190, 195, 196
  UULA and, 241–2
socialism, 10–11, 12–16, 20
  in Belfast, 71, 72, 74
  Catholicism and, 178–80, 183–4, 189–90, 190–2, 194–5
  Christian Socialism, 178, 179, 181, 193–4, 208
  culture and, 199, 200, 201–2, 204, 206–8, 209, 210–13, 214–16
  James Connolly and, 13–15, 66, 74
  Labour Party and, 171, 189–90, 193, 194–6
  left wing press, 204, 206–8, 209
  left wing theatre, 210–13
  republicanism and, 66, 74
  trade unions and, 240, 245, 252
  Ulster Unionist Party and, 241, 248–50, 252, 253
Socialist League, 10–11
Socialist Party of Ireland (SPI), 15–16, 75
socialist realism (Soviet Union), 201, 210, 213
sociology, 20
Soviet Union, 161–2, 170, 201, 210, 211, 213, 215
Spanish Civil War, 4, 183, 184, 195
  Catholic Church and, 183, 205–6, 207–8
  cultural responses, 200, 205–6, 207–8, 211, 212, 213, 214–15
Spender, Stephen, 202, 213
Spinning the Threads of Uneven Development: Gender and Industrialisation in Ireland during the Long Eighteenth Century (Jane Gray, 2005), 21

Squire, Rose, 109, 114
Squire v. Sweeney case, 115
Standard, Catholic, 186
Stepinac, Cardinal (of Zagreb), 191
Story of Irish Labour, The (Joseph M. MacDonnell pamphlet, 1921), 16
street preaching, evangelical, 59
suburbanisation, 54
Sullivan, A.M., 11
Swift, John, 18, 182
syndicalism, 75

T

Taff Vale judgement, 72
Tale of Three Cities: Comparative Studies in Working Class Life, A (John Lynch, 1998), 20
taxation populaire, 28, 29, 30, 31
textiles industry, 12, 21, 55, 67, 68, 77, 119–23
   in Lurgan, 118, 119–33
   rural outworking, 104, 105, 106–7, 108–16
theatre, 209–13
Thompson, E.P., 27, 28, 30, 45, 130–1, 133
Thompson, William, 15
Thorne, Will, 71
'Time, work-discipline and industrial capitalism' (E.P. Thompson article), 130–1, 133
time-keeping in factories, 118–19, 122–4, 127–9, 132–3
   Lurgan strike (1899), 124–9, 131–2
   Puritanism and, 130–2
Times, The (London), 42
Titanic, the (ship), 141
Toller, Ernst, 210
Tone, Wolfe, 170
Topping, Colonel, 247, 249
Torch (weekly paper), 185
Trade Union Advisory Committee, UUP, 251–3
trade unions, vii–viii

amalgamated unions, 2, 78, 83, 85–6, 88, 97, 138, 141, 145–7, 171
   see also Amalgamated Society of Carpenters and Joiners (ASCJ)
Articles of Agreement (Harland & Wolff, 1914), 140, 145–6, 153, 154
in Belfast, 51, 66, 67–72, 74, 75–9, 239
in Belfast shipbuilding, 71, 78, 138–42, 144–7, 149–54, 239, 240, 245
British orientation, 2–3, 67–8
building trades lockout (Dublin, 1896), 83, 84, 88–100
disciplining of own members, 141, 147
First World War and, 15
historiography, 18, 19, 20, 21
home rule and, 70, 76, 77
inter-union relations, 138, 139–40, 145–6, 149–50, 153, 154, 186
IRA and, 157–66, 167–72, 173–4
James Connolly and, 13, 158–9
Labour Party and, 74, 159, 171–2, 185–6
legal status of, 72, 87
metal trades, 67, 69, 77
nationalism and, 2–3, 68
new unionism, 12, 70–1, 72, 83–4
religion and, 68, 181
socialism and, 16, 17, 240, 245, 252
textiles industry, 67, 77, 122, 129
time discipline and, 132–3
unionism and, 51, 67, 77–8, 243, 250–3
unskilled workers and, 12, 83–4, 96, 98, 100
UULA and, 239, 240, 245, 250–1
white collar workers, 151–2
Trade Unions in Ireland, 1894–1960 (Charles McCarthy, 1977), 19
Trades Union Congress, British (BTUC), 68, 69, 70, 71, 79
tramway system, electric, Dublin, 87
Transport and General Workers

Union, 150
Trew, Arthur, 50
Trinity College Dublin, 2, 9, 19, 182, 187, 200
Truck Acts and amendments, 104, 109, 110–16
Twomey, Moss, 161, 163
Tyrone, County, 39–40

U

Ulster
  economy, 12, 66–8, 252
  southern Catholics and, 244–5
  see also Belfast; Ulster Unionist Party
Ulster Covenant (1912), 253
Ulster Unionist Council (UUC), 60, 61, 77, 243, 246, 247, 251, 253
Ulster Unionist Labour Association (UULA), 79, 239–54
Ulster Unionist Party
  Conservative Party and, 80, 242, 246, 248, 249, 250
  electoral politics, 240–1, 242, 248
  Ian Paisley and, 254
  social class and, 246–53
  socialism and, 241, 248–50, 252, 253
  Trade Union Advisory Committee, 251–3
Ulster Volunteer Force (UVF), 243
Ulster Workers' Trade Union, 79
Union and Industries Defence Federation, 57–8
unionism, 10
  British Labour Party and, 65–6, 72–4, 242
  Conservative Party and, 80, 242, 246, 248, 249, 250
  Labour Unionism, 77–80
  Protestant middle class and, 55, 61, 62, 246–8
  Protestant working class and, 59–60, 61, 62, 65–6, 246, 247–9, 250–3

trade unionism and, 51, 67, 77–8, 243, 250–3
see also loyalism; Ulster Unionist Party
Unionist Labour (UULA news-sheet), 241, 244, 245
Unionist Municipal Reform Party, 61
Unionist Party, Irish, 50, 51
Unionist Registration Association, 60
Unionist Society, 249–50
Unionist Trade Union Alliance (UTUA), 253
Unionist Trade Union Organisation (UTUO), 252
United Builders Labourers of Ireland (UBLI), 84, 88, 93, 98–9
United Irishman, 167, 169, 170–1, 172
United Kingdom Pattern Makers' Association (UKPA), 138
United Trades Council of Belfast *see* Belfast Trades Council
Unity (communist newspaper), 241
Unity Theatre (London), 211, 212, 213
universities, 9, 10, 19–20, 21, 22, 182, 187, 194, 200, 214
  John W. Boyle and, 2, 5
University College Dublin, 187, 194, 214
unskilled labour, 12, 147–50
urbanisation, 12

V

Vatican Council, second, 179
Victoria, Queen, death of (1901), 59
vocationalism, 186
Voice of Labour, 180

W

Waiting for Lefty (Clifford Odet play, 1937), 211, 212
Walker, William, 68, 71, 72, 73–4, 75, 80

Wallace, Colonel R.H., 65
Waller, Bolton, 32, 37
Walsh, Archbishop William J., 94, 95–6, 98, 100
War of Independence, 159, 204
Ward-Perkins, Sarah, vii
Washington Post, 171
Waterford, 29, 30, 36, 40, 41, 44
Wealth of Nations (Adam Smith), 29
weaving industry, 118–33
Webb, Beatrice and Sidney, 10
weights, under standard (in grocers' shops), 41
Wells, Roger, 30–1
Wesley, John, 27
West, Alick, 200
West, William, 60
white collar workers, 150–2, 219, 220, 223, 224, 229–30
Whitelegge, Arthur, 114
Wilkinstown, 42
women
   The Boyles and, 1, 4, 5
   Catholicism and, 184
   clothing and, 231–2
   low career expectations, 219–20
   middle class, 223, 224, 234
   money and, 218–35
   widowhood, 228–9, 234
   working class, 21, 219, 220–2, 224, 225, 234
   see also women and money; women and work
women and money, 218–35
   caring for next of kin, 219, 228, 234
   credit arrangements and, 232, 233, 235
   earnings after marriage, 226–8, 229, 234–5
   frugality and thrift, 219, 229–33, 234
   household management, 224–8, 229–33, 234–5
   husbands' earnings and, 225–6, 234
   marital status and, 218, 219, 220, 221, 224, 225

   moneylenders and, 233, 235
   social class and, 218, 219, 220–2, 223, 224, 225, 234
   see also women and work
Women and Paid Work in Ireland, 1500–1930 (ed. Bernadette Whelan), 21
women and work
   agricultural work, 107–8, 219, 226–7, 231
   domestic service, 219, 220, 222, 226, 231
   industrial, 103, 219, 220–1, 230
   parental control of earnings, 222–5, 234
   professional, 219, 221, 223, 227, 228
   rural industrial, 103, 104, 105, 106–16
   shipbuilding industry, 152
   shop service, 219
   time discipline and, 128–9
   truck legislation and, 104, 109, 110–16
   weaving industry, 120, 121
   white collar/secretarial, 219, 220, 223, 224, 229–30
Workers' Education Association, 252
Workers' Republic constitution (Labour Party, 1936), 183, 185, 195
Workers' Republic, the, 206–7
Workers' Theatre Movement, 210
Workers Union of Ireland (WUI), 160, 171, 186
working classes
   consumption culture, 133
   culture and, 200, 202, 203–4
   enfranchisement, 56, 69, 71
   historiography, 9–22
   Labour Party and, 161
   Labour Unionism, 77–80
   NILP and, 250
   Protestant, 49–63, 65–8, 69–71, 74, 77–80, 79, 210, 239–54
   sectarianism and, 3, 49–52, 53–4, 55–62, 66, 67, 79

shipbuilding industry, 67, 68, 71, 78, 135–54, 239, 240, 245, 250
trade unions and, 79
unionism and, 59–60, 61, 65–6, 246, 247–9, 250–3
UULA and, 239, 240, 241–2, 243, 248, 249, 250–2, 254
women, 21, 219, 220–2, 224, 225, 234
see also trade unions
Workman Clark, 135–6, 137, 143, 147, 148

Workmen's Compensation Act (1897), 87
Wyndham, George, 59

Y

Yeates, Pádraig, 173
Yeats, W.B., 10, 62, 210